Praise for *After t*

Winner of the J. Anthony Lukas Book Prize
A *New York Times Book Review* Editors' Choice
The "Understanding the World" Book of the Year at *World Magazine*
A Best Social Science Book of the Year at *Library Journal*

"Required reading for anyone trying to understand the challenges of getting to and surviving in the United States in the Trump era . . . What makes this book so different from other works that tell similar stories is the talent and doggedness of Goudeau, who . . . brings an insider's authority to the page."
—*The New York Times Book Review*

"Thorough reporting combined with a novelistic attention to detail and plot create a work of nonfiction that reads like the best novels. . . . Deeply moving."
—*San Francisco Chronicle*

"A bracingly empathetic portrait of two refugee women's struggles toward resettlement . . . A masterfully detailed portrait of the refugee experience."
—*The Texas Observer*

"Jessica Goudeau . . . has done what few journalists and fewer policymakers have been able to accomplish: bring the extraordinary tales of two war survivors . . . into the everyday normality of life in the United States. . . . Goudeau approaches these contentious issues as a gifted storyteller and diligent reporter, carefully building a historical backdrop while also following the stories of Mu Naw and Hasna where they lead, without smoothing the rough parts or making the women sentimental archetypes."   —*World Magazine*

"Absolutely breathtaking. A story of the unbelievable resilience of two refugee families, worlds apart, and the desperate humanitarian crisis that brought them to our doorstep."
—Kate Bowler, *New York Times* bestselling author of *Everything Happens for a Reason: And Other Lies I've Loved*

"*After the Last Border* is the rarest of books: a history, and collection of stories, that manages to be both deeply moving and deeply explanatory of a system that's foundational to our national identity. It feels like the culmination of a decade of work and friendship with refugees who trusted Goudeau enough to tell the stories. It feels like the work of a writer with a PhD and a deep, detailed understanding of the American project. It feels like that because that is precisely who Goudeau is: a person uniquely capable of writing this necessary book."

—Anne Helen Petersen, senior culture writer at *BuzzFeed News* and author of *Too Fat, Too Slutty, Too Loud*

"*After the Last Border* is a tale of our times and for our times. . . . Goudeau is not merely reporting; she is writing from a place of friendship, care, and heart."

—Kao Kalia Yang, author of *Latehomecomer: A Hmong Family Memoir*

"LOVELY . . . Jessica Goudeau's spectacular writing turns the struggles of each family into saga, enabling us to feel their predicaments and their progress as our own. The author does full justice to the sweeping drama of resettling from one side of the globe to the other. This is a captivating book about bravery, dislocation, and human resilience."

—Helen Thorpe, author of *The Newcomers: Finding Refuge, Friendship, and Hope in America*

"Profound, electric, and necessary. These two closely observed stories of women who have been duped by the American dream is our universal crisis. Goudeau skillfully blasts open our eyes to the plight of humans treated like cattle on the road to 'salvation.'"

—Sophia Shalmiyev, author of *Mother Winter*

"Goudeau, a gifted listener and writer, [takes] readers deep into the love, faith, loss, and astonishing strength of families who endure horror but never surrender hope. The result is an inspiring work of great beauty and profound humanity. You'll find yourself unable to put this book down and wishing that every American reads it, too. This is the kind of storytelling about refugee experiences that the world needs now."

—Wendy Pearlman, author of *We Crossed a Bridge and It Trembled: Voices from Syria*

"A revelatory and compassionate account . . . At a time when it is more important than ever to recognize that closed borders shrink a country's moral compass, *After the Last Border* reminds us of the human cost, seen through the heartbreaking stories of Mu Naw and Hasna."

—Sarah Weinman, author of *The Real Lolita*

"*After the Last Border* is essential reading for this moment; skillfully weaving in her meticulously researched history of refugee resettlement in the United States, Jessica Goudeau tells a gripping, fast-paced story of trauma, struggle, and the fierce hope of those who cross borders for the sake of their children. Read it with tissues close by."

—Amy Peterson, author of *Where Goodness Still Grows: Reclaiming Virtue in an Age of Hypocrisy*

"*After the Last Border* is a powerful testament to the U.S. refugee resettlement system. By illuminating the journey of two families and delineating the history and scope of refugee resettlement in the United States, Goudeau illustrates the perilous journeys refugees undertake, and the critical importance and ethical imperative of the U.S. resettlement program. In this political moment, when embracing those fleeing from war and violence is being replaced by walls and policy barriers designed to keep people out, Ms. Goudeau's book reminds us of what is at stake, and reminds us that this is not who we have been, and not who we are."

—Russell A. Smith, LMSW, CEO of Refugee Services of Texas

"In *After the Last Border*, Jessica Goudeau has written a history of refugee resettlement in the United States that is masterful in its sweep and novelistic in its attention to the human details that animate that history. I read it transported, appalled, and inspired by the courage of the refugees whose stories she so vividly tells. *After the Last Border* should be required reading for any U.S. citizen: it is stories like these that allow us to understand who and what we are as a nation."

—Louisa Hall, author of *Speak*

"Jessica Goudeau's reporting and storytelling in *After the Last Border* are extraordinary, giving her the abilities to grab ahold of the reader and make them see connections between policies and people. This is nonfiction that reads as dramatic and grand as the best fiction. You cannot read this book and remain unchanged."

—Pamela Colloff, *The New York Times Magazine* staff writer and *ProPublica* senior reporter

"A richly detailed account of the resettlement experiences of two women granted refugee status in the US. . . . Her excellent interview skills and obvious empathy for her subjects make the family portraits utterly engrossing, and the history sections provide essential context. This moving and insightful dual portrait makes an impassioned case for humane immigration and refugee policy."

—*Publishers Weekly* (starred review)

"In a detailed text that moves smoothly around in time, Goudeau effectively humanizes the worldwide refugee crisis while calling much-needed attention to a badly broken American immigration system. Sharp, provocative, timely reading."

—*Kirkus Reviews*

"It's obvious that Goudeau was able to gain the two women's trust . . . Their histories emerge through alternating chapters broken up by excerpts that provide social and political background about American refugee resettlement from the nineteenth century to the present day. These profiles are sympathetic and ultimately profoundly moving."

—*Booklist*

PENGUIN BOOKS

AFTER THE LAST BORDER

Jessica Goudeau has written for *The New York Times, The Washington Post, The Atlantic,* and *Los Angeles Times,* among other places, and is a former columnist for *Catapult.* She produced projects for *Teen Vogue* ("Ask a Syrian Girl") and *A Line Birds Cannot See,* a documentary about a young girl who crossed the border into the United States on her own. She has a PhD in literature from the University of Texas and served as a Mellon Writing Fellow and interim Writing Center director at Southwestern University. Goudeau has spent more than a decade working with refugees in Austin, Texas, and is the cofounder of Hill Tribers, a nonprofit that provided supplemental income for Burmese refugee artisans for seven years.

Penguin Reading Group Discussion Guide available online at penguinrandomhouse.com

AFTER THE LAST BORDER

*Two Families and the
Story of Refuge in America*

JESSICA GOUDEAU

PENGUIN BOOKS

PENGUIN BOOKS
An imprint of Penguin Random House LLC
penguinrandomhouse.com

First published in the United States of America by Viking,
an imprint of Penguin Random House LLC, 2020
Published in Penguin Books 2021

ISBN 9780525559153 (paperback)

THE LIBRARY OF CONGRESS HAS CATALOGED THE HARDCOVER EDITION AS FOLLOWS:
Names: Goudeau, Jessica, author.
Title: After the last border : two families and the story of refuge in
America / Jessica Goudeau.
Description: New York : Viking, 2020. | Includes bibliographical references and index.
Identifiers: LCCN 2019033736 (print) | LCCN 2019033737 (ebook) |
ISBN 9780525559139 (hardcover) | ISBN 9780525559146 (ebook)
Subjects: LCSH: Women immigrants—Texas—Austin—History. |
Immigrant families—Texas—Austin—History. | American Dream. |
Emigration and immigration—Government policy—United States—History.
Classification: LCC E184.A1 G66 2020 (print) | LCC E184.A1 (ebook) |
DDC 362.83/98120976431—dc23
LC record available at https://lccn.loc.gov/2019033736
LC ebook record available at https://lccn.loc.gov/2019033737

Printed in the United States of America
2nd Printing

Book design by Daniel Lagin

All names and identifying characteristics have been changed to protect
the privacy of the individuals involved.

To "Mu Naw," "Hasna," their family and friends scattered around the world,

and the refugee resettlement community in Austin—with all my love.

Where should we go after the last border? Where should birds fly after the last sky?
Where should plants sleep after the last breath of air?

—MAHMOUD DARWISH, "EARTH PRESSES AGAINST US"
(TRANSLATED BY MUNIR AKASH AND CAROLYN FORCHÉ)

The world has got very good—very skilled and very adept, really—at spotting these great mass abuses of populations. But only from a distance of about 40 years. Up close it's different. . . . The thing about it is that it is happening—*now*, to real people. And the world—including and especially the world that could help—can't quite get the thing in focus. . . . This is a question of moral right and international responsibility—and one from which neither the United States nor the rest of the industrial countries should be permitted to look away.

—EDITORIAL ABOUT THE INDOCHINESE HUMANITARIAN CRISIS,
". . . AND REFUGEES," *THE WASHINGTON POST,* JUNE 22, 1979

Contents

Author's Note   xv

Character Maps   xviii

Prologue: MU NAW (MYANMAR/THAILAND BORDER, 1989)   I

PART 1

Chapter 1: MU NAW (AUSTIN, TEXAS, USA, APRIL 2007)   7

Chapter 2: US REFUGEE RESETTLEMENT, 1945–1951   14

Chapter 3: HASNA (DARAA, SYRIA, MARCH 2011)   22

Chapter 4: MU NAW (AUSTIN, TEXAS, USA, APRIL 2007)   38

Chapter 5: HASNA (DARAA, SYRIA, MARCH 2011)   47

Chapter 6: MU NAW (AUSTIN, TEXAS, USA, APRIL 2007)   57

Chapter 7: HASNA (DARAA, SYRIA, MARCH 2011)   71

Chapter 8: MU NAW (AUSTIN, TEXAS, USA, MAY–AUGUST 2007)   79

Chapter 9: HASNA (DARAA, SYRIA, MARCH 2011)   87

Chapter 10: US REFUGEE RESETTLEMENT, 1880–1945   94

Chapter 11: HASNA (DARAA, SYRIA, MARCH–APRIL 2011)   101

Chapter 12: MU NAW (AUSTIN, TEXAS, USA, SEPTEMBER 2007)   113

Chapter 13: HASNA (DARAA, SYRIA/RAMTHA, JORDAN, APRIL–JULY 2011)   124

Chapter 14: MU NAW (AUSTIN, TEXAS, USA, OCTOBER 2007–APRIL 2008)   139

PART 2

Chapter 15: HASNA (RAMTHA, JORDAN, DECEMBER 2012–FEBRUARY 2013)   149

Chapter 16: US REFUGEE RESETTLEMENT, 1950–1963   163

Chapter 17: MU NAW (AUSTIN, TEXAS, USA, APRIL 2008–MARCH 2009)   167

Chapter 18: HASNA (RAMTHA AND IRBED, JORDAN, FEBRUARY–DECEMBER 2013)   175

Chapter 19: US REFUGEE RESETTLEMENT, 1965–1980   184

Chapter 20: MU NAW (AUSTIN, TEXAS, USA, OCTOBER 2011)   194

Chapter 21: HASNA (IRBED, JORDAN, DECEMBER 2013–JULY 2016)   199

PART 3

Chapter 22: MU NAW (AUSTIN, TEXAS, USA, AUGUST 2014, JANUARY 2015)   217

Chapter 23: US REFUGEE RESETTLEMENT, 1980–2006   224

Chapter 24: HASNA (AUSTIN, TEXAS, USA, JULY 2016)   235

Chapter 25: MU NAW (AUSTIN, TEXAS, USA, MAY 2015)   243

Chapter 26: US REFUGEE RESETTLEMENT, 2008–2015   249

Chapter 27: HASNA (AUSTIN, TEXAS, USA, OCTOBER–NOVEMBER 2016)   260

Chapter 28: MU NAW (AUSTIN, TEXAS, USA, MARCH 2016)   268

Chapter 29: US REFUGEE RESETTLEMENT, 2015–2018   272

Chapter 30: HASNA (AUSTIN, TEXAS, USA, JANUARY–JULY 2017)   284

Epilogue: MU NAW (AUSTIN, TEXAS, USA, JANUARY 2016)   295

Afterword   299

Acknowledgments   309

Notes   313

Further Reading   333

Index   335

Author's Note

This book tells the stories of two women resettled through the refugee resettlement program to the United States. Mu Naw arrived in 2007, at the beginning of the program for refugees from Myanmar, one of the most successful and widely supported resettlement initiatives in US history. Hasna al-Salam arrived in 2016, with the first wave of Syrian refugees, during one of the greatest moments of upheaval since the establishment of the federal resettlement program.

I gathered the details of these stories through intensive interviews every two weeks or so over a period of two years; in addition, I had been friends with Mu Naw for almost a decade when I began writing the book. The Afterword provides a more in-depth look at our interview process and my methods in writing their narratives. At their request and with their direct input, some identifying details, including names, have been changed to protect Mu Naw, Hasna, and their relatives and friends, many of whom are still in danger currently.

This book is also the story of the American resettlement program itself, from its roots in the immigration debates at the end of the nineteenth century to its dismantling in 2019 at the hands of the government branch that once promoted and protected it. Refugee policy is not a single, monolithic piece of legislation, but a series of programs and practices shaped by one of the most powerful forces in the American republic: the will of the people. Too often we focus on the opportunities the US provides immigrants in the land of the

"American Dream," and not on how our mercurial national moods lead to small and large policy shifts that radically affect real people. Americans' national fight for identity—the wrangling about who we once were, how we will define ourselves for each generation, and who we want to become—is the single greatest determiner of who we accept for resettlement.

After years of friendship with refugees and countless hours of research into one of the most remarkable, if imperfect, federal programs, I have come to believe that refugee resettlement is a bellwether of our country's moral center—how we respond to the greatest humanitarian crises of our time reveals our nation's soul.

AFTER THE LAST BORDER

CHARACTER MAPS

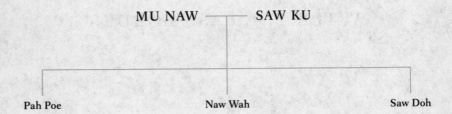

MU NAW —— SAW KU

Pah Poe   Naw Wah   Saw Doh

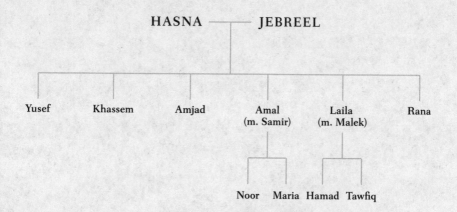

Prologue

MU NAW

MYANMAR/THAILAND BORDER, 1989

Mu Naw is five and she is running. Thick wet grass rises higher than her chubby thighs and she lifts her legs as if she is marching, almost jumping to keep up with the frantic adults. Her mouth is silent, but her body makes noises because she hasn't learned yet how to run and hide well in the woods. Her mother is carrying her baby sister; her toddler brother is with her aunt. Mu Naw struggles valiantly, pushes back tall plants, breathes hard, but she cannot keep up. Her young uncle swings her up onto his shoulders and she wraps her arms under his neck, lays her cheek on his head to keep it out of the way of slapping branches, and holds on.

They run for three days. On the back trails in the mountains, they encounter another family. They are wary at first, but soon realize they are prey hunted by the same predators. They run together. There is safety in numbers. They pool what knowledge they have. Someone heard there are openings at a refugee camp across the river in Thailand. They set off in that direction.

At night, in the darkness, in hushed voices, they share their stories.

Mu Naw overhears her young uncle whispering to another man about what happened; he had waited until his sister, Mu Naw's beautiful aunt, was out of earshot to speak. Mu Naw's beautiful aunt is married. She caught the eye of a soldier in the Tatmadaw; not just any soldier, a dangerous soldier with burnished stars on his green sleeve.

Mu Naw remembers a man with stars on his sleeve. From her uncle's whispers, she learns those stars probably mean he was a general in the Tatmadaw, the Myanmar Armed Forces. The villagers are Karen, one of the many ethnic minorities that the Burmese junta is targeting on a variety of fronts. All over the country, everyone who is Karen—or Kachin, Karenni, Rohingya, Chin, or many of the other groups of people who are not ethnically Burmese— will run. Or they will think about running. Or they will wish they had been able to run. They will pour into camps in Malaysia and India and Thailand, depending on how the vicious scythe of war cuts through their villages and cities. When the scythe sliced through Mu Naw's village, that general held it.

Mu Naw understands from her uncle's tone that the stars on the general's sleeve mean her aunt could not refuse. If she told him she loved her husband, if she said politely, with her eyes down respectfully and her teeth bared in an uncomfortable smile, that she would rather *not*—she and all of her relatives had better run the second he turned his back.

Her aunt turned him down. Now Mu Naw and her family are running. They love Mu Naw's beautiful young aunt more than they love their village. Leaving is safer for now, but true safety does not exist in Myanmar.

Mu Naw's country is in free fall, a state of bewildering, breathtaking conflict. It feels as if everyone is fighting everyone. Families like Mu Naw's—a Buddhist woman married to a Christian man, neither of whom wanted to fight—are caught in the crossfire from every side.

Fleeing is hard on the children; they must be carried and cajoled and whispered to. It is hard on Mu Naw's aging female relatives, all referred to as "grandmother" with the deference and love she gives to all older women. It is hard on the young adults, jumping like rabbits at every sound in the forests, aching with fear for the children and the grandmothers, bearing the weight of packs bound in woven cloth with everything they can carry.

It is hard on Mu Naw's father. Years ago, his right leg was blown off by a land mine, and though his body has adjusted to the makeshift crutch he fashioned then from a branch, his back and arms ache as he pushes through the damp, sticky branches that cling to him and pull at him. Once, when they stop to rest, he tells Mu Naw that the forest where he walked into a land mine was the same as this one, that she should stay close to him. As they walk again, she can see that sameness wears on him, warns him. He speaks sharply to his wife all day, but not to Mu Naw. At night, he is silent.

Mu Naw's mother, terrified for her children and for herself, turns her anger on her husband. The sight of his blown-off leg depresses her. Her abrasive tone sets everyone else on edge. One of the grandmothers chides her gently, but Mu Naw's mother only snaps back. The other grandmothers murmur among themselves—they do not approve of a woman who is so angry, who speaks her mind to her elders.

Mu Naw is unaware of the whispered conversations curling through the camp. She tucks herself next to her father, who leans back against a tree with his amputated leg stretched out. He strokes her hair behind her ear, and she sleeps, mouth open, her small body weighed down with exhaustion.

Her parents' tension is her country's war in miniature. Mu Naw does not know it yet, but her family has already shattered. Like broken glass in a frame, the cracks spread, deepen, divide, but the glass stays in place. For now.

The next day, Mu Naw crossed her first border.

PART 1

Chapter 1

MU NAW

Mu Naw stood on the landing above the airport baggage claim–area at Austin-Bergstrom International Airport and wished she had on different shoes. She shifted the plastic International Organization for Migration bag from her left shoulder to her right and grabbed her daughter's hand. There were two escalators leading down; she and her husband, Saw Ku, had instinctively paused, not sure which one to take. People passed them on the right and left, confidently moving through space as Mu Naw never had. Mu Naw's shoes, the black rubber slide-on sandals everyone used in Mae La camp, felt dusty, undignified. She was proud of her skirt and shirt—these were her nicest clothes. They were red and handwoven in the traditional Karen style, a long straight skirt with braided fringes brushing the top of her feet, a tunic with a diamond-shaped hole she slipped her head into. She looked at her daughter Naw Wah, who was two, in her pink Karen dress, and her other daughter, Pah Poe, who was five, in a turquoise one. Even Saw Ku, holding Pah Poe's hand, had a green tunic that he wore with jeans. In the tiny airplane bathroom, Mu Naw had rebraided the girls' hair, and Saw Ku had slicked his hair down with water from the tinny sink.

She had heard from friends at the camp that she would get a black sweater and new shoes on the bus to Bangkok. There had been no shoes and no sweaters, though Mu Naw had looked behind the bus seats to make sure. She was too shy to ask the UN workers at the time, but she had not stopped worrying about her rubber sandals in every airport, afraid they seemed shameful to the IOM worker guiding them, that the lack of new shoes meant that she had missed some important step everyone else knew that she did not.

Now the IOM worker was gone. That was another piece of information they had heard in the camp, this one accurate: They would know they were boarding their last flight because the IOM worker would not go with them. Mu Naw had barely known the woman, but now felt bereft without her.

That woman had been certain and knowledgeable, guiding them through their travels by reading the long lists of names on huge signs overhead in each airport and then translating them into their native dialect, Karen, from Bangkok to Los Angeles. Mu Naw could read several things in English already, but she could not understand why the large A22 meant you were on a flight to Dubai, and A23 meant you were going to Hong Kong, but A24 meant Los Angeles. It was one of thousands of things Mu Naw did not grasp.

Mu Naw's entire life had been spent with people who looked like her. Occasionally, a white UN worker or volunteer came to the camp, but that was it. Everywhere she turned were people with different eyes, ears, hair, noses, clothes, skin, mouths, purses, hats, hijabs, necklaces, bracelets, wallets, suitcases, books, food, water bottles, headphones, scarves, pillows, sweaters, shoes. Even when her eyes were down to shield her from the onslaught of strange sights, the languages assaulted her ears, snatches in tones she had never heard, musical, guttural, loving, rude. The smells of perfume, food, sweat, air-conditioning kept her from breathing in deeply.

Now, in Austin, standing in her last airport at the top of two escalators going down, she wished desperately for one brief minute that they were back in Mae La camp. She wished the IOM woman were still with them. She wished she had her new sweater and shoes.

They had only seen an escalator a handful of times, most of them in airports within the last twenty-four hours. She turned and gazed blankly at her husband for a minute. Saw Ku walked to the escalator on the left, almost running into a white businessman pulling a suitcase behind him. Mu Naw fell into place behind him. She stumbled for a minute, eyes down to keep her balance, clutching the rail that made her hand move slightly faster than the stairs on which she stood. She made sure Naw Wah's tiny feet were centered in the metal striped step. When she finally reached the bottom of the stairs, anxiously avoiding the steps submerging into each other, Mu Naw took a firm step with Naw Wah over the line that ended the escalator, then looked up. She didn't have time to worry; a man was already greeting them in Karen, standing beside a tall white woman with a wide smile.

"Are you Saw Ku and Mu Naw? We're here to take you to your new home! Welcome to Texas!"

Mu Naw's face broke into a relieved grin.

The white woman and Karen man helped Mu Naw and Saw Ku get their bags from the revolving circle that spewed luggage out of a large metal mouth. Their bags were easy to spot: multicolored plastic zip-up bags they had purchased from a store in the refugee camp. Just a few days before, Mu Naw had approached a hut where the owner had opened the front wall to form a makeshift storefront. Rusted shelves held snacks and sodas, soap and toothbrushes and combs, rubber sandals in dusty plastic sacks, and a rotating inventory of whatever items he could sell. The store owner's children watched, squatting in the front of the store, their cheeks white with thanaka to protect them from the sun. Mu Naw tried not to smile too broadly when she walked up and asked the store owner respectfully for the Western bags. He turned and rummaged through the back of his hut, his children looking on solemnly. He handed her two, asking her where she was going.

"Taxi! We are going to go live in Taxi!" He nodded in response, as if he knew exactly where Taxi was. It would be years before she would realize the difference between the yellow cars you could hail on the street and the state where she lived, or laugh at the fact that she had confused the two.

Mu Naw held the bags proudly slung on her shoulder back through camp, deftly jumping along the uneven packed dirt paths, up the hill lined with huts on large bamboo stilts, past the concrete bathroom area with the trickle of water where everyone—women on one side and men on the other—bathed discreetly, covering themselves with longyi while they washed. Her neighbors eyed her. A few friends waved. The large square bags were a symbol of the trip she was taking, of her new status in the world. She had seen others walking with those bags before they disappeared from the camp forever.

The camp where she had lived in Thailand, Mae La, was supposed to be a temporary stop. After the infiltration of Laotian and Hmong refugees on the eastern border of Thailand in the 1970s and 1980s, the country had very little patience for the refugees arriving from Myanmar on the western border. Thailand had remained stable in spite of war in Vietnam, genocide in Cambodia, unrest in Laos, persecution of Hmong people wherever they lived in the region. The longest-running civil war in the world was not the problem of the Thai people. They designated land where those who crossed illegally into the country could live in ramshackle huts, packed together like pickled fish in a can. Mu Naw had not spent her entire life in the camp; she was unusual among her generation for that. Many of them could barely remember life in Myanmar and most left the camp only by sneaking out and avoiding roads with Thai police or military officials. Leaving the camp was illegal, and capture usually meant being returned to Myanmar. They lived cheek by jowl together, until rumors spread through the camp that doors were being opened for them in other countries. UN officers interviewed them, suddenly interested in their stories, verifying again and again that they were refugees—of course they were, why would anyone live here if they could live anywhere else? More officials came, from Canada and Sweden and Australia and the United States. Mu Naw stood outside the community center beside the dirt road, jostled by what felt like half the camp, when the first two groups of Karen people boarded rickety buses, everything they took with them in their coveted colorful bags. Everyone wanted to wave good-bye, to witness them actually leaving. Mu Naw waved and teared up when one woman wailed, watching her daughter and young grandson wave good-bye through the bus window. But she also felt a rush of excitement as the bus wheeled away in a whirl of dust and exhaust.

Their empty huts were now fair game—daughters-in-law living in one room with their husbands' entire family moved happily into an abandoned hut down the row. But Mu Naw didn't even try. She knew as soon as she saw the first group leave that she and Saw Ku would go. There was no life in this camp.

When it was her turn, she and Saw Ku were chosen to be among the first groups to resettle in the United States from Mae La. Her Buddhist mother called it luck; her Christian mother-in-law praised God's hand in the UN selection process. Mu Naw thought perhaps it was a bit of both. There were thousands of people in Mae La camp who would give anything to be her, walking purposefully past her neighbors with bright plastic bags on her arm.

WHEN THEY ROUNDED THE CORNER ON THE BAGGAGE CAROUSEL, MU Naw was surprised that the bags that had felt foreign and new just days before now seemed intimately familiar, as if they had been with her all of her life. In her IOM sack, tucked inside her own woven bag, she had her passport and her daughters' passports and the important documents they brought with them. In the checked bags, they had packed what was left: T-shirts, tunics, and two pairs of jeans for Saw Ku, woven tunics and skirts for Mu Naw and the girls, a few extra for them to wear as they grew. There were albums with pictures of each of their relatives, a jar of thanaka for the girls' faces, cream for Mu Naw's skin, a few clips for their hair, underwear and combs and toothbrushes. And that was it. There was nothing else to take.

Seeing their bags, Mu Naw felt a pang for the box of letters she had left behind. Two days before she left, she found a tree near enough to her hut that she could find it again someday but far enough away where it would not be disturbed by her neighbors. She had dug a small hole in the hard clay dirt and placed a tin box near the roots of the tree. In it were all of the letters she and Saw Ku had written to each other over the months when they first admitted they liked each other when they were fifteen, saying on paper what they were too shy to express out loud. She had thought about taking the box, but she was not sure what would happen in their new place. This camp seemed more constant, more real than the fantastical new life she would lead in America.

As she watched the white woman and Karen man talking to Saw Ku about the bags, at the end of an exhausting journey that spanned endless, monotonous hours, Mu Naw suddenly knew with a deep certainty she had made the wrong choice. She had thought she would go back with her daughters to dig up the letters in a few years. The idea of ever returning now seemed impossible; the English that had been a novelty spoken only by UN workers now engulfed her. The loss hit her in a powerful wave of grief. She could close her eyes and see the sun shining through the expansive green leaves of the tree, feel the muggy air on her skin, the claylike dirt beneath her sandals. It was perfectly clear in her mind but the tree was on the other side of the world, standing vigil over the teenage love she had shared with her husband; the tin box would rust, the letters disintegrate. Her daughters would never read them. She moved forward numbly, feet shuffling on the cold linoleum.

THE CAR RIDE FROM THE AIRPORT TO THEIR NEW HOME WAS A DIZ-zying, exhilarating experience. They had walked on a crosswalk where cars paused politely. The white woman led them around to the side of a dark van and showed them how to buckle their children into the car seats. The children slept, mouths open in exhaustion. They skimmed the smooth highway into town, the lights and buildings whizzing past at a rate that left her dazed. Mu Naw gripped the armrest, body hunched against the window in an effort not to throw up or cry or succumb to the powerful emotion she could not name that pressed down on her. She had only ridden in a car a handful of times in her life and it was nothing like this, the flight of an efficient machine through an electric landscape she had never imagined existed.

They parked their car in a circle of light under a street lamp at an apart-ment complex with iron gates that were open. The air smelled like asphalt and clean laundry. The white woman and the Karen man took their bags and led them to an apartment on the first floor with a faint hint of cigarette smoke.

The lock on the door stuck for a minute, but then they got it open and walked into a living room with a brown couch and a chair, some empty shelves, a tall floor lamp leaning slightly to the side. There was a table in the small kitchen, appliances on the counters, a refrigerator that whirred gently. In one bedroom was a large master bed with a red and white comforter. The other bedroom held two twin beds covered in white comforters. The sheets were already on the beds; the woman showed Saw Ku how to lock the door and put up the brass chain that would keep everyone out. She made him try several times, watching until he got it. The children slumped on the couch, staring at their father opening and closing the door and fastening the chain.

Finally, they started to leave, the Karen man translating for the white woman that a church group had gathered all of this furniture for them, that everything was theirs to keep, that the refrigerator had some food in it. He added that the group had prayed over the apartment, a fact that pleased Mu Naw. They smiled warmly and Mu Naw tried to speak her new language, her "thank you" a bit garbled, but the woman understood and, after an awkward second of jostling, they hugged. Mu Naw barely came up to the woman's shoulder. The Karen translator repeated his invitation—they would come eat dinner with him later that week. After they left, Saw Ku hastily locked and chained the door. No one mentioned when someone would be back to get them. They didn't think to ask.

They looked at each other and smiled. This was it. They were here. They dug through the bags for squashed, wrinkled pajamas; when Mu Naw unfolded them, the scent of wood smoke, clay floor, dried bamboo rushed past her. They brushed their teeth in the bathroom where the water ran inside the house any time they wanted. They tucked the girls into the large queen bed between them, a little unit of four.

As she crawled into the bed beside Naw Wah, Mu Naw imagined getting ready to sleep in their small hut in Mae La camp, laying out the mats, pulling the mosquito netting away from the wall, fastening it around them. The leaves in the trees outside would rustle; their neighbors' conversations would seep muffled through bamboo walls until the thick night settled around them. The rice mat would smell pleasantly like earth; it would be flat and cool.

This new bed was soft. The sheets were stiff and held the crisp wrinkles that Mu Naw would later know meant they had been unfolded from a package. The blanket was thick. The blinds above the headboard gapped slightly at the bottom and the light from a street lamp shone through the meager tree outside her window, forming shadows when the wind blew that made her jump. The white noise of the nearby highway was a motorized river, the constant stream disrupted by horns or loud engines. She could hear voices outside the apartment speaking in a language that did not sound like English, voices that spiked into an argument in the middle of the night. She lifted her head to see if Saw Ku was awake; he lifted his head too. He silently reached over their girls and took her hand.

Chapter 2

US REFUGEE RESETTLEMENT,
1945–1951

A profound public awakening following World War II shaped American refugee resettlement policies in the twentieth and twenty-first centuries. US lawmakers, with the unprecedented support of constituents across the country who were horrified by the scale of the Holocaust, worked with the global community in shaping international agencies and programs, legislation and conventions, that would remain in place for generations. And all of it happened within a handful of years. The pace of the change was extraordinary.

World War II left more than 10 million displaced people in Europe alone. On June 25, 1948, President Harry S. Truman and the US Congress passed the Displaced Persons (DP) Act, a landmark bill that provided special visas allowing about four hundred thousand European refugees to find new lives in the United States over a four-year period. At the time, the US immigration system was controlled by quotas; only a certain number of visas were available each year for people arriving from a handful of designated countries, which were almost entirely European. During the war, the government launched a few ad hoc policies that allowed some Jewish refugees and others fleeing the Nazi occupation to come to the United States, but there was nothing on the scale of the DP Act. It was one of the earliest instances of the American government's officially recognizing refugees' unique circumstances as victims of war and creating a separate immigration policy—not yet a program—to bring many of them to this country.

Before the act was passed, in his State of the Union on January 6, 1947, President Truman praised the way the United States had provided aid and supplies to people "reduced to want by the ravages of war"—more aid since the end of the war "than all other countries combined." But still he pressed Congress to continue to "fulfill our responsibilities to these thousands of homeless and suffering refugees of all faiths." In an address to Congress six months later, he laid out the clear need for American resettlement to go hand in hand with foreign aid. He called it "unthinkable" that refugees "should be left indefinitely in camps in Europe." Every other option was equally impossible for humanitarian reasons ("We cannot turn them out in Germany into the community of the very people who persecuted them"), economic reasons ("the German economy, so devastated by war and so badly overcrowded with the return of people of German origin from neighboring countries, is approaching an economic suffocation which in itself is one of our major problems"), and security reasons ("Turning these displaced persons into such chaos would be disastrous for them and would seriously aggravate our problems there"). Through it all, he appealed to Americans' sense of obligation: "our plain duty requires that we join with other nations in solving this tragic problem" in order to "enable these people to take roots in friendly soil."

The arguments Truman and other lawmakers relied on after World War II would be repeated for the rest of the century whenever questions about refugee resettlement rose to the national level. After World War II, the moral imperative underlying Truman's reasons felt especially charged: Americans owed it to our allies to keep them from bearing the burden of millions of persecuted people in need of immediate assistance. Americans owed it to the displaced people, who had already endured so many atrocities. And Americans owed it to the Allied soldiers who had fought, even died, to free these refugees; any national sacrifice US citizens would make was minuscule in comparison.

The American public listening to Truman shared memories of a time in the recent past when they had not supported refugee aid, in what a later president would call a "stain on our collective conscience." Less than ten years before, in 1939, President Franklin Roosevelt personally received telegrams from Jewish passengers of the MS *St. Louis,* a luxury liner that held 937 people fleeing the Third Reich. Their Cuban visas, which had been legal when they left the dock, were revoked while the passengers traveled. A Cuban official had been embezzling funds, selling visas to desperate refugees, and pocketing the money. While the refugees sailed, blissfully unaware, the Cuban government caught up with the official and negated the visas he had issued, driven by a public deeply fed up with the large number of refugees coming to their island nation. Despite diplomatic wrangling and hasty international negotiations, Cuba remained unbending—the MS *St. Louis* passengers were not allowed to disembark.

The MS *St. Louis* sailed on to the coast of Florida, hoping for asylum in the United States. The passengers tried valiantly to explain their plight. Their telegram to President Roosevelt begged, "Help them, Mr. President, the 900 passengers, of which more than 400 are women and children." Newspapers across the country covered the story. The subheading on the story for the *New York Times* captured the tension of that political moment: "Rumor That United States Will Permit Entry Is Spread to Avert Suicides—Company Orders St. Louis Back to Hamburg." Refugee advocacy groups worked tirelessly in Cuba and in the United States; feverish behind-the-scenes political efforts ramped up in the White House and outside it, to no avail. The US did not allow them in. As the ship moved toward Europe, one headline read baldly, "Ship Steams Away to Return Refugees to Reich."

Eventually, through diplomatic negotiations, American representatives found four European countries willing to take in some of the ship's passengers. More than a month after they first boarded the ship, 288 people arrived in England; almost all of them lived to see the end of World War II. The rest of the passengers who disembarked in Belgium, France, and Holland seemed to be safe; many had good reason to assume they would eventually make it to the United States. But within the year, Nazi troops invaded those countries. Of the passengers who stood on the deck and saw the shores of the United States, 254 died in concentration camps.

Their journey came to be called "the voyage of the damned." At the end of the war, the memory of those refugees and others who had begged for safety during Hitler's genocide haunted the American public.

THE UNITED STATES ENDED WORLD WAR II WITH A FIRM SENSE OF THE country's role as a new—if not *the* new—world leader. It was a message hammered in the 1940s by radio shows, newspaper headlines, magazine articles, and political speeches, but especially at the movies. During and after the war, movie executives viewed it as their patriotic duty to work closely with the government to make movies in keeping with US foreign policy or public propaganda campaigns. The message about US preeminence was in such escapist films as *The Gang's All Here* and *Weekend in Havana*—the blonde actresses wore Technicolor red, white, and blue, and the American good guy always won in the end. It was in more serious fare, such as *It's a Wonderful Life* and *The Best Years of Our Lives*, which explored the struggles of postwar American identity, always ending with their characters' choice to do what was right even if it was hard. It was in every scene in which John Wayne led the cavalry or the troops or the cowboys to victory; one of his most famous lines summarized the mettle Americans would need: "there are some things a man can't run away from." The underlying message of these movies shaped the imagination of the American public about the sobering responsibilities required of strong leaders in service to the common good.

Before each movie, short newsreels would play. Newsreels after 1945 showed the plight of European refugees to American audiences. In one film, a cheery newscaster voiced over black-and-white footage of women in skirts and headscarves, men in suits, small children walking along a road: "These are some of Europe's stranded millions; displaced persons, participants in the largest, swiftest mass migration in history." The films asked Americans to sympathize with the devastation caused "by the heedless greed of Nazi overlords, who pillaged the country and brought down upon its people the terrible burden of war." The music underlined the pathos of the footage; in one newsreel a violin plays underneath the narrator's voice as the camera zooms in on specific faces: "Footsore and weary, they await patiently, anxiously. This mother wonders where she will get milk for her baby. . . . This little girl will have to sleep in a ditch again tonight."

Newsreels showed the refugee camps, often repurposed from the very concentration camps from which refugees had been liberated. The camp model provided a central location for distribution of food and clothing "expedited by the United Nations Relief and Rehabilitation Administration, using United States Army trains and trucks." There, nurses examined children "orphaned by the bombs of battle, the deadly aim of the Nazi firing squads, the hot flames of an oven inside a German death factory" for signs of typhus. People with "stomachs gnawed with hunger and ruined with a diet of grassroots and leaves, and bread mixed with sawdust" receive gruel and vitamins. The film depicted refugees looking at a community message board outside a large building where they have classes and receive orientations.

"Why do we help?" the narrator asks—is it only for humanitarian reasons, or because Americans are "suckers"? He immediately dismisses those ideas: We help because "we realize that our half of the world cannot remain well if the other half is sick. We realize that we must rehabilitate these displaced persons for our own interests and preservation, as well as theirs. If we don't help these people now, then the chaos will continue indefinitely, and the seeds of a third World War will take root."

In the 1940s, that was the most compelling argument. It grew out of the country's shared sense of its identity and its solemn duty to prevent another war. The US would do what was right, even if it was hard.

IN 1945, PRESIDENT TRUMAN SENT AN EMISSARY, EARL G. HARRISON, to visit these camps and report back on conditions there, particularly for Jewish refugees. Harrison's letter belied the chipper tone of the newsreels to the American public: Jewish refugees felt that "they, who were in so many ways the first and worst victims of Nazism," were "neglected by their liberators." The horror of remaining in some of the "most notorious of the concentration camps, amidst crowded, frequently unsanitary and generally grim conditions, in complete idleness, with no opportunity . . . to communicate with the outside world" was unconscionable. Harrison wrote that Jewish refugees often had a choice only between concentration camp uniforms and German SS guard uniforms—both options equally disturbing. At the end of 1945, their most pressing concern was finding their relatives again, a complicated task that had been barely addressed by the time Harrison arrived. He warned the president that there was insufficient food and the living conditions were "clearly unfit for winter use." The threat of death was as overwhelming following the war as it was during the Holocaust; one rabbi "personally attended, since liberation 23,000 burials (90 per cent Jews) at Bergen Belsen alone." According to Harrison's report, the former concentration camp still housed 14,000 displaced people, more than half of whom were Jewish.

No wonder, when he addressed Congress less than a year later, President Truman called those camps "unthinkable."

RESETTLEMENT BECAME A CRITICAL TOOL IN THE GOVERNMENT'S FOR-eign policy arsenal, with international negotiations about how many refugees the US would resettle going hand in hand with diplomatic talks about foreign aid. The same year the DP Act was passed, the 1948 Marshall Plan committed $15 billion over four years to help rebuild Europe after the war. And in moving toward an internationally-agreed-upon, legal definition of refugees as victims of targeted persecution on a massive scale, the world also identified the perpetrators of a new type of crime—"crimes against humanity."

After World War II, for the first time in history, Allied countries agreed during the Nuremberg trials to prosecute other sovereign states for violating a newly adopted system of international laws. There was widespread international consensus that a sovereign country could not just do whatever it wanted to its own citizens.

Though the US might have seen itself as leading the charge, these conversations were happening on a national scale in other countries as well. The Nuremberg trials were a start; fifty nations met in San Francisco in October 1945 and established the United Nations. In 1948, the UN voted on two landmark declarations: On December 9, the UN unanimously ratified the Convention on the Prevention and Punishment of the Crime of Genocide. The next day, the UN passed the Universal Declaration of Human Rights, which stated "the foundation of freedom, justice and peace in the world" is the "recognition of the inherent dignity and of the equal and inalienable rights of all members of the human family." It laid out the fundamental idea that "all human beings are born free and equal in dignity and rights" to which they are entitled "without distinction of any kind, such as race, color, sex, language, religion, political or other opinion, national or social origin, property, birth or other status." The identification of crimes against humanity and genocide as internationally criminal offenses, and the declaration of rights not based on citizenship but on basic humanity, were the foundation of the modern refugee resettlement program in the US and other countries around the world.

Three years later, the United Nations ratified the 1951 Refugee Convention. A core tenet of the document, signed originally by twenty-six countries and later by the United States, is "non-refoulement," which states that countries cannot send asylum seekers or refugees back to any country in which they face threats to their life or freedom. Non-refoulement became a routine part of laws protecting the rights of displaced people in various countries, including the US, for the next seventy years.

The 1951 Refugee Convention defines a refugee as anyone with a "well-founded fear of being persecuted for reasons of race, religion, nationality, membership of a particular social group, or political opinion." The signatory countries, of which many more would be added over the years, established their duties to protect refugees at all cost.

A filmmaker captured one of the first ships bringing refugees to the United States from the port city of Bremerhaven, Germany, after the passage of the Displaced Persons Act. US soldiers assisted women and children carrying cardboard suitcases, with coats and hats, onto the gangplank. A handful of refugees look down at the camera, leaning over a banner that reads "SHIP TO FREEDOM!" The October 20, 1948, headline from the *New York Times* stated, "813 REFUGEES SAIL FOR THE U.S. TODAY. First of Displaced Persons Admitted Under New Law Will Leave Bremerhaven."

The images of those passengers surely evoked memories of photos from the MS *St. Louis*—the ship to freedom attempting to redeem the voyage of the damned. With the departure of the first passengers out of Bremerhaven, the American refugee admissions process began. Following World War II, through the dips and shifts of refugee resettlement policy over the next several decades, one of the principles of American identity would remain the same: The United States viewed itself as a country that provided defense for the defenseless, welcome for the war-battered, and home for the displaced people of the world. This identity was shaped by an American public that, along with much of the world, felt a deep resolve to prevent a crisis like the Holocaust from ever happening again.

Chapter 3

HASNA

DARAA, SYRIA, MARCH 2011

Hasna al-Salam absently picked a dying flower off her jasmine plant. The cool morning wind stirred her still-damp hair; she would not put on her hijab for a few more minutes. This was the time of day Hasna liked best, puttering alone in her home sipping her coffee before beginning the work of the day. In the early years, when the older children were babies, she could not have dreamed of a pause after breakfast and before cleaning the dishes, time to listen to music on her record player or prune the plants. But as the children went off to school one by one, these quiet mornings became completely hers. Daraa, her beloved city, came awake around her—the deep rumble of trucks and the high whine of a motorcycle, her neighbor scolding a small child, birds calling to one another.

She turned on an album by Fairuz. The singer's voice always accompanied Hasna in the mornings, as it did so many women—the rhythmic drive of the piano and the snappy drums, the soulful violin that infused her lyrical trills with nostalgia. Fairuz captured the heartache and joy of being a mother.

The high walls lining the courtyard of their home, which allowed her to be both outside and private, were covered in vines. The jasmine plant was in a deep pot in one corner on the smooth concrete bench skirting the entire courtyard; the heavy scent filled the yard. Metal poles set in the mosaicked tile floor held an awning above. Grapes grew along the awning and kept the courtyard shaded for much of the day. The courtyard was filled with plants both practical and beautiful—she could make tea from the jasmine and the roses. She had pots with lemon trees, olive trees, and sage to cook with, aloe for her children's and grandchildren's scrapes. The begonias and amaryllis she kept because she loved them. Whatever she planted grew; the region of Horan, in which Daraa was the biggest city, was well-known for its agricultural wonders. And Hasna was especially good with plants. She adjusted the chairs around the table where later in the day someone would set up a backgammon game; sometimes her husband, Jebreel, and their neighbor would stay up until three in the morning before someone won. Sometimes, on holidays, their sons Yusef and Khassem and their friends would come over, filling their home with laughter and stories.

The courtyard took up half of their home. In Daraa, there were few days out of the year when they needed to remain indoors. They slept and prepared food inside the house; they hosted formal clan gatherings on the rugs and pillows in their large living space. But their life as a family happened in this courtyard. In the years when her children all lived at home, before the girls had married and Khassem gone off to the army, they ate their meals on the long table in the middle of the courtyard. The children would pile in from school and from working in their father's shop. Hasna imagined them again, all long arms and legs, bickering and laughing together, as she sat down to finish her coffee on the part of the bench she liked best, her back against the wall by the kitchen door, the record player within easy reach.

Her children were only the latest generation to grow up in this house, where dozens of al-Salam children had been raised over the decades. The houses in the streets surrounding the small Al-Salam Square, which was what everyone called the small plaza around which their clan life revolved, changed with every generation. Each family added balconies and second-floor apartments, took out some walls and added others in a complicated hodgepodge that defied any sort of architectural order. The result was a labyrinthine neighborhood where the houses were joined in an elaborate system of connected garden walls and alleyway shortcuts that the children innately understood and that was all but incomprehensible to outsiders.

Hasna loved that her friends and neighbors lived within a stone's throw of one another. One of her best friends from childhood, Um Ahmad—her title as

Ahmad's mother—married a cousin of Jebreel's who worked at a guard's station near the border with Jordan. Hasna saw Um Ahmad almost every day. She missed her parents, who had died years before; her brothers and sisters and their families lived in Damascus and Aleppo and United Arab Emirates and visited a few times a year. But her days were full with neighbors, especially Jebreel's many sisters and cousins, slipping back and forth to one another's homes when the men were at work, cooking or shopping or lingering over coffee.

Hasna had been a teenager when she married into Jebreel's clan. She could still remember the al-Salam men tromping to her house for the jaha; she was supposed to remain upstairs as the traditional engagement ceremony took place among the men, but she had snuck a look at her husband-to-be when the men walked up the long, olive-tree-lined drive. He was in the middle of the group, laughing nervously with his cousins. His older relatives, led by the richest of his uncles, had been invited to show off the strength and respectability of their clan.

The al-Salam men were known throughout the region of Horan, all around the city of Daraa, for their fierce clan loyalty. She watched them as they walked, men sure of themselves and of their place in the world, feeling proud that his family had chosen her as a good match.

When the requisite ceremonies and the parties were done, Hasna had found herself in charge of a small dominion—as the only brother's wife, she had a place of respectability in their family that she had not had as a younger daughter in her own home. Jebreel and Hasna had been shy with each other in those first few months, careful, polite. She was little more than a girl and he seemed so much older in his midtwenties. Hasna, who had secretly dreamed of becoming an architect or an engineer—she was good at drawing and was fascinated by the houses and streets that gnarled around them like arteries—never questioned the fact that marriage came before education, not in those early years. Better to question that harvest came before winter; some things were part of life. Women bore children, men worked outside the home, the world continued.

The most important thing to both of them and to the clan living around them was to prove that their marriage was fruitful. Their initial shyness wore off; the children came. First a son, Yusef, a sign of Allah's favor and a blessing on their marriage. With his birth, Hasna became Um Yusef. He was quiet and serious from birth. He took his time to accomplish any goal, thoughtfully contemplating the floor before him before crawling or walking. His brother, Khassem, born a year later, was Yusef's opposite in every way—all fire and drive, running almost before he walked. Both boys were smart, but Yusef was almost always content to be home and Khassem was perpetually bored; if he wasn't entertained, he would find ways to make his life interesting. Hasna spent much of her late teen years trying to keep toddler Khassem out of trouble.

Those were tumultuous years, when Syria was still defining itself as a nation. Syria had been a French colony until it gained its independence in 1946; before the French, the nation was under the Ottoman Empire. A series of dizzying power changes followed independence as the region roiled and churned. Like the other Arab nations, Syria had become a pawn in the chess game of global dominance that played out in the Cold War between the Soviet Union and the United States. The other countries in the region were involved in boundary skirmishes, civil wars, and an ever-shifting series of alliances as the Arab states jostled for position in relation to the newly established country of Israel and as their own alliances shifted. Hafez al-Assad came to power in a series of coups that ended all that. His "Corrective Revolution" ended in 1971, firmly cementing Assad and his party as the rulers of Syria.

It was a relief, in a way, to remain under the same leader—there was a certain stability in that, at least. But Hafez al-Assad ruled with an iron fist. Jebreel and Hasna, along with most of their neighbors, learned early on that political engagement in Syria under Hafez al-Assad was a high-risk game they'd rather not play.

Jebreel and Hasna were not Alawites—the ethnic minority in Syria that had risen to power with Assad—which meant they had two options: to join the ranks of the non-Alawites who bought or schemed their way into positions of power and success within the country, or to stay out of politics entirely. To openly resist Assad was not an option; everyone knew people in Syria who had disappeared, sometimes for years. A distant relative of Hasna's had made an off-color joke about Assad and had never come home from work. Twenty years later, after his infant grew up, got married, and had a child of her own, he showed up one day at their family home. There were rumors of where he had been for the last two decades, but no one spoke of it. His wife and family welcomed him back as if he had only been gone a few days. To repeat the story was to risk the possibility of being disappeared. Still, everyone had developed codes and shorthand for saying what needed to be said, and the story spread, a warning of what could happen to anyone at any time in Syria under Hafez al-Assad.

Jebreel and Hasna decided to stay politically unengaged, to never even speak of politics. It was a choice they agreed on completely. In Syria, even the walls had ears.

Their family might not attain the same successes that they could have if they had played into the often-corrupt system, but at least they would not be subjected to the mercurial changes of fortune that followed so many who did. They led as independent a life as they could.

Hasna tried hard not to pay much attention to the conflicts that turned her country into a pressure cooker during the years her babies were being born. In 1980, when Israel took advantage of President Hafez al-Assad's efforts to eradicate the Muslim Brotherhood in Syria in order to formally annex the Golan Heights and solidify their defiant position against Syria and other Arabic countries, she was pregnant with Yusef and setting up her new home. A year later, when Khassem was only a few months old and Yusef was echoing his mother's voice with his first words, Hafez al-Assad's troops began targeting the Muslim Brotherhood in Hama, slaughtering thousands of civilians. The Assad regime learned that brutal repression could eradicate any external threat, a lesson they would not forget.

Hasna, a teenage mother with two small boys, kept her head down, spoke of other things when the neighbors came for coffee or tea. Still, she heard about the deaths of the Syrian civilians at the hand of their government. It was the political event that would define the nation—thousands of young people died, even more fled the country. But the event that defined Hasna's life came two years later in 1983, when baby Amjad—her third son—was born with asthma. Her older sons had also had asthma as babies, but there was a medication she had given them to ease their symptoms. When Amjad was just a few weeks old, she asked the doctor for that medication along with formula; breastfeeding had never been easy for her. He told her sorrowfully that both were no longer available because of sanctions against the country, collateral of the complex relationship between Syria and Lebanon and the continuing conflict with Israel. Hasna neither knew nor cared about this tangle of international relations. Such things were in the hands of Allah. But her body was not producing enough breast milk to keep Amjad alive. He was three months old when she held him, starving and struggling for breath, and watched him die.

Amjad's death deeply affected her. Months passed. Her relatives and neighbors gave her unsolicited advice about how to move past her grief: babies came and went—better not to be too attached before you knew they would live past the first year. Hasna could barely hear them; her body ached for her son. She woke up to the sound of his plaintive cry in the night. Her living sons' toddler bodies seemed tainted with her grief. Instead of being the energetic and active playmate she had been, she was now withdrawn. The boys were clingier and whinier than before. Eventually, the grief dimmed, but she no longer assumed that she could live out a normal life and avoid what was happening in her country—eventually, the politics in Syria would come for them all.

It was four more years before she could welcome another baby. By then the economy in Syria had improved; Hafez al-Assad, after the bloody assaults in Hama and the wars against Israel and in Lebanon, seemed to want to create a secular state more like Turkey than like fundamentalist Iran. In 1987, Hasna's first daughter, Amal, was born into a more prosperous Syria where formula and medicine were now plentiful again.

Amal was serious like Yusef and smart like both of her brothers. From an early age, she showed a deep and abiding love for the scriptures; she would become the delight of the sheikhs in Daraa because of her thirst for knowledge and her love of Allah. She was quiet and reserved, which most of their neighbors read as natural goodness and obedience. Only her family saw the depths of her stubbornness, the ways she could play her brothers against each other. Hasna tried not to let her daughter get out of the trouble she sometimes caused for her brothers, but she also adored her brilliant mind. Watching Amal gave Hasna the first intimation of a revolutionary thought that would become one of her lifelong passions—her daughter should have the same educational opportunities as her sons. It was a thought she kept silent about for years. To speak it aloud might make her seem more radical than she felt, might sound as if she were questioning the very structure of her life. But the thought never went away.

Her second daughter, Laila, only confirmed that desire. From the beginning, Laila barreled through life; where Amal assessed and strategized, Laila charged. She became especially close to Yusef, who was a decade older. They were complementary opposites—he was grave and reserved, she was lively and loud. Their family—with two boys and two girls—felt balanced and complete.

When Amal decided at the age of eight after reading the Quran and listening to the sheikhs that she wanted to wear a hijab, Hasna took up the hijab as well. Hasna had not worn it before that—in Assad's Syria, to be overly religious could have implied a suspicious relationship with the Muslim Brotherhood. But Amal was growing up in a time when those connotations were more and more a thing of the past and she wanted to do what was right. Hasna was pleased at Amal's pure relationship with Islam; she was proud to tell others she wore her hijab because of her devout young daughter. She felt only a pinprick of resentment that her educated, passionate, devout daughters could have the things that she did not. Hasna would have liked to have spoken her mind as easily as Amal did, would have loved to have gone to school, would have loved to be as knowledgeable about scripture as all of her children were.

Yusef was preparing to leave high school when Hasna had her last baby, eighteen years younger than Yusef and eight years younger than Laila. Having a baby in her late thirties felt very different from her earlier pregnancies; she was more tired than she remembered being. After the baby was born, however, her body surprised her: She exclusively breastfed Rana, something she had not been able to do with any of the other children. She thought she might begrudge Rana, happily suckling the milk that might have saved her older brother Amjad so many years ago, but it was impossible to feel anything but delight for this baby with the black-brown eyes. Amal, who was twelve when her baby sister was born, was beginning the preparations she would need to care for her own house someday and loved to cook when her mother allowed it.

Amal, who always did what was expected of her, finished her high school degree as her mother had wished. It was Laila who gave her parents headaches, who asked more questions than she should, who refused to acquiesce or give in.

IN A REGION WHERE MOST MARRIAGES WERE ARRANGED, LAILA MARried for love. Nothing about the unorthodox courtship should have surprised Hasna, but it did. Laila was still young and full of plans, and it never occurred to Hasna that those plans might include marriage at seventeen. Hasna had been unsure about Laila's adamant dreams of becoming an engineer—even the young men who made it all the way through college were not able to find engineering jobs in Syria, which was still recovering from a drought that wrecked the country in 2007 and the worldwide recession that started in 2008. But it never occurred to her to worry that Laila might be willing to walk away from her plans.

One Friday evening, Amal's husband, Samir, sat down with Hasna and Jebreel, the whole family lingering over the late afternoon meal in their courtyard. He and Amal had not been married long, but the whole family loved the jovial Samir—he was easy to get along with, secure in himself, quiet but assured in his love for Amal. He told Jebreel and Hasna that his friend Malek al-Salam was interested in Laila. Malek was a member of their clan, a very distant cousin, and a handsome teacher at the boys' school associated with Laila's girls' school. He taught Quran to children on Friday afternoons and had a reputation in their neighborhood for holiness that was untouched.

Hasna was pleased—it was no small thing to have one of the most eligible young men in the area be interested in her daughter. But she was quicker to speak than Jebreel, who often took time to deliberate on such important decisions. She told Samir "no" immediately. Hasna was adamant: Laila was too young. She could talk about marriage after finishing high school in two years.

Jebreel and Hasna went to bed that night mulling over the situation. They had sent a similar rejection with Jebreel's relative who approached them about Amal when she had been Laila's age. Hasna felt a twinge of regret—Malek really was smart, good, and handsome. He would have made a remarkable husband for Laila. But her reasons were sound. She went to sleep with a good conscience.

She should have known better.

THE NEXT DAY, AMAL CAME OVER IN A RUSH, TOO HURRIED TO WAIT till her mother had heated the stove to boil water for coffee.

"Laila's going to marry him anyway," she blurted as she unpinned her hijab.

"What?" Hasna sat down, pulling out a chair for Amal.

"Laila was at the house this morning—"

"Instead of going to school?" Hasna rose to get out of her seat, and Amal gestured for her to sit down. "Yes, but that's the least of our problems. She says you can either approve of Malek or not, but she's marrying him anyway."

"Do they . . . ? Have they . . . ?"

"*No*, of course not, Mama. No. It's Malek and *Laila*. They're just—they love each other."

"What do you mean, they love each other? They don't even know each other."

"Mama, honestly. They do. Malek's been over here for years with Khassem; they were in our cousin's wedding together."

"Have they talked?"

"No! They're making us do it! Samir and I are stuck in between and it's getting ridiculous! You should see what it's like, the way Samir and I laugh that they've taken over our conversations—Malek loves her and she loves him, and we tell each other what the other one says."

Amal and Hasna looked at each other for a moment. It was not appropriate for a man and woman to be alone together, and it was pushing the boundaries for a sister and brother-in-law to act as a conduit. The consequences, if Malek and Laila went further, could be dire—her reputation, his job prospects, their ability to set up a life in the city they loved.

"Mama, she's serious. She loves him. I've never seen her like this. She almost threw my best teacups, she was so mad that you said no. I told her I'd come talk to you. Please, will you let them talk about marriage? I'm not sure

Samir and I can take this much longer!" And then Amal was laughing and Hasna was laughing with her.

Hasna sighed. "I'll talk to your father."

Amal grinned. "You have to admit, he's really good looking." She already knew if Hasna were convinced, Jebreel would be easy to bend—he cared about his daughters' educations because Hasna did.

"And he's a good man. She could do worse." Hasna patted Amal's hand, getting up to put the hot water on. She called out over her shoulder, "Let's drink our coffee, huh? And then you can tell your sister to come home and tell me this to my face."

Hasna's voice was light. Laila had already won.

The men of the al-Salam clan packed into their living space for Laila and Malek's jaha. Malek brought his brothers, his father, his many uncles and cousins. Jebreel had brought his brothers-in-law and their sons, Hasna's cousins and her cousins' husbands, and of course Laila's brothers. Hasna was grateful to her father-in-law once again for the foresight in building a home that was cool in the summer and warm in the winter—the men sat on her expensive Iranian rugs, settled into the comfortable cushions, and smoked as they discussed the fates of the children. The disagreements were minor and affectionately bartered—the men of the clan always enjoyed the chance to gather together and catch up. In the marriage contract negotiation, there had been only one sticking point, and Hasna had quietly discussed that before the official jaha took place.

She extracted from Malek a promise: If Laila did not finish her schooling, Hasna had the right to have their marriage contract annulled. This was no small concession on his part—he knew it would cause a minor revolution in his household; his sisters-in-law and his mother would hate it. But Hasna was unbending. The men teased Jebreel about life with a stubborn wife, but it was lighthearted—which of the men in Daraa did not have a wife whose heart was flint?

The night before the wedding, the men left the house and their women neighbors and relatives came over to help the bride prepare for her wedding day. They danced and ate. The girls giggled and whispered stories to a blushing Laila of what was coming. The older women lingered over a table filled with platters of half-eaten baklava and cake and sang the songs that had been handed down for generations. Traditionally in Daraa, mothers prepared the bedding for their daughters and the songs drew out of that custom, when women banded together to help a mother sew what her daughter needed, when a bride spent one last night with her sisters and cousins.

The next day, Laila and Malek were married. The wedding celebration separated men and women. Malek danced dabke with the male relatives at noon in the Al-Salam Square; the older men wore traditional long white tunics and headscarves, but the young men mostly wore trousers and crisply ironed shirts. They put their arms around one another and leaned into one another while they danced for hours. The dabke wove together the fabric of a new family; at a clan wedding like this one, it reinforced the bonds that already held them together. For generations, men had danced the dabke, held hands and hugged one another with an easiness Western men might never understand. The brotherhood of these men went deeper than almost any other social bond—no political leader or economic hardship could break it.

That morning, before the men danced dabke, Laila, her mother, and her sisters had their hair styled and their nails done. In the mirror, Hasna critically examined the wrinkles around her eyes—a series of home remedies for skin care, including combining rice water with frankincense, or using aloe vera, kept her skin smoother than that of many other women her age. Her honey-colored hair—a result of her own concoction of hair dye, which relied heavily on bleach—offset her hazel eyes. She glanced at her daughters in the mirrors around her: Laila had her mother's nose but a thinner version. If she could have sketched Laila, it would have taken a few angular lines—nose, jawline, cheekbones, slash of eyebrow—to capture her face. Amal's face would have been all curves. Amal inherited Hasna's cheeks but her father's dark brown eyes. Laila radiated intensity, Amal warmth.

Rana was all curiosity. Her eyes, shaped more like Amal's with a face more angular, like Laila's, were wide with interest in the day around her. Her mother had always cut her hair and done her nails. Pampering in a salon was something Rana would not have remembered from Amal's wedding. Rana could barely sit still in the salon, turning constantly to see what was happening with her sisters and mother. Hasna spoke sharply to her a few times; the stylist shot her a grateful glance and they shared a look of amusement. They had been young girls once too.

Afterward, they went to the rented dance hall and partied for hours with the other women of the clan—even the servers were women, so that they could take their hijabs off and dance together. They giggled and sang and cried together. They ate and ate, food that for once other people had prepared. They admired one another's hairstyles and ornate dresses.

At the end of the women's party, Malek came to get Laila. She embraced her mother and sisters, her aunts and cousins and friends. They helped her put on her abaya; the folds of the white cloth draped around her head and shoulders. She went with Malek to his parents' home, to the small suite of rooms they would share together, where they would begin their new life.

THE START OF THEIR MARRIAGE WAS ROCKY. AS HE PREDICTED, MALEK'S promise to Hasna was not received well by the rest of the family—they did not feel that Laila should be able to get out of serving the family just because her mother wanted her to go to school. And within a few months, she was too sick to go to school and too sick to serve the family, and that caused tension too.

The next-to-oldest brother's wife banged on the door of Laila and Malek's suite one day, demanding that Laila come help them with the feast for the day's guest. "I can't! I feel awful!" Laila yelled back. The idea of slaughtering and preparing a lamb sent her running to the bucket she kept near her bed.

In disgust, her sister-in-law went to their mother-in-law. Malek's mother did not bang on the door, but her quiet knock was imminently worse. "Laila, every woman in this house has been pregnant and we have all felt sick. In this house, you will get up and do your duty and that is that."

Laila got up and walked, not to the kitchen, but past her mother-in-law, out the door, straight to her mother's home. There she cried and dry heaved before curling up in her childhood bed for a nap. She was sleeping when Malek came to find her. Hasna answered the gate to Malek's knock with her chin jutted out; he had the presence of mind to look chagrined.

"Is this what we agreed, then? That my daughter would spend every day of her life working for your mother, always cooking, always cleaning, with no breaks to go to school? I know she is pregnant, and that school might need to wait until she feels better, but this sickness will pass in a few weeks, and then what? You promised me more than this, Malek." Malek agreed with Hasna at once. She had been prepared to invoke the clause erasing their marriage, but he respectfully asked her what to do.

Two days later, they moved into their own apartment. A few weeks later, Laila went back to school, riding there and back on the back of Malek's motorcycle, her pregnant belly pressed against his lower back while he drove.

It was not common, the level of love Malek and Laila held for each other. Their passion was evident to everyone around them; he was always proper, but Malek's eyes were never far from Laila. He adored her and, seeing this, Hasna adored Malek as much as her own sons. And no woman could question the love Malek showed for Laila when she gave birth to his son.

Laila only had a few months left on her high school degree even with a baby; she would be the second woman in their family after Amal to finish high school. Amal's daughter, Noor, now a bustling toddler, and Laila's baby, Hamad, a curious seven-month-old, stayed with Hasna often. She was proud of the good lives her daughters were building.

THE BOYS, THOUGH, WERE STILL STRUGGLING. YUSEF WANTED TO GET married; he was already older than Jebreel had been when he had married Hasna. But he wanted a business of his own first, and they were still struggling to keep Jebreel's business afloat.

Hasna often reminded Yusef that he was lucky to have any source of income at all, something he readily acknowledged. When his friends came over on summer evenings after dinner, they carried a palpable frustration with them. Yusef's friends were almost all from their neighborhood and Hasna had known most of them since they were in diapers. They should have been able to get jobs, should have been working in their chosen professions and thinking about marriage, but most of them were not. Yusef worked with his father, but the business was not his passion. He labored for his family unquestioningly— he was not Laila, to rail against the system until it changed. He would do his duty first. Hasna knew this was a good quality but she saw with sadness how much it cost him. She would give anything she could to help Yusef live out his dreams. But that would have involved leading a different life, one that was politically connected, and the risks outweighed the advantages.

Khassem had done well on his exams; like Yusef, he could draw, but he wanted to use that ability to become an architect. There were few architects in the country but Khassem was not worried—he had always been at the top of his class. He would attend a four-year college in Damascus and set himself up there at an architecture firm.

And then, in his last year in high school, after the exhaustive battery of college-entrance tests were finished, the school announced who would be accepted to the university in Damascus. The students in the top three spots received not just a guaranteed enrollment but full scholarships with room and board provided. The results were a surprise to everyone: Khassem was in the fourth slot. The girl who edged him out for third was someone he had gone to school with his whole life. He had tutored her; he knew what she was capable of. There was no possible way she had scored higher on the tests than he did. At home, inside with the doors closed, they all acknowledged: It was her father, an Alawite with connections deep in the Assad regime. Khassem and his family could not do anything about the fact that they were Sunni Muslims. What had been an occasional practice of picking Alawite children over more qualified Muslims or Christians under Hafez al-Assad now seemed to be the norm for his son Bashar's administration. Slowly, over years, the second Assad regime was ensuring that people utterly loyal to their family held every position of power in the country.

Jebreel and Hasna knew that they could have started months or years before, placing bribes and working their way into the inner circle of the people who supported the government. Some of the pro-government people were good men, like the husband of Hasna's dear friend Um Ahmad.

But they had set their path long ago. To begin giving bribes after a lifetime of remaining neutral might have cost them even more dearly; they might have ensured Khassem's place but jeopardized Jebreel's business. Or they might have stepped inadvertently into an intrigue they did not understand and one day one of them would disappear. Hasna was surprised at how angry she felt. She did not speak it, barely thought it, but the resentment bubbled below the surface. If she felt it, she knew that the young men gathered in her courtyard on summer evenings must be boiling over with frustration.

Yusef worked in part to pay for Khassem to go to college. They were good boys. Hasna could choose to feel anger that one son was forced to work so the other son could go to school, or she could feel grateful to have sons who were unselfish.

Hasna admitted to herself what she would never have voiced: she was most frustrated at the mandatory military service in Syria that caused both her sons to put their dreams on hold. Khassem had put it off as long as possible, going to school first and joining the military at the end. He had not wanted to enter the army—had even prolonged his last two classes in college since, as long as he was a student, he could delay the service that all Syrian men were legally required to partake in. Finally, he signed up for the army himself rather than waiting to be drafted, finishing the remaining college credits in Damascus. Hasna did not want her sons in the hands of the Assad regime. She prayed five times a day that Allah would stay with Khassem and protect him. She had been intensely grateful when Yusef made it out of the military. She lived for the day when Khassem was finished.

Everyone knew about the unhappy young men in Tunisia and Egypt and many other countries in the region. She had heard of a protest in Damascus just a few weeks earlier. When the next call to prayer sounded at midday, she would pray that Allah would be with the unhappy young men of Syria, that they would be wise and full of peace. She would pray for Khassem, that he would come home that Friday, and every week, for prayers with his father at the Omari mosque, and Mother's Day the following week, with a heart that was lighter than it had been recently.

Thinking of Mother's Day brought Hasna back to her day. She wiped her hands on her knees resolutely and walked into the kitchen to start on the breakfast dishes, flicking the towel over her shoulder. Laila and Amal were coming over soon to pickle eggplants with her. When the boys married, she thought with joy, there would be more little ones. She could picture herself here, surrounded by small children, and felt content. All she could want was here— a family that loved to be together, that ate midafternoon lunch on Fridays and lingered around their table under the fairy lights Rana had convinced her father to hang. When the dishes were done, Hasna stood in the open doorway of her kitchen and caught the last strands of Fairuz's warbling voice before the record finished. Then she snapped the towel once briskly and laid it over the wooden dowel to dry.

Chapter 4

MU NAW

AUSTIN, TEXAS, USA, APRIL 2007

The heat that first morning was the worst part. Their jet-lagged bodies had finally relaxed into sleep as the sun was rising, so Mu Naw and Saw Ku woke in the late morning drenched in sweat in an airless box of a room. The caseworker had shown them how to adjust their thermostat, but when they tried it, a terrifying whooshing noise frightened them, and they turned the dial up again so that it would stop. They combated the sweltering heat by taking cold showers, a marvel of their new home. Showering in the refugee camp was a communal activity, something done in public with a plastic bucket and a ritualistic movement of the thin longyi cloth to stay covered and still get clean. The water had come from the mountains through a pipe to the corner of the camp designated for bathing; the lines were always long. In this new place, they had an entire room for themselves. They could close the door and be entirely naked. Mu Naw giggled uncontrollably after her first shower, continually catching glimpses of her body in the large mirror when she dried off with the towels someone had supplied. She had never been completely uncovered when she bathed before. She had seen movies in the camps in which the people showered in bathrooms and slept in beds. The first day felt as if she were living on a Hollywood set.

After pulling on her skirt and tunic and slipping into her black rubber sandals, Mu Naw walked back into the bathroom to comb and braid her hair. The room still felt damp; the paint on the door felt tacky under her fingers. She knew what bamboo felt like when it rained in Thailand, the way the fibers thickened on the walls of her home. This new sensation, of dampness isolated to one room, fascinated her. The lights over the mirror were bright and she stared at her face in the mirror. It's not that she hadn't seen her face before—they had a small handheld mirror she had propped up in the hut in Thailand every day, there were mirrors in some of the shops in the camp market—but this brightly lit enormous mirror felt almost intrusive.

She studied her face in this new light. She smiled and then frowned and noticed how her face changed. When she smiled, her eyebrows lifted and her cheeks pulled back, bringing her cheekbones into prominence. When she did not smile, her cheeks looked fuller. Mu Naw could see in her own cheeks the echo of the baby cheeks she loved to kiss on Naw Wah, who looked more like her mother than Pah Poe, who took after Saw Ku. On herself, Mu Naw had always despised those full cheeks. She wished she were taller, that her skin were lighter. In the light of the rounded bulbs above the mirror, she could see that the thanaka she normally wore when she was outside had left her cheeks and forehead slightly lighter than the skin around it. Her eyebrows were shaped like bamboo halved longwise—a gentle, even curve arching above her eyes. Her lips were not much darker than her skin. Her chin ended with a point; her face was like a heart. She was quietly pleased with her nose, the tip slightly rounder than many of her friends' growing up. Her black hair reached to the middle of her back, and it smelled like berries from the shampoo. She parted it severely down the middle, pulling her plastic comb through it and braiding it at the nape of her neck. She decided she had had enough of seeing herself for the day and went to make breakfast for her family.

Mu Naw opened the refrigerator in the kitchen. The air inside it poured out, chilling the room. It smelled faintly of stale food. Inside, there was one roasted chicken in a plastic tub with a cardboard label she could not read, and four apples. When she peeled off the cardboard label and opened the plastic cover, she saw the chicken's legs were tied together with twine and it was sitting in congealed fat. The apples set on the shelf beside the chicken were small. She took both chicken and apples out of the refrigerator. There was a large bag of rice sitting on the counter but, when she dug through the cabinets, she could not find a way to cook the rice. The girls, who had been stoic the night before in the face of the strangers who escorted them from the air-port, were now whining with hunger, heat, and fatigue. Mu Naw cut one of the apples with a knife she found in a drawer and laid an equal number of slices on thin white plates on the table for each girl.

The chicken should be hot and should be served with the rice. She looked at the stove and wondered how to get fire out of it. In her home in Mae La camp that Saw Ku had lovingly constructed from bamboo he cut behind the camp with his machete, she had cooked over a charcoal stove in the outdoor kitchen nook in the back. Their stove was a large clay vase with a metal grill on top. She lit coals in the lower part and cooked sizzling meat over the fire. She pre-pared rice in the metal-and-bamboo rice cooker that was a staple in everyone's home there. The coals heated the water in the metal base of the rice cooker; steam rose through the bamboo cone, trapped by the lid on top. The rice cooked evenly, retaining the earthy hint of bamboo and smoke from the charcoal fire; it was flavorful and filling. She often added vegetables, chilies, and spices. Even with the limited food available in the camp, she was an excellent cook; just thinking about the rice made her stomach growl.

She looked distastefully at the lemony-scented chicken wrapped with soaked twine. Hesitating, she turned each of the four knobs on the front of the stove and nothing happened. She opened the large metal door; the burned remnants of the previous tenants' dinners lined the corners with ash. Also cold. She turned all of the knobs: it remained cold. She turned them off again. She looked underneath—was there a coal compartment she could not find? Saw Ku came in and sat with the children munching solemnly on their apples at the table. They watched Mu Naw turning the stove handles; Saw Ku got on his knees and looked under the stove. Nothing worked. It was another mystery they would have to add to their list of questions for someone to address. Some-one would come soon, surely, so Mu Naw sliced the greasy chicken legs off for each of the children and deftly divided the remaining meat onto the white plates. They had not eaten last night and had not had breakfast that morning; the chicken was at least full of protein and they ate their fill, sucking on the bones afterward to get the last of the meat flavor.

Mu Naw bathed and dressed the girls after their unsatisfying meal. They pulled the red and white covers up on the bed and went into the living room. They sat down on the brown couch to wait. They did not speak. They listened to the sounds of the apartments around them—children playing in the courtyard outside, their upstairs neighbors moving around, someone running up the stairs. Someone shouted out a name. They could hear cars starting and radios playing. Pah Poe and Naw Wah soon tired of sitting, so they played together quietly. They knew better than to disturb their parents. Saw Ku and Mu Naw sat stiffly on the brown couch waiting. At some point, Mu Naw began to cry, the tears rolling silently down her cheeks, afraid to frighten the children.

After hours of waiting, the sun began to set. There were three apples left. Mu Naw sliced two of them for the children's dinner, leaving the last apple alone in the refrigerator. She thought regretfully of the chicken bones that they had already sucked clean and thrown into the small garbage can under the kitchen sink. Her mother might have dug them out for the children to suck on further, but Mu Naw knew that her mother lived dirtily and that Saw Ku's family had been clean. She did not want to ever be dirty when she could be clean. She left the bones in the trash. They nibbled apple slices.

They took showers again to cool themselves off. They climbed into bed together. Again, Saw Ku and Mu Naw could not sleep. Saw Ku's belly grumbled; they had not had a great variety of food in Mae La camp, but the rations of rice and golden beans and the cans of catfish that they could fry or grill had been regularly delivered and their children had never starved.

That night, lying in bed, Mu Naw felt a formidable anger rise. She had been promised a new life in this country. No one came to their house today. How would they find the food they would need if no one delivered, gathered, or harvested it? Were the stores big or small, and how would she know the right English words to say so she could ask for the things they needed? She knew theoretically that there would be jobs and food and schools in this new life, but how was she to find these things? Had they been lied to this whole time?

She felt abandoned and deceived. She tried to keep her heaving sobs from shaking the bed so that the children would stay asleep. Saw Ku's hand found hers again and she clung to it.

SHE MET SAW KU FOR THE FIRST TIME WHEN THEY WERE FIFTEEN. They were both in the fifth grade, along with many of the others their age who had lost years of education to the civil war. Mu Naw thought Saw Ku was cute, with his square jaw, pale skin, artfully unkempt hair. She assumed that he would like her friend, a tall, long-haired beauty whom all the boys in Mae La camp seemed obsessed with. So, when, a few weeks into the start of the new school year, she got a note through a friend from Saw Ku, she was shocked. The love note to her was elegantly written, though the description of her beauty seemed a bit off to Mu Naw; later he confessed that he had written the note for her beautiful friend and not Mu Naw, but at the last minute, had a sudden change of heart. He called back their mutual friend who was acting as messenger and told her he had decided to send the message to Mu Naw instead. Saw Ku and Mu Naw laughed about it together over the years. Saw Ku knew of several other boys who already liked the other girl and suddenly he realized he would rather have a life with the girl who looked fun, who was comfortable in her skin, than the beautiful girl who would probably never return his affection. And that was it, a decision made swiftly in a schoolyard at the age of fifteen.

They kept their relationship a secret for a year; Mu Naw's family was an obstacle to be overcome rather than a source of pride to either of them, and the gossipy camp life was exhausting to both of them—secrecy felt easier. They wrote each other letters and slipped them discreetly to each other. Mu Naw was still quietly sure that Saw Ku had made a mistake, that he would regret declaring his love for her on a whim, but he did not. He found her insightful and full of joy. She did not complain like many of the other girls. Her mind was swift, making connections he often marveled at. Her eyes half-mooned with mischief when she teased him. He loved her effortlessly.

The other girls, not knowing Saw Ku was her secret boyfriend, pined after him at school, whispering all the things they would do if Saw Ku asked them out, and she passed the information along, giggling, to her boyfriend in the grove under the trees where they met some afternoons. One day, with no warning, he came up and said in front of her friends, "I want to talk to my girlfriend." She followed him, a blush overtaking her face, while her friends squealed.

When she met her future mother-in-law for the first time, Mu Naw was deferential and polite, eyes cast down, every movement showing her respect and docility, every line on her body communicating her desire for Saw Ku's mother's blessing. Later, Mu Naw would become Christian for them. She would leave her mother for them. She would raise her children to be clean rather than perpetuating the messy chaos of her mother's home. Her mother-in-law was duly impressed. They were married two years later and moved into the one-room bamboo hut Saw Ku built for them.

Saw Ku got one of the few available jobs in the camp, helping the NGO that educated people about hygiene, a critical part of living in a camp like Mae La. People who did not boil their water died of diseases that ripped through their bodies and often infected others. People who did not use the prescribed bathrooms put everyone at risk of cholera. People who did not correctly bank their cooking fires caused homes to blaze, a disaster for a camp built entirely out of bamboo. Saw Ku was an earnest part of the NGO campaigns, knocking on his neighbors' doors to teach them or invite them to educational plays put on by Karen people with Westerners' direction. Mu Naw was proud of her young husband, but they both chafed with the boredom and limitations of life in a permanent refugee camp.

ON SUNDAY, THEIR SECOND MORNING IN AUSTIN, THEY ATE THE LAST apple. Mu Naw sliced it thinly so that it would take longer for the children to eat. By midafternoon, they had showered and dressed and sweated through their clothes again in the airless apartment, waiting for someone to come. Naw Wah could not stop crying, a fretting noise that was not like her. Naw Wah was not a fussy toddler, but she was hungry and there was nothing to eat. The bag of rice sat tauntingly on the kitchen counter. Naw Wah finally fell into a fitful sleep on the big bed. Saw Ku was visibly sweating through his T-shirt. He told Mu Naw he was going to take a cold shower again. As soon as he closed the bathroom door, Mu Naw opened her hand-woven bag and made sure the envelope that held the money the IOM woman had given them—$25 for each person in their family, $100 total—was still inside. She put the bag across her body, grabbed her older daughter's hand and slipped out of the house, closing the door behind them. She was going to find some food.

Pah Poe was five and very quiet, exhibiting the almost stoic behavior of a well-trained Karen daughter. She did not protest when her mother pulled her along. The bright afternoon sun bounced off cement sidewalks. The buildings were painted brick red with dark blue trim; on closer inspection the red walls held gloppy remnants of the blue trim paint and the cement foundation was splattered with dried paint in both colors. The squat buildings were situated close enough together to hold the spring heat between them. When they walked into the courtyard, a breeze picked up and lifted Mu Naw's hair off her face. It was good to be in moving air again. She strode toward the big road that she could see past the buildings. On the sidewalk, she passed a group of young men in T-shirts smoking cigarettes. Sweat prickled at the back of her neck. She held Pah Poe's hand and walked swiftly. She had no idea what they said as she moved down the sidewalk littered with cigarette butts and pieces of trash that had clearly been left in the sun for weeks.

Mu Naw moved across the parking lot to the edge of the driveway. It was on a curve of the road and cars raced by. They stood there for a minute, unsure what to do, and continued down the sidewalk rather than crossing the street. She and Pah Poe walked past the edge of the red and blue apartments, past a yawning parking lot, past a tall sign with words and a graphic of a dove and a sun, past two houses made out of brick with brown-shingled roofs. She came to the end of the block and stopped, unsure where to turn. Across the street, she saw a canary yellow sign with black writing. The first word and third word were not ones she recognized, but she knew the second word from her English classes in Mae La camp: "Food."

Holding Pah Poe's hand resolutely, Mu Naw crossed the street when a pickup truck stopped at the stop sign, walking carefully between the white lines as she had done two days before at the Austin airport. She watched the driver nervously the whole time, the exhaust from the engine filling her nostrils, but he waited for her. She put her hand on the metal bar of a door plastered with brightly colored advertisements that Mu Naw didn't even try to decipher. Boldly, she pushed the glass door open.

There were stacks and rows of things that neither of them had ever seen, entire aisles full of items that Mu Naw's eyes slid past because she did not understand them. She smelled coffee that had been left too long on the burner, unwashed bodies and smoke, the metallic scent of air-conditioning, the sweet smell of cakes. She wanted cake.

Pah Poe let go of her mom's hand and raced toward the chips, ones in the same kind of crinkly bag they sold in the hut store at Mae La camp, asking in a higher-pitched voice if they could have some.

"Let's get some!" Mu Naw told her, grabbing bag after bag. She had no idea how much they cost, how to even measure the numbers on the small signs in front of the items in relation to the $100 in cash she had in the envelope in her purse—it would be weeks before she understood the words for "dollars" and "cents." She held the chip bags close to her body with her left hand and reached for other items that looked familiar: packaged cakes and juice boxes. There were no fruits or vegetables and she did not know what the other cans or the other bags held in them.

She and Pah Poe took their armfuls of items to the front, waited in line behind a woman buying a Coke and a pack of gum, and then spilled their purchases onto the counter in front of the startled clerk. He said something to Mu Naw, and she neither acknowledged his remark nor asked questions. She took the cash out of the envelope inside her bag and slid it to him. He asked another question and she looked back at him expressionlessly. She would not show fear. Without another word, he began to swipe over the items with a black plastic box in his hand; a red light shone on each chip bag and, when it pinged, he would set it aside in a small plastic bag. When he was done, he said something to Mu Naw again. She gestured tersely with her chin, pointing at the money in a pile on the counter beside him. She prayed silently that the money was enough. He handed her back several bills and a handful of coins, which she tucked carefully back into the envelope.

Pah Poe carried one plastic bag and Mu Naw carried four as they walked back carefully hand in hand. Mu Naw knew she had arrived at the right apartment because there was nothing in front: no plants or towels or bikes or shoes. She set down her bags to open the door.

Saw Ku threw the bathroom door open quickly, his hair still damp from spending so long in the cool water.

"Did you leave? Where were you?" His voice was startled and relieved.

"Pah Poe and I went to find food." She gestured with her chin at the bags she had brought in as she set them down on the table.

"Food! Where did you find food? Did they come back and bring it to us?"

Mu Naw told Saw Ku about walking along the sidewalk and recognizing the word "food" on the store sign; Pah Poe punctuated the story with her own contribution: "I saw the chips!"

They sat down at the dining room table and pulled item after item out of the bags and ate with no preamble, stuffing themselves with the chips and cake, washing it down with the juice Mu Naw had found for her family. When Saw Ku smiled at her, a potato chip crumb clung to the corner of his mouth. She laughed and he swiped at his mouth, spreading more crumbs across his cheek. The children giggled and Saw Ku blew out his cheeks at them, waggling his eyebrows and his ears. Pah Poe folded over with laughter and begged him to do it again and again. Every time he agreed, until their laughter faded into comfortable, homey silence broken only by the crinkle of foil wrappers and the rustle of cellophane.

Chapter 5

HASNA

DARAA, SYRIA, MARCH 2011

The morning of March 18 was like any other Friday before it, the sunlight coruscating through the grape leaves over the courtyard, causing dappled shadows on the table where Hasna and her family gathered for their usual Friday morning meal. Hasna normally made her own bread, but that morning she hadn't—Jebreel took Rana with him in the morning to their bakery to pick up the pita bread, the humid warmth fogging the plastic bag wrapped around it. Rana hugged it to her as she walked, holding her father's hand, through the streets that were filled with fewer cars than on weekdays. Rana was a coltish twelve-year-old with big eyes and a smile always set to please her mother and sisters. Rana loved Friday mornings, the leisurely breakfast, the chance to walk alone on the street with her father, looking forward to the large afternoon meal when the whole family came over.

Hasna made ful for Yusef, Khassem, Rana, and herself, a staple of their Friday breakfast; she diced tomatoes and scooped them carefully into the center of each of the bowls, a bright balance to the fava beans. Khassem was home for the weekend from Damascus; he had arrived Thursday night, as he did every week, and he would go back that night in time for work on Saturday morning. Khassem pecked her cheek and took the bowls of ful from her hands to the table; she went back to the kitchen to finish setting the table.

They ate, their conversation desultory. Afterward, her men left as they normally did for Friday prayers, kissing her on the way out and leaving a lingering scent of shampoo and aftershave. She cleared the table, did the dishes, pruned the plants, listened to Fairuz, sipped her coffee. Hasna danced slightly as she moved around the house, her heart light, her body moving through her beloved home without really seeing the familiar objects, as she had done every morning for years. The meal only seemed remarkable later, the last normal meal in their house.

When the call to prayer sounded, she wished—as she did occasionally— that she could be at Friday prayers. She would not want to be in the Omari mosque with Jebreel and Yusef, that big mosque frequented by the officials and police officers and many of the important people in Daraa, but she would like to go to the smaller neighborhood mosque that Malek attended. She could picture him now, as she washed her right hand three times and then her left— the sheikh imam would be standing in front of his congregation, men on one side, women on the other, and beginning the salah with "Al-salamu alaykum," wishing them peace.

When she thought of going to a mosque, she remembered attending as a young girl with her grandmother. She could still smell the lotion her grandmother used on her hands, the musky dry scent of the well-used Quran her grandmother always carried. She centered herself within that memory as she tugged on her prayer covering, the elastic waist of the leopard-print head covering and skirt lying lightly over her clothes—imagining herself in the mosque with her grandmother and the other women she had grown up with helped her stay focused when she made prayers.

She walked to her navy rug spread out in her prayer corner, the arrow pointed toward the Holy Kabah in Mecca. She stood at the edge of the rug and made sure the folds of fabric covered her completely. She put her hands to her ears, began with "Allahu Akhbar," then crossed her arms right over left on her chest to pray the Surah al-Fatihah. During the four repetitions of the midday prayer, when she knelt and praised God the Great, "Subhana rabi alazeem," her hands were on her knees. When she prostrated herself and praised the God above, "Subhana rabi alaala," her hands remained just below her chin on the rug beside her. At the end of prayers, she prayed for Abraham and Moham-mad and finally wished peace to the angels, whispering "Al-salamu alaykum" first over her right shoulder and then her left. Then she remained kneeling, hands on her knees, and presented her petitions to God: prayers for her children and grandchildren, and especially for Khassem as he journeyed back to Damascus that night.

When she had removed her prayer covering, she hurried to finish her dishes. After her prayer time, she would only have a few minutes before Amal arrived. Hasna had every intention of enjoying her Friday without working all day. They would begin preparing the large meal in the early afternoon, as the men came home from the mosque, but the late morning was one of the few leisurely times she had during the week with her girls.

THEY HEARD THE SHOTS FIRST. AMAL HAD BEEN THERE FOR OVER AN hour, her feet up on a chair to keep them from swelling, chatting with Hasna over tea while Rana played with little Noor. At first, they thought that someone must be having a wedding; there was always someone shooting off guns in celebration of weddings on Fridays. They barely registered the shots until they heard the angry voices. Those were not the celebratory yells of happy wedding guests, they were the outraged, determined shouts of a mob. There were more shots—direct, repeated, intentional.

Hasna and Amal ran outside. The air was filled with the voices of the women in the street, the metal clanging of gates up and down the street as more women came outside. They clumped together in front of her neighbor's house, where there was a good view of the main road; the women talked in low voices as they waited for the men to come home.

Jebreel, Yusef, and Khassem were with the first group of men to make their way up the street, shoulders hunched, heads down, their desire to avoid trouble evident in their determined walk. Samir was not with them. Hasna could feel Amal's body stiffen. As the men joined them, the clump of women dissolved. Amal did not move from her post by the road.

Hours later, Samir made it back to his in-laws' house. A few minutes after Samir, Malek and Laila slipped in; Laila clutched baby Hamad. Hasna pushed coffee and tea on everyone, set out plates of cookies and fruit. No one ate; their drinks cooled in their hands. The gate was open and neighbors and relatives came in and went out all evening, repeating what they had heard and seen.

The walls in Syria might have ears, but what had happened was so portentous, her normally nonpolitical neighbors now spoke openly.

Over their collective renditions, Hasna pasted her own perceptions. Soon the tale was fused so firmly together that it became a thing in its own right, a monument to this day and the days that would come, fabricated from scraps of gossip and layered with whispers spoken behind closed doors, a story with weight and heft that she would carry with her to every new place, that she would center the rest of her life on.

At the Al-Abbas mosque, as the sheikh imam was finishing his khutba, he spoke the final blessing, the same as the first: "Al-salamu alaykum," so they could begin and end their time together with peace. "Al-salamu alaykum," they should have replied, and some of them did, the words barely leaving their lips before thirty men rose as one and answered his blessing decisively: "ALLAHU AKH-BAR!" It was not what they said—Allahu akhbar, Allah is greatest, which could be breathed out in recognition of Allah's manifold goodness a thousand times a day or sighed in response to a story or spoken out in praise. It would be the prayer on the lips of thousands of people in the next few days. In the Al-Abbas mosque, it was the way they said it: When the sheikh imam stood, hands raised to bless his congregation, and received back the fierce, guttural response of a multivoiced act of defiance, the sheikh knew, they all knew, what it meant.

It was a battle cry.

The men marched out of the mosque, down the street, yelling loudly, "ALLAHU AKHBAR! ALLAHU AKHBAR! ALLAHU AKHBAR!" Their voices rang out with the boldness of those who had been utterly wronged, who were done being silent, who knew that all good men would join them in their cause. The men made their way down the streets from the Al-Abbas mosque to the Omari mosque, where Jebreel and Yusef and Khassem were walking out into the sun. The protesters wanted to end in the clearing beside the large Omari mosque, so that the government officials and mukhabarat officers who regularly attended it on Fridays would be forced to reckon with their accusations.

At first, Jebreel told Hasna, he, too, thought it was a wedding. Then they saw the first marchers turning the corner, into the clearing, their faces set in anger, their fists raised, and they realized it was a demonstration. Jebreel,

Khassem, and Yusef ducked down a back road to home. They were walking quietly, heads down, when they heard the first gunshots. A man running past them told them two men had already been killed.

But it was the story of why the men had protested that day that was the most unbelievable to Hasna—the reach of it felt too vast, too unlikely. She hoped fervently that they were all wrong, that all of this would blow over in a few days.

THE EVENTS OF THAT FRIDAY IN MARCH BEGAN, IN MANY WAYS, ALMOST exactly three months before in another country. A shopkeeper named Mohamed Bouazizi set himself on fire in a market in Tunisia on December 17, 2010. He was protesting his treatment by a government official, a protest born out of unshakably hopeless poverty. It was the spark that ignited a region. By December 19, police in Tunisia were using tear gas to disperse hundreds of young men in the city of Sidi Bouzid, protesting high unemployment and lack of promised political reform. After ten days of violent clashes, the president of Tunisia appeared on national television to promise, "The law will be applied in all firmness" to all protesters. Two days later, protests began in Egypt: On January 1, 2011, a Coptic church was bombed, and Christians took to the streets. Six days later, on January 7, 2011, it spread to Algeria—the protesters demanded access to jobs and affordable food like their Tunisian and Egyptian counterparts. On January 9, protesters in Tunisia were setting fire to cars and engaging in violent scuffles with police. On January 13, a man in Algeria lit himself on fire like Mohamed Bouazizi, while rebellion in Tunisia flared beyond anyone's ability to measure, much less control.

Riots started in neighboring Libya and Muammar Gaddafi took to the national airwaves on January 14 to tell protesters to stop. His warnings were overshadowed by the triumphant news that the Tunisian president had fled to Saudi Arabia, an early victory that only increased the spread of the Arab Spring. Yemen's protests spiked on January 23. The morning of January 25 saw massive protests in Lebanon and Egypt, followed by thousands of protesters in Jordan and in Palestine on January 28.

Despite the repeated efforts of the many repressive leaders, the people were undeterred. Leaders whose legacies had seemed secure just weeks before were falling: Tunisia, then Yemen. Egypt's Hosni Mubarak hovered on the brink. In February, protests flared up in Algeria. Bahrain. Morocco. Iraq. The region was succumbing quickly.

Syria was one of the last places where the Arab Spring had not ignited. And Bashar al-Assad, celebrating ten years in power after taking over the country at his father's death in 2000, was determined that it would remain that way. The Assad regime would not be toppled by unruly young men. He had watched his father during the raids on the Muslim Brotherhood in Hama; Alawite leaders who had retained power despite their minority status for years were all around him. They knew what to do; he had already issued orders that every spark from the Arab Spring would be stamped out immediately, irrevocably.

IN A REGION GOVERNED BY DICTATORS, THERE HAD INITIALLY BEEN signs Bashar might be a benevolent one, certainly less cruelly strategic and more accepting of the outside world than his father before him. Bashar's older brother, Bassel, had been groomed for the presidency from an early age, getting a PhD in military studies and cutting his teeth on his father's brand of warfare through Syrian involvement in the Lebanese Civil War in the late 1970s and '80s. Bassel was a reckless womanizer with a fast and loose reputation; privately, Syrians worried about his taking power. Bashar was off at school in England to become an ophthalmologist in 1994 when Bassel was killed in an accident, heading to the airport in Damascus—he had been driving too fast. Bashar spoke fluent English and decent French. He married a beautiful Sunni woman, which signaled to his people that after his father's insular, Alawite-only regime, things might change. His wife, Asma, had been raised in the United Kingdom and retained her British citizenship, which the world took to mean the isolated Syrian government was now interested in being part of the global community again. Even if these things were not true about Bashar, how much damage could one eye doctor do?

Bashar al-Assad carefully curated his image to the outside world as an educated, cosmopolitan family man who just wanted to do right by his people.

He hired a Western PR firm to help his reputation in the outside world—Brown Lloyd James, founded by Peter Brown, who had once managed the Beatles. Brown Lloyd James wooed travel and fashion journalists to cover the country at the time, to show that people were happy and the leader was a savvy man of the world. With an eye toward bringing in tourists, they worked to sell the beautiful countryside, the ancient landmarks, the culture and language that stretched back unchanged over thousands of years. They invited a long list of celebrities to come and have their pictures taken with Bashar and his family: John Kerry and Sting, Angelina Jolie and Nancy Pelosi.

In December 2010, Joan Juliet Buck, once the editor of French *Vogue*, traveled to Syria to write a cover story on Asma al-Assad for *Vogue*, attempting to peer beneath the surface of the image the Assad regime was aiming for. She could sense a Syria that, she said, "oscillated between untrustworthy rogue state and new cool place." Toward the end of their visit, Buck was treated to a Christmas concert with the president's family. The concert was clearly Christian, and included Arabic rap and some Broadway show tunes, another display of inclusive worldliness. In the middle of it, the president leaned over and whispered to Buck: "This is how you fight extremism—through art. . . . This is how you can have peace!" Unable to fully articulate or prove the rigidity beneath the surface, Buck wrote the piece she was sent to write. By the time the article came out in *Vogue* in February 2011, Bashar al-Assad's statement would be profoundly ironic.

By then, Assad was perfecting another image inside of his country, one that was very familiar to the Syrian people—that he, like his father, would respond swiftly and completely to every threat that arose.

ON FEBRUARY 16, 2011, A GROUP OF LITTLE BOYS STAYED OUT TOO LATE and wrote in chalk on a school wall. Hasna's neighbors told her that they were elementary school students, fourth and fifth graders like Rana, who walked across the street to write on the wall of the al-Banin school where older boys attended. They borrowed one of the incendiary phrases from the Arab Spring, "The people demand that the president be deposed," and changed it to insult the principal: "The people demand that the *principal* be deposed."

The next morning, the mukhabarat, the secret police, led by Atef Najib, Bashar al-Assad's cousin, were at the school; Bashar had not deviated at all from his father's tactic of giving key positions to family members and unquestioned loyalists. The boys were arrested immediately. There was no trial. It didn't matter if it was a prank, that the boys were children.

They were tortured, their bodies mutilated. Neighbors told Hasna that the secret police cut off some of the boys' penises. They ripped out their fingernails, hooked them up to electric currents and electrocuted them almost—but not quite—to the point of death. They shot them and then prevented them from dying, allowing them to live only to be tortured more.

In the city of Daraa, which had around three hundred thousand citizens in 2011, and the larger region of Horan, almost everyone could trace their ancestry back to a few families. They could tell you stories that went back generations of feuds that originated with incidents that became legends. Enmity, too, is passed along from generation to generation, with the tenacity for which the people of Daraa are famous throughout Syria. They did not take insults lightly. An insult to a citizen of Daraa was an insult to his entire family, all of his cousins and aunts and uncles, and their relatives in turn. And since many of the people of Daraa are related in a complex web that is all but indiscernible to an outsider, every citizen of Daraa knew, understood in his or her bones, that what happened to those boys affected all of them.

Things only got worse. The parents went to the mukhabarat and demanded the release of their sons. They were told—in an insult designed for maximum offense—that they should go home and forget those sons. In fact, they should make new sons. And, if they were not men enough to sire new sons, they should bring their wives to the mukhabarat, who would happily fuck them to make new sons on their behalf.

IT WAS THAT INSULT, ON TOP OF THE CAPTURE OF THE CHILDREN, THAT caused thirty of the boys' relatives and neighbors to plan the first Friday afternoon demonstration that Hasna and Jebreel mistook for a wedding, to yell "ALLAHU AKBAR!" in reply to the sheikh. The men planned their protest to end with Friday prayers at the Omari mosque. They wanted enough time for their demands to be heard before being fired upon by the army or the police.

At the funeral for the two men shot on the first day, other protests flared up. Other demonstrators died. Their funerals begot more protests. The days of rage were beginning.

Hasna knew, as any mother of young men did, that the protests that began that Friday were about the al-Banin boys, but that they were also about other issues that had been brewing for a long time. There were too many young men with no opportunities, too much pent-up fury, too many whispered stories of toppled leaders and revolutions in neighboring countries.

Hasna kept a kettle of hot water simmering on the back of the stove ready for coffee or tea with the neighbors who came by. The walls with ears no longer kept them from speaking out about what was happening as they tried to stay abreast of the news.

Late in the afternoon, her cousin—who was married to someone who knew the families of the al-Banin boys—told her a rumor that set the hair on Hasna's arm standing. The families who began the protests on that Friday did more than start the riots in the street—they met with Bashar al-Assad himself and laid out four demands: First, that the boys who were captured and tortured be released immediately if they were alive; if they were dead, that their bodies be given to their families for burial. Second, that the officers who had tortured and killed the boys be hanged in front of everyone. Third, that Bashar al-Assad's cousin and the head of the secret police in Daraa be publicly executed. And fourth, that Bashar al-Assad himself come to Daraa and apologize to everyone in the town.

Hasna liked her cousin; they had been close since they were children. She trusted her enough to voice her terror: Were these men naïve, thinking that these demands would sound reasonable to the government officials or to Bashar al-Assad himself? Were they thinking of the most outlandish things they could say as a calculated opportunity to vent their rage—were they spoiling for revenge and hoping to have an excuse to fight with the government forces that had wronged them? Did they really think that Assad would acquiesce? Did they not know that they were waving raw meat at a rabid dog?

After the cousin left, Hasna closed and locked the gate. She knew now what she had suspected but had not wanted to face: The government would not back down. This would not blow over.

KHASSEM ARRIVED HOME LATE THAT SUNDAY NIGHT, LONG AFTER THEY had all gone to bed. The sound of his motorcycle woke Hasna and Jebreel, Hasna's heart racing as she put on her housecoat and ran out to meet him. She kept him up and cooked him a late meal. His face was pale, and he ate without paying attention, speaking without fully chewing, telling his story as quickly as possible in a hushed voice. He had been planning to come back for Mother's Day the following morning, but he decided that he could not wait.

When Khassem asked, Jebreel confirmed that the families of the boys and their supporters had adopted the Omari as their unofficial headquarters. Families were camped out along the grounds where the protests had ended on Friday. They were waiting to hear the government's response to the family representatives who had gone to Damascus.

"That's what I was worried about." Khassem swallowed his mouthful of food, drank a large glass of cool water, wiped his mouth with the back of his hand. Hasna did not point out the napkin folded beside his bowl. Khassem leaned in, his voice as low as it could be so that the neighbors could not hear. He told them why he had ridden through the night on his motorcycle, unable to use the phone, where the government was always listening. What he knew could not wait even a few more hours.

He had been walking on the street near the barracks when he passed a general getting into a chauffeur-driven car. Khassem heard the general say the word "Daraa," and he surreptitiously moved closer so that he could hear. The general was repeating the story—like a joke—to one of his officers. They were laughing about it, standing in the street, not worried who heard them, mocking those country bumpkins from Daraa and their outlandish demands on the president.

Khassem kept his face straight as he turned away from them, turned up his collar, put his hands in his pockets nonchalantly. He could just hear the general say as he got into the car: "Those people in Daraa have no idea what's about to hit them."

Chapter 6

MU NAW

AUSTIN, TEXAS, USA, APRIL 2007

On Monday, Saw Ku's frantic voice in the bedroom doorway roused Mu Naw. A woman was at the door speaking Burmese. He did not speak Burmese well; even though Burmese was the language of education and communication between the various ethnic groups, Saw Ku's mind stayed stubbornly loyal to Karen, his mother tongue. Mu Naw rushed through, putting on her skirt and tunic, pulling her hair back into a ponytail as she left the room, afraid this Burmese woman would leave and they would be alone again.

The woman stood in the doorway, her lips pursed slightly. She tucked her hair behind one ear as she walked into the room. She wore a brown tweed blazer with a brown pencil skirt and low brown pumps that clicked slightly as she moved toward the table. She was a study in earth tones. Mu Naw was to learn that this woman always spoke emphatically, but that first day all Mu Naw understood was that they must have done something wrong.

"I am Rita. I am not your caseworker, but I am the only person who speaks Burmese. Do you speak Burmese?" She looked up and pointed with her chin at Mu Naw.

"I speak Burmese, but my husband only speaks some."

"That is fine. It is easier if at least one of you does. Come with me, we're going to your first-day orientation. I will take you to meet your caseworker."

"I'm sorry, this is our third day."

"It is Monday. This is your first day with us."

"We have been here for two days with no food." Mu Naw's voice rose slightly at the end. She instinctively curled her shoulders as Rita raised the edge of one eyebrow.

"You had something to eat." Rita held up a chip bag with two fingers. Mu Naw's brave solo trip to the store suddenly felt commonplace.

"Yes, we found a store where we bought some things, but we are still hungry. The children have only had chips and cake to eat."

"Your caseworker did come by Saturday?"

"No."

"Or Sunday?"

"No one has been here."

Rita's face softened a fraction. "We will go buy you some food now and I will make sure your caseworker sends someone to you to show you where to go shopping. Did you already have a volunteer come by?" She said "volunteer" in English and Mu Naw shook her head slightly, confused. Rita's eyes scanned the kitchen, taking in the packages of half-eaten processed foods, the wrappers folded over neatly to save what remained for later.

"This was all you had to eat? Do you have rice? Vegetables? Meat?"

"There was a chicken in the refrigerator and three apples." Rita pursed her lips, but this time Mu Naw suspected Rita was not frustrated with her. Mu Naw caught a glimmer of admiration on Rita's face and wondered if she had imagined it.

"There was no bag of rice?"

"Yes, but there was no rice cooker and look. . . ." She indicated the oven. "This isn't working. We tried it and we can't get it to heat up."

Rita fiddled with the knobs, looked inside at the cold metal interior, and then closed it. "I'll call someone to take care of this. It seems to be broken. And before we go to the RST office, we will go buy you a kind of beef meal with bread. It will not be what you are used to, but it is filling and I will make sure you get more today or tomorrow." She said the letters "RST" quickly, tripping over them lightly in Burmese, so that Mu Naw understood that "aresti" was another English word she did not know, like "volunteer."

Mu Naw dressed the children and they followed Rita, carefully locking the door of their apartment. Saw Ku put the keys self-consciously in his woven bag, sliding it across his body and behind his hip as he had every day in Mae La camp. Rita was already on the phone, speaking rapidly in English. Mu Naw and Saw Ku buckled the girls into the car; he sat in the back and left Mu Naw the front seat. As Rita maneuvered out of the parking lot, Mu Naw felt a sense of trepidation—the apartment sheltered them from the onslaught of sights and sounds that now dazed her. She had left only once in three days and Saw Ku had not left at all; with one part of her mind, she noticed how quickly the apartment had come to feel safe to her. She sat up and moved her head around to see the apartments, cars, street signs, people. Then a wave of nausea came on and she leaned her head against the window with her face in the cool stream of air-conditioning, clutched the door handle, and breathed in.

Rita pulled into a parking lot beside a building that had a large yellow and red sign above it. Their car waited in a line for a few minutes. Rita spoke out her window to a large black box, where a disembodied voice responded to her. The line continued and then Rita pulled in two paper sacks and two red boxes with English writing and pictures all over them. The whole time, Rita remained on the phone, moving it away from her mouth only to thank the woman who took her plastic card and to tell Mu Naw they would wait till getting to the aresti offices before eating. Mu Naw's stomach rumbled as the exotic aroma from the bags filled the car; she could feel the heat of the food through the bag where it touched her elbow.

The nausea had just reached the point where Mu Naw was beginning to worry she would vomit on the velvety seats of Rita's car when they arrived at a low concrete building with tall windows. She instantly felt better when they stopped moving. She and Rita took the bags and the drinks and Saw Ku helped unbuckle the children and they walked into the building. Rita led them past several desks with low walls separating them from each other to a room with a table. There she opened the bags and handed out yellow-wrapped bundles and small red cups with fried strips to Saw Ku and Mu Naw, unhooking the tops of the red cardboard boxes for the girls. She even opened the straws, though Mu Naw had seen straws before, and inserted them in the drinks for them. Mu Naw loved the beef and the starchy saltiness of the fries but did not care for the sauce-soaked bread that stuck in the back of her tongue. She wiped sauce off the meat and ate it alone, sipping gratefully at the Coke, which was at least familiar. The girls ate without stopping. Saw Ku dipped his finger into the corner of the French fry container and brought his finger to his mouth to taste the last of the salt.

After they ate, Rita took them to the desk of the woman she told them would be their caseworker, a white woman shuffling through papers on a messy desk. She finally found what she was looking for—two pens—and looked up with a toothy grin.

For the rest of the afternoon, Saw Ku and Mu Naw sat in wooden chairs listening to the caseworker, whose words Rita translated into Burmese, explain each paper in the pile and what it would mean for them. Gradually Mu Naw realized that the things they had built or gathered or received in Mae La camp—bamboo huts, vegetables for dinner, rice from the bimonthly food deliveries—came to them in the United States through these papers. It seemed an odd concept—why did signing a paper ensure that she would have a place to live or that she would be able to go to the doctor? But they formed the English letters of their names diligently, so that the papers could bring what they needed. No one said anything about why they had been left alone for three days other than the fact that the office had been closed. Mu Naw thought that perhaps Rita was angry with the caseworker, but the woman seemed undeterred, so maybe Mu Naw was misreading the situation.

They received bus passes and Rita told her someone would come by the next day to show them how to use the bus. When she dropped them off back home, Rita came in and taught them how to adjust the thermostat. She did not mention dinner and Mu Naw did not bring it up, so they made do with the last of the cake and chips for dinner. It was surprising how familiar, even welcoming, the apartment felt after being gone. They left every light blazing all evening. They took long showers. Saw Ku squeezed Mu Naw's hand when she dissolved into tears again after the children were asleep.

MAE LA CAMP WAS THE LARGEST OF THE NINE REFUGEE CAMPS ALONG the Thai-Myanmar border. But large is relative: almost fifty thousand people lived in a camp that measured less than one square mile from end to end. Every household received a ration of rice and cans of fermented fish every two weeks—the comparison of the people in the camp to the packed tin cans of fish felt inevitable.

Mae La was intended as a temporary existence, but the metropolis built of sticks became permanent as the decades stretched on.

The camp was divided into three zones. In zones A and B, there were small stores like that of the store owner from whom Mu Naw bought her bags; zone C held the larger marketplace, with over a hundred huts selling food and goods from the outside world. The enterprising refugees knew how to supplement their diet with goods foraged from the forest around them; some figured out businesses where they made food in their homes and sold it to their neighbors desperate for anything to break up the monotony. Even without the extra food sold in the market and by their neighbors, there was enough to eat if they rationed it carefully, but the options were limited. Nutrition was always a concern.

Mae La camp was made up mostly of Karen people because it was the camp closest to the Karen state across the border in Myanmar. Missionaries, tourists, anthropologists, and teachers had adopted the term "hill tribes" in English to describe the various ethnic minorities in the region: Karen, Hmong, Karenni, Chin, Shan, Kachin, and others who lived throughout Southeast Asia and faced various forms of abuse and persecution in many countries, not just the wholesale slaughter in Myanmar. Though lumped together as "hill tribes," the groups had very little in common in terms of language or culture; it was the same way that Cherokee, Choctaw, Shawnee, and Sioux all became "Indians" to their colonizers, despite being ethnically and culturally diverse.

Karen people were part of a discrete culture that viewed itself as a nation without a homeland—thus one of the conflicts within the civil war. Mu Naw understood that she was viscerally Karen in body, in language, in clothing, in habits, in worldview. Because of this, she was also permanently without a home. She had papers that said she had fled Myanmar, that she was a refugee in Thailand, but those granted her permission to live on a temporary basis in Thailand. She was not Thai. She was certainly not Burmese. Being Karen, her only state was temporary-permanence, liminality, never-belongingness.

Karen people were mostly either Buddhist or Baptist; Mu Naw's mother was Buddhist, but Mu Naw converted to being Baptist before marrying Saw

Ku. Missionaries from the West had come to various parts of the country in the nineteenth century. Entire regions had been Christian for more than a century; their Christian faith put them further at odds with the Buddhist Burman rulers.

North of the Karen state in Myanmar, the Shan state and the Kachin state bordered on China, which was even less welcoming of refugees than Thailand. There were no officially sanctioned camps on the Chinese border as there were in Thailand, only informal sites that cropped up precariously. Refugees from the Kachin state often made the much harder journey west, joining Chin refugees from western Myanmar in escaping toward India, as word eventually spread about how stuck the refugees in Thailand were. Kachin refugees fleeing the fighting in northern Myanmar also felt it was worth the higher risk of paying smugglers to run with them at night across Thailand's peninsula—near popular tourist destinations like Phuket—and into Malaysia, where they might not be legally recognized and would never have rations, but could work more easily in cities and therefore hope to make some kind of new life.

Any of the members of Myanmar's ethnic minorities could run a nuanced cost-benefits analysis of the various escape routes—China, India, Malaysia, Nepal, Thailand—and whether it was better to live a half-life in a camp or a hunted life in a city, based on the rumors they heard. Many more of them took their chances and stayed in Myanmar, part of the millions of internally displaced. Whatever choice they made held high risks.

In all of her journeys, Mu Naw had had very little choice: She was five when she crossed into Thailand and ended up in the small camp where she lived out much of her childhood. Circumstances dictated most of the journey that led from that small camp to life in Mae La years later. The only choice she had really had was a yes or no one: to accept the UN offer of resettlement in Texas. Choice was not a thing Mu Naw thought about much at all.

THE DAY AFTER RITA TOOK THEM TO RST, AN ASIAN WOMAN SHOWED up at their apartment midmorning. She did not speak Burmese or Karen, but she smiled often and spoke several words in English that Mu Naw did not understand, except for "food" and "bus." Saw Ku stayed behind with the children and Mu Naw followed the woman outside the apartment complex, turning left instead of right, away from the convenience store with the canary yellow sign that sold only junk food. They stopped at the bus stop that was to become Mu Naw's lifeline to the outside world. The woman showed her how to slide her bus pass into the small machine and wait for a green light and a beep before boarding.

Mu Naw had slipped one of the shopping bags from the convenience store into her purse just before leaving. As discreetly as possible, she leaned into the wall and threw up into the bag as the bus halted to a stop. The woman made sympathetic noises and patted her back occasionally. Embarrassed, Mu Naw avoided the woman's eyes until she had had a chance to throw the sack away and wash her hands inside the grocery store.

Her nausea easing, Mu Naw exclaimed joyfully as each new aisle brought items she recognized: chili paste, sticky rice with a label from Thailand, vegetables, fruit, spices. The woman did not understand her words, but she smiled as Mu Naw made her discoveries. The woman put almost all of the things Mu Naw recognized into their cart, as well as a number of other things she needed, including two kinds of rice cookers—the machine to make regular rice and the bamboo steamer for sticky rice. Mu Naw would not have dreamed that this new country would have a store with sticky rice and lychee so close to her house. As the cart filled up, she began to worry whether the bills in her envelope would be enough, but the woman smilingly pushed her hand away when she pulled out the envelope at the checkout line.

Mu Naw wondered if one of the papers she had signed at RST would grant her a small card like the one the woman slid, as she had the bus pass, to pay for the items. Mu Naw could see herself, clad in jeans like this woman, pulling out her plastic card and sliding it confidently to pay for the food her family would eat. She almost giggled, but stopped herself.

After their bus ride home, laden with sacks they could barely manage, the woman came inside and turned the knobs on the stove. Gas came out immediately. Someone had come while they were gone and connected the oven to the gas, showing Saw Ku how to turn it on. By the time the woman left, they had rice bubbling gently in their new rice cooker, strips of chicken sautéing in oil with chili paste on the stovetop, and a green mango salad chilling in the refrigerator. The familiar smells made Mu Naw hungrier than she could remember being in her life.

Two-year-old Naw Wah ate four bowls of chicken and rice that night, dribbling the juice down her chin.

BY THE END OF THE WEEK, THEY COULD GO TO THE REFUGEE RESET-tlement agency by themselves on the bus. Mu Naw was racked with debilitating nausea, but buses were still better than cars. The Karen man they had met the first night invited them to come over for dinner, carefully writing out the stops to the south part of Austin, where the six Karen families in Austin lived. Saw Ku and Mu Naw were the seventh family to arrive. More would be coming soon, he told them.

That Friday they spent the night surrounded by Karen people. All of the families cooked in big aluminum pans with plenty to share; they stuffed themselves and told stories late into the night. Mu Naw was so overwhelmed by sights and smells of home she cried twice before the food was served. They treated one another like long lost relatives, any shyness lost in finding one another in the shared loneliness of this new place. The man and his wife had rice mats for them to sleep on and Mu Naw slept all the way through the night for the first time since arriving.

They spent the next morning lingering together over breakfast while the children played, finally climbing back onto the bus toward their isolated apartment. When they unlocked the front door, the apartment now seemed strange, almost hostile. For the rest of the day, Mu Naw was taciturn, cooking woodenly. In the hours in between meals and cleaning, she sat and looked out the window, watching the comings and goings of her neighbors with a vague detachment. A woman shook a rug out on her front porch. Children ran past in shorts and flip-flops. A young man lugged a bicycle up the stairs and chained it to the iron railing on the apartment across from her.

After dinner, once the children were tucked in bed, the grief came upon her all at once. While Saw Ku showered, Mu Naw buried her face in a kitchen towel still damp from drying dishes to quiet her sobs. She could feel the terry cloth with the edges of her teeth. She gripped the refrigerator handle fiercely.

Once when she was a child, missionaries came to visit the camp where she lived with her parents. They handed out brightly colored balloons on white string to the children. Mu Naw had felt the gentle tug of her green balloon on her wrist after the man had tied it; his hands were warm and smooth and had a soft down of blond hair.

Another child near her had untied his string. Mu Naw watched his yellow balloon as it drifted slowly toward the sky, past the tops of the trees, past the height at which the birds flew, into the wispy clouds above her until she could no longer see it.

She felt then if she did not hold on to the refrigerator handle, she might become that yellow balloon—untethered, moving aimlessly, inexorably toward a desolate sky.

SHE COULD REMEMBER CRYING AS SHE DID THAT NIGHT ONLY ONCE before in her life. She was around ten or eleven; the passage of time in her childhood went largely unmarked, without birthday parties and school grades to note the change from one year to the next. Her family lived in Nu Po, the small refugee camp where they had ended up after fleeing across their first border. They had lived in Nu Po for six years.

Life was rhythmic and uneventful—cousins and siblings and neighbors to play with, dirt floors to sweep, rice and canned food deliveries to sort and cook every two weeks. Mu Naw spent many days at her great-grandmother's hut a few doors down from them. Mu Naw's great-aunt lived with her, caring for her aging mother; both women adored Mu Naw and her younger sister and brother and, without small children around their own hut, were always ready to help her mother out.

Mu Naw's mother and father took turns leaving the camp to find jobs and provide some income for their children and for the many grandmothers who relied on them. For Mu Naw, those intervals when one of her parents was off trying to find work were peaceful—her parents' intense fighting was renowned throughout the camp. Her father, like most of the men she grew up with, disciplined his wife by beating her. Mu Naw's mother was sullen and critical; Mu Naw heard the other women of the camp remark on more than one occasion that her mother deserved the beatings because she yelled back at her husband, did not submit to him as she should. Mu Naw felt that her mother's actions were shameful in some way that she did not understand. Her father never raised his hand to Mu Naw and only a few times to her sister and brother, but she learned that when his eyes flashed, she should leave at once. Mu Naw spoke with her eyes down, anticipated his need at night for a seat and balm for his arm where his makeshift crutch rubbed it raw. She knew when to fetch him cool water, how to serve his food in a way that he found pleasing. As the years passed, she wondered sometimes why she should know these things and her mother should not; at some point she realized her mother knew them, she just refused to do them. Mu Naw decided, after hearing it from a few of the aunts, that her mother was a very bad wife.

Mu Naw cooked when her mother was gone, and helped her mother when her father left. Most of the time, her great-grandmother and great-aunt were the grandmothers who made sure she had clothes, that she learned to read, that she went to the schools that missionaries would start up, often lasting for a year or two before discontinuing.

No one seemed very interested in doing more than containing the Karen refugees pouring out of Myanmar. Buddhists fought Christians and both fought the Burmese, and the Karen people who did not want to fight fled. Because Nu Po was one of the smaller camps, it received less aid and less attention than larger ones. As the years passed with no plan for employment, no real schooling for the children, no system in place to ensure the people could go back to Myanmar safely, Mu Naw's parents and other adults grew increasingly restless. Mu Naw's father stopped looking for jobs and journeyed alone back into Myanmar to check on relatives.

He came back unexpectedly one day and confronted his wife over something that Mu Naw did not understand, their blazing argument audible several huts away. Later, when the screams and thumps had died down, Mu Naw snuck back in. Her mother's face was unmarked—he never hit her face, because he thought she was beautiful—but she was limping and she did not move her left arm away from her ribs. Mu Naw's father was stretched out on the bed, his snores evidence that he was drunk and would not be awake for several hours.

Without saying a word, Mu Naw watched her mother as she moved clothes around, put a few things in a small bag, including some of her gold necklaces. The rest she put into a small woven purse stuffed behind the supply of rice on the shelf in the kitchen. She showed Mu Naw, indicating that Mu Naw was not to tell her father where the bag was hidden. Mu Naw nodded, not understanding. It was only when she realized that her mother had packed some of her shirts and skirts that she realized her mother was leaving. She followed her mother out of the hut; her sister and brother were still with the grandmothers. Her mother cupped her face for a moment.

"I'm going to go to Bangkok to find work. I will be gone for a few weeks, maybe a few months, but I will find a way to send you money if I can. Here." She took one of her gold stud earrings out of her ear and put it into Mu Naw's. "Do not sell this unless you absolutely have to."

And then she walked away, limping slightly and holding her arm pressed against her torso. She did not say good-bye. She did not say she loved Mu Naw.

That afternoon, while her father slept, Mu Naw sat in a semicircle with some of the other children from the camp around a television set in the dirt, watching a movie of white children singing Christian songs Mu Naw did not understand but that she loved anyway, with catchy tunes she tried to remember as she walked back to her great-grandmother's hut. She did not want to be at her home when her father woke up. In the movie, the children sat and sang and animals came up to them, animals that Mu Naw did not recognize but that seemed soft and snuggly. She wished she had animals like that to play with and pet.

The next morning, when she woke up at her great-grandmother's hut, her father was there eating breakfast. Though her great-grandmother was related to her mother, all of the camp grandmothers approved of her father.

"Have you seen your mother?" he asked around the bite of rice and fish that he was chewing.

"She left yesterday to go find work, she said. She'll be back soon."

His crutch leaned against the wall. He ran his fingers along his mustache. He sat back, tied his longyi more tightly around his waist, tucking it close to his amputated leg.

"She didn't go to find work. She left me."

Mu Naw felt her vision narrow as she tried to catch up to what her father said, as if he were speaking a language she did not understand. Dim light shone through the cracks in the bamboo. The window was open, letting in an anemic breeze. A glob of food clung to the end of his mustache. A fly buzzed around him, landed once on his shoulder.

"Your grandmother thinks she went to Bangkok."

"Maybe she just left to go find a job. She said she was going to find a job."

"No, she left me for another man. I'm going to go find them."

His face was grim. He hugged her briefly, his hand on her ear, her cheek against the top part of his bare belly. He went outside and called to her brother and sister and explained to her great-grandmother his half-formed plan. He gave her some money to continue to care for the children for a few weeks until he could come back. He packed up what he could and then he was gone. He did not find the gold behind the rice bag. Mu Naw went after he was gone to check; she pushed it farther back so that it was hidden and then pulled the door shut tightly.

The next morning, when the early dawn light had begun to shine through the cracks between the bamboo, her great-grandmother shook her awake. Mu Naw smelled acrid smoke, different from the homey cook-fire smell that always hung low over the camp. She heard popping noises. Mu Naw sat up at once. The camp was burning. Men were firing guns. Her great-grandmother's voice was low. "The Tatmadaw are coming. We have to leave here right now. Go to your hut and get what you can. I'll stay here and get your sister and brother ready to go. Come straight back. Don't speak to anyone."

Mu Naw didn't pause. She threw on the few clothes she had and raced to her family hut. She opened the door silently and walked into the shadowed interior. Open cabinets and strewn clothes told her she was already too late. Looters had taken what little they had; she had missed them by minutes. The rice was gone, as well as the sack of gold hidden behind it. She touched the earring her mother had given her and grabbed a few shirts for her brother and sister in a heap at the bottom of the niche they used as a closet. There was nothing left of her childhood home. It felt already as if it were empty, as if it were rotting back into the jungle, erasing every trace of the family who had lived there for six years.

She rushed back to her great-grandmother's. They ran behind her hut through a slim hidden path. The next four days they spent squatting and lying beneath the undergrowth, watching the camp, the fighting a distant rumble in the background as the Tatmadaw tore through the camp looking for men who had fought for the Karen armies, sporadically burning down huts. When the soldiers came too close, they retreated into the woods. Her great-grandmother had packed food, but it was not enough.

Mu Naw did not speak for several days. Her sister and brother were equally unobtrusive. They had all heard the stories of what those soldiers could do. A baby cried once in the jungle a few hundred yards away. Mu Naw, her sister and brother, her great-aunt and her great-grandmother moved closer to one another, their breathing shallow, their eyes wide. Their bodies nestled low among the leaves around them. They did not dare to move their bodies until it was almost too dark to see; by then, Mu Naw's feet were asleep, her back numb.

The soldiers did not destroy the camp—there were too few of them and they didn't want to risk the attention of the Thai army or international peace-keepers. After four days of sitting in the jungle and observing the camp, Mu Naw and her great-aunt took a chance. They walked around the sprawling perimeter, keeping their bodies low and their footsteps silent. When they were sure it was secure, they walked confidently into the open square on the opposite side of the camp from where their hut had been. It was food delivery day and, if they could receive an allotment of rice for their household, they could sell it and have some extra money for the upcoming journey.

The UN officials were there, undeterred by the raid. They handed out giant sacks of rice as they did every two weeks; Mu Naw's aunt showed them her papers and received her allotment. Mu Naw helped her carry the unwieldy sack. When they were far enough away from the truck that they would not be observed, Mu Naw's aunt offered to sell the rice to a man with a large family. They haggled politely for a few minutes, and he gave Mu Naw's aunt a handful of coins. Mu Naw was hungry, but she saw her great-grandmother's excitement over the coins. They ate root vegetables and leaves in the jungle that tasted bitter but filled their stomachs, moving back into the cover of the trees. This time, there was not a group of people working together. Two old women and three small children picked their way across miles of jungle.

That first night, as the darkness enfolded them, Mu Naw felt the sobs come with no warning. She buried her face in the bag she had been using to carry her belongings, the one that smelled like wood smoke and spices from her mother's home.

As the sobs bent her body nearly double, she held on to the roots of the tree behind her. She did not know when she stopped sobbing, only that her face in the morning was swollen and hot, and that it would be days before she would have consistent food and water again as they made their way back into Myanmar, into the heart of the war.

CLUTCHING THE REFRIGERATOR IN AUSTIN AND HOLDING THE DISH towel to her face, Mu Naw remembered again the grass under her legs, the roots in her grip, the sounds of her great-grandmother and great-aunt breathing, the rustle of the wind in the trees. She had not wanted to go back into Myanmar without her parents, but her great-grandmother had held her hand while they walked. She had tethered Mu Naw along that journey, back to the village where their mother came from, where the Tatmadaw had gone and Karen people were once more living a half-life haunted by war. She had had her grandmothers around her to give her what her parents would not, though it was not and never would be enough. Looking back now, Mu Naw realized she had always known that this moment would come again—not in the United States, not by a refrigerator holding a dish towel with a slightly faded daisy on it. But she had expected and feared it all of her life.

The intensity of her aloneness shook her. She wondered how she would know if she had drifted away, or if it had already occurred, if an essential part of her had stayed behind at the camp, had been lost in the journey to Austin.

Chapter 7

HASNA

Hasna did not feel like celebrating Mother's Day on Monday morning. She was glad to see Khassem again, but his fevered drive and unexpected appearance late on Sunday night only spiked the fear that had coursed through her for two days. His warning felt worse because it was vague: What was coming? What would the government do? They had spoken late into the night, speculating freely in whispers as they rarely allowed themselves before, not even inside their home. Worst-case scenario, they all knew, was a repeat of Hafez al-Assad's assault on Hama thirty years before. They could not decide what the general had meant, what they should do, whether they should say anything to anyone.

More people had died in Daraa since Friday. Enraged crowds pulled down statues of Bashar al-Assad and his father. The fact that Monday was a holiday only gave the protesters license to destroy the city—by the end of the night, the courthouse downtown would be burned to the ground. That morning, Khassem begged his mother to get away for the day. At first she said no, but he was persuasive, smiling the sweet smile he reserved for her. After lunch, when he asked again, she raised her eyebrows, smirking, and then rolled her eyes.

They went, as their family always did, to Lake Muzayrib. He skillfully guided the motorcycle around each of the curves, the potholes, the other drivers. Hasna clung to him. He was out of uniform that day, in a collared shirt and jeans, looking again like her son and not the property of the Syrian army. The edges of her long black coat flapped around her legs as they left town and he picked up speed. She laughed once and Khassem half turned his head, grinning.

The first glimpse of Lake Muzayrib was her favorite—the water, held reverently between steep verdant hills, reflected lacy clouds above. Exuberant new grass asserted itself around winter's scrubby landscape. The road rimmed the lake and Khassem slowed the motorcycle as they circled. They pointed out to each other again the sites they knew perfectly well. There was the road that led to Muzayrib castle. There was Rana's favorite waterfall. There was the place they picnicked with the cousins from Damascus.

Hasna looked and looked, taking it all in, turning her head like a child to see every sight anew. Eventually they stopped and found a place to sit by one of the sites where the water poured from pipes into the lake at an incredible rate. They were not waterfalls, not in the traditional sense, but they were beautiful and powerful and most of them had taken on a life of their own, the water leaving the pipes to create natural causeways. Somewhere on the other side of the lake, someone was playing a flute; over the thrumming water, she heard snatches of the minor melody when the wind shifted.

Sitting in this ancient valley, one of the most beautiful and fertile in a region that had been the hub of civilizations since history began, Hasna felt she could come to grips with her place in the world. She was small, her family was small, her time in the world would come and go. The water underscored this notion coursing through her—this water did not care that her beloved city was falling, that her son was in an army she did not trust, that forces beyond her control were moving toward her at an inexorable rate.

It was as if every color were crisper than she had ever seen—kelly-green grass bursting from buff rocks, opaque lake turned coral and fuchsia and lemon-yellow by the setting sun, cerulean sky bruising into indigo as the last light lowered behind the hill.

When the sun was gone, she turned to Khassem: "Everything is about to change, isn't it?"

He nodded.

They rode through the dark in silence. When it came time for Khassem to set out for Damascus, the grief she had managed to avoid all day caught up with her. She was almost sobbing when she hugged him good-bye, thanking him for a perfect afternoon. He clung to her for a moment and he was not ashamed of his tears when he kissed her fiercely on her forehead.

It was the last time she would ever see Lake Muzayrib.

KHASSEM WENT BACK TO DAMASCUS THAT MONDAY NIGHT. TUESDAY passed in a semblance of normalcy—school and work punctuated by neighbors' visits and reports of what was happening in town. The protests continued to center on the Omari mosque; Hasna avoided her usual market so she would not be caught in the streets. Wednesday was the same. She felt listless, tense. She baked bread and went to the market away from the protesters and listened, ears straining for she did not know what.

In the middle of the night on Wednesday, she sat up in terror. For several seconds, she was not sure what had disturbed her sleep. Then she realized the usual light from the streetlight outside was gone, the gentle whirring of the refrigerator in the kitchen was silenced. She pulled out her mobile phone and saw that it was 1:00 a.m.—the phone was charged, but there was no service. The hairs on her arms rose as she sat up.

Jebreel was stirring from his sleep. She heard Yusef's door open, the sound almost alarmingly loud. Hasna put on her house robe, moving instinctively through the darkness, and checked that Rana was sleeping. She had to lean in close to see her daughter in the dim room. She brushed a lock of hair off Rana's forehead and felt her own hand tremble; she noticed the fact almost objectively, as if she were removed from the trembling hand, from the lingering touch on her daughter's face. She closed the door gently and said a prayer that Rana would continue to sleep. She could hear Jebreel and Yusef shuffling in their rooms, getting dressed. She thought of putting on her clothes, but she felt an overwhelming urge to see what was happening outside. She pulled her robe more tightly around her and went to the stairs leading up to the second story of their home.

The stairs were bricked in with ornate cement blocks. The decorative holes in the blocks allowed fresh air and light to come into the stairwell but kept outsiders from seeing in; like the high-walled courtyard, the stairwell was designed to allow a woman without a hijab to move freely in her home while giving her access to outside space. Hasna wedged her fingers into the openings of the blocks at waist level, pushing her body against the wall so that she could turn her head to the right and the left.

The skyline of her city was as familiar to Hasna as her mother's face had been. From her vantage point, she could usually see the skyline partially, the face half-turned; the enveloping darkness gave her more sense than sight. But she did not need light to envision the Omari minaret that rose imposingly above the dun-colored buildings around it, its square shape formed by irregular, hand-built bricks and topped by a slim dome. Electric lines creased like wrinkles at every intersection; spiked wires protruded from the pillars of half-built walls where construction had halted on a building nearby. The wide bridges, the open soccer fields, the verdant Hameeda Altaher park, the ridge of mountains around them—all were too far away for her to see, but she could feel them, as if she were nestled against the shoulder of her city, as if it shared the shuddering rise and fall of her fear, their hearts racing as one.

For one agonizing moment, all was still. The evening breeze toyed lovingly with her hair, the soft wisps around her face, the ends that hung lustrously down her back. She tucked her cheek against the bricks and breathed out a muffled sob.

And then a flare below the Omari mosque lit the minaret from the side away from her, so that the tower was backlit, black and ominous. The sound was delayed by a full second, the boom coming shortly after the light. And then another flare, and another. Gunshots rang out from various points around the minaret. She could see flashes from the tops of buildings surrounding the mosque, a brief yellow spurt she thought she imagined at first until she saw it dozens of times—snipers had taken places all around the Omari.

The night was instantly a cacophony—men screaming in the mosque, neighbors shouting in the streets, guns blaring, explosions. She could make no sense of the noise. The objectivity she had noticed when touching Rana returned—she felt as if she were removed from what was happening, observing herself as she observed the attack on her city.

Down in the street, she heard a voice louder than the others: "Help! Help him! He's hurt!" Without thought, she was moving down the stairs, wishing she had taken the time to get dressed earlier.

The darkness of her room was deeper after the flashing lights outside; she dashed around the bed and opened the wardrobe, pulling on pants and a shirt and her hijab by feel, grabbing her coat as she went. There was no time to check on Rana because she could hear Jebreel in the courtyard calling her name. "Hasna! Hasna!" His voice rose sharply on the second syllable. Her husband's audible fear shook her. He met her just inside their gate and gripped her arm: "Get some water boiling and bring some rags. We're next door."

He was gone into the street before she could ask any questions. She filled three of her largest pots with water and used a match to light the gas burners; the pilot light went out with the electricity. When the water churned rapidly in the smaller pot, she wrapped the handles with an old towel and walked swiftly, keeping her elbows stiff so the water did not slosh. She tucked a bundle of old rags under her arm and went the way Jebreel had. People ran past her and she made her way next door. For a minute she stood in the doorway, watching. She could not bring herself to cross the threshold.

A man was laid out on the table where Hasna had drunk countless cups of coffee during mornings at home with her neighbor, Um Ibtihal, whose husband was a veterinarian. Candlelight skewed the scene. Um Ibtihal's husband held a towel to a man's chest; his shirt had been ripped away. Blood soaked the edges of the towel. The veterinarian's voice was firm as he directed Um Ibtihal, who stood at the end of their dining room-turned-operating table, and the men around him. Hasna could not see Um Ibtihal's face through the shadows.

The man on the table groaned and Hasna moved, taking the water to his feet where Um Ibtihal was using bleach and boiling water to clean the utensils her husband used every day on animals. Hasna laid the towels in a heap beside it and went back for the other two pots boiling fervently on her stove.

That moment pausing in the doorway was the last time she stopped that night.

The victims kept coming—some were already dead, but many others made their way to the veterinarian's house as word spread that he could help. Some came propped up by their relatives or friends; some hobbled along, others were carried. Hands grasped armpits and knees, heads lolled against shoulders, eyes squinted and closed, mouths shrieked and bawled and exhaled.

Hasna boiled water, ripped sheets into rags, filled glasses with water. She was mercifully free of feeling, her body an automatic thing that moved quickly, competently, while her mind watched dispassionately. Later, the horror of watching her neighbors' sons bleeding on a kitchen table would wake her up night after night, but in the moment, her mind did nothing. Her body obeyed the orders of those who seemed to know what they were doing, supplying bandages and water for Um Ibtihal to clean the surgery tools and drinks for those whose throats were parched from smoke and from screaming.

HASNA LEARNED ONLY MUCH LATER THAT KHASSEM HAD GOTTEN word the next morning when he woke up in the army barracks that the entire area around the Omari mosque in Daraa had been destroyed by the government forces that moved in at 1:30 a.m. The way his roommate mentioned it—casually, slyly—made it sound as if Daraa were completely obliterated, a repeat of Hama so many years ago. The soldiers in the rooms all around him heard his bellow of rage. They were witnesses to the uncontrolled torrent of anti-Assad profanities Khassem did not even try to control. His government-informant roommate was only too happy to pass on the exact words Khassem had used. He was huddled, weeping, in a corner of his room when the army officials came to take him in for questioning.

The investigating officers let him call a relative who was a lawyer in Damascus; the phone lines into Daraa were all shut off. The lawyer tried to help, but the incriminating evidence about Khassem's critical views of the government had already been sufficiently observed. It was too late to regret his actions later, when he eventually heard that his family was safe. The investigating officers interviewed Khassem on and off for two weeks before taking him to Sednaya Prison. Hasna was never sure how their lawyer relative even learned that information, whom he paid or what it cost him—very few people would get the same information about their sons who disappeared into Sednaya.

A word-of-mouth communication system emerged quickly over the next few weeks. But it was hard to decipher truth from rumor. It would be weeks after Khassem was incarcerated that Hasna learned of the location of her second son.

THE MORNING AFTER THE ATTACK ON OMARI, RANA WOKE LATER THAN usual. She was a heavy sleeper and her bedroom had thick basalt walls that had shielded her from the noise of the night before. She emerged tousle-headed to see her mother washing her hands vigorously in the kitchen sink. Hasna's shock was only beginning to wear off; she jumped when Rana walked in.

"Habibti, are you hungry?" She grabbed her daughter's face, held her shoulders, hugged her, pulled back to examine her face again. Disconcerted by the force of her mother's affection, Rana took a step back, but nodded. Hasna pulled a large bowl of ful from the refrigerator, closing the door quickly so that it did not lose its coolness. Rana watched her light the stovetop with a match.

"Is the electricity out again? Am I going to school?" she asked warily.

Hasna paused and looked at her blankly, utterly undone at the thought of explaining this night to her daughter. Finally, she gestured for Rana to sit down, chopped up half of a tomato while the beans heated through, and filled the bowl to the brim. She would feed her well first, she decided, and then tell her.

Leaving the pot to simmer on the stove for when Yusef and Jebreel came back from helping to clean up at Um Ibtihal's home, she carried Rana's bowl to the table, her mind jumping unbidden to a few hours ago, when she had run swiftly through the dark courtyard with boiling pots of water. Her hands were shaking visibly again by the time she set the bowl in front of Rana. She watched Rana eat with an attention that clearly irritated her daughter.

"What? What's going on?"

Hasna was trying to find the words to explain to her daughter what had happened when a loud banging noise began. Someone was pounding on Um Ibtihal's gate next door. Hasna froze. She heard a deep voice ringing out, "Open up! In the name of Bashar al-Assad!" Hasna motioned for Rana to stay at the table and quietly slipped out of her own gate.

She had taken a few steps toward the veterinarian's house when she saw soldiers emerging from the house leading some men, including Jebreel and

Yusef. The soldiers carried machine guns and Jebreel, Yusef, the veterinarian, and a few other neighbors walked with their hands on their heads. Other soldiers were emerging from houses down the street, pushing men in front of them to form a group in the middle of the road. Hasna watched for a moment, then ran to her house to meet the soldiers walking in. She explained in as calm a tone as she could that her husband and son were already in line. She opened the gate and let the soldiers enter the courtyard and look around. Rana blanched, rushing to her mother. The soldiers did not tarry; when they exited the house, one barked at Hasna to point out her husband. Jebreel nodded, never moving his hands, and the soldiers moved on to the next house.

Hasna caught Jebreel's eye and held it. His eyes widened and he opened his mouth to say something but he stumbled a bit and Yusef dropped his arm to catch his father and a soldier snapped at them and they no longer looked at Hasna but away from her and whatever Jebreel had been about to say was lost. And suddenly she remembered her first glimpse of Jebreel from her window when the men came for their jaha and how they had walked like this in an imposing group of al-Salam men—strong men, good men, men who danced dabke and played backgammon and worked hard and took care of their wives and children and grandchildren, who held all the hope and promise and pride of their clan—and she knew now that she had loved him from that very first moment. Next to him walked their son who had not had the chance for his own jaha, their gentle Yusef who liked to draw and who never complained about helping his family.

She watched them as they marched on, unable to move, unable to reach them, and it was only when they were gone that she realized Um Ibtihal's arms were around her waist, restraining her, keeping her from running. She knew then she might have attacked the soldiers—she might have done anything. When Um Ibtihal released her hold on Hasna, the restraint became an embrace and Hasna sobbed onto her neighbor's shoulder. Um Ibtihal's hijab held the scent of smoke and the coppery, gamey smell Hasna would always associate with that night.

Chapter 8

MU NAW

AUSTIN, TEXAS, USA, MAY–AUGUST 2007

Mu Naw and Saw Ku started English classes the following week. At 7:15 a.m., they packed the children out the door to take the 240 East/West bus along Rutland, followed by the 801 bus headed down North Lamar to the Central Presbyterian Church downtown, briskly walking the three blocks to the church for the 8:00 a.m. class. During rush hour, the bus ride could take over an hour, especially if any of the buses were running late, which they always seemed to be. Outside Central Pres, they joined refugees from all over the city walking up the steps on one side and the long cement ramp on the other. Most of the time they had to step over someone sleeping on the sidewalk. The pavement retained a pungent aroma of piss and accumulated body odor. The courtyard outside the church held scraggly plants and picnic tables under the large arms of a live oak. They walked past the strollers banked in the foyer, up two flights of stairs, dropped the children off at child care, and then up again to the third floor to the adult English classrooms. They sat down at the long tables as close to the board as they could get.

Mu Naw loved English classes. They cheered and grounded her, gave her days rhythm. Saw Ku endured them and returned at the end of each day drained and frustrated. Many of their classmates were from Burundi and Somalia. Saw Ku and Mu Naw were the only Karen speakers in their entry-level class for the first three weeks. And then it felt as if every week or so, another family from Myanmar moved to Austin.

It began with Saw Ku's brother and sister-in-law, Jaw Jaw and Deh Deh. The brothers were close in age to each other and they had always done everything together. Some snag with the paperwork had given them departure times three weeks apart. But it was his brother's arrival, rather than English classes, that grounded Saw Ku. Mu Naw had always gotten along well with Deh Deh, but here they forged a newly strong connection. Their apartments were only a few doors apart. Their girls were close to the same ages. Soon there were other families, several in their apartment complex, who went to English class together and shopped with one another when they needed. The six families from south Austin whom Mu Naw and Saw Ku had spent the night with also moved into the same apartment complex. Soon a sizable group waited for the 240 bus every morning, a tiny diaspora in the middle of the chaos.

For the first few weeks, speaking Karen, sharing information, helping as she could, provided Mu Naw almost immediate relief from the oppressive loneliness. She found that arriving a few weeks earlier had made her the local expert on the culture, and she became determined to save the new women from her initial isolation.

But the community and camaraderie did not eliminate the complexities of their daily lives. The surprises kept coming. It began with their first bills a month after they arrived. First, they received their rent bill, followed shortly by their electricity/water bill. Their caseworker came with a translator one day and explained to Saw Ku and Mu Naw how their bills worked—these were the papers they had signed on the day they ate their first hamburgers. The loss of $700 for rent and $70 for electricity and water was a steep blow. Their caseworker showed them the rent and then told them that, for four months, the resettlement agency was paying their rent, but the bills were supposed to come out of their $120 a month stipend. That left only $50 for them to pay for groceries and did not include their phone bill, which was $50 a month for a Cricket phone plan. The choice between phone and groceries was one that would come up every month for years; some months they chose food and were out of touch with relatives in Mae La camp or friends in Austin. Mu

Naw's fantasy of walking through the grocery store, buying faraway fruits and extra boxes of Pocky with a plastic card, faded immediately.

They shifted their lives. They no longer used electricity at night; they lived in almost complete darkness—not a major change from the camp. They spread the word in the community that the electricity was something they would all have to pay for; it was summer, so she and the other women sat outside as long as they could stand the heat, soaking up the natural light before entering airless, dusky apartments and going to bed early.

They learned that the building next door, the yawning parking lot with the large sign with a dove, was a church that gave out food on Monday nights. Those regular allotments of canned goods and fresh produce helped reduce the grocery bills Mu Naw worried about. Used to waiting in line for canned rations, Mu Naw felt no shame at receiving free food from the church. But she was confused about how to cook the stringy green beans and the overly starched corn that came in the cans. The rice and dark beans were not that different from what she had gotten in Thailand. And the fresh fruits and vegetables she occasionally received were very welcome. She tried some creative recipes with the free food; some were less successful than others. They all hated Spaghetti-Os and she passed those cans on to her neighbors.

Some of the surprises were serendipitous. One day Mu Naw found a television set out by the big green Dumpster in the corner of the parking lot behind the apartment complex. She picked it up herself and lugged it into their apartment. She plugged it in and tried to turn it on; the screen lit up but all she could see was a gray scramble. Her across-the-courtyard neighbor only spoke Spanish, but she smiled and waved at Mu Naw every time they saw each other. Mu Naw saw her neighbor outside and pulled her into the apartment. They laughed and used hand gestures and managed to communicate that there was something missing from the TV. The neighbor left and returned a few minutes later with thin metal antennae that she hooked up to the top of the TV. That night, Saw Ku came home to an apartment filled with noise and light. Mu Naw kept the TV on during the day when she was home with the children. The crisp images buoyed her. Here was the America she had expected, contained in the neat borders of the small box.

Still it felt to Mu Naw that not a day went by without her crying. It became a normal part of their routine, like brushing their teeth and bathing. Usually it was at night; after the children were in bed, while she was wiping down the kitchen, Mu Naw would succumb to her grief. Saw Ku's stress manifested instead in irritation and anger. At first it was not directed at her; he would blow up over minor things or get frustrated at situations neither of them understood or could control. Saw Ku's anger seemed to be focused mostly on English class. He was tired of learning the letters, of feeling like a child. He could still barely write his own name in the baffling English alphabet. Progress was too slow: their four-month support window was ending soon and rent and bills would all be his responsibility. Mu Naw was adding new vocabulary at a speed Saw Ku found dizzying. The cleverness he had always loved now grated on him—he could barely admit to himself that his wife was better than he was at languages.

Their caseworker helped him fill out the papers that meant he could get a job on the cleaning crew at a hotel. He and Mu Naw strategized together: If he could start working before the end of their stipend ran out, they could get ahead just enough to build a buffer into their budget. When the caseworker called and told him he had been hired, he happily left English class.

Things felt more comfortable for both of them when Saw Ku got a job; the idea of this small cushion brought them hope. A few weeks later, a volunteer at the church next door, an older white man with glasses and a slight paunch, knocked on their door. Mu Naw had seen him when she was picking up free food on Monday nights. He introduced himself as Bob and said that the church had asked him to help the refugees in any way he could. Paperwork, grocery shopping, English tutoring—he was semiretired and glad to be of assistance. His blue eyes behind the glasses were kind and Mu Naw invited him in. Soon he was coming most afternoons, helping her and her neighbors with the bills and with their English homework. She tried out new words with him and he explained some of the thornier grammar rules she felt stuck on. He was great with their children. And as every new family came—Mu Naw becoming the center of a loosely connected web of Karen people—she would tell their names to Bob. He would pull out a piece of paper he kept in the breast pocket of his shirt, lick the tip of his pencil and adjust his glasses, then add them to the ever-growing list.

The families were relieved to have an American uncle they could rely on in these new lives full of traps waiting to ensnare them. The boon that Saw Ku and Mu Naw expected from having both a job and a stipend did not come. They had not understood that as soon as he got a job the stipend would end; the caseworker told them kindly—Saw Ku thought condescendingly—that she had already explained that part. Perhaps she had. Perhaps Mu Naw had misunderstood when Rita translated. Somewhere along the telephone game of communication between the caseworker in English, Rita in Burmese, and Mu Naw translating into Karen for Saw Ku, they had missed the fact that they would now be solely responsible for their rent.

They couldn't make the math add up. Saw Ku earned just over minimum wage: $8 an hour. Working forty hours a week, he earned around $1,200 a month. Their rent, bills, and groceries added up to just over $1,000 if they were careful, if they turned off all the lights, if they mostly ate rice and beans, if they went every Monday for free food. They talked to Deh Deh and Jaw Jaw, made plans for what would happen when the children started school in August. Jaw Jaw was waiting to get a job till after his stipend ran out, having learned from Saw Ku's mistake. Deh Deh and Mu Naw would stay in ESL classes with the children through August, when Deh Deh's older daughter and Pah Poe would be in school. Then they would try to find jobs and either share child care or one of them would pay the other to watch their younger children. Mu Naw left every morning for ESL class with renewed purpose—it was her one chance to learn English before starting work in a few months. She saw how exhausted Saw Ku was and knew she would lose the will to master the language when she had two small children and a job every day.

Her nausea had become debilitating. She could barely function most days. Riding the bus sent her into a spiral of vomiting that she could barely push through to focus on vocabulary lessons. Her eyes had bags under them; her face looked hollow when she caught a glimpse of herself in the mirror in the strange bathroom where she undressed to bathe every day.

One day her caseworker came to their house with a notice. She had brought

Rita, but even so, Mu Naw did not understand—was it her fault? the casework-er's? a bureaucratic snag they all missed? Mu Naw only grasped the most basic point: Their Medicaid application had not gone through and they would not be able to go to the doctor. She asked Bob to look over it later and he shook his head; there was nothing they could do but reapply and wait.

Since they could rarely afford to pay for a Cricket phone once a month, Mu Naw knew she could not pay for the doctor. And she had already learned the hard way that the fact that she did not know how much it cost probably meant it was much more, not less, than she anticipated.

ONE MORNING SHE WOKE UP WITH A START AND REALIZED SHE COULD not remember the last time she had had her period—weeks earlier, if not a couple of months. The stress from her daily life had so absorbed her mind that it never occurred to her that she had missed it. She had assumed the increased nausea, the crying jags, the hollows under her eyes were a result of stress, but her body had responded this way when she had been pregnant with the girls, without buses and cars to exacerbate her morning sickness. She did not take a test; even if she could have afforded it, or found the package in the grocery store, she would not have needed it. She could feel the familiar return of her body to pregnancy.

Saw Ku came home that night from a long shift and found his wife waiting for him on their brown couch. She sat with only the lamp on, her knees pulled up to her chin. The TV was off. The silence was oppressive.

When she spoke, her voice was a monotone: "I'm pregnant."

"No, you can't be."

"I am." She looked up at him and it was as if they were strangers. She remembered, incongruously, that at their wedding he had curled his fingers around her elbow.

"What . . . what can we do?" He sat down heavily. They began to lay out the costs—medical bills they could not afford, delaying her starting a job by months or even years, adding another mouth to feed. They could not make the money stretch any further than it already did.

Deciding that night to end the pregnancy felt like the only option. It was the first time in a few weeks that they felt completely united. Despite the fact that they were Christians, they did not debate the morality of it at all. All she felt was the crushing pressure of her everyday life. There was no space, not even the tiniest crack, for a new life. She could not imagine giving birth alone in this hostile new place, much less parenting three children. They went to bed and she slept hard. The nausea would be over. They would wait for a year or two, when they could pay their rent and bills, then have another child. It would be sad but okay. She worried that she should feel more angst, but she couldn't bring herself to care.

She took the children on the bus to the refugee agency the next day rather than to Central Presbyterian for English classes. She waited over an hour to see Rita, her feet scuffing the concrete floor while the girls played with the other children from Iraq and Somalia in the waiting area. When they finally sat down in Rita's cubicle, Mu Naw burst into tears. Annoyed at herself, she hastily wiped them away with the heel of her palm. Rita said nothing.

"I'm pregnant."

"How many months?"

"It can't be more than two. I need to go to the doctor."

Rita put her hand on Mu Naw's and held it there for a moment. Mu Naw could not bring herself to say what she had planned. Rita called a number and wrote down an address for Mu Naw, noting the bus transfers she would need to take to get there. When Mu Naw left, Rita hugged her in the cubicle, out of sight of the other clients.

Mu Naw knew she needed someone to go with her whose English was better than hers. She went to the Karen-speaking man who had met them at the airport; he now lived a few buildings over. She nervously explained her situation and asked him to accompany her to the doctor. She was clear with him about the intention she had hidden from to Rita. His face was pained but kind.

"Sister, I cannot do this with you. I'm sorry. I wish you would change your mind. You know that's not what God would want of you."

"I know, but how can we do this? My husband has a job and we can't pay the rent, I need a job, we already have two children. What choice do we have?"

His tone was gentle but still he refused. Mu Naw felt ashamed to tell Deh Deh and the other women, afraid they would talk her out of it or judge her for it. She went back to her apartment and cried for the rest of the day, for once not hiding her tears.

Saw Ku had to work. There was no one else who could go with her. She would ask Deh Deh to watch her girls and tell her she had an appointment. She would go alone.

A few months ago, she had wondered if she had lost some essential part of herself, but she did not wonder now. Not even when the Tatmadaw came and burned down her camp, when she had lost both father and mother at once, had she ever felt this alone.

Chapter 9

HASNA

DARAA, SYRIA, MARCH 2011

The soldiers took Malek, too. Laila flew to their house with baby Hamad in her arms, her sobs so hysterical that Hasna took her into the courtyard to calm her down, putting aside her own grief and terror. She closed the gate and took off Laila's hijab, giving her room to breathe. Hamad, distressed at seeing his mother cry, began his own wailing. Rana came over and hugged her mother's waist while Hasna put cool hands on Laila's crumpled face, held her for a moment. But it did not work. Hasna felt something malicious pulling at her core, as if she and everything she loved were being uprooted.

Women wailed in the streets. All over the city, a cry rose out as the soldiers moved through. It was a guttural, primal response. All the male citizens between the ages of twelve and sixty were taken.

The women eventually joined one another in clumps on the streets. Rumors tore through like foul wind—soldiers were going to gun down all of the men in rows, they were going to pick out just the young men, they would shoot only the leaders of the demonstrations, they would bomb all of them in one fell swoop. Hasna prayed for Amal and Samir; she assumed Amal had stayed with her mother-in-law but did not want to leave her home to find out.

Finally, in the afternoon, some of the men began to come home. The older men were first. Jebreel was part of the first clump of men that rounded the corner from the main road; Hasna saw him and rushed to him, black dress rushing around her legs as she ran. Laila and Rana were behind her and they clung to him. Hasna looked wildly around him for Yusef.

"They're not here. They're not here!" And stoic Jebreel was crying in her arms. His face had aged in the handful of hours they were apart. "Samir they let go, but Malek and Yusef are still there. They shot those boys, Hasna. They shot them right there. Someone told them who the protesters were and there was no trial, they just held a gun to their head and shot them."

"Do they know that Yusef and Malek did not demonstrate?"

"They know that Malek was there at the Al-Abbas mosque when the protest began. I heard someone point him out to the soldiers."

Laila's scream was otherworldly. She would not stop. Hasna took her home. They had no comfort to give each other.

THROUGHOUT THE DAY, OTHER MEN MADE IT HOME, AND THE RUMORS began to solidify into a coherent story: The soldiers had taken the men of the city to the soccer field, the only place large enough for so many people to gather. There they had killed many of the young men. They arrested several of the others and took them back to Damascus.

By nightfall, it was clear that Yusef and Malek were among either the dead or the group taken to Damascus. By Hasna's count, there were nineteen young men still missing in their neighborhood. In addition to Yusef and Malek, also unaccounted for were some of Yusef's best friends—the loss of these bright young men, the pillars of their families, beloved and treasured, was incalculable.

Time seemed to have escaped its boundaries. Hours felt like years. Laila looked younger and Rana older, the eight years between them erased. Jebreel's face and hunched shoulders were those of an old man. Hasna felt hollowed out. She saw the circles under her neighbors' red-rimmed eyes when they brought her food and knew she must look the same. The food remained uneaten. One neighbor gazed at her compassionately: "Um Yusef, I have never seen you like this." She sat outside in the street or inside in the courtyard. She rose distractedly at times as if she were missing something, before sinking down again. People spoke to her and sometimes she responded.

One day Jebreel went to Laila's to pack up some things so that Laila and

Hamad could live with them for the time being; she could not stay alone in a house with no husband. Hasna was sitting with her back against the wall on her favorite part of the bench with no coffee and no Fairuz record when she heard a knock at the gate. She jumped, her heart racing.

The hinges squeaked and she heard the voice of her childhood friend, Um Ahmad, hesitant and polite: "Um Yusef?" Her voice was high-pitched and airy and never seemed to Hasna to fit her sturdy, compact body.

Hasna's own voice felt raspy and foreign: "Welcome, peace be upon you."

She gestured for Um Ahmad to come in. The two women embraced and kissed cheeks. Um Ahmad's face always reminded Hasna of a small owl—her angular nose too small for her round cheeks. Her wide eyes were a striking gray-green color. They were more like sisters than neighbors. Hasna's dark-eyed children had grown up with Um Ahmad's gray-eyed ones—Khassem and Ahmad were the same ages, Um Ahmad's married daughter was a year older than Laila. Today her nose was red, her eyes puffy.

Um Ahmad sat down at the table in her usual chair while Hasna went to make the coffee. After a few minutes, Hasna brought in a brass tray with two porcelain cups and the silver pot of strong Turkish coffee. She poured for her friend—black coffee the way Um Ahmad liked it.

Looking at each other, they both teared up. Um Ahmad took her hand. "I am praying every moment that Allah will spare your boys. Allah be merciful."

"Allah be merciful."

"Um Yusef, I have to tell you something that you cannot tell anyone else."

"Of course." The tears coursed freely down Hasna's cheeks; she could not seem to check them.

"The soldiers came to our house today. They put a mark on it, an 'X' just above the door." And now they were both crying, their coffee cooling between them. "I think something else is about to happen."

"What?"

"I don't know, but I think they are marking all of the houses that are . . . that will be . . . I think everyone who works for the government or for the police like Abu Ahmad will be safe. And I think . . ."

"The other houses will not."

"Yes." They gazed at one another for a minute, contemplating what that meant—the neighbors they both knew so intimately, the impact on their houses, the relatives and friends who were in danger.

"What is going to happen?"

"I don't know, but I want you to be ready. I want you to pack some things and have them in a bag. Tonight I want you and the girls to come stay with me. Please come through our neighbors' houses, so that the soldiers will not see you in the street. You can pass through the alley on the other side of the square. You can tell our neighbors that I am feeling nervous because my husband's services have been required by the army—that is true—and that I asked you to come. We are old friends; everyone knows that. I want you in my house tonight." Her eyes filled again with tears.

"Where is Abu Ahmad?"

"He and the other officers are out trying to keep the protesters . . ." And she stopped. Hasna understood—Abu Ahmad was trying to do his job to stop the protesters without hurting anyone. These were his neighbors and friends; he did not want anyone killed. The lines were not clear in this battle, there was no black and white. Good men had worked for the government for a long time; it did not mean they didn't share their neighbors' frustrations. Hasna wished again, passionately, that the protesters would stop, that the government would back down, that they could all sit down over coffee and have a reasonable conversation.

They talked over their other neighbors who had already fled to relatives' houses outside of town. And then they made plans. Hasna would cook dinner in her own home; she wanted to use up the rest of the meat she had bought at the market two days before because it would not last any longer without electricity. After today, they would have to rely on bread and rice, chickpeas and beans to keep them full. Her gas canisters had been filled recently; they could at least cook for the next several days if they were judicious. She would bring food when she came that night. She realized as she was talking that she already assumed the electricity would not come back on, that the situation might last for a while. She fought against a sinking depression.

Um Ahmad's forehead wrinkled as she stood, a sign that she was trying to find the right words. Hasna touched her arm. "My friend, you can say whatever you need to. Let us not mistrust one another now. You are my sister."

Um Ahmad nodded. "I trust you. I'm trying to decide if I am being ridiculous. But I think it would be a good idea for us to hide our valuables. There's no way to know what will happen. I think it would be best to be prepared."

Hasna hugged her friend and kissed her cheeks good-bye. She was grateful for a task to break up her stupor. She stood in the dim house, assessing what she needed to hide in case things got worse. But what could "worse" be? She shook the thought from her head. There was much to do before tonight.

SHE BEGAN BY CLEANING THE HOUSE, SWEEPING AND WIPING DOWN surfaces as best she could by the light from the windows. She doubled the amount of bread she would make and set it out to rise so that they could eat it for dinner and over the next few days if they did not have access to more food. She packed a bag for her and for Rana with enough clothes and toiletries for three days; she would tell Laila to do the same with enough diapers to last Hamad for some time. She also picked up Rana's pillow and some blankets to make pallets on the floor for her and Hamad.

She created a new hiding place for her valuables. In between her bedroom and the room where her young children had slept, now occupied by Rana, there was an open bookshelf so that she could hear them if they cried at night. She rearranged the rooms so that the open space between the walls was now covered. She stacked pillows in Rana's room to cover up the bottom half of the space and arranged them to look like a small couch. When Jebreel came back with the girls and the baby, he helped her move the floor-to-ceiling wardrobe in their room so that it covered the open bookshelf. From their room, it looked like one continuous stone wall with a wardrobe; from Rana's room, it looked like a wood-backed bookshelf built into the wall. She surveyed her work when she was done—the pillow couch made it appear as if the bottom shelf were the base of the bookshelf. If no one looked carefully, they would miss the hollowed-out portion below it.

There she put the gold that was their entire life savings. No one really trusted the banks in Syria; gold was the only stable investment. They had almost 35,000 liras' worth of gold in the form of bracelets, necklaces, earrings, and rings. She put them in a sack hidden behind some books at the bottom of the space, and then her children's pictures on top of that. They had other valuable possessions—artwork and Persian rugs and their family motorcycles—but she did not see how she could hide them. They would have to be taken care of later.

She baked the bread and seared the meat and sliced the last of her fresh vegetables for a salad. They ate outside while it was still light. Hasna did the dishes quickly, packing up a basket of food to take with her to Um Ahmad's. She went with Jebreel to make sure that all of the windows were shuttered and locked, and that the gates were securely fastened—he would not think of leaving if their home were in danger. If anyone came, it would be easy for one man to hide, much harder to hide the children.

Hasna showed him twice where the food was wrapped up for him. When she mentioned it for the third time, he pushed her gently toward the internal gate; she would make her way from neighbor's to neighbor's until she reached Um Ahmad's house with the small "X" etched over the door on the other side of Al-Salam Square. They hugged and he kissed the girls and she felt as if she were leaving on a long journey rather than just going across the square.

When she passed through her neighbors' homes, she told the few neighbors who asked that Um Ahmad had requested she come spend the night to amuse the younger children and keep her company while her husband was gone. She also mentioned that perhaps it was best for everyone to lock their doors and gates that night; her neighbors nodded—the rumor of another attack had made the rounds. Hasna passed through a dozen houses before crossing the alley and knocking on Um Ahmad's gate.

Um Ahmad pulled them quickly into the kitchen. Her friend's urgency made Hasna fearful again. Within minutes, there was a low rumble that shook the walls, and then a series of explosions. The tanks had arrived.

AFTER THE GRIEF AND FATIGUE OF THE LAST FEW DAYS, THAT NIGHT took on the ragged, surreal quality of a nightmare. Laila, Rana, baby Hamad, and Hasna sheltered in Um Ahmad's kitchen with Um Ahmad's younger children, away from the windows, trying to keep Hamad as quiet as they could. They hoped, but were not sure, that the "X" on the door would deter the soldiers they could hear moving through the city. Hasna's lips formed prayers almost constantly.

They could hear the shouts and screams of their neighbors all around them, the pounding on the doors, the shots that rang out through the night. Rana slept fitfully, her head cradled in Hasna's lap. Laila, Um Ahmad, and Hasna stayed up all night. Hasna felt sick with worry for Jebreel and their home. She should have insisted he come with her.

By the time the sun rose the next morning, Hasna's head buzzed with exhaustion and shock. The city had been silent for over an hour. She left Laila with the children at Um Ahmad's and went back to her home, this time along the roads instead of through the back way. The gate to their house was untouched—a good sign. When she unlocked it—something she could not remember doing, because they had always left their house unlocked before— Jebreel was sitting at the table drinking coffee. Soldiers had come through the house quickly, opening cabinets and looking under beds; Jebreel had lain behind the couch cushions in the living space and no one had checked there. The soldiers had not found anything.

A few minutes later, they went back to Um Ahmad's to get Rana and Laila and Hamad. Two soldiers now stood, hands gripping their machine guns, on the corner of the main street out of their neighborhood. They watched Jebreel and Hasna, who kept their eyes studiously in front of them. She felt sweat prickle her scalp.

Daraa was under siege.

Chapter 10

US REFUGEE RESETTLEMENT, 1880–1945

The 1940s brought a transformative shift in the American political landscape. The Displaced Persons Act, the Marshall Plan, the Nuremberg trials, the establishment of the United Nations—the years following World War II were extraordinary not only because of the fast pace of change. They also signaled a new direction in the immigration debate.

In the decades preceding World War II, isolationism, blatant racism, and fearmongering guided immigration policy in a way that is almost unparalleled in American history.

Almost.

THE POSITIONS IN THE IMMIGRATION DEBATES SOLIDIFIED IN THE 1880s with the rapid influx of newcomers from around the world. From the 1880s into the 1910s, more than 20 million immigrants arrived in the United States. Many of the newly arrived people were not from Northern and Western Europe, as had been the case in decades past. Historians have identified two distinctive sides of the immigration debates that were established in those years and that would remain in place for more than a century. The sides divided often (but not only) along partisan lines: The "restrictionists," led by the Democratic Party, wanted national quotas and limited admissions; the

"liberalizers," led by the Republicans, favored more open immigration policies. For decades, Republican liberalizers managed to win many of the immigration battles, though not all. The sheer number of people who came to
turn-of-the-century America demonstrated the liberalizers' political victories. But as the numbers increased, so did anti-newcomer resentment.

The more effective restrictionist arguments at the time paired economics
with racism. In op-ed pieces and political cartoons, in congressional debates
and town hall meetings, in conversations and letters and pamphlets, restrictionists created a fill-in-the-blank formula that would be trotted out in almost
every debate about immigration that followed: "These _____ immigrants are
taking our jobs and we need to stop them." Over time, that blank would be
filled with a number of nationalities: Irish, Polish, Italian, Vietnamese, Mexi-
can, Honduran, and Haitian, to name a few.

The Chinese Exclusion Act of 1882 was a massive restrictionist victory; it
was the first US immigration law to limit an entire group of people based on
their ethnicity or country of origin. While economic arguments probably per-
suaded the public, the act didn't really save jobs. Chinese people made up a
tiny percentage of the population and excluding them from the US did very
little to mitigate the lack of employment in the West, where the majority of
Chinese immigrants lived, and where they were disproportionately blamed
for economic woes. Restricting all Chinese immigrants was clearly much
more about race and culture. The lack of strong Chinese lobbying groups, or
community ties among business leaders with influence in Washington, meant
that it was relatively easy to push through the bill. Certainly, anti-Irish and
anti-Italian sentiment was high at the time, and yet there were no correlating
anti-Irish or anti-Italian bills. In part this was because liberalizers effectively
blocked other restrictionist legislation. But the lack of opposition to the Chinese Exclusion Act had to do with the racialized hierarchy that viewed Chinese immigrants as a cultural threat, one that liberalizers weren't generally
concerned about overcoming—it was a battle they were not willing to fight.

One political cartoon from the years leading up to the Chinese Exclusion
Act shows how race and culture trumped other factors. The cartoon features
an Irish man (wearing a tattered hat and coat with a bundle at his feet) and a

Chinese man (with a long pigtail coming from the back of his head) consuming "Uncle Sam." In the first frame, the Irish man is eating Uncle Sam's head and the Chinese man, his feet. In the second frame, they have almost finished swallowing him whole. In the third frame, the Chinese man is depicted wearing the Irish man's hat and coat; the Irish man's feet dangle from his mouth. The cartoon reads: "The Great Fear of the period—that Uncle Sam may be swallowed by foreigners." This cartoon was one of dozens, possibly hundreds, in major newspapers, local publications, or partisan magazines that used stereotypical markers to show that immigrants were a threat to "naturalized" US citizens, and that some were greater threats than others.

Liberalizers might have conceded defeat with the Chinese Exclusion Act, but they were winning the overall immigration policy war. A year later, in 1883, to raise money for the Statue of Liberty, the poet Emma Lazarus wrote "The New Colossus," a poem that could have been the liberalizer anthem at the time. Declaring the statue the "Mother of Exiles" who offers "world-wide welcome," Lazarus imagines her speaking out to other countries: "Give me your tired, your poor, / your huddled masses yearning to breathe free, / The wretched refuse of your teeming shore. / Send these, the homeless, tempest-tost to me, / I lift my lamp beside the golden door!" The poem was permanently affixed in bronze to the Statue of Liberty in 1902, a powerful symbol of America's liberalizer movement.

The cartoon and Lazarus's lines point to the lack of distinction and the use of stereotype in US politics and rhetoric about immigrants by both sides in those years. The debates lumped together people who fled targeted persecution and those searching for more economic opportunities, portraying them as either a massive influx of people coming to take jobs or the desolate and destitute in need of American benevolence. The precise immigration categories that determined actual arrivals would begin to be parsed out only after World War II, when "refugee" shifted toward a specifically defined legal term. People who would have met that later definition—like those escaping the Armenian genocide from 1915 to 1917—were not differentiated from other immigrants. The conversations raged as the American public decided not just which foreigners were welcome, but how the United States would define itself.

Immigration debates have always been about American identity.

FROM 1900 TO 1914, THE WAVE OF IMMIGRATION BECAME A FLOOD; 15 million new arrivals in that fourteen-year period taxed even many liberalizers' goodwill. As Europe became increasingly tumultuous, fears over an impending war made national security one of the more persuasive arguments against open immigration. Public opinion began to turn.

Liberalizers had effectively blocked bills in 1895, 1903, 1912, and 1915, but in 1917, they no longer had the political power to resist the growing restrictionism. The 1917 Immigration Act listed a significant number of "undesirables" that the American government did not want to allow into the country, including what it termed "idiots" and people deemed "mentally or physically defective." On the list of "undesirables" were not just people from China, but now from every country in the "Asiatic Barred Zone" except for those from the Philippines—who had been US nationals since America colonized their country—and Japanese immigrants, who were bound under other restrictions. It also mandated that all potential immigrants pass a literacy test and gave immigration officials wide freedom in denying entry to anyone they wished. The act blatantly described the kind of immigrant the people in leadership within the US valued: literate, upper-class, white, Northern Europeans without disabilities.

By the time the next major immigration bill passed Congress seven years later, the racism was not only overt, it was masquerading as cutting-edge science. Politicians argued for the Immigration Act of 1924 based on eugenics, the science of population control and human breeding. Eugenicists argued that white people were scientifically, biologically, and culturally superior and that one of the ways to preserve the best aspects of the human race in the United States was by limiting nonwhite immigration. In an April 9, 1924, speech, Senator Ellison DuRant Smith of South Carolina encouraged his fellow senators to read eugenicist Madison Grant's 1916 work, *The Passing of the Great Race*, and touted Grant's arguments about the superiority of "pure, unadulterated Anglo-Saxon stock" to "shut the door" and "breed pure American citizens" rather than allowing the US to be "an asylum for the oppressed of all countries."

When it passed, the bill stated that the number of immigrants from each country would be limited to 2 percent of the population of each of the countries represented in the US during the 1890 census—before the large wave of immigration brought more people from Southern Europe. The 1924 act was an attempt to allow in more people from England and Austria than from Greece and Italy. The act also almost completely excluded arrivals from Asia, South America, the Middle East—and of course the entire continent of Africa, since most African Americans in 1890 had arrived as a result of being trafficked through the Atlantic slave trade routes. The act also actively barred the admission of people who were "likely to become a public charge."

THE GREAT DEPRESSION IN THE 1930S SOLIDIFIED THE RESTRICTION-ists' hold, since anyone coming to take scarce jobs was now especially unwelcome. As the decade went on and the conflict in Europe increased, national security became a rising concern. The racist views of the 1920s remained largely unchecked; eugenics was a mainstream view in the US and Western Europe until the Nazis took the philosophy to its logical, awful end in the Holocaust.

By the time the MS *St. Louis* arrived off the shore of Florida in the summer of 1939, the American public was still largely unwilling to accept even the most "tempest-tost" refugees. There were floods of sympathetic articles across the nation advocating for these refugees and others, personal and political appeals from desperate relatives who told alarming stories of what was happening as Hitler's forces moved through Europe. But whether those stories were dismissed as rumors or disbelieved, the attitude of the American public toward refugees remained against arrivals even in the early years of World War II. The prevailing public view was a kind of restrictionism that could be summed up by the very American phrase, "better safe than sorry."

The brand of "better-safe-than-sorryism" from the late 1930s through the early 1940s presented national security, racialized, and economic fears as commonsense policy. It rationalized dehumanizing tactics as a necessary political move to protect US citizens. It quelled the impulses of people who might have been uncomfortable by arguing that it was more important to defend the rights and safety of the American public (even if the people affected were also US citizens or their relatives).

Better to be safe by turning away thousands of panicked refugees fleeing the Nazi regime than be sorry if one of them turned out to be a German enemy alien. Better to be safe by forcibly detaining almost 120,000 Japanese Americans in internment camps along the West Coast than to be sorry if US information leaked across the Pacific. Better to be safe by arresting, indefinitely holding, or even deporting patriotic Italian citizens than to be sorry if rumors in their local neighborhoods turned out to be true.

Better-safe-than-sorryism was the staple of such groups as "The America First Committee," established in 1940. Their spokesman, Charles Lindbergh, used blatant anti-Semitic language in Iowa in 1941 to argue that the "greatest danger to this country" comes from the "large ownership and influence in our motion pictures, our press, or our radio and our government" of "the Jewish." As he framed it, these "war agitators" pushed the US to enter the conflict "for reasons which are not American." While he nodded to the suffering of Jewish people and others under Nazi rule by acknowledging that intervention by the United States was "understandable from their viewpoint," he spent much of the speech laying out the case for why the US entering the war would only lead to "chaos and prostration." By resisting their "misinformation" and "propaganda," the US could avoid "sending our soldiers across the ocean to force a landing on a hostile coast against armies stronger than our own." The reasoning of Lindbergh, an established Nazi admirer, relied on the fact that the Nazis were the superior race, had superior technology, and would certainly defeat the US Army. In his configuration, while it might be regrettable for the victims of the Holocaust, the best policy for US interests was that it was better to be safe than sorry.

The backlash against Lindbergh's speech was immediate. Over the next four years, the tide of public opinion rose in favor of US investment in humanitarian endeavors, including resettling refugees. The obvious ramifications of better-safe-than-sorryism became clear: The cost of "sorry" was the humiliation and dehumanization, the lost livelihoods and freedom, of innocent Japanese or Italian Americans. The cost of "sorry" was the lives of the 532 passengers on the MS *St. Louis* who ended up in concentration camps. The cost of "sorry" was a genocide so horrifying, affecting so many millions of people, it needed an entirely new word. The cost of "sorry" was the displaced faces haunting Europe after the war, hoping for news of their loved ones and a safe place at last.

That was the political ground in which the unprecedented refugee policies following World War II had their roots. The profound American desire to prevent better-safe-than-sorry restrictionism from occurring lasted almost a decade, until the memory of gas chambers and pogroms faded, until the country forgot there had ever been a time before the word "genocide" existed. But some of the core values of the years following World War II remained, especially our shared identity as a global leader with the strength and responsibility to help others. The argument of the Army-Navy newsreel that "our half of the world cannot remain well if the other half is sick" would become so well-worn, it would seem that it had always existed—that refugees were always a part of our national consciousness. What changed over the next few decades was the nation's definition of the "other half of the world."

Chapter 11

HASNA

DARAA, SYRIA, MARCH–APRIL 2011

Within days, it felt impossible to Hasna that there had been a time before the soldiers came to Daraa, before tanks menaced every crossroad, before fear of what was happening to Malek and Yusef infused her every waking moment with dread. The government forces had returned the bodies of the young men who had been killed so their families could bury them. There was no word on the dozens of other young men who were missing.

Hasna hated to find hope in the other families' grief, but the return of the other men's bodies seemed further proof that Malek and Yusef were among the men carried off to Damascus. No one had seen them killed. Some people who had remained at the soccer field after Jebreel was sent home told Hasna that they thought they had seen the two of them among those who remained behind. Hasna clung to the thinnest scrap of hope, rubbed it to tatters beneath anxious fingers, felt the edges fray and unweave as each day passed without their boys.

A large building several blocks from their home had become the headquarters for the soldiers in this section of Daraa. Because there were soldiers near them, their grocery stores still had food. The electricity in their area of town returned and remained on. There were no raids on their already-occupied block.

Their luck was relative, of course. They lived every day in a state of occupation in a city with no communication with the outside world. No journalists documented what was happening; the only news was being propagated by the government-owned media outlets. Immediately after the attack on the Omari mosque, the government released video in which they claimed that they had saved Syria from outside dissidents who were planning an attack. Hasna thought it was ludicrous—everyone in Daraa knew government forces staged the video with their own guns, propped innocent Syrian men up and made them lie to the camera under threat that their families would be killed. But because it became the official story on the government news, people outside Daraa believed—at least for a time—that the Syrian government was only trying to stop terrorists, rather than killing innocent civilians. Without free journalists, rumor and hearsay were the only counterweight to the official story.

Hasna heard reports that mercenary soldiers from Iran and Hezbollah had been seen elsewhere throughout town—they were easily differentiated from the clean-shaven, modern-Arabic-speaking Syrians either because their beards revealed they were in Hezbollah, or because they spoke the classical Arabic of the Quran—fusha—indicating their first language was Persian. Hasna heard reports that these mercenaries were telling people they suspected could be dissidents that they could turn in guns and receive amnesty, but when they turned the guns in, the soldiers killed them for confessing. Anyone who was assumed to be taking part in the protest was shot on the street. The government imposed a curfew and officials often kept suspects out until just minutes before the curfew, when government snipers would shoot any men seen out in the street, even the innocent ones who had just been released and were trying to get home.

In the parts of town where known dissidents lived, foreign soldiers knocked on doors and told the residents they had five minutes to get out. At the first houses they went to, the residents did not leave. Why should they, when it was their home? What was the worst these hired men would do? The soldiers threw white phosphorous bombs into the homes, jamming the doors shut behind them so the residents could not escape.

The bombs melted the walls within seconds.

The horror of melting alive in her own home turned the blood in Hasna's body to ice every time she thought of it. She could not sleep. She roamed the house, touching the walls with the palms of her hands as if their solidity might reassure her, running her fingertips over the leaves of her beloved plants, gray in the moonlight. She haunted her own home like a ghost, desperately searching for some measure of peace. The sleepless nights left permanent smudges under her eyes.

And yet, every day, with surreal routine, they went about their lives. They ate and they tried to sleep, they talked to their neighbors. Rana went back to school. Jebreel went back to work. It was astonishing how quickly they adjusted to this new reality.

On Fridays, the city erupted into protests and the demonstrators clashed with soldiers. At the funerals on Saturdays, more protests flared up, which only led to more deaths, which only created more riots, in an ever-escalating cycle.

ONE MORNING, HASNA COULD NOT STAND IT ANY LONGER; THERE seemed no worse fate than waiting and not knowing. Every day that she went to the bakery or to the store, she watched young soldiers on the street.

She had seen something in the demeanor of a few of them that reminded her of Khassem and his cousins, who were also soldiers. She and her neighbors whispered among themselves that the Syrian regime could not have complete control of their army. Why else would they be dependent on Hezbollah and Iranian mercenaries already?

According to one persistent rumor, the first shot fired at the Omari mosque was at a conscripted Syrian soldier who had refused a direct order to enter a sacred space and shoot unarmed young men. He had been shot by his commanding officer.

Hasna bet that the soldiers who looked at her with kindness, who respectfully spoke the words of blessing and peace each time they saw her, were true sons of Syria caught up, like Khassem, in a situation beyond them.

As she left the small bakery that had the best bread in town, she passed by some soldiers lingering outside. She asked one of the tall young soldiers to help her carry her bread home. When he came to her house, she offered him coffee and sat with him for an hour. He told her his name was Fahad al-Homsi, and he was deferential and gracious. They did not speak of the political situation—she would not put him in that position—but by the end of the coffee, Hasna was convinced that he did not want to be doing what he was doing and that he would, if pressed, err on the side of helping the people of Syria.

When Laila came out to the courtyard and saw her mother entertaining a soldier, her small shoulders set rigidly and her eyes narrowed. She slunk away quickly after Hasna introduced them. Their argument after Fahad al-Homsi left was cataclysmic. Perhaps screaming at each other would have released some tension; instead their hissed whispers only seemed to magnify the pressure. Hasna was the worst kind of traitor, Laila said. Hasna tried to form her strategy in words—if they could befriend the soldiers, find the cracks in their professional demeanor, they could find out information. Laila wouldn't listen, wheeling away and slamming the door to her room, the only way to express her raw fury. She woke the baby and Hasna could hear her shushing him back to sleep. When it was time for dinner, Laila came out to help her mother, but her mood was black. Later, when they were calmer, Hasna tried to broach the subject again, but Laila snapped and walked out of the room. Hasna did not bring it up again. She watched Laila warily, worriedly.

The house had often seemed too small for their seven children over the years and now it felt stiflingly full of their collective anger, anxiety, and fear. Only Hamad and his peals of laughter brought any of them joy.

DESPITE LAILA'S CENSURE, HASNA DEEPENED HER STRATEGIC FRIEND-ship with Fahad al-Homsi. He brought other soldiers over to her house one day. They brought her bread and she served them coffee. She had often gone to other bakeries, depending on the day and the deals available, but she took to frequenting only the bakery by the soldiers' station on the street. She noticed that Fahad al-Homsi was often the soldier posted at the entryway to their neighborhood or making the rounds through the narrow streets and alleys around Al-Salam Square. Soon she spoke to him at least once a day.

The earnestly handsome Fahad al-Homsi became an almost constant focus of the giggling neighborhood girls. He was kind to them, but it was Laila he followed with his eyes every time she and Hasna left to go to the store or sat on the street with their neighbors. Catching his eyes on her only seemed to make Laila angrier. She and Hasna were both aware of the direction of his eyes, but they never spoke of it.

One day, he brought a loaf of bread to Hasna's gate early in the morning. He knocked gently and, when she answered, leaned his head down briefly so his voice did not carry: "Good morning, Um Yusef. Peace be upon you."

"Peace be upon you, Fahad."

"I hope you are well this morning."

"I am as well as I can be, thank you, son."

"Um Yusef," and here he looked over his shoulder for a brief moment, "I've gotten . . . I heard . . . Yusef and Malek are alive. They are in a prison in Damascus with some of the other men. All nineteen of the men from this neighborhood are alive."

She put her hand to her heart, felt it beating raggedly. She took a step back from the door, making room for him to come inside, but he did not. He spoke low, just above a whisper.

"I am not the one who told you. But they do not have proof against them and, if they do not find any in the next few days, they have to let them go."

"And they will come home?" She tightened her grip on the metal gate and felt its edge bite into her palm.

His eyes shone with what she thought might be tears, but his hat shadowed his face and she could not be sure.

"There is a very good chance they might be coming home. I will do what I can to get you news."

"Thank you, son. You are very kind." They looked at each other, all of the things they could not say laid bare between them. "I will pray for you, my son."

"Thank you, Um Yusef. I would appreciate that."

"May peace be upon you."

"Peace be upon you and your family."

Hasna rushed to tell Jebreel and Laila what the soldier had told her. They all cried, with relief, but now with added worry—when would they come home? And what were they enduring as each day passed in captivity in Damascus? Underneath, though, Hasna felt a spike of triumph—her strategizing had paid off.

As quietly as they could, without revealing the source of the information, Hasna and Jebreel told the mothers and fathers of the other nineteen young men what they had learned. Laila went back with Jebreel to her house to get a few more things, to make sure their valuables were hidden, and to get Malek's clothes in case he came back to the house. They also told Laila's in-laws. Word leaked out slowly, like spilled oil, that all of the boys were safe.

NOW EVERY DAY WAS PASSED IN A FEVER PITCH OF HOPING THAT YUSEF and Malek might come home. Hasna spent all day on the road in front of her house, sitting with the neighborhood women, watching from the red plastic stools that served as extra seating in everyone's houses. They began within an hour of the sun rising. They spent their days keeping vigil together beside the wall she shared with Um Ibtihal. If their boys came into the neighborhood, they would see it from this vantage point. She left her stool only to take Rana to school and to cook quick meals for all of them.

Hasna was sitting on the stool near the road one morning, leaning her back against the wall, when she saw a group of women gathering just down the block from them, in the entrance to the neighborhood, preparing to walk down the wider road toward the warehouse with the soldiers.

They were all wearing the long black dresses and hijabs that most women in Daraa wore. They leaned into one another for a moment, and then they turned. They pulled out cardboard signs from beneath their long dresses and coats and held them up. Hasna's heart lurched—there in the front, the small form with a sign held up high, was Laila.

She felt paralyzed for a second as their voices rang out: "Free our boys! Let them go! Peace, peace, we want peace for Daraa!"

For a few moments, it felt as if nothing would happen. The women shouted and their voices resonated with conviction and indignation. Hasna ran to follow them, staying back so it was clear that she was not with them. The group moved as one down the street. Time suspended as they yelled the grief of all of the mothers, daughters, and wives who were waiting.

Then a contingent of soldiers turned the corner. Soldiers were thick behind the first group, as if the entire army had been waiting for these women.

Soldiers poured and poured and poured into the streets. Tanks turned the corner, two of them, their ambling progress toward the clump of women all the more menacing because they were slow.

To Hasna, they looked like a colony of ants racing toward a crumb. And that crumb was her daughter.

She ran faster than she had ever imagined running in her life. There had been women behind Laila, but Hasna saw only her daughter. Laila stood, alone, her cardboard sign still held high above her head, shouting out her explosive rage in the face of soldiers thundering toward her.

Hasna snatched her arm, pulled her rapidly back into the neighborhood, into the gate of a neighbor's house, through that side gate to another and another, through the honeycomb of gates designed to allow women in hijabs to visit during the day, now serving for the second time in their lives as a secret passage to safety. She did not even give Laila a chance to speak but pulled her by the arm through house after house.

Her own internal gate was barely closed and locked behind her before she was stripping Laila like a child. She pulled her hijab and her dress off her body as if they were toxic, snatched her cardboard sign and folded it savagely into tiny squares, stuffing it at the bottom of the pile of clothes in the basket of laundry, and shoving the black dress inside the middle of the pile. She found Laila's pajamas, bunching the shirt in her hands so Laila could put it on over her head swiftly. When she pulled it down over Laila's naked torso, she realized her daughter was weeping silently.

"Enough. Enough! You have to look like you've been asleep. Quick! Get into bed!"

She swatted her daughter's bottom as she turned, the swift spanking of an exasperated mother to her little girl.

Hasna made herself take a deep breath. She waited until she heard Laila's bedroom door click shut before walking, deceptively nonchalant, out her front door. She gathered her stools as if she were utterly unconcerned with the soldiers who were breaking up into groups and running to knock on the doors of the houses around her.

The neighborhood women saved Laila's life. The soldiers said they were really only looking for the one woman who organized the protest, the small one in the front. Um Ibtihal said she had no idea who that was, that none of them did—perhaps she was a dissident from outside the neighborhood who came to cause trouble for them. Theirs was not the only neighborhood where young men were missing; all across Daraa, mothers and sisters and wives waited for men to come home. Hasna joined her voice with those of the other women in telling the soldiers—none of the women here would protest, they were patriotic Syrian citizens and would never speak out against their government. It was truth; Hasna would never have dreamed of protesting against her government. Hasna invited some soldiers to search her home, where her sick children slept, but they declined, convinced by the women's tones that it had been outside protesters.

When Hasna finally went back inside, Laila was asleep, holding Hamad, who had napped the entire time his mother was bringing the soldiers down on all of them. Hasna pulled a blanket over them both.

THE INFORMANT WHO TOLD ON LAILA WAS A GIRL WHO HAD NEVER liked her. She was the daughter of the man who owned the small grocery store used by everyone in their neighborhood and her insecurities made her sharp; she was constantly spreading gossip and rumors about other girls in school. The girl was thrilled that the soldier who came to her house was the handsome one she had been making eyes at for weeks. She happily told him what no other woman in the neighborhood would: "Oh, of course I know who that was! That was Laila al-Salam. She lives just down the way—her family's gate is near the main road. I'll show you if you'd like."

"No, thank you, I know which one you're talking about. I'll go check on it now."

And Fahad al-Homsi went straight to Hasna's house.

"YOU'RE LUCKY IT WAS ME SHE TOLD," FAHAD AL-HOMSI CONCLUDED, this time sitting at the table. "No one has accused Um Hamad but the girl down the street."

Laila walked into the courtyard silently, her hijab fixed firmly in place, and listened.

Fahad al-Homsi went on as if she weren't there, but his tone shifted, became more formal. "There is nothing we can do, nothing we will do, since it is evident that the girl who informed on your daughter was wrong and that the person who led that protest is from another neighborhood. But we wanted to let you know that these false rumors were being spread by someone in the neighborhood, just so you are all aware."

Hasna's voice was as formal as his. "We take these rumors very seriously. When my husband gets home, he will go and speak with that girl's father. Clearly it was not my daughter, who was sleeping all morning with her infant son; they have both been sick. The grocer's daughter is a known liar. Her father will discipline her for it. We will make sure of it."

Fahad al-Homsi nodded and got up to leave. Laila walked with him to the door and this time, she spoke the words of farewell: "Peace be upon you."

Fahad al-Homsi turned his face fully toward her when he responded, "And peace be upon you."

Hasna offered to keep the baby for a few minutes.

The story became legend in the neighborhood by that night. Laila walked resolutely over to the grocer's house, knocked on the door, and walked in when the daughter opened the gate.

Then, without saying a word, she beat the girl up savagely.

The grocer tried to pull Laila off his daughter, but she spat in his face: "You should be ashamed to call yourselves Syrian."

And Laila left as swiftly as she had come.

After that night, no one in the neighborhood went back to that man's grocery store again.

When Laila came the next morning to sit with Hasna and the other women in their prolonged vigil on the red stools, they made room for her, patting her shoulder and her knee.

FAHAD AL-HOMSI SAUNTERED UP TO THE WOMEN GATHERED OUTSIDE on the fifteenth morning without Yusef and Malek. "Good morning, Um Yusef. Peace be upon you."

"Peace be upon you."

He looked up as if he were checking on the weather. "There is a small chance that there will be a bus of prisoners coming back from Damascus today, and that it will come at the end of this street, perhaps within the next few hours."

He walked away casually. She did not have the words to speak the usual blessings of peace. She sat down again.

Within hours, the whole neighborhood joined the red-stooled vigil keepers. Even the men joined them, everyone waiting in the streets, all pretense of casual loitering gone. It was a dangerous game, to gather like this, but they could not bear to miss the moment when the boys came back.

THE BUS PULLED UP, STOPPING WITH A MECHANICAL SIGH. THE DOORS opened and a handful of people got off—women in hijabs, older men, some children.

And then they were there, nineteen young men, limping off the bus.

Hasna ran. Jebreel ran. The whole neighborhood ran, as one, to welcome them home.

The soldiers stood on the main road and watched them.

Hasna hugged Yusef and he was crying and she was crying and she could see how filthy his face was by the tracks his tears made on his cheeks. She pulled him close to her, cradled his thin body against hers, and then he was holding his dad, and then he was pulling his mother back to him.

After a moment, she stopped to look for Laila and saw her, chin on Malek's shoulder, their son nestled between their bodies. Laila's eyes caught her mother's and they did not have to speak the forgiveness they felt for each other. It was already granted and gone, washed away in the joy of having Malek and Yusef safely home.

After several minutes, the neighbors left the street. Laila saw the grocer, standing back in the welcoming crowd, and she walked up to him and spat in his face. "You do not deserve to be here."

No one said a word as Laila walked with her husband back to her mother's home.

THAT NIGHT, ALL OF THE NEIGHBORS AND RELATIVES BROUGHT FOOD
over to Hasna's house. Yusef and Malek showered and changed and their hair
was still damp when they came out to join the party. Amal and Samir came
and Hasna's daughters and nieces helped her serve coffee and tea to everyone
who walked in; she borrowed cups and teapots from Um Ahmad and the veterinarian's wife and other neighbors. They could not make enough coffee and
tea. Her neighbors brought huge heaping portions of chicken and basmati rice,
falafel, hummus and pita, dolmas, baklava. She turned on the lights strung
from the pillars when it started getting dark, softening everyone's faces so the
stress and sleepless nights were no longer visible.

The house was full, as Hasna loved it to be; people packed the bench surrounding the courtyard and the table was overflowing. While she was pouring
coffee for one of Jebreel's cousins, Hasna overheard someone telling Malek
the story of how Laila had faced down the soldiers, and how Hasna had saved
her. It was the first time Hasna could remember any of them speaking so
openly about sedition, but she was caught up in the fervor like the rest of them.
When the story was finished, Malek joked that they should start calling Hasna
"Lebweh"—The Lioness. The neighbors loved it; they passed the name around.
Hasna was embarrassed and pleased. A lioness knew when to watch and wait,
and when it was time to strike. A lioness was cunning, able to ascertain the
situation effectively, watching for potential danger, sensing the undercurrents
around her. A lioness was fierce in protecting her children, moved on instinct
without thought for her own safety, and when she moved there was no one
who would dare stand in her way. Hasna caught Malek's teary eyes across the
courtyard. He smiled at her, holding Laila's hand with one hand and baby
Hamad in the crook of his arm.

Hasna knew even then that this evening might be the last celebration in
her home for a long time. She was not the only one who wiped away tears when
they threw candy in the air and watched the children scramble to get it. She
was not surprised that the neighbors lingered later into the night than usual.
They all wanted the respite from stress, all wanted the happiness to stretch out
as long as possible before they had to face the days to come.

Before it was fully dark, Hasna slipped out to take candy and baklava to Fahad al-Homsi and the men standing watch on the street corner.

That night, Laila slept in her own home and Yusef slept in his room. And Hasna slept fully for the first time since Khassem had come home with his warning. If only she could have had Khassem home, the evening would have been perfect.

The next morning, she awoke with one thought—she would do whatever it took to get her children to safety. She would prove her nickname right. They needed to leave—there was too much suspicion already cast upon them by Yusef's detention and the informant's aspersions against Laila. They could be detained again, or disappeared. She could not bear to have any of her children in Syrian jails ever again. She and Rana would have to wait until Rana's school year was over, because even in the midst of the escalating revolution, Hasna clung to her tenacious desire for her girls to be educated. But her focus narrowed to the single goal of saving her family.

Chapter 12

MU NAW

AUSTIN, TEXAS, USA, SEPTEMBER 2007

Mu Naw rounded the corner toward her apartment door where she saw a sheet of paper hung precariously by a single piece of tape. The walk through the arid heat was one of the most excruciating parts of her day. Little Naw Wah sat blandly in the umbrella stroller, sweat beading along her hairline, watching the world move slowly past while Mu Naw shuffled behind her and stood with the other mothers waiting for their children. The kindergarten classes came out and Mu Naw waved at the teacher as Pah Poe spotted her. They would walk home together, Mu Naw slowing perceptibly as they neared home.

The late summer heat refused to break. Day after day of temperatures in the high nineties or low hundreds sapped what little energy Mu Naw had left. She woke up every morning thinking she might go to English class, but she could barely move off her couch or bed. The hour-long commute both ways was overwhelming. Everything made her throw up, but cars and buses were the worst. She hated the fumes that spewed out of them, the fact that there was no air that did not reek of them; riding in them had become an almost insurmountable hurdle. At home in the dark apartment, she and Naw Wah could sit for hours and watch the television or spend time with their neighbors, her distractions from grief and nausea.

It had been several weeks since she had told Saw Ku that she was pregnant. The squatty red buildings now held several Karen families. More came every few days. Not all of the families from Myanmar were Karen; some were Karenni and a few were ethnically Burmese. Many other refugee families moved in, too—tall women in flowing headscarves from Somalia; effusive families from Burundi. She smiled at them when she passed the same women in her walks to and from school. Sometimes their presence helped her feel less alone; sometimes their inability to communicate with one another contributed to the heaviness of her depression.

The other Karen families were her only source of joy. To hear her language spoken, to eat familiar foods, to catch up on news from home—she could forget, for a few minutes or even a few hours, everything that she had lost. She had become good friends with the woman who lived in the apartment just behind her, Meh Bu, who spent many afternoons at Mu Naw's house watching TV. They ate lunch together and helped each other with the paperwork that defined their lives.

Mu Naw had come to rely on Meh Bu's translation skills; though Mu Naw had come here first, her new friend was confident and assertive with the English she had learned back in her camp in Thailand. Mu Naw was happy to defer to Meh Bu on most things. In turn, Mu Naw shared what she had and what she had learned about navigating their new world: She gave Meh Bu food stamps, took her on Monday nights to get boxes of nonperishable food from the church next door, taught her which buses took her to the refugee services office or to English class. There were some things that she noticed about Meh Bu—the way she pointedly helped some of the families and not others, her tendency to criticize many of the women—that did not sit well with Mu Naw, but she had already become family within a few days in the way that people did when they had no family nearby and no one else they could speak to.

Mu Naw had grown up the daughter of the camp pariah; she assumed without question that the same gossip and whispering that had followed her around Mae La camp would come with her to the United States. But it did not. No one here knew that her mother had divorced her father and remarried someone else. No one else looked at her every move as proof that Mu Naw, like her mother, was "not a good girl." To be the closest friend of the most educated woman in the apartment complex was surprising to Mu Naw, but delightful nonetheless. She felt unworthy of Meh Bu.

It felt perverse that the apartment manager had come during the one hour she was gone to leave a note. Mu Naw pulled it down, leaned over to unbuckle Naw Wah, used the door frame for support while she fumbled with the lock. She rushed inside, the children moving aside as she scrambled for the bathroom. Afterward, she flipped the TV on for them, lying down for several minutes before she felt ready to look at the note in the manager's scrawled handwriting.

Everything related to the apartment was her job, a designation that never bothered Mu Naw because Saw Ku was the one going to work every day. He went five or six days a week—as many as they would let him schedule—to a restaurant where he and his brother scrubbed piles of pots and pans for hours. The bus route to get to their job was circuitous and the buses notoriously unreliable. He had to take multiple buses to get from his apartment to the restaurant, which meant many days he spent as many as twenty-four hours gone from his home. The posted bus route times seemed more of a suggestion than an actual schedule; he had missed his bus a few times in the beginning and then missed all of his subsequent connections. In order to make it to work in the morning on time, he had taken to sleeping some nights at the bus stop, curling up on his backpack with his jacket pulled over him. Mu Naw worried about him on those nights sleeping rough in this new country, but there was nothing they could do. The alternative—losing the job because he missed the bus—was unthinkable.

MU NAW COULD NOT REALLY EXPLAIN THE FACT THAT SHE WAS STILL pregnant to herself—she did not want to bring another child into the world, another mouth to feed, more bills to pay, the spiking nausea that only grew worse. She did not want to give birth in this new country. And yet she could not bring herself to call the number the nurse at the health care clinic had given her. She knew that waiting only made things more complicated. It was a conundrum she endured only by withdrawing further into herself.

The inescapable isolation that she had worried about now seemed inviting, the cold emptiness of it comforting. Alone, she did not have to wonder what the women around her would think if they knew she wanted to end her pregnancy. She could return to what had been familiar to her for most of her life—shameful daughter of a shameful mother, somehow marked by choice or birth or skin color or place in the world as less than the others around her. She could accept that; in fact, as her feelings seemed more and more out of her control, she embraced that shame and the release of detachment. She had no control of the world around her, of the inexorable forces of apartment managers and bureaucratic papers and language differences. She couldn't even control her own body. She couldn't help anyone. She couldn't help herself. She couldn't help her children. Who was she to think she could? Better to drift alone, lost, empty. It was the fate she had been moving toward since the minute her mother let go of her at the age of eleven.

AFTER SHE RETURNED WITH HER GREAT-GRANDMOTHER AND GREAT-aunt to her parents' home village in Myanmar, she lived there for a year; her great-grandmother died not long after the journey. Word came from another relative—Mu Naw's father had a cousin in a village a few hours away willing to take Mu Naw; her sister and brother were shipped off somewhere else. No one mentioned Mu Naw's mother.

Mu Naw went to live with her father's cousin—also called "grandmother" in Karen—in a rural part of northern Karen state. From the first day, she was cruel to Mu Naw. Mu Naw was beaten with a bamboo branch for the smallest infraction. The years she spent in the home of this grandmother were hopeless, full of grueling work and endless repetitions of her worthlessness.

All around them was the grinding tension of war. People fled like furtive deer past Mu Naw while she was working in the fields. One woman told Mu Naw that she hid underneath the bushes and watched soldiers rape all of the women from her village. Mu Naw picked out hiding spots in every place she went; she held herself tensely every time she saw soldiers—Karen or Burmese, militia or military, they all frightened her.

One day, about three years after she arrived there, Mu Naw unexpectedly ran into a friend of her mother's in the tiny village near this grandmother's home. They greeted each other the way that many Karen people did in those days—surprise at finding each other here, relief that they remained alive. As they were catching up, the friend mentioned that her mother was living in Mae La camp.

After years of wondering, Mu Naw's face flushed with an intense relief. She was glad, later, that she had felt that way; it was evidence to her in the years to come that she had loved her mother underneath it all. There were rumors that the war was coming to this region of the country again and those rumors had been reliable in the past—many of the people around her were beginning to pack up their things. Her mother's friend told Mu Naw she was crossing the border into Thailand and Mu Naw asked to go along.

Mu Naw sold the gold earring her mother had given her to cover her part of the expenses. She left without telling the cruel grandmother; she showed up at the appointed time with her mother's friend, reveling in the knowledge that the grandmother no longer had the power to control her movements.

The drive across the country was very different from the two journeys Mu Naw had made on foot through the jungle. Her mother's friend was warm and nurturing, confident Mu Naw's mother would be glad to see her. She was solicitous of Mu Naw's emotional state, the difficult years she had spent with the grandmother, the way she had worked so hard only to receive regular beatings, the separation from her entire family. It was a relief to share the things she had endured with an older woman who cared to listen. The car, an ancient Volkswagen bug, drove jerkily over potholed roads, but the sun turned the leaves jade green and the open windows let in a breeze that smelled of growing things. When they arrived at the border, they abandoned the car and snuck across a broken-down bridge, making a shadowed midnight approach to the camp.

And then they were there. The friend knocked on the door of a hut. Her mother answered. She started when Mu Naw stepped behind the friend into the dim hut, lit only by a bare bulb. But then her mother uttered a hoarse cry and clutched at Mu Naw, her hands clawing at Mu Naw's arms and hair, moving all over her as if to see that she was whole, that she was real. Mu Naw laughed and her mother kissed her cheeks.

It was only the next morning that Mu Naw and her mother examined each other in the daylight. The four years of their separation had not changed her mother at all. She seemed smaller to Mu Naw, but her face was the same. They grinned at each other when Mu Naw woke up, but they did not hug again.

A baby cried in the hut and Mu Naw's mother went to console her and a man Mu Naw had never met emerged from behind the mosquito netting on the shadowed sleeping platform. It was only then that Mu Naw realized what living with her mother would mean. The friend had mentioned that her mother had remarried and had a child, but she had not focused on that fact. Had she intentionally not wanted to think about it? Her mother had been living in a new hut with a new family while Mu Naw worked and was beaten by a distant relative who did not care about her, who housed her because her father paid a fee. Her brother and sister were off with other relatives in the war zone of Myanmar. Mu Naw's mother whispered to the new baby as it suckled at her breast and her husband dropped a kiss on her head as he tightened the longyi around his waist to go bathe in the community bathhouse and Mu Naw felt rage dry up her relief like dew in the hot sun.

That rage would be the lens through which she would view her mother and this adulterous and disgraceful new life—in which her mother had the audacity to be happy—for years. Her mother's husband was never unkind to Mu Naw, did not seem to resent her coming into their new home. He never beat her mother or even threatened Mu Naw. But she hated him from the beginning, hated his chin and his thin arms, so different from her father's bulky build. She hated his quiet voice, the way he asked her mother what she thought, not man enough to make decisions. Only her little half sister was not a source of rancor for her. The baby was sweet and dimpled and looked most like Mu Naw. She cared for her sister whenever her mother asked, but she could barely bring herself to look at her mother's husband.

At the cruel grandmother's house in the Karen state, Mu Naw's actions had revolved around a desire to avoid beatings. Now her life took a new turn. She wanted to love her mother, to be a good daughter. But she found herself unable to overcome her anger, resentment, and shame. Eventually she sank into her rage. She yelled and screamed and talked back. She criticized her mother's hygiene, the often-dirty dishes, the subpar cooking. Outside the hut, she spoke demurely, eyes down, clothes neat, hair washed, desperate to communicate to everyone around her how different she was from her mother, that she was an unwilling by-product of her mother's home.

Gossip was the lifeblood of the camp. Perceived slights, social snubs, revealed secrets, repeated insults—they were the only new fodder of conversation for people in a deeply stagnant life. To change the gossip about her became one of the few goals of Mu Naw's life. She spent most of the day out of her mother's hut. When school started, she went early and stayed late. She spent hours lounging with her friends under trees at the edge of camp. She received Saw Ku's note and dated him for a year in secret. It never occurred to her to confide in her mother about their relationship.

IN THE APARTMENT IN AUSTIN, THESE WERE THE THINGS MU NAW COULD still control: Every day, Pah Poe made it to and from school. There was food on their table, even if it came from packages or cans. The apartment was clean. Their bed was made. Their shoes were organized by the front door. Their hair was clean and combed. Their teeth were brushed.

The apartment manager's note belonged in the category of things she could not control. Mu Naw had gone over the figures several times. They had paid in full; she had asked Bob to help her look at the bills and he agreed with her.

The day she saw the note on her door after school, she walked over to the office again, a low building near the main parking lot. She held Naw Wah's hand with one hand; the other gripped the note from the apartment manager and a copy of her bank statement to prove that she was not late on the rent. Pah Poe trailed along behind them.

The apartment manager took off her glasses, which Mu Naw suspected were fake, and tapped the bills with long fuchsia fingernails to emphasize her points: Mu Naw owed money from last month and this month, as well as some indeterminate fine that she threatened but did not clarify. She scarcely glanced at Mu Naw's bank statement, only barked at her, looked distastefully at the children, and returned to her computer to clatter away at the keyboard.

Mu Naw planted herself, chin jutting out, in the cheap particle-board chair covered with pilling gray fabric. Five minutes passed and then ten and Mu Naw still sat, arms crossed, while the children stared at the manager with curious eyes. Finally, she caved and told Mu Naw to come back in Monday and she would see if there was anything she had missed in their records. It was not what Mu Naw wanted—she had not been told they did not have to pay—but it was a concession that might lead the woman to change her mind, a small victory. Mu Naw left without saying a word, resolving to be in the office first thing Monday morning and to track down a willing English-speaking volunteer to stand with her.

Mu Naw knocked on Meh Bu's door, barely giving Meh Bu a chance to greet her as the door swung open before launching into her frustrations with the apartment manager. At the end of her story, Mu Naw put her hand on Meh Bu's door frame, assuming her friend would move so she could walk inside as she had so many times before.

"Can you go with me?"

"Right now?" Meh Bu glanced behind her in the apartment as if looking for something that she needed to do.

"No, Monday morning."

"No, not on Monday."

"But I need help!"

Something shuttered in Meh Bu's expression. "Everyone needs help. Do you know that? Everyone needs something all the time. I can't go Monday and I can't go Tuesday."

Mu Naw felt the tears that she was trying so hard to hold at bay rising up. "Please! Saw Ku is coming home and I need to tell him we have a plan to make sure we don't have to pay this fine!"

"Then go tell the manager yourself!"

"I tried but she's not listening and I don't speak English."

"That's your fault. You don't go to English class. I see you every day, sitting at home in your apartment while the rest of us go to class. You think we want to go? You think we like the bus? You're lazy. You've been here longer than anyone and your English is no better than it was when you arrived. It's time for you to figure out what to do by yourself. Go tell her yourself or go home, I don't care, but I'm not helping you."

She shut the door firmly on Mu Naw. Mu Naw stood there for a long time, breathing. Finally, she picked up Naw Wah's hand, put her other hand on Pah Poe's shoulder, and went around the corner to her front door.

Saw Ku arrived home that night to a dark apartment; the television illuminating the children's upturned faces was the only light. Rice simmered in the rice cooker and a covered pot of vegetables and meat sat on the back of the stove. It took him a minute to locate Mu Naw, huddled under the blankets in the bedroom, her racking sobs silent except for an occasional gasping breath.

"What happened?" His hand on her arm was gentle. He turned on the lamp beside the bed, then knelt down beside her. His eyebrows beetled with concern. She cried harder for several minutes and he stroked her arm, then her hair, brushing it behind her ear with his thumb.

She told him what Meh Bu had said, her voice choking on the word "lazy." She told him about the apartment manager, about paying double rent, about the fine she knew they did not owe, about her inability to end the pregnancy. His hand still on her arm, he waited until she was done, until her breathing had become calm. Then he went to get her some toilet paper from the bathroom to dry her eyes. Coming back in, he moved to sit beside her on the other side of the bed.

"Well, first of all, I think Meh Bu is right."

"What?" Mu Naw pulled herself onto her elbow. Saw Ku handed her the tissues.

"Not about your being lazy. Not at all. But that no one can help us but us. Remember when we sold food at Mae La camp?"

"Yes." She sat up, pulling her hair back into a ponytail. They had decided their first year of marriage that they could use her ability to cook well to make some extra money, going door to door selling rice and bamboo.

"Honestly, I never told you this, but I didn't really think we could make any money, even though your food was delicious. I sold it to our friends and neighbors, but you took yours further, to the houses of people we didn't know. You are so good at talking to people. You are stubborn. And you made us money that we wouldn't have had otherwise. You did that. I can go to work, but there are things you can do, even if . . ." he gestured to her belly and swallowed. "Even if we're going to have another baby. You are good with people, good at learning things. You can learn English, even without classes. You will figure out a way around this apartment manager. You can do this."

It was a long speech for Saw Ku. He was not shy with Mu Naw, as he was with other people, but he still often spoke in short sentences. But his eyes bored into hers while he spoke and he gestured with his hands and it felt like a revelation to Mu Naw. He was right and Meh Bu was wrong.

She washed her face while Saw Ku went into the living room. When she came out of the bathroom, the lights were on and the table was set. Saw Ku told her to sit down and he scooped rice and steamed vegetables onto her plate. They ate dinner around the table together. She brought out a box of Pocky she had been saving for dessert and the children happily snapped the chocolate-dipped cookie sticks. Mu Naw nibbled hers to make it last longer. She let herself, for the first time, imagine a third child at their table. She realized that without speaking of it, she and Saw Ku had acknowledged the decision they had already made: She would be keeping this baby. She was surprised that her only emotion was joy.

ON MONDAY MORNING, AFTER WALKING PAH POE TO SCHOOL, MU NAW took Naw Wah back to the apartment manager's office. She sat in the chair, pulling the stroller tightly up against the wall so it would not take up too much room. She kept her eyes down, a smile on her face. The apartment manager told her she did not have time to meet with Mu Naw that day. She said, "Okay, no problem." Then she sat there. An hour later, the manager came out again and said something with an exasperated air. Mu Naw replied, "Okay. It's Okay! No problem!" But she did not move. For three hours, she and Naw Wah waited. They played finger games. She told Naw Wah stories. Naw Wah took a nap in the stroller. Finally, the apartment manager opened the door. "Fine, what do you need?"

Mu Naw pushed the stroller into the office. She pulled the bills out of her bag, pointing to Bob's careful notes, and informed the apartment manager that it was all paid, that there was nothing more. The manager turned to the computer and typed for several minutes with her lacquered fingernails, looking closely, taking her glasses off and putting them back on again. Finally, she turned back to Mu Naw. "Okay. It is all paid. No more."

Mu Naw hid her triumphant grin. Lowering her eyes respectfully, she murmured, "Thank you." When the door closed behind her, she lifted her face to the sun, then meandered behind Naw Wah as the toddler pushed the empty stroller all the way back to the apartment.

Chapter 13

HASNA

DARAA, SYRIA/RAMTHA, JORDAN, APRIL–JULY 2011

Malek and Laila moved to Jordan first. They left a few days after Malek was released to find an apartment in Ramtha, the small city right across the border from Daraa, that would be large enough for Laila's whole family. Malek's parents and his larger family did not want to leave, but they began scouting anyway for locations if his parents and siblings changed their minds. What had once been just a few minutes' drive to Ramtha now took Laila and Malek several hours with the new infusion of soldiers.

One of their neighbors had a van rental service and he took Malek, Laila, Hamad, and their few suitcases. They had to pack lightly so their story of going to visit Malek's uncle seemed reasonable to the border patrol officers. The van driver was one of the few people whose businesses prospered in the next few weeks as relatives and neighbors kept him busy between the al-Salam neighborhood and Ramtha. He reported back to Hasna that he had delivered Malek and Laila safely to Ramtha a day after they left. She breathed a sigh of relief—one child out, four left.

But that relief was short-lived. A few days later, another relative brought word from their cousin in Damascus about Khassem's imprisonment. In an instant, the shortness of breath and irregular heartbeat that had plagued Hasna during the fifteen days of waiting for Yusef and Malek returned. Hasna and Jebreel were plunged again into panic, but this time they felt more alone: They did not wait with the entire neighborhood, did not have a friendly soldier giving them word about whether Khassem might return.

The neighbors who had filled her home on the night when Yusef and Malek returned were slowly exiting Syria. The neighborhood already felt empty. Hasna left to take Rana to school and to do her essential shopping; she did not go outside unless it was absolutely necessary.

For the next few weeks, the government only doubled down in its attacks on the city of Daraa. Every day, rumors passed that outside forces were on the brink of intervening—Jordan, which could not want war at its doorstep; Israel, which must be concerned at the missiles so near their country; the United States, which had interfered in Iraq because of the hint of chemical weapons; the UN peacekeeping forces, which would not allow these atrocities to stand. Hasna held out hope that these rumors were true.

She woke up in a sweat most nights dreaming of white phosphorous bombs. Sometimes the soldiers in her dreams were from Hezbollah and sometimes they were Syrian—once it was Fahad al-Homsi who fixed her with a look of profound maliciousness, tossed a grenade into her home, and laughed while the walls melted.

She could not shake her terror. Her home felt like a deadly trap and the only safe place. It was filled with so much goodness and warmth and she could not imagine a world without this haven where she had lived for almost four decades. Its basalt walls still held the bouncing echoes of her children and her neighbors and the traffic in the streets, which all now seemed infinitely precious, which she wanted back with a desperation that came from the deepest parts of herself.

SOLDIERS BANGED ON THE DOOR OF HASNA'S HOME ONE MORNING IN late April. Rana was already at school; Jebreel had returned home from taking her and was gathering some tools in the shed on the side of the house before heading out for a construction job. Yusef was still asleep. Every morning, they let Yusef sleep in if he could. He often woke up screaming and shaking, with dreams he would never tell his mother about. The bouts of insomnia after those dreams were often worse than the nightmares. She knew some essential part of her son had been altered in those two weeks in Damascus.

When she heard the pounding on her door, her heart stopped for a moment. She held on to the back of the chair, then ran to the door, spurred by the thought that Yusef would wake up to the voices of soldiers. Perhaps it was Fahad al-Homsi or another soldier she knew and she could send them away. Perhaps they were looking for someone else.

Hasna lost all hope the minute she opened the gate. Soldiers with guns aimed at her face and at her heart stood on her doorstep. She backed slowly inside. She glanced down once to see if any of them held grenades in their hands but could not tell for sure.

"What do you want?" Her voice sounded steadier than she felt; without taking her eyes off their guns, she tugged her dress away from her shaking knees so they would not know how scared she was.

The commander barely glanced at her. "None of your business." He strode in as if it were his home, his boots thudding on the tile floor. He nodded at his men; almost fifteen of them filled her courtyard. A few kept their guns on Hasna, others on Jebreel, who was standing in the doorway into the courtyard.

"Who is in the house?" The officer's voice was clipped.

"Me, my husband, and my son, who is sleeping." She indicated the closed door to Yusef's room, visible from the courtyard inside the shadowed hall. Soldiers were already spreading out; she could hear them opening drawers and cabinets in her kitchen and bedroom. She prayed silently that Allah would keep them from the bookshelves where her gold was hidden. She could hear one man going through her wardrobe, shoved over the open space between the rooms. If he moved the wardrobe to look in the back, he would discover their stash. She willed herself to keep calm.

The officer moved toward Yusef's door.

"No!" Hasna ran and put her body in front of the door. There was a sharp rush as the guns moved to her. "I'm not going to let you in there with those guns in your hands." Her voice was so calm—how was that possible? She was quivering inside.

The officer was lazily unconcerned. "We have orders. If you don't let us in, we're going to shoot him. You know that, right?"

"Yes, I know, and I know you will do it. I'm asking for you to let me wake him first. You can talk to him, but you cannot go in there."

He moved toward her and without thinking, she put her hands on his shoulders and shoved.

She heard the safeties go off on the rifles around her, the multiple clicks perhaps the last thing she would hear.

And then Jebreel's calm voice sliced through the tension: "No, my sons. This is your country. We are your people. You are good sons of Syria and you cannot do this to people who love our country."

The officer stepped back. She had felt the warmth of his shoulders with her palms, under the same thick uniform cloth as the one Khassem wore. She flashed back to what it was like the last time she hugged her second son. She wondered, in a stomach-dropping instant of despair, if Khassem was still alive, and if she was going to lose her oldest son today, and what it would be like to go from being a mother of two living sons to a mother of none.

Behind her, Yusef opened the door.

The guns trained on her now turned swiftly to him and she stepped in front of him without thinking.

The officer's voice rang out. "Have you been asleep this whole time? How could you possibly sleep, with all of us shouting outside of your room?"

Yusef's voice was insolent. "There are so many fireworks every day, what's one more?" Hasna almost moaned out loud. Yusef managed to imply that the officer was all noise and no danger. Hasna wanted to turn and take Yusef's face in her hands—this was her quiet and reserved son, who was always polite and easygoing. What had happened to make him talk back with such rudeness and rage? What had he lost in that prison?

The officer looked at his soldiers and almost laughed: "What do you think, should I shoot him? Who is going to stop me?"

Hasna's voice was quiet. "Your patriotism."

The officer looked at her, head cocked slightly to the side, giving no indication of what he was thinking as he contemplated her answer. Time suspended as they all waited for the officer to move.

"Sir!" A soldier who had been searching the room beside hers, the one with the open space and the hiding place with the gold, came in. "Sir, we found this in the closet."

He held up Khassem's military coat.

"Where did you get this?" The officer's tone was accusatory and Hasna knew he was insinuating she had killed a soldier to have the coat.

"My son is a soldier in Damascus." When the officer looked skeptical, she quickly gave Khassem's officers' names. As she kept talking, the officer leaned back slightly, putting his weight on his heels rather than the balls of his feet. She allowed her voice to waver only for a moment, a sliver of vulnerability slipping into her words: "What do you imagine it would be like if my son went into the home of your mother and threatened her like you are threatening me?"

Now he was backing up, his shoulders nonchalant, suddenly uninterested in her: "Other people, when we come to their house, they offer us breakfast and lunch, but you treated us like enemies from the moment we walked in."

She responded, still keeping her body in front of Yusef: "When you come as guests, I will offer you hospitality, but when you enter like enemies, I will treat you like enemies."

"Next time treat us as guests, and we will not respond like enemies." She almost retorted, but Jebreel was by her side with his hand on her arm and Yusef was behind them and the officer was opening the front door, taking his soldiers with him. Jebreel was gracious and diplomatic, his voice carrying over their boots echoing in her home: "Peace be with you, my sons."

And, as abruptly as they had come, the soldiers were gone.

Two days later, Yusef was with his sister and brother-in-law in Jordan.

YUSEF LEFT JUST IN TIME. IN LATE APRIL, A MONTH AFTER THE ATTACK on the Omari mosque, following the "Great Friday Protests" that spread from Daraa to all of Syria, the Syrian army completely surrounded Daraa. The phone, electricity, and internet that had been restored to some areas of the city, including Hasna's neighborhood, were cut off once again. The government shut off humanitarian supplies and all communication with the outside world, beginning a full-scale military operation against the city.

They brought a rumbling line of tanks, driving with malicious carelessness, tearing through houses and over streets. Amal was huddled with Samir and Noor at her in-laws' house when they heard a tank crash through their garden wall. The tank destroyed half of the wall, backed up, and left. Samir took Amal to live with Laila as soon as they could safely cross the border into Jordan.

The government set up a ground-to-ground missile base in the soccer field at the north of town, in the same field where they had rounded up the men of Daraa. The city of Daraa was built in a valley that had sustained life for generations; by positioning the tanks and missiles on the ridges around the city, the Syrian army was able to control it easily. At the time, the protesters were still carrying rocks and cardboard signs. There was no organized resistance—these were grief-stricken people who had nothing left to lose.

Days later, government forces massacred people from the surrounding towns who had come to bring milk and bread to the citizens of the besieged city. They were from other parts of the Horan region, villagers and farmers with relatives or friends in the city. That day, many people had their phones out in what would become one of the hallmarks of this twenty-first-century revolution: They filmed the entire battle and later put it on YouTube. It was one of many battles that would make it out to the world not through a free press, but from the phones of the witnesses. As the war in Syria progressed, everyone became a journalist.

Two boys were arrested in what came to be called the Massacre on Saida Bridge—Hamza al-Khatib and Thamer Muhammad al-Shari. They were tortured and killed in the same mukhabarat headquarters as the al-Banin schoolboys. Hamza's and Thamer's bodies were released to their families, who shared their photos on social media. Soon the images of their battered, swollen, bruised bodies were on protest signs around the country. The government forces intended for the siege of Daraa to finally put an end to the protests in the country; instead, they poured gasoline on the fire of their citizens' rage, giving the people a pure cause to rally behind.

The unrest that had been escalating around the country exploded. Hasna's blood pressure did not go down. With Khassem in jail, Yusef, Laila, and

Amal in Ramtha, and Rana going to school every day in a war zone, Hasna's life felt fractured. She tried to find solace in the fact that three of her children had made it to safety, but there was no comfort to be found in the entire country.

Surely, she told herself every morning, this could not go on much longer.

FOR A FEW WEEKS, HASNA WAVERED ON WHAT TO DO ABOUT HER youngest daughter: Was it time to send her with her sisters and brothers to Jordan? To do that meant taking her out of school; there were no guarantees that she would have access to school in Jordan.

The government imposed a curfew that made it almost impossible to do any shopping or work; food and fuel became increasingly scarce. Missiles rained down with a regularity that was mind-numbing—they were loud, but they did not fall in the streets around Al-Salam Square, centering more in the neighborhoods where the protests had begun.

Life started up again. Many soldiers who were kind to them, like Fahad al-Homsi, commented on the obstinate strength of the women of Daraa who still fed their families, took their children to school, and shared tips about the best routes to take to get around checkpoints and which streets were under siege that day. They somehow made an impossible situation livable.

Hasna never thought of Jebreel leaving; someone needed to stay to protect their home and try to earn money for the family so that they had someplace to come back to when this all passed. Their neighbors who remained talked through the same sort of calculated decisions; most of the men stayed and sent their wives and children out of the country if they could. Um Ibtihal had left already and Hasna invited her husband over often to eat dinner in their home. Um Ahmad stayed because her husband worked for the government; sometimes she quietly shared news with Hasna. Everything Hasna heard pointed to the fact that this siege would end sometime soon, perhaps by the end of the summer if not earlier. If everyone left, looters would take their valuables and the things they had worked so long to accumulate over the years. And a lifetime of keeping their heads down and their mouths quiet had instilled in Jebreel and Hasna an odd sort of confidence—they had done nothing wrong. Hadn't the government released Yusef and Malek? Surely when the government had taught whatever lesson it wanted to the protesters, they would end these attacks.

And Hasna could not think about leaving while Khassem was still detained. So they stayed on, evaluating every day whether that was the right decision.

THERE WAS A CHECKPOINT OUTSIDE RANA'S SCHOOL THAT SHE COULD see from her classroom window, a kiosk where soldiers stopped and checked every car or motorcycle that passed. Rana was watching it out of the window of her fifth-grade classroom one day when a motorcycle drove too fast toward the checkpoint kiosk. The driver did not stop. Rana watched, horrified, as the driver blew himself up.

She saw the whole thing like a movie, framed by the window. One minute, the air was clear. The next, it was filled with black, billowing smoke, and shrapnel from the explosion—bits of metal, wood from the kiosk, the arms, legs, and fingers of the people whose bodies had been decimated.

The teacher yelled for everyone to duck down. Rana moved just in time. A stray bullet from the fighting that erupted outside struck the radiator pipe right above her head, missing her by inches.

In her kitchen, Hasna heard the massive explosion and dropped everything to run to the school. It was her first real taste of the fighting she had heard about but had avoided for weeks. Bullets flew around her. She kept her head low and kept going.

As she ran, she saw the other mothers she knew from school pickup, dodging in the shadows by the walls, ducking in the entryway of houses as soldiers chased resistance fighters down their street. The mothers nodded at one another but did not stop, their black dresses billowing around them like vengeful angels—Allah help anyone who got in their way.

Hasna found Rana with her teacher, huddled in the classroom. Hasna held her daughter for a few minutes until Rana stopped sobbing, pulling her head close so that Rana could feel her calm breathing, murmuring blessings and prayers. As Hasna kissed Rana's head, she could smell the sour sweat under the smoke. She would bathe her, Hasna thought, as she had when she was a little girl. She would pull out her best shampoo, let Rana apply the expensive rose-scented lotion she always wanted to use. She would put on her softest pajamas, tuck her into her own bed. If they could make it home first.

Hasna watched all around them, waiting for pauses in the shooting to make it a few feet at a time. They picked their way over shrapnel from the blast. Everywhere were body parts—fingers and feet and globs of flesh.

Hasna noted the body parts coldly, her mind in that strategic mode she had discovered when the mosque had been attacked and when Laila had protested alone. She was the Lioness again. Through her cunning awareness, they made it a few streets over, ducking and racing, before she could hear the gunshots coming closer, around the corner. Men's voices shouted and she ran to the nearest metal gate, clutching Rana's hand. Banging on the gate, she put Rana in front of her so that if the soldiers came, Hasna's body would shield her.

The gate opened. A woman Hasna had never met did not hesitate—she pulled them in as if she had been expecting them and they ran to join the family huddled at the wall farthest away from the windows. They could hear people being killed just on the other side of the wall. Hasna held Rana's head to her, her hands wrapped firmly around her ears to muffle the sounds of guns and the screams of the dying men. Rana did not make any noise; silent sobs racked her body.

They spent the evening huddled with the family. Later, when the fighting moved on, the woman of the house made them coffee. She offered them food, but both Rana and Hasna felt too sick to eat. They exchanged information as they sipped the strong Turkish coffee the woman served them—Rana knew the woman's children by sight from school. The caffeine combined with the adrenaline shooting through Hasna's body made her hands shake so that she could barely hold the small plate beneath the porcelain teacup. As quickly as felt polite, they left—she and the woman hugged as if they had known each other for years. Afterward, Hasna would not remember her name.

She and Rana moved swiftly through the night, shadows in the street. They were out after curfew, but Hasna could not bear for Jebreel to wait another minute. The snipers must have been looking elsewhere, or angels protected them—they made it home safely. When she unlocked her gate, opening it slowly so that it did not creak, she found Jebreel sitting alone at the long table, tears pouring down his face. He could not speak when she hugged him; he clutched at Rana and Hasna.

"No more. She is going to Jordan immediately." He kissed Rana's face and held her to him. "You are my habibet-albi, the darling of my heart." Hasna knew his baby girl, born in his old age, was precious to him.

She packed a small bag for Rana; it was ready when their friend arrived in his van early the next morning. Hasna and Rana wore as much as they could on their bodies; Hasna's voluminous black coat made it easy to hide layers of clothing without drawing suspicion.

The journey took hours, but they made it to the apartment in Jordan. Hasna stayed for a few days to set Rana up with her sisters.

Hasna was struck, walking into the city for the first time with Rana that evening, at the difference between Ramtha and Daraa. Before the war, Jordanians would often cross the border into Daraa because the fruits and vegetables were more plentiful and much cheaper, and it was often faster to go shopping there for those near the border. In the evenings, people from Daraa would stroll across the border into Ramtha to eat dinner and then come home. Jebreel's sister had lived in Ramtha and they had gone to visit her occasionally. Hasna had been to Ramtha more than most Syrian cities. Now it felt a world away. The peace in Ramtha over a weekend only made her angry: What right had these people to go about their lives, within view of her city, unaffected by the things that were tearing her family apart? She knew it was unreasonable; the Jordanians she met were unspeakably gracious, but Hasna sensed a separation, as if she were infected, the war a disease that Jordanians tutted about sympathetically from a distance.

In the new apartment, Rana was petulant and weepy; she talked back at every small thing Hasna said and threw fits as she hadn't since she was small. Hasna responded sharply; she seemed to have no patience.

When she returned home without Rana, Hasna was bereft. Her neighborhood felt barren; the women and children she had known for years were mostly in Jordan now. There were only a few women who remained. The weeks lingered on, the fighting ebbing and flowing. But still Hasna stayed. She could not leave without Khassem.

ALMOST THREE MONTHS AFTER HE WAS IMPRISONED, KHASSEM appeared at the gate and walked in as if it had been merely a few days. Hasna gasped and dropped a plate and did not clean it up for hours so that she could hold him. He seemed shrunken, his eyes hollow. The bruises on his arms, legs, and torso were yellowing.

He stayed inside, soaking in their home, as Hasna cooked as many of his favorite meals as she could with limited supplies and unreliable electricity. He always had been mellow with her but this time there was a toxic edge to his mood, as if he could not stop from falling into himself. She worried frantically about him, but she chatted brightly and fed him meal after meal, splurging on overpriced gas canisters so that she could cook as much as she wanted.

His expression did not change when they told him the story of how his military coat saved them. All he said was, "At least it was good for something." He wore his regular clothes again around the house. Hasna could hardly bring herself to touch the uniform when she washed it.

Quietly they plotted his escape, more dangerous than that of his siblings because he was still in the military. His leave was only for a few weeks; he was shocked they had let him out at all. He was guilty of what they accused him of, after all—he was traitorously angry at the government. Even though he said he denied his true feelings in the many interviews, which Hasna took to be a euphemism for torture sessions, they all knew he was a painfully bad liar. Every thought that was in his head was easily detectable on his expressive face; he was always authentically himself, her overgrown boy. Every knock on her gate made them jump; they kept the gate locked at all times now.

When he entered the service, Khassem had had to relinquish his civilian ID for his military one. He could not use the military one to leave the country; he would be immediately recaptured, if not shot on the spot. Jebreel began making discreet inquiries and found someone who made black market civilian IDs, and within a few days, Khassem's was ready.

Hasna went with him, crossing the border into Jordan so that it seemed Khassem was a good son escorting his mother and not a maverick soldier fleeing from the government. Hasna was aware that she herself was a danger point at every checkpoint—if the soldiers checking their papers suspected that Khassem was not a civilian, they would threaten his mother first, and Khassem would never endure it. His forearms were tense and a vein on his jaw flared, but he kept his face carefully neutral, looking off unconcernedly every time they had to stop at the many checkpoints between Daraa and Ramtha.

Hasna's knees almost buckled with relief when they finally made it across the border into Jordan. Khassem went to join Yusef in the small apartment he had found in the center of the city and Hasna went to join her daughters in the larger apartment at the bottom of a villa on the outskirts of Ramtha. It was already becoming crowded. She stayed for three days and her children begged her to stay longer. But she refused—now that her children were safely across the border, she could go back to their house and prepare it so that she could be gone for several weeks. In time, she knew that some country or outside force would intervene—surely the government of Syria would not be allowed to attack their people like this with no response from the rest of the world.

Every day, they lived with expectation that something would change, that this would all be over, that life in Daraa would begin again.

SHE HEARD ABOUT THE VIDEO BEFORE SHE SAW IT, BACK IN DARAA with no access to internet or phones. Electricity came and went sporadically, so that she could not often charge her phone. She could not get on social media as she could in Jordan, but friends could still text things to her. Huddled in the darkest part of Hasna's bedroom, away from any windows, she watched on the tiny screen as her beloved Fahad al-Homsi defected publicly from the Syrian army. He spoke out in a firm voice against the Syrian government's acts of cowardice in attacking innocent people. It was spectacular, a glorious blaze of courage. Weeks before, seven defecting officers—highly trained, career military men who did not leave their positions lightly—started a trend among conscience-stricken soldiers when they created a video that announced the creation of a new force: the Free Syria Army.

The civil war had officially begun. In organizing themselves into an army and declaring that they would no longer side with the government and its unprovoked attacks on civilians, the founders of the Free Syria Army proved themselves to be patriotic sons of Syria. They also painted targets on their backs. They would be killed—all of them—over the next few months, and they knew when they released the videos that they were sealing their death warrants. And yet they did not waver.

When she saw the video again later, in Jordan on Facebook, Hasna passed her thumb over Fahad al-Homsi's face. Miles away from his own mother, while her sons were in jail, he had become her son. And she would mourn him for the rest of her life like a mother. When his death was confirmed later, in the obituary pictures that became ubiquitous on her Facebook feed, listing his birth and death dates with a picture of his dead body, she wept and wept.

The creation of the Free Syria Army cemented the fact that this conflict might not last a few days or weeks. She walked every day down streets that bore the ghosts of the life she had known, of the people who had always been here, of a Syria that already no longer existed. Syria was her beloved home. Syria was her heart.

FOR ALMOST A YEAR, THEIR NEIGHBOR THE VAN DRIVER BECAME THE conduit between the two sides of Hasna's life. He brought news from the children and took back treats from Hasna—well-iced meat from her favorite butcher and fruits and vegetables when she could find them. Sometimes, when she felt that there was a break in the fighting, she would leave with the van driver to go to Jordan for a long weekend. She got Rana established in a local school, helped the girls clean the villa apartment in Ramtha well. Yusef and Khassem had established a bachelor pad in a tiny apartment in downtown Ramtha and she would sometimes clean it for them as well. Samir, Malek, Yusef, and Khassem all worked as much as they could, painting, constructing, teaching—whatever day labor jobs they could find. Samir left for several weeks to work on a construction site in another city. They pooled their money to pay the rent on the two apartments in Ramtha and sent some home with Hasna when they could. Her sons and sons-in-law were strong workers. Hasna stayed for a week when Amal had her second baby girl, Maria. Laila planned to enroll in the local high school and Amal would go find a job if Hasna would come watch the babies for them.

WHEN HASNA FINALLY LEFT, SHE PACKED FOR ONLY A FEW WEEKS. THE war was escalating. There were rumors of the kinds of weapons the Syrian government was moving into Daraa—missiles that could target houses, bigger bombs, more tanks; the government was planning a longer campaign to root out the rebels now arming themselves as part of the emerging Free Syria Army. She and Jebreel agreed: he would stay and protect their home, doing what work he could, and she would move in with the girls in the villa in Jordan. It would only be for a couple of months, they told themselves. She clung stubbornly to that belief.

The electricity was back on again and she made full use of it. Jebreel was not like many men, who did not know their way around the kitchen—he did not mind helping out and he could cook for himself. But still, she stocked their freezers. Hasna stuffed both the freezer in the kitchen and the deep freezer in the back of the house. She made kibbeh, she roasted eggplant, sautéed peas, blended hummus, she even froze grape leaves. She bought flour for bread, extra olive oil. She stayed up late canning baby eggplants and olives, the briny smell reminding her of so many days spent with her daughters or neighbors. How many meals had she prepared in this kitchen, rising early or staying up late, making the favorite dishes of the people she loved?

She prepared a months-long feast for Jebreel, rich foods that were his favorites, delicacies that he could enjoy, everything that he could ever need. She endured hours in store lines, begged for the last sacks of flour, schemed to find the freshest vegetables. Finally, when there was not an inch of space left in the freezer or refrigerator or cupboards, when the meat was seasoned and wrapped well, when the jars were sealed and the kitchen was spotless, she packed up the things she would take: her teacups, the white ones with painted yellow-gold designs around the edges. Her children and grandchildren had sipped from these, her neighbors had wrapped their hands around them for warmth on the cool winter days in Daraa while they lingered over black tea after lunch. She protected them well to survive the van ride into Ramtha.

She packed up her everyday dresses—why would she need to dress up in Ramtha?—and packed her nicer clothes away so the moths would not get to them while she was gone. She stored their family pictures in the space where her gold had gone and put her ounces of gold in a special purse she would keep very close to her. Some of her jewelry she wore, the rest she wrapped with the gold ounces, her entire life's savings contained in one precious purse.

She paused, looking at her expensive Iranian blankets and her antique rugs. They were some of the nicest things she owned. She folded the blankets, piling them in the hiding place on top of the pictures. The rugs she could do nothing about. If the soldiers or looters wanted to roll her rugs up and take them away, she supposed she would have to let them. She left behind her nicest dishes, her best dresses, her books of poetry, her Fairuz records, and the record player that had been her morning companion for years.

On the last morning before the van came, she walked Jebreel around her garden, giving him instructions about how to water her plants, pulling dead leaves off with her expert hands. She spent the last few minutes as she always had, a cup of coffee in her hand, the jasmine joining the lingering aroma of breakfast in the corners of their courtyard.

The van driver honked, earlier than she expected, and she scrambled to get her bags. Jebreel carried them to the van, then stood and waited for her beside the gate while she pinned her hijab one last time in her bedroom mirror. Hasna only had time for a quick glance around the house she had lived in for four decades, checking to make sure everything was in place, before giving Jebreel a swift hug and climbing into the van.

Later, she wished she had walked around the rooms one more time, taken in the breeze on their rooftop terrace, trailed her fingers through the grape leaves, held one of the Persian blankets, packed up the pictures of her children, soaked in the last sight of Jebreel loading the van and walking with both arms held out to her as she stood in the door of the home they had loved, where generations of al-Salam children had grown up and thrived, where she now realized they had been exquisitely, deliciously happy for years and years and years.

Chapter 14

MU NAW

One Monday night, when Mu Naw was at the community church collecting a box of nonperishable food, she met a woman named Jane. Jane asked a question Mu Naw did not understand with a hand gesture that indicated pregnancy. It took them a few minutes to get the details straight: that Mu Naw was pregnant, that she was not always able to go to the clinic on the bus, that she would love some help. Mu Naw showed Jane her ID, with her address on it, and hoped she had said everything correctly.

Jane, who was retired, arrived the next day and took Mu Naw to the next and every other doctor's visit for the rest of her pregnancy. To sink into the seat of Jane's air-conditioned sedan was a luxury Mu Naw could never have imagined; it was such a far cry from the bus that her nausea, which had been getting better in her second trimester, only flared up mildly while they drove. It was a source of enormous comfort to have an older woman beside her in each appointment, listening and asking good questions, and then patiently explaining things slowly to Mu Naw. Mu Naw found she could understand Jane better than most people, because of the modulation of her voice and the deliberate way she formed her words. She still only fully got about a quarter of the information, but it was more than nothing. Jane helped her with the last of the Medicaid paperwork and sent it in; Mu Naw prayed for weeks that the paperwork would go through in time so they would not have to pay for the hospital bills. Jane assured her that the church would help and Mu Naw felt relief rise within her. She trusted Jane.

A new group of people had started an evening English class once a week at the church community center. Mu Naw was grateful to be able to walk there. She took home the worksheets they gave out every week and worked through them assiduously.

A few weeks after they met, Jane drove both Saw Ku and Mu Naw to a doctor's appointment. They went into a dark room where a woman in scrubs poured transparent jelly on Mu Naw's bare belly, and then showed them their baby kicking on the ultrasound screen. They both understood when the sonographer said, in an excited singsong voice, "It's a boy!" Saw Ku beamed and Mu Naw turned her face to the wall for a moment to hide her tears. The sonographer continued to rub the machine along her belly for a while, talking to Jane, until Jane turned to them and said, "Everything is fine. The baby looks good." "Good" was another word they both knew.

PAH POE HAD BEEN BORN TEN MONTHS AFTER THEY GOT MARRIED. Unlike most of the adults in the camp around them, whose marriages had been arranged by family members, Mu Naw and Saw Ku married for love. They thought that they would wait for a few years, since Saw Ku aspired to go to the mission school, which married students weren't allowed to attend. It was far more selective than the nonprofit-run camp school, and his only chance at a real education. After the day he told her friends that they were dating, she told her mother and he told his parents and it was understood that they would get married without their ever having an engagement ceremony.

Mu Naw spent as much time as she could with Saw Ku's family, hoping to show through her polite language and helpful subservience that she was very different from her mother. While they did not openly disapprove of her, she felt their tacit judgment, especially his sister's, in their stolen glances—sometimes she felt that they stopped gossiping about her just as she walked into a room. She wanted them not just to approve of but to love her.

One day Saw Ku got sick and Mu Naw took some nourishing soup to his homey hut near his mother's. He was good with his hands and had fitted the bamboo together snugly so that it was watertight and kept out the elements. They ate the soup together in the light of the electric bulb. When they were finished, he told her he did not want to spend another day without being married to her.

Within a few days, the marriage contract was negotiated, and Mu Naw came to live permanently in his tiny hut. His dream of attending the mission school was laid aside, regretfully, by both of them. He was smart and he should have had more opportunities to learn; neither of them ever thought once about whether she should have had more schooling.

Surprisingly, Mu Naw's marriage brought her closer to her mother—the first time she heard one of Saw Ku's sisters-in-law make a disparaging remark about her mother, the stony expression of rage on Mu Naw's face stopped it instantly. She was stunned to realize that she felt defensive of her mother. Her love for Saw Ku, their simple joy in being together, was such a sharp contrast to the way her mother had been forced into her first marriage. Mu Naw began to suspect that perhaps her mother was not as selfish as the grandmothers had always insinuated, as the rigid camp morality made her out to be. Theirs was still not the kind of relationship Mu Naw wanted to have with her own daughter someday. She would do almost everything better than her mother—love her husband, make a home, be close to her children. But she felt a softening toward her mother that was new.

Naw Wah was a squishy newborn and Pah Poe almost three when they applied for the resettlement program. UNHCR workers had approached Saw Ku while he was passing out hygiene pamphlets to see if they were interested in being among the first to go to America. They had talked it over in hushed tones that night in their home; it had not taken them long to come to the decision to apply. Their girls were so intensely curious about the world. Mu Naw could hardly bear for them to be raised as she had been, scuttling like mice in the woods or stuck like fish in a net.

The interview process took two years and they had to tell their story again and again to various officials—what it was like to flee the war, where they were from originally, what would happen to them if they went back. They learned things about each other in the interview process; Mu Naw had never told Saw Ku all of the stories about the cruel grandmother who beat her, or escaping the fire in Nu Po camp. Their case was fairly straightforward—they were Karen and all Karen people in Mae La camp could prove easily that they were persecuted for their ethnicity by the Burmese Tatmadaw. They went where they were told and answered the questions honestly and eventually got word that they had been accepted to come to Austin, Texas.

It was always for their children, this new life. And now Mu Naw worried a new child would bankrupt them before this life had even begun.

A FEW WEEKS BEFORE THE BABY WAS BORN, THE VOLUNTEERS AT THE community center, including Jane, threw a baby shower for Mu Naw during evening English class. They tried to tell her what they planned the week before, but she didn't fully understand: "shower" as in, standing up to bathe? They laughed together about how funny the word was. That night, instead of having class, they circled their chairs and showered her with presents. She and Saw Ku unwrapped each one in wonder: small onesies and shoes, mostly in gray and blue, more diapers than she had ever imagined, a dark-blue portable baby crib, baby bottles and wipes, a large black bag to hold everything in. The Karen families brought diapers too, and they drank the punch and munched on cake together happily. Bob was there, laughing in the corner. Jane cleaned up tissue paper and passed out refreshments. One of the English volunteers dressed her toddler daughter in the traditional Karen dress someone had given her—the turquoise offset the little girl's blue eyes—and the children danced together when someone played music from their phone.

In her entire year, that night might have been Mu Naw's happiest—here was proof of the friendships she had built, both with Karen people and American people, at an American baby shower with a blond white baby in woven Karen clothes. It felt like a glimpse of what her life could be like, a beautiful blend she could find between past and new future.

WHEN THE PAINS BEGAN EARLY IN THE MORNING IN LATE APRIL, SHE called Jane. Saw Ku took the girls to his brother's apartment and returned, his hand gentle on her back as she bent over and breathed, the first big contraction

racking her body. Within fifteen minutes, Jane arrived and they were climbing into the backseat of her sedan with the bag they'd packed at her direction.
Jane drove them to Brackenridge Hospital in downtown Austin. Jane was
watching the clock; as she dropped them off before parking the car, she said,
"Tell them 'seven minutes.' They will understand." So when she walked in,
pausing to breathe roughly for a minute, Mu Naw told the nurse at the desk:
"Seven minutes." She repeated it again, no matter what they asked: "Seven
minutes, yes, seven minutes." And then Jane was there, answering all of the
doctor's questions, pulling copies of all of their documents out of her large
purse, Saw Ku nodding wide-eyed as if he understood the doctors. Jane filled
out paperwork while a nurse helped Mu Naw change into a gown that opened
at the back, revealing her bottom and making Mu Naw giggle between contractions.

The nurses connected her to various machines, raised the back of the bed
and added pillows until Mu Naw nodded that she was comfortable. They measured her blood pressure, pressed on her belly, checked her progress, made
notes on clipboards and on the whiteboard in the wall by the door. Mu Naw
withdrew into herself as the contractions increased, stopped noticing what the
nurses were doing after a while, concentrated on her body and the breaths that
grounded her through the sweeping pain.

Saw Ku's face was infused with love for her, and Mu Naw saw with
intense clarity, as the pain of the largest contraction yet passed, that she
loved him and he loved her. The last few months had been hard. They were
in the midst of such stress, this impossible life they were building. She saw
them both—so young, so earnest, so out of their depth—and she could not
believe all that they had done in the past year. She knew, suddenly, that
everything would work out fine. She tried to tell Saw Ku that, but she
couldn't find the words, and the pain made it hard to speak. Instead, they
looked at each other and the years melted away and they were back in that
small clinic in Mae La camp when Saw Ku stood beside her as she gave
birth to Pah Poe.

They had been so young then and they were young still and this was their
third baby and they could do it all again, parent together again, walk forward
in this new life with their daughters and now with their son.

HOURS LATER, MU NAW TUCKED HER BABY BOY UP TO HER BREAST AND he suckled greedily. He was so big. They kept repeating it—"Look at his size!"—to each other, neither quite believing the difference between the tiny babies their daughters had been and this grand, chubby boy.

"He is an American baby." Mu Naw laughed with Saw Ku. She said the baby's name because she liked the sound of it. "Saw Doh."

"Yes, it's because you've been eating American food and Saw Doh knew he needed to be big to live in America."

"He will be tall. He will be taller than me."

"Everyone will be taller than you, sweetheart." Mu Naw swatted at her husband and he kissed the top of her head. The birth had gone fine. It had been, in the end, almost like birthing her daughters, except she was in a pristine hospital with a white male doctor and white nurses. She had pushed out her son just like her daughters—her body knew what to do.

She had not even paid attention to the doctor, who had apparently had someone write the word "Skoo!" in ballpoint pen on a folded-over brown paper towel, and tape it above her bed so that he knew the right word to say when it came time to push. Saw Ku told her about it later; she didn't remember the doctor saying anything that sounded like Karen in the garbled instructions from behind his face mask. She wondered who had told him the word. Saw Ku said it was not him—he could barely understand the doctor in English, much less speak to him. Had it been someone on the language line the hospital used? Was it something he had learned from an earlier patient? It was a mystery she would never solve; she had no way to even frame the question. Still, she liked the story, an American doctor who cared to try to learn the right words.

Her body was sore, her belly twinging as she pulled the satiated baby off her breast and handed him, milk-drunk, to Saw Ku to burp. At her request—with Jane's help—the doctor had agreed to tie her tubes during the birth. Later, when the numbness wore off, she hurt more than when she'd had her daughters. She watched Saw Ku hold his son, the last of their children, their first little American.

Smiling nurses buzzed around them every hour or two. They weighed

and measured the baby, put ink on his feet and hands to press against a piece
of paper, pricked his feet with needles, put massive headphones on him, felt his
belly and his thighs. One woman, who was not in scrubs, came and watched
Mu Naw breastfeed the baby. He ate without stopping, but still the woman
shifted him around, putting her hand to adjust Mu Naw's breast in his mouth,
squeezing his cheek to move his head slightly. Mu Naw was amused that the
woman seemed to think she might not breastfeed this fat boy—Naw Wah, at
two, was still breastfeeding at home and Pah Poe was almost four when she
had weaned. Did she think they would want to spend money on formula? She
took the pamphlets the woman left for her, tucking them into her bag to show
to Jane.

They spent two nights in the hospital. At night, the nurses took the baby
with them, wheeling him out in his plastic bed with transparent sides, and
then wheeling him back in to eat. The lit-up, beeping machines made it hard
to sleep, the strange, moving bed was disconcerting, the food was almost ined-
ible. But two days with just Saw Ku, to focus on their new baby, were an unexpected benison. He was grateful and attentive, the same way he'd been after
the girls were born, too, and she relished seeing that side of him again.

On their last day, Jane came in and sat down. She told Mu Naw that the
Medicaid paperwork that they had filed a few months before had gone through.
Mu Naw made Jane repeat it a few times until she was sure she understood.
The entire stay was paid for. Mu Naw felt the enormity of debt lift off her
shoulders. Having this son had not bankrupted their family. Everything had
worked out in the end.

It was only as they were wheeling her out of the hospital, Saw Doh snuggled firmly against her, toward Jane's car that Mu Naw imagined what it would
have been like to have had her mother there, to see her small frame coming
around the car where Jane was now, opening the door, helping her in. Her
mind couldn't even form the picture of her mother in this place—she had
never seen her mother near a car, much less in American clothes. The idea felt
ludicrous. She felt a pang of familiar sadness—not that her mother was not
there, but that she was a daughter who had never known what it was like to
have a mother she could rely on.

Saw Ku helped the nurse put the baby in the car and then solicitously watched as she buckled up from the other side of the car seat. He reached for her across the baby.

His hand was warm: "Are you okay? How do you feel?"

Tears pricked her eyes: "I feel good. I love you."

"I love you too." Their hands rested lightly on the soft blanket covering their sleeping son as Jane pulled away from the hospital.

PART 2

Chapter 15

HASNA

RAMTHA, JORDAN,
DECEMBER 2012—FEBRUARY 2013

Malek waited for Hasna to arrive in Ramtha; they overlapped by one night before he went back to Syria. His parents and siblings had sent word with the van driver that they were finally ready to come to Jordan. He and Laila had decided that he would apply for graduate schools in Egypt, where schooling was free for Syrians, so that the next few years would not be a total waste if the conflict did not end quickly; he needed some paperwork back in Daraa to finish the applications. And while he was grateful to be safe, he was also yearning to be back in Daraa to see for himself what was happening.

Laila understood; she felt the same tension he did. Only concern for little Hamad kept her in Jordan. Malek would leave just long enough to prepare his family to move to Ramtha and then join them back in Jordan. They had all heard the rumors that the Jordanian government had been cracking down on Syrian immigrants. Jordan had already enfolded thousands of Palestinian refugees into their population over decades and as the conflict in Syria seethed on, most Jordanians felt there was a limit to how much they could do to help more refugees. But Hasna had been going back and forth between Daraa and Ramtha for over a year and Jebreel had joined them for some weekends. And their part of the Jordanian border was fairly porous for those who knew how to get back and forth, despite the land mines.

The morning he left, Malek pulled Hasna aside and asked her to protect

Laila. She promised, smiling at him—Laila was her daughter, of course Hasna would look after her. He nodded gravely.

At the end, Amal, Rana, and Hasna left Laila and Malek and Hamad alone outside to say good-bye. When they walked back into the apartment, Laila put a CD into the stereo; she pressed repeat over and over, weeping over Hamad. It was a song about a father's love for his son. Hamad, who was at the toddler age where he rarely liked to sit still, nonetheless clung to her and cried. Hasna gave them space for a few hours. Eventually Laila came into the kitchen, eyes puffy, and silently began helping prepare lunch. Hamad could reach the button on the CD player and he pressed it when the song was done.

For the next several weeks, Hamad played that song—how proud the father was of his son, how much he missed and loved his son—until Hasna heard the minor refrains in her dreams.

HASNA THREW HERSELF INTO TASKS AROUND THE APARTMENT TO DIS-tract herself from the rumors that the war was escalating. Their apartment was on the bottom floor of a split-level home built into the side of a hill in a new neighborhood on the edge of the city. Jordan was under a massive water short-age and their neighborhood had running water only on Saturdays; the other six days, they made do with the large jugs of water they bought in town, which the seller assured them came from Syria.

Saturdays were busy with cleaning and laundry and bathing, but for the next few weeks, as she settled into this new life, the days between dragged on. She struggled to find a rhythm that worked. Everything either took too long or left her with too much time to worry.

Walking to town was one of the tasks that took too long. There was no regular bus route and they had to make a long trek through scrubby brush to get anywhere. There were snakes, big poisonous spiders and scorpions, and entire herds of street dogs; Hasna, who had grown up in the country before moving to Daraa when she married Jebreel, had a healthy fear of wild things. She carried a stick and yelled or clapped at the dogs when they came too near. In the mornings and afternoons walking Rana to school, Hasna was diligent about the dogs. But it was more difficult with arms full of grocery sacks on the way back to the house. The neighbors around them were kind, constantly offering rides into town, but Hasna found it galling to always be dependent on others, no matter how hospitable they were.

Others in town had very little patience for Syrians. She often walked quickly past political conversations in the street, keeping her head down so that she would not hear any censure of her country, but it was difficult. Although women in Ramtha and Daraa dressed similarly—she looked like any Jordanian housewife going about her errands—she figured it was clear to everyone around her that she was Syrian, that somehow her grief for Daraa was etched onto her face.

One day in a hardware store, Hasna overheard the owner talking to another man near the counter.

"What do those Syrians want with us? Why can't they fix their own country?"

The customer, an older man leaning conspiratorially across the counter, nodded in agreement. The owner continued, leaning back on his stool and putting his hands across his ample belly, settling into his rant. "Do they think they're going to come here, go to our schools, eat our food, take our money, and we're not going to do anything about it?"

Hasna noticed that her hand trembled as she located the elbow bracket that she needed. She was not sure until she pulled out her bills to pay for the part whether she would actually respond but the words were forming before she could pull them back.

"Your footsteps are all over our country." Her voice was so low that he did not register that she was speaking to him for a moment.

"I'm sorry, what did you say?" His look was polite, slightly condescending.

"Your footsteps are all over our country, you Jordanians. You came to us for food when it was too expensive here. You drank our water. You bought our clothes. You've taken advantage of us for years and now you blame us when we need your help."

The man laughed incredulously, turning to his friend at the counter to make sure he was catching what she said. "You? You're not Syrian! Look at you!"

Hasna looked down at herself then back up at him. "What do you mean, I'm not Syrian?"

"You're not . . ." The man gestured up and down at her.

"Living in a camp? Wearing dust and dirt? No, I'm not. I'm here paying for an apartment. My sons are working in jobs your sons don't want. We are spending money, buying your vegetables and meat. We are just trying to survive. You think I would have left if I had any other choice?" She slammed down the money she owed him and walked out without another word. His look had shifted from condescension to hostility. She would not return to his shop. It was several minutes into her walk before she realized she had not been watching for scorpions, spiders, or snakes, that her hands were still shaking, that her heart rate had not slowed.

She placed the part she had purchased on the bed she shared with Rana; Amal and Laila were not at home. The walls of the apartment felt too close; she longed for the coolness of the breeze in her courtyard at home. Listlessly, she climbed to the rooftop of the villa, where their laundry dried to stiff crispness on Saturdays in the Jordanian sun. A pile of leftover tile formed a makeshift bench and she sat down. The tiles crackled slightly, the edges biting into the back of her legs through her dress. She leaned back against the rough brick wall.

From the roof, she gazed over the hills that separated her from Daraa. She was only a few kilometers from her home. The wind over the roof was a different kind of chilly than the damp winter shade of her home. She pulled her black coat close around her.

She came to the roof sometimes, mostly at night after she put Rana to bed. Over the low hills, she could see explosions of light; the walls at the villa shook a few seconds after the missiles hit. She endlessly tried to guess what parts of the city were under attack.

Today there were not many smoke plumes above the hills. She wondered again how she would know if anyone she loved was hurt, unless the van driver brought word. Would she feel it somehow? Would there be some awareness in her that Jebreel was gone? That something had happened to Malek?

These slow parts of her day were torturous. Amal would be back soon; it was her turn to make lunch that day. If Hasna went downstairs now, she knew she would just fight with Amal or Laila. It suddenly seemed a miracle that they could have lived all of those years so peacefully when the girls were at home—they bickered, of course, and she was angry when they misbehaved as children, but she had always gotten along with her kids. Now the grandchildren were whiny, her daughters petulant, and she was tense. She looked again at the horizon, searching for some measure of peace in the dusty hills and low trees surrounding her.

A bird hopped curiously on the wall a few meters from her elbow. Utterly still, Hasna watched out of the corner of her eye as another bird joined her. The first was the female and the second the male. They were hoopoes, small birds with brownish bodies, distinctive black-and-white striped wings, a peaked orange crest that looked as if it had been dipped in black; the birds could fan out or flatten their crest at will. Now they were flattened into a pointy spike that balanced out their long, thin beaks. While she watched, the male flared his crest at the female, displayed his wings, and called out. The noise sounded like someone blowing on the lower register of a flute: two notes and then another two notes. The female played coy and flew off a few minutes later. The male, determined, flew after her.

Longing for her home overwhelmed Hasna. She questioned, as she did every day, if she had made a mistake in leaving Syria. She was glad Rana could continue her schooling in Jordan; she did not want her children and grandchildren in danger. But to set up a new life in this new country felt like a betrayal. Grief and guilt stalked her, and she could not evade them the way she did the dogs or snakes outside her home. On the rooftop, she cried where her daughters and grandchildren could not see.

WHEN SHE WENT TO PICK RANA UP FROM SCHOOL, THE TEACHER pulled her aside and asked if she had registered as a refugee yet.

"Of course not! We're going home as soon as this is over."

His face was sympathetic. "I understand. But we cannot allow Rana to continue to go to school until she has paperwork saying that she is a refugee." He said he had allowed Rana to stay as long as possible, but the Jordanian government was beginning to check in on all of the children. They received funding only for educating refugee children, not for Syrian children who did not have refugee status.

Hasna walked back to the house with Rana and left her downstairs playing with some of the children in the apartment next to theirs. She returned to the roof.

To register as a refugee would be to admit that things in Syria might not change. If she filed, would the Syrian government let her back in her country? She could barely breathe when she thought of being gone so long from Daraa.

And it also felt like begging. They were proudly self-reliant. Samir, Yusef, and Khassem were working construction day jobs in Mafraq, a nearby city; the boys had moved their small apartment there and Samir stayed with them during the week, coming to be with Amal and his daughters on Fridays. Jebreel sent money from Daraa sometimes with the van driver. If they ever needed it, Hasna had her cache of gold with her, hidden in the apartment; with that alone, they would be secure for months. They did not need government assistance—their family unit was a well-oiled machine, with each of them doing their part.

During the evenings in the breezeway, the Syrian neighbors in the four apartments that made up the bottom floors of the villa pooled their knowledge, sifting through the rumors to discover the kernels of truth. They could speak openly here in Jordan as they never could in Syria, though a lifetime of wariness made it difficult for many to voice their opinions. One neighbor with relatives from Aleppo said that the Free Syria Army had successfully defeated government troops several months before and that they were receiving outside support from the United States and Israel and France. One of the younger men seemed positive that Jordan, backed by the US, would rise up against Syria. The older people were more hesitant, but Hasna couldn't help hoping he was right.

The conflict in Hama when Hafez al-Assad razed the Muslim Brotherhood and wiped out any political opposition had lasted eighteen months, from 1982 to 1983. It had been almost two years since the first protests had started in Daraa. Of course, the conflict in Hama had remained relatively isolated and this conflict had now spread throughout the country. The neighbors debated whether that meant it was more likely to end swiftly or not, and whether the rumors about outside interference meant that Assad would remain in power. If he stayed, they all grimly agreed, Assad would never let refugees come back unpunished.

Hasna, who had spent her entire life remaining as apolitical as she could in Syria, now found herself hanging on every word, weighing sides, taking in sources, strategizing her next moves. The decision that she made next could have dire consequences on either side—a daughter who stopped her education in the fifth grade, or the door shut to her country, to everything and everyone she loved in it.

During the day, she spent more and more time on the roof watching the hoopoe couple build a nest together. Evidently the male had won the female over. They worked quickly, finding choice bits of grass and constructing a nest in a hollow in the stones in the corner of the wall. One day when she came up, the mother was in the nest. Hasna did not disturb her as she incubated her eggs.

HASNA COUNTED EACH PRECIOUS DAY THAT RANA MISSED SCHOOL while she deliberated. She called the number the schoolteacher had given her, learned where in the neighboring city of Irbed she needed to go to fill out the refugee paperwork. Rana loved her days at home—what child would rather go to school than play? Hasna found herself criticizing Rana more often and tried to stop; it was not her daughter's fault that Hasna couldn't decide.

One day, five young heads appeared above the edge of the hoopoe nest, mouths open, vociferously demanding to be fed. She laughed conspiratorially when the exhausted mother glanced at Hasna once and then decided to ignore her. Seeing the hoopoe babies was one of her few purely happy moments in Jordan.

Jebreel came to visit that weekend; Hasna did not show him the hoopoe nest. His brother-in-law watched their house while he was gone. Looters had been roaming through the neighborhoods, taking whatever they wanted out of abandoned houses. Jebreel had carefully hidden their family's motorcycles. Hasna asked him about her Persian rugs and dishes and he snapped at her. The tension only grew from there. She told him she was thinking of registering as a refugee because of Rana's school and he exploded—he worked even in the middle of war, their boys were scouring the country for jobs, and she was thinking of signing them up for government assistance? They did not need it. They would not be burdens in Jordan.

She tried to lay out her thinking—that school was critical at Rana's age, that there was a good chance from everything she had heard that Assad would be defeated, that maybe being a refugee wouldn't affect them at all. He railed that he was on the ground in Syria and if she thought Assad was going to be defeated, she had already been living in Jordan too long. She yelled back that she would love to return home but that they had both agreed that she should stay with their daughters. Their voices reached a fever pitch; a string of spittle formed in the corner of his mouth and Hasna felt a visceral revulsion toward him. She lived on her own with the girls for weeks at a time, strategizing and scheming and protecting them all, and he came in for the weekend and upended all of it.

She did what she had never done before: She screamed at him to leave, aware of the way her voice echoed shrilly from the tile walls, to go to Mafraq with their sons. Gone was his look of warm approval and affection from that day she proudly showed him the well-stocked refrigerator and freezer to keep him fed through the siege. His face now wore the haunted look of a man who had lived the last several weeks through a hellscape of war. She felt that he did not even see her, that he had become nothing but wrath and spit. She hated him then, and she hated herself more, this vile shrieking woman.

The minute he left to go to Mafraq, she regretted it. But it was too late. Even if she wanted to call him and tell him to come back to Ramtha, she knew he would not.

She thought the girls would be angry with her, but instead they were solicitous and gracious. Hasna wished that she could have been a strong pillar for them to rely on. Instead, she was pitifully grateful that they fed her dinner and took over all of the household chores for the next few days. Seeing that she was weak only served to make them stronger; seeing their competence allowed her to rely on them rather than always trying to protect them. Her daughters were extraordinary. Hasna prayed that they would soon be in safe places where they could thrive, Malek and Laila in Egypt, Samir and Amal home in Daraa. She prayed Jebreel could forgive her, that she could forgive him—that she could forgive herself.

A WEEK AFTER JEBREEL LEFT, RANA GOT INTO A FIGHT WITH THE BOYS who ruled their end of the street like one of the dog packs. They did not hurt her—one of the boys pulled her hair and she kicked him before the older boys intervened—but when she came home there was dirt on her face, her knees were skinned, and her hair was disheveled.

The next day, Hasna left Rana with Amal and took the bus two hours away to the refugee office in Irbed. She waited in a concrete room with vinyl couches for a woman to call her name. She received a packet of paperwork in a manila envelope from a woman with short hair, a white shirt, and a gray pencil skirt. She walked back to the bus stop and took the two-hour bus trip home, holding the paperwork in her lap without looking at it.

That night, she meticulously filled out the papers with a black ballpoint pen and wrote the address on the envelope. She took it to the post office in Ramtha. She held the papers for a moment before sliding them into the post office slot. The envelope disappeared with a metallic snick. Walking back through the scrubby forest, she wept. The dogs left her alone. She did not see any snakes.

WORD CAME THROUGH THE VAN DRIVER: MALEK AND HIS LARGE FAM-ily would be arriving in Ramtha in a few days. It had been three months, longer than any of them expected—the apartments Laila had found for them had been let, so they found others. Laila, whose mood had been somber, was overjoyed. It was as if they had opened the windows to let in spring air.

Hasna felt that Malek's family coming to Ramtha only confirmed her decision—if Malek's conservative, traditional family felt it was time to leave, then she would not be going back to Daraa any time soon. The paperwork offi-cially granting her and Rana refugee status arrived a few weeks later in the mail. Hasna took it to Rana's schoolteacher. Rana went back to school the next day.

That afternoon, waiting to get Rana from school, she sat on the tile bench on the roof. The hoopoe babies were now at the awkward, squawky stage where they were into everything but could not fly yet. Their demanding voices made her laugh out loud.

AT 1:00 A.M. ON THE NIGHT HE WAS SCHEDULED TO ARRIVE, MALEK
called—the first phone call he had been able to make for months, which meant
he was in Jordanian space. Hasna had gone to bed, but Laila had stayed awake
on the couch, searching through social media—a novelty none of them had
had in Syria and now the most reliable source of their news—and texting over
WhatsApp with Malek's parents and siblings. They texted as soon as they
arrived; all of their families had made it past the border, thanks be to Allah,
but the guards had stopped Malek—only him. He should have been a few
minutes behind them. Their group text had gone quiet after a while and they
did not reply to her repeated questions.

They had crossed at Zataari camp, two hours away from Ramtha, where
officials were now rerouting all refugees trying to enter Jordan.

When she heard Laila's voice, Hasna came out of her bedroom, pulling
her hair back with a scrunchy and tugging her housecoat closed around her.
Yusef was visiting from Mafraq for a few days and he was asleep on the floor
of Hasna's bedroom. Hasna could hear the rough timbre of Malek's voice. Laila
clutched at the phone, her tone rising with each response.

"What?"

"What do they want?"

"Now? It's two hours away—can you wait?"

"Make them wait. We are coming. I love you, habibi. Hold on, we are
coming."

Laila hung up and Hasna was already moving. Laila was still dressed. She
did not keep her voice down: "Mama, they've detained him. Get Yusef. I'm
getting Hamad. They have to let him stay." Her voice at the end of the sentence was a squeak.

Yusef awoke immediately, pulled on his clothes, and splashed water on his
face. Amal came out of her room as well and they walked down together. Yusef
pulled the motorcycle he shared with Khassem out of the shed on the side of
the villa where he had locked it away. Laila straddled the back of the bike, took
Hamad from her mother, and tucked him between her body and her brother's

back. Hamad held on to Yusef's coat with his tiny fists. Hasna kissed them all.
The motorcycle roared away into the night.

Amal and Hasna went to their prayer rugs and began to pray. They did
not stop until the sky was graying into morning and the children woke up.

YUSEF TOLD HIS MOTHER LATER WHAT HAPPENED. THEY HAD FOUND
Malek's family first, and they pointed to the guard's station a few meters from
the border. Laila walked over to the guards, holding Hamad.

Malek had all of his paperwork in order; he had left legally, there were
no concerns against him. What was the reason that he could not enter? she
demanded of the guards. They shrugged. No one was sure—it was someone
else's decision. She tried to reason with them, but none of the guards would
listen. They were obdurate. They pointed to a bus idling nearby, where she
could see Malek's face pressed against the window. The bus faced toward
Syria.

"He's right there! Please, let me at least say something to him! Can I at
least see him? Can he hold his son?" The soldier began to look away. Her begging only made things worse, but she couldn't help herself. Hamad began crying for Malek, who held his hand on the glass as if the window might dissolve
and allow him to join his son and wife in safety.

Everything welling up in Laila burst.

Her voice ringing out over the guards, she cursed every inch of the country of Jordan. She began with the soldier in front of her, cursing his mother and
his sons and every one of his brothers. She cursed the officers of the Jordanian
army, who could look at a devout woman and tell her that her son's father could
not be with them. She cursed the land around them, this godforsaken desert
that would never enjoy the verdant landscape of her beloved Syria, she cursed
it that it might never produce fruit of any kind. She cursed the camp they had
set up to keep the people of Syria out of cities and away from the help they
needed. She cursed the government that did not intervene when Bashar al-
Assad began bombing Daraa and Homs and Aleppo and Damascus. And she
cursed the Jordanian king, the fucker of too many wives who sat in his palace

doing nothing, surrounded by his fat lazy sons, while these soldiers were taking her son's father away, were watching with their hands on their copious bellies while her country was destroyed.

By then, Yusef's hands were on her shoulders. The bus was starting up and the acrid smell of diesel fuel mixed hotly with the snot pouring out of her nose. Tears tracked through the dust on her face. She let out a primal scream as the bus pulled away. Malek was right here in front of her. And then he was gone. The bus rolled back toward Syria.

NO ONE WAS SURPRISED WHEN LAILA ANNOUNCED THAT SHE WAS going back to Daraa. It would be easier to negotiate peace with Assad than convince Laila to stay away from her husband. Hasna was not sure it was the right decision, but she knew it was not hers to make.

Hasna spent almost every moment of the next two weeks near Laila and Hamad, soaking them in. She held Hamad while he napped. She toyed with his dark curls. His eyelashes against his cheeks were long and thick. The hair at the base of his neck was damp with sweat and he breathed with his mouth open slightly. She prayed ceaselessly that Allah would protect this little man, that his feet would be swift if he needed to run, that his mouth would be quiet when he was in danger, that his eyes would not see anything that would hurt him, that his hands would pass kindness to the people he met, that his heart might remain pure no matter what happened.

She did not fight with Laila in their last days together. She helped them pack, bought her the clothes and shoes she and Hamad would need for the next several months. She gave Laila a few ounces of gold, some insurance for the months to come.

When the morning came for them to leave, Hasna and Laila hugged each other tightly before she clambered onto the van. Amal openly sobbed; she had never lived more than a few blocks away from her sister. Noor and Maria wailed—their cousin had felt more like a brother for the last year and they could not understand his leaving. Hasna told Laila over and over again that this was not the last time they were seeing each other, that they would find a new way to come back, even if it wasn't through the legal channels—she and Malek were two of the savviest, strongest people she knew. They would find a way.

The words were hollow in her mouth. As Laila pulled away in the van, Hasna felt guilt stab her heart. She had promised Malek she would keep Laila safe and she had already broken that promise.

TWO DAYS LATER, ONE OF THE BOYS WHO LIVED IN ANOTHER APART-ment in the villa knocked on her door. His hands cupped around something held against his shirt: "Auntie, we are sorry. We have hurt your bird." He opened his hands and she saw the mother hoopoe blinking dazedly. Her legs dangled at impossible angles.

"What happened?" Hasna's voice rose.

"We were throwing rocks and we hit the birds. They"—here the little boy gestured with his chin to three boys standing sheepishly behind him—"they didn't know those were your birds. I told them, but it was too late—we've hurt this one. I'm so sorry."

Hasna looked in his gray eyes and wondered what would happen to this boy who was not afraid to confess, who had observed her closely enough to know that she'd grown to care about these birds. He could have left the bird to die; no one would ever have known.

"I'll take her." Hasna tugged on the dish towel that she had put on her shoulder and wrapped it gently around the bird. The bird's chest rose and fell shallowly; Hasna was careful not to touch her legs, hanging limply from her body. She was unsure what she could do, but she nodded gravely at the boys and closed the door with her heel.

In the kitchen, she laid the bird out on the dish towel beside the stove, where she had the best light from the picture window. No wild creature succumbed so easily to being touched by humans unless it was past the point of fighting. They had remained apart for so many weeks and now here they were, improbably beside each other in this kitchen in Ramtha.

Hasna wrapped the broken legs carefully with a paper towel, securing the tiny bandages with a bit of electrical tape. She had no idea if the makeshift leg braces would stay, but she had to try. Hasna gathered the bird up, held it cradled against her belly, carried her up the stairs.

She had never gone this close to the nest before. She could barely see through the tears streaming down her face: There were the five gangly babies. They would not be able to take care of themselves. Those boys and their rock had condemned the children to death with their mother.

Tenderly, she placed the mother inside the edge of the nest. The babies screeched in terror as Hasna's enormous shadow blocked out the sun. When she pulled back, they pushed against their mother's familiar body with their beaks, searching for food or comfort or her familiar scent, now mixed with Hasna's. They would never see their father again—Hasna knew that male hoopoes left the area when their mates died, never to return.

Hasna sat down on her pile of tiles and her body shook with sobs, her face turned toward Syria. She could hear the frantic cries of the five baby birds. She sat vigil with them as their mother died. She stayed up on the roof, back aching, as the sun set.

Eventually the babies were silent as well. She could hear occasional cars, the street dogs snapping and barking at each other in the field below, the wind through the low trees around her, the muffled explosions as the missiles started up in Daraa again. That night, the only lights were from the city of Ramtha behind her, the bombs flaring in Daraa before her, and the stars above.

Chapter 16

US REFUGEE RESETTLEMENT,
1950–1963

As the globe glacierized into the Cold War, the definition of "refugee" shifted again. Europeans displaced by Nazi rule gradually left the camps—returning to their homelands, moving to the newly established Jewish territory in Israel, or resettling in new countries—and the US government turned its attention to those affected by communism. For the twenty years following World War II, "refugee" would be a term applied by politicians, news anchors, writers, and advocates in the United States almost exclusively to anticommunist dissenters and victims, especially white European ones.

The disproportionate focus on Europeans was a hallmark of the political whiteness of the decades following World War II. The Immigration Act of 1924, with its eugenicist language and racialized quota system, remained the law. Refugee resettlement into the US and refugee aid outside it continued to ignore the plight of millions around the globe.

There was no Marshall Plan for the 14 million displaced Indians and Pakistanis in 1947. There were no airlifts for the 750,000 Palestinians who became refugees in 1950. There were no US-government-promoted PR campaigns for the 385,000 Chinese citizens relocated by the Chinese Cultural Revolution between 1950 and 1954. There were no visas allotted for the 1 million Vietnamese forced from their homes when the communist government formed a new country in North Vietnam, or for the 1.2 million displaced Algerians during the Algerian war of independence in 1960. That is not to say that those places did not receive aid, CIA involvement in their political embroilments, or foreign policy consideration from the US government. But none of those people became "refugees" in a way that would grant them special program assistance or immediate new lives in the United States.

However, the Hungarians did.

IN OCTOBER 1956, STUDENT PROTESTERS IN BUDAPEST LAUNCHED A revolution against the Soviet Politburo. On November 4, 1956, the Soviet military responded with an assault designed to crush the resistance: The Soviets intended Hungary to serve as an example to other nations of what happened if they resisted occupation. In the bitter winter following those battles, more than two hundred thousand refugees fled on foot to safety in Austria and Yugoslavia.

At the time, the US was deeply involved in a political, cultural, and rhetorical battle with the Soviet Union on a number of fronts around the world. The space program was one of the ways the United States tried to prove cultural dominance during those years; the arms race was another. With the Hungarian Revolution, refugee resettlement became a weapon in the argument that capitalism was superior to communism. To present it more effectively to the American public, the Eisenhower administration partnered with the "Mad Men" of New York in an impressive PR blitz in early 1957.

A newsreel from 1957 followed the format of the postwar newsreels. The announcer relied on lyrical language thick with alliteration to show "battered Budapest under the brutal Russian boot" over a violin-laden soundtrack. Filmmakers smuggled the footage out of Hungary to show the world the "grim evidence of the brutality and savagery with which the red tanks blasted a defenseless people and their city." Soviet soldiers "blockaded highways and destroyed bridges in a desperate effort to halt the mass exodus," but these "proud people" were not deterred on their "flight to freedom." The film showed a father carrying his son through shoulder-high grass, refugees balancing on a tree-trunk bridge over a border canal, guards waving Hungarians into Austria. There, representatives of the "free world, which suffered through Hungary's gallant struggle for freedom, opens its hearts to the homeless masses," assisting refugees as they headed to temporary camps, and from there to resettlement in Switzerland and other European countries.

President Eisenhower responded almost immediately with extraordinary levels of aid—he launched Operation Safe Haven, a joint effort by the air force and navy in which they eventually brought over more than ten thousand refugees by transatlantic air and sea transportation into the United States. The newsreel section on the displaced people ended with refugees arriving at McGuire Air Force Base in New Jersey: "Stepping out into the crisp air of America, the refugees have found the freedom for which their countrymen yearned, and fought, and died."

As part of the PR blitz, in coordination with Operation Safe Haven, the January 7, 1957, cover of *Life* magazine featured a smiling Vice President Richard Nixon embracing two small Hungarian girls in a crowd of refugees; there was a Norman Rockwell quality to the cover photo as one little girl lovingly gazed up at Nixon with a beaming smile, touching his cheek, while another girl, clutching a baby doll in a bassinet, looked on. The magazine featured an eight-page photo spread of black-and-white pictures, beginning with Hungarian women being lifted into wagons in the snow after fleeing Soviet oppression. It followed one family's arrival in Indianapolis with images of a small girl pledging allegiance to the American flag on her first day of school, families embracing one another after being reunited on US soil, a woman enjoying washing machines and television sets. The photo series ended with the children starting school and the man kissing his wife before going to work at Anheuser-Busch.

The *Life* photo series used what would become the standard tropes for presenting refugees to the American public: images of a bleak journey; crowded photos indicating hordes of people hoping for scant resources; relieved faces when refugees realize they were accepted for resettlement in the United States; moments of joyful reunions with loved ones; pictures of smiling refugees in their new homes and at new jobs. The American Dream, granted to the deserving few.

IN THE 1950S, RESTRICTIONISTS (STILL MOSTLY DEMOCRATS) AND LIB-
eralizers (still mostly Republicans) hammered out refugee policies and rhetoric as the postwar surge of goodwill began to dissipate. The nationalist quota

system of the Immigration Act of 1924 remained in place, bolstered by the McCarran-Walter Act in 1952. Eisenhower and other liberalizers created a separate track for refugee admissions in 1953 with the Refugee Relief Act and the resulting federal program. The Refugee Relief Program lasted three years, until 1956; with restrictionists wielding power in Congress, the executive branch had limited options for refugee resettlement. During his tenure, Eisenhower "paroled" thousands of refugees to the United States in an attempt to go around Congress. But the short-term nature of the crisis-driven acts and programs in those years made resettlement especially difficult; the lessons learned with each of these initiatives did not necessarily carry over to the next crisis. A series of ad hoc solutions followed in 1957, 1958, and 1960, patching the issue without fixing it.

Beginning with the Refugee Relief Act, restrictionists made sure that national screening protocols were in place—vetting refugees would be a critical part of every resettlement policy from the 1950s on. McCarthyism and the Red Scare were in full effect in the early 1950s and in the beginning, officials worked to keep out almost everyone in the 1953 Refugee Relief Act, not just Soviet spies. The Eisenhower administration eventually intervened and, in that act and others, worked to prevent over-vetting and to regulate the program. It took some time and some political finagling, but vetted refugees arrived in fits and starts throughout the decade.

The 1950s were a tumultuous time in terms of American identity, and that played out in the immigration debates. The back-and-forth, stop-and-start nature of resettlement reflected the mounting tension that would erupt with the civil rights movement. Still, those years provided fundamental building blocks for the program when it finally stabilized a few decades later. Liberalizers who argued that resettlement numbers were never high enough to address real refugee needs and restrictionists who wanted to ensure that national security vetting was always included—both paved the way for the program that would come.

Chapter 17

MU NAW

AUSTIN, TEXAS, USA,
APRIL 2008–MARCH 2009

A year after Mu Naw gave birth to her son, Saw Doh, they moved from their first apartment, 1-1-2 (she always said each number individually and carefully, so that Americans could understand her, knew where to find her), to the glorious upstairs apartment, 2-1-6. 216 was next door to an older Karen couple who were soon like the grandparents her children had never had. They came over for dinner, spent time chatting outside on the porches. After the birth of her son, with so many families around her, life in this new country, while not easy, was becoming familiar. Most days, she was glad they had come.

Each week brought even more new families as the refugee resettlement program for Myanmar expanded. Austin was highly receptive to refugees—housing was expensive, but jobs were plentiful. Churches and other groups were quick to meet the needs of the new families; there were people around all the time. After those first lonely months, Mu Naw found it refreshing. She loved to be needed and busy. She and Saw Ku were thriving.

There was a women's cooperative that began and quickly grew as new women moved into the apartment complex. Some of the women were deft artisans and American volunteers worked to find the right yarn and to replicate the backstrap looms of the more experienced weavers. The new yarn was from Maine, stiff and mostly in earth tones. The women did not like it as well as the supple, bright cotton from Myanmar, so they mixed the two together in dazzling new combinations: fuchsia with coral, emerald green with brick red, neon orange with black. The white women figured out how to sell the bags and the weavers profited, and Mu Naw became their go-between, explaining the cultural significance of Christmas and Halloween colors, why the earth tones would do better in the United States. When they were gone, the women talked about the ridiculousness of white people's taste: Who would want to weave only in brown and gray? Didn't Americans know these colors were ugly? But the women were glad for the money. They enjoyed spending time together. Daily the courtyard of the apartment complex was filled with the women who were too old or had children too young to work, weaving on their porches. Mu Naw was the unquestioned leader of the daytime group.

They banded together in everything from child care to sorting out bills and Mu Naw felt, for the first time, that the bonds that had restricted her for her entire life were truly gone. She could never have done in Mae La camp what she was doing here.

Some place inside of her healed in that year. Pah Poe was in elementary school and Naw Wah in pre-K. She had a fat, happy son. Her husband adored her, could not always keep his hands off her, especially now that they knew they would have no more children. They giggled as they had as teenagers, not so many years and yet a lifetime ago.

The new second-floor apartment had wider windows and laminate floor-ing. There were more shoes by the door than the year before, neatly stacked onto low shelves. On the porch were two chairs, the mesh seats slightly frayed, where she could sit and visit with friends or watch the birds in the branches in the courtyard's only tree.

ONE DAY THE WHITE WOMEN FROM EVENING ENGLISH CLASSES CAME to the apartment complex with some of the caseworkers from Refugee Ser-vices and a new interpreter. Mu Naw did not know these caseworkers; the agency had hired more people as more Burmese people moved to Austin. The caseworkers showed them a piece of paper with two pictures of Bob behind a white backdrop with some numbers listed; in one, he glowered at the camera, and in the second he looked to the side.

Usually informal and always laughing, the white women were serious, teary. The interpreter repeated himself several times, in a variety of ways: Bob was dangerous. He hurt children. The police had caught him inappropriately touching a young boy. If their children had ever been alone with Bob, they should come and talk to RST immediately.

A few weeks later, all of the refugee families who lived in the apartment— from Burundi, Somalia, Iraq, and Myanmar—were asked to come to a meeting in the conference room at RST. It was the only time they had all been called together and almost everyone came. The refugees made a circle in the room; mixed in with them were many familiar faces—the ministers who spoke at the Karen Baptist church, one of the white men with a beard who played the guitar, the RST caseworkers, the white women who brought them yarn. The room was overcrowded and stuffy.

The director of RST, a woman with straight dark hair and intricate dangling earrings, stood in front of a whiteboard and spoke loudly in a firm voice that surprised Mu Naw. Mu Naw had been asked to be a translator for the meeting and she stood with the other translators in an inner circle facing the group of people near her.

They divided the room based on language, so the Burmese were in one part divided up into subgroups based on dialect; the Karen speakers were in front of her and the Karenni speakers were to her right in front of another translator. The director of RST would say a sentence and then pause. Then, simultaneously, the translators would translate what she said into the first language, then the second round of translators picked it up. For the Iraqis, the phrases were repeated once in Arabic. For the Burundians, twice: in French and then Kirundi. For the refugees from Myanmar, four times: Burmese, Karenni, Po Karen, and Ska Karen. Mu Naw was the Po Karen and Ska Karen translator, which meant that her voice was the only one at the end of each statement, the large group of people listening expectantly for her to be done saying each phrase twice before the director of RST began speaking again. Mu Naw could feel her neck and cheeks flush the first time her voice rang out alone in the silent room, but she repeated the phrases faithfully in two languages.

The director enunciated each word: "This man, Bob, who said he was your friend, is not your friend—he is a dangerous criminal who has lied to all of us.

"The police are helping us. In other countries, it is not always a good thing to have the police involved. In the United States, this is a good thing.

"Bob wants to touch your children in sexual ways, in ways that only a husband and wife should use with each other.

"Bob was arrested, but the police do not have enough proof to keep him in jail. The fact that the police suspect him makes Bob especially dangerous right now.

"If you see Bob at the apartments, you need to call the police.

"Do not let Bob into your home. Ever.

"If the police want to speak to you about Bob, that is okay! Do not be afraid! It is okay to speak to the police! If you think that maybe Bob has already hurt your children, you can tell your caseworkers privately and we will help.

"Right now, the police do not have any way to keep Bob away from the apartments. They are working to get everything they need to keep Bob in prison for a very long time, but those things take time.

"You must tell the police if you see Bob—for the sake of your children."

Mu Naw's voice finished last. In each of the languages, the word echoed: Children. Children. Children. Children.

THE MEETING DID NOT STOP BOB FROM COMING, BUT IT DID MAKE her neighbors less likely to open the door to him, at least some of them.

Mu Naw understood why it was hard for refugees, who had always lived in countries where uniforms implied danger, to now trust that the police and their caseworkers were telling the truth. One of the white women explained that the detectives had arrested Bob on suspicion of child abuse—that was the picture they had shown at the community meeting, what they called a "mug shot"—but that the little boy who accused Bob was now no longer willing to tell his story. The detectives had called the white women and told them that, on the day they went to arrest Bob, they had found several Burmese boys hidden under the bed and in the closet of his home. But those boys were not willing to speak to the police either. Translators were working with the woman and the RST caseworkers and other volunteers, trying to convince the families to tell the detectives if Bob had ever touched their sons. The police knew that Bob had molested the children, but they could not prove it, and without proof, there was little they could do in a country where they were bound by civil laws. Bob could keep coming and the only deterrent was the will of the community, unless someone gave them the proof they needed.

Two of the white women saw Bob leave in a pickup truck loaded with Burmese boys. They called the police and then went to Mu Naw's house. Later that day, uniformed officers knocked on the doors of the families that had let their children leave with him. No one answered their knocks; the lights inside the apartments were all turned off.

A FEW WEEKS LATER, A KAREN FRIEND INVITED MU NAW TO COME OVER for another meeting with another group of white people. This time it was a man who was coming to tell the people in the apartment complex about new jobs. The pudgy white man sat in her neighbor's living room and spoke loudly so that the people gathered outside on the porch could hear: He worked for a company that wanted to hire all of them, right now, to work in a meat processing plant. It was a good job—you did not have to speak English. Husbands and wives could work. The children could go to school and they had places where young children could go. The apartments were cheap. They would all be paid good wages. They just needed to be ready to go in two weeks. The company would send a bus to come get them; they would move all of their furniture, too, for free.

When he was done, Mu Naw looked around and realized that she had heard something totally different from most of her friends. That night, she talked it over with Saw Ku. They felt that God had called them to Austin, and they were beginning to like it here, finally finding their way. And, as Saw Ku said, "Cheaper does not always mean better. In fact, cheaper is often worse." His brother and sister-in-law felt the same. They would stay, they all agreed.

Only one other family stayed too. For the next two weeks, Mu Naw watched in disbelief and then despair as her new friends packed up their houses to move. She could barely speak for crying when the couple next door—the ones who felt like grandparents to her children—told her they were going too. She begged them to stay, but the promise of good jobs for both of them was too tempting.

Mu Naw helped them pack boxes, received lamps and desks and chairs that people did not want to take, cried and cooked and prayed.

On the designated morning, when two charter buses pulled into the parking lot outside of her building, she woke her children so they could say goodbye and stood with Saw Ku, his brother, sister-in-law, and their children, and the other Karen family by the door of the bus. Each person filed by and hugged them or shook their hands.

Two years before, she had been the one boarding the bus that would take her to the airport and then to the United States. She had hugged her mother and her relatives and Saw Ku's relatives just like this. She had held her daughters out to be kissed one more time by their grandmothers. She had gotten on the bus, nervous but excited, preparing for a new life that was nothing but a promise, nothing but a whiff of hope.

As the buses pulled away, the depression that Mu Naw thought she had moved past settled at once and immediately on her shoulders. She wrapped herself in it again, pulling it tight around her.

Seeing a man in the shadows who looked like Bob only increased her despair. She cried for hours, days. She cried as she had when she first arrived. She cried for herself, alone again except for two other families, in this apartment complex that had been full and almost felt like home.

Until now she had never considered what her mother had gone through when she had watched her daughter get on that bus that would take her to a new life a world away. She felt a rush of empathy.

Her mother deserved to be here, to be out of the camp, to take showers, eat hot food from an oven, wear new clothes.

Mu Naw made an appointment with a caseworker—she had not been a client of RST for years, but after the community meeting about Bob, she worked for them as a translator sometimes. The caseworker told her that her mother would have to apply for resettlement first.

But when she spoke with her mother later that month over her Cricket phone, her mom balked. What would she do in a foreign country? She was glad Mu Naw was doing well, but her life was here in the camp. Mu Naw tried to convince her to apply for resettlement, but her mother was uninterested. Eventually they stopped speaking about it.

Mu Naw and Saw Ku stayed until their lease was up in the apartment complex that felt gutted without her friends, then moved to another apartment complex for a year, then to another. They stayed near Jaw Jaw and Deh Deh, but the loss of their little thriving community—her found family—revealed a complex minefield of fears that Mu Naw had not realized still lay submerged beneath the surface of her life.

Her fears did not go off all at once. But when the explosions came, her anger pocked the terrain of her family. She seemed incapable of stopping herself.

She felt her mind divide—one part of her felt immense satisfaction at the results of these explosions, as if they were inevitable and it was better to have done with it. The other part of her lived with dawning horror, working to mitigate the damage, trying to stop it. The mental divide deepened as the destructive force of her anger found a target: Saw Ku. By the time they moved to their last apartment complex, it was hard for her to remember the sweetness with which they had held each other's hand over their new baby just three years before.

Ironically, in that last apartment complex, Mu Naw began to find the kind of community she had known in their first one. The women were not Karen like all of her first friends, but they were all from Myanmar, and Kachin and Karenni were not that different, it turned out. She was still friends with some of the white women from before and they began to start passing out looms and yarn again. Mu Naw connected them with people who wanted to weave; some of the women wanted to make jewelry and she helped with that too. She was at the center of things again, eager to help them all connect and make new lives but, this time, intimately aware of how quickly it could all evaporate.

She continued translating for RST as well as Caritas, another agency that took care of refugees in Austin. She could translate from English now, not just from Burmese, which meant she was in high demand. The white women paid her to pass out yarn and looms and translate for them; they held English classes and artisan meetings and homework help in the evenings for the kids at an apartment they called the Village Center. Dr. Salai, an incredibly skilled Burmese translator in his eighties, whom the whole community revered and called "grandfather," praised her work. Mu Naw shone with pride.

Outside the doors of her home, her life appeared to be one of the success stories of the refugee resettlement program. The teachers at Central Presbyterian who taught English to refugees in Austin took a portrait of Mu Naw and her children on World Refugee Day. They mounted the picture on cardboard and it hung in their office for years. When new refugees arrived, they pointed to Mu Naw, grinning and wearing her traditional Karen clothes. You can be like her someday, they told the new arrivals. This woman is now one of our translators. She and her husband both have good jobs. They are paying their bills. Their children go to school and they are happy. Theirs is a very happy home.

Chapter 18

HASNA

RAMTHA AND IRBED, JORDAN, FEBRUARY—DECEMBER 2013

Enough neighbors and friends from Daraa came to Ramtha over the next few weeks bringing news from home that Hasna was able to piece together a sense of the life that Jebreel, Malek, Laila, and Hamad were leading. Laila and Malek had moved in with Jebreel to help him protect their house; their own apartment had been damaged in the shelling. The government attacks ebbed and flowed—this she knew from observing the city from her rooftop perch.

Occasionally, Laila or Malek would slip away to go stay with cousins for a few days in the rural areas near the Jordanian border, where they could occasionally get cell phone service to call Jordan. She lived for those days. The calls often dropped and they could not really say how they were doing in case their words were overheard, but to hear their voices—to tell Hamad she loved him, to send messages of love to Jebreel—was bittersweet.

One of the phone calls carried news that devastated Hasna for weeks—while Malek and Laila were at relatives' homes and Jebreel was working, looters had gotten into their house. They had taken all of Hasna's clothing, all of the porcelain dishes, the Persian rugs, the paintings she loved from the walls, her table. Even though she was far away, Hasna felt violated. She could see every inch of those rugs, the pulls in the weaving, the stains from where her children had spilled things, the corners that were curling up slightly after years of use. She knew every curve of the porcelain, the dishes she only used for formal occasions. She could feel the clothes against her skin, the long black dresses that she had loved, with glittery edging designed to separate them from her everyday clothes. And the loss of her table felt symbolic—it was nothing special, just a plain table of dark, smooth wood, long enough for a dozen chairs, but every important conversation in her adult life, every meal with her children, every coffee or tea with relatives and friends, all of it happened around that table.

Hasna tried to imagine what her city was like now and she could not. This lawless place Laila described had nothing to do with the city of peace and neighborliness that Hasna loved. All of the neighbors around her—Um Ibtihal, Um Ahmad, all of their cousins—everyone was gone. No one noticed, or at least they did nothing, when looters carried away her belongings in broad daylight.

She recognized now that, of all the forms of grief she endured, this was the most agonizing: to be safe while her home and her family were not. It was a wound that could not heal, that was searingly fresh every day.

ONE DAY, A CALL CAME TO HER CELL PHONE FROM A NUMBER SHE DID not recognize. It was a Jordanian number and she answered it at once, thinking perhaps Laila had found a way into the country. Instead, it was someone from the office of the United Nations High Commissioner for Refugees. The woman on the phone introduced herself and asked Hasna if she would be interested in applying for refugee resettlement somewhere in the world. Hasna almost laughed out loud; the woman might as well have told her she could enter to win a free trip to the moon. Hasna had never been on an airplane and spoke no other languages. She only ever imagined travel in the more fantastical moments of her life, but even those dreams were in the Middle East—Mecca, of course, possibly Beirut, maybe Abu Dhabi.

"Sure," she responded. "Why not?" The conversation was short. She assumed the woman was misinformed or had gotten her file confused with someone else's. She thought about the phone call a few times over the next several weeks but eventually forgot about it in the stress of the next few months.

THEY MOVED TO IRBED, JORDAN. CHANGING CITIES FELT LIKE A FUR-
ther act of admitting that their life in Jordan was not temporary. But in Irbed,
Amal could take the final classes to finish her computer science degree and
Rana could go to a school that was closer than the one they trekked to every
day in Ramtha. Most importantly, Samir, Yusef, and Khassem could find better work there than in Mafraq.

They found a three-bedroom apartment full of white tiles and light.
Hasna watched Noor and Maria while Amal went to classes and Rana was in
school. When Amal finished her classes, Hasna spent the afternoons shopping
for furniture to replace what the looters had taken. The apartment in Ramtha
had been furnished with particle-board items and Hasna took some plea-
sure in buying things for their new home with a small portion of her gold—
everything she bought in Jordan, she pictured in her home in Daraa. When the
war was over, they would rent a truck, and she would come back from Jordan
with a gleaming wood table and porcelain dishes that might not have the same
sentimental associations as the ones she had lost, but that would still serve her
loved ones.

Her new kitchen was big enough for a large stove that needed six gas canisters, and Hasna cooked again for her family, gathered as often as they could
around the table at night. They left Jebreel's traditional place at the head of the
table free; there was room at the end of the table where Malek and Laila would
one day sit. Hasna tried to keep herself in a positive frame of mind. Either they
would all find their way to this apartment in Irbed, which was not ideal but
which was still much better than what most refugees in Jordan had—she still
struggled to picture herself as a refugee—or, if Allah willed it, Assad would
be overcome by the Free Syria Army or the UN would get involved, and she
would take all of this furniture home. Amal, with her new degree, would get
a good job; her sons, with the savings they were accumulating in Jordan, would
start a business. They would rebuild out of the ashes of this war.

Khassem came back to the apartment one day and told her that he had
met a friend from Daraa whose little sister was at a marriageable age. His eyes
gleamed and, when Hasna asked if she was pretty, he picked his mother up

and twirled her around the kitchen. She swatted him until he put her down and they both laughed. He had asked his friend to see, quietly, what her parents might think of a potential match. Hasna grinned to see her taciturn son hopeful.

Word came from Syrian neighbors around them that Assad had used chemical weapons in Ghouta, a suburb outside Damascus, against rebel forces. At first, Hasna was confused—had they not been using chemicals throughout the war? The white phosphorous grenades continued to haunt her dreams. She looked up the news on her phone—the ability to read news from around the world never ceased to amaze her—and was horrified. Her Facebook feed, made up of Syrians outside the country, was full of images of bodies of those killed in the attack. She could not bear to turn away; one of the pictures of a father holding his son looked so much like Malek holding Hamad that she burst out sobbing before she could stop herself, scaring Rana and the little girls.

Fellow refugees told her about the president of the United States, who declared that Assad had crossed a red line. Hasna felt nervously optimistic— she was afraid of what would happen to her country if it became a pawn between Iran and Russia on one side and the United States, France, and England on the other. But she desperately hoped that the people in Ghouta had not died in vain. If the pictures compelled her, she could not imagine their impact on the people in the US—now they would finally do something to save the children of Syria. She began to pray that the coming war would be better for her country than the US war in Iraq had been, that Assad would leave peacefully without killing anyone else.

After the chemical attack in Ghouta, Syrians spilled out of the country like water from a split barrel. Those who could not leave at least moved, so that eventually most of the rebels were concentrated in a few key areas—including Daraa. Suddenly there seemed to be many more Syrians in Jordan than there had been before. Hasna knew from listening to the stories that her situation was unusual. The fact that she had most of her children with her was a blessing she did not take lightly; Amal and Samir, Yusef and Khassem all worked together to pay rent while Hasna watched the children and kept their home.

Syrians were still not legally supposed to work, but there were contract jobs for those willing to take them. Wages were lower and rent was higher for Syrians, but it was a life. And working in the city seemed infinitely better than receiving aid in the refugee camps blooming in the desert. Hasna could not fathom the degradation of having to live off handouts in a tent.

Hasna remembered the story told by Scheherazade of the old fisherman who cast his nets only four times. That was how the options felt for Syrians. Each one worse than the next—a dead donkey, a pitcher of dirt, a netful of glass shards were like war or flight or a refugee camp or a precarious life in an apartment in Jordan that could be taken away at a moment's notice. But suddenly, for Hasna, it was as if an improbable jinni leaped into the boat in which she sat, opened its own bottle and offered her the most outrageous thing she could imagine.

A representative from UNHCR called her again, several months after the initial call, and asked her to come to the office in Irbed for an initial interview. She almost turned him down. Resettlement was of no use at all if peace in Syria was right around the corner. But he suggested that she at least come to the office and hear more—she did not have to take resettlement if she didn't want to, but why not at least keep her options open? The process took at least two years; many things could change in that time. She agreed to come, but in a way that made it clear that she was humoring him. She hung up and left the house to spend a few hours shopping for throw pillows with her granddaughters before picking Rana up from school.

HASNA WENT TO THE FIRST INTERVIEW ALONE. A WESTERN MAN— American or German or Swedish—asked her questions in passable Arabic in a small room and jotted her answers down on white paper that he put in a file. He wanted to know when she was born and where, the year she was married, what her children's names were, and when they had married. He asked about their schooling and some questions about their relatives—her sisters and Jebreel's family. She was surprised that he asked questions about their parents and grandparents, about their family's hospitalizations, even about the baby she had lost that she rarely spoke about now. When it was over, he repeated her answers back to her, and that was it. He told her a few things about the process—that there would be several more interviews, that there was no guarantee that she would be resettled anywhere, but that if she was, her family would be more likely to be resettled with her since most of the countries, especially the United States, valued family reunification.

Family reunification, he explained, struggling a bit with the vocabulary in Arabic, just meant that if one of them was resettled—ideally with her husband and Rana, maybe her sons—then the rest of the family would be flagged in the system and notes made to keep them together. If they were doing a background search on her, they would also learn information about the rest of her family and could vet them at the same time. Most countries felt that refugees did better with their families; in fact, of the refugees he had interviewed who were offered resettlement, almost all of them said that family reunification was the main reason they chose to go to a new country across the world.

She asked him why they had called her and he told her that women traveling alone were often more likely to be resettled than men because it was harder for them to make it in countries like Jordan. She told him her husband was alive and they were separated by the war, but he urged her to at least go through the process a bit further. She found she liked him, his open face and his endearing Arabic, which she corrected only a few times. She appreciated his effort and by the end, Hasna felt they were almost friends.

Hasna left the building in time to walk to Rana's school. The UNHCR official gave her the feeling that she might have been something of an anomaly; most people when asked if they wanted to go to North America, Europe, or Australia were immediately interested. But Hasna felt some concerns—she had no desire to leave Syria and, if they had not called her, would never have thought of resettlement. Still, she recognized the man's wisdom—she would continue to go to the interviews, keep her options open. She stopped at the butcher's before going to Rana's school and exclaimed, as she did every time, about the price of meat in Jordan—things were half as expensive and twice as good in Syria.

THE CALLS CAME WITHIN MINUTES OF EACH OTHER, AROUND 2:00 A.M.
in late October 2013, a few months after they set up the big apartment in
Irbed.

The first call was from Khassem, who was staying with friends on a job in
a nearby city: "Mama." His voice broke and he began sobbing and she was
instantly awake, sitting straight up in bed, not bothering to lower her voice.

"Khassem? What is it?"

"Mama, it's the house. There was a missile." He held the phone away from
his mouth and she could hear him sobbing. "Father is injured. Someone called
me and told me that our uncle had given them my number—they're rushing
Father to the field hospital now. It doesn't look good. The house is gone."

"Laila and Hamad? Were they there? Are they okay?"

"They were there." He paused again. "I don't know, Mama. I don't know."

And then Amal was banging on Hasna's bedroom door, her phone in her
hand, her hair escaping in tendrils from her low ponytail. She held up the
phone and kept speaking: "What does that mean? Will he be okay?" She
gripped her mother's hand and listened, cradling the phone to her cheek while
she closed her eyes.

The call ended. She told Hasna what she had learned: Jebreel was about to
go into surgery. No one knew what had happened to Malek, Laila, and Hamad;
just that they were in the house when the missile landed.

Hasna and Amal began the longest wait of both of their lives. Rana woke
up but the little granddaughters slept. Hasna made coffee that no one drank,
set out spiced bread that no one ate. They waited. The sun lightened the skies,
the birds began to chirp, the earliest shopkeepers opened their doors and rolled
out their awnings before the next call came in.

It was Malek. The line crackled and almost dropped, but she could hear
him. "We're safe, Auntie. We're okay."

"Where are Laila and Hamad?"

"They're here."

"Please, let me hear them."

There was a pause, then Laila's voice, "Mama! Mama, we're okay! Hamad was scared, but he's fine, aren't you, you good brave boy?"

Hasna told them she loved them through her sobs and sat down hard on the floor, and after a few minutes the call dropped.

And then she could finally face the truth. It was gone. Her home, her life, all of it—nothing but rubble, nothing but dust.

THE MISSILE HAD HIT THE BEDROOM WHERE JEBREEL WAS SLEEPING. It was a small missile, or he might not have lived. Still, he credited Hasna for saving his life, as well as his father, who built a home intended to last. When Hasna moved the cupboard in their bedroom to hide her gold, she placed it in such a way that, when it fell, it protected him from the worst of the shrapnel. The walls, with their huge basalt stones quarried from the mountains around Daraa, absorbed the impact of that missile. He should have died. Instead, he lost his left arm from the elbow down, a portion of his cheek, his ear, and part of his torso. The doctors told him later the major miracle was that he did not lose any of his organs.

Malek, Laila, and Hamad—sleeping on the other side of the house—were bruised and dazed, but otherwise fine. They had gone to the field hospital with Jebreel, sitting with their relatives who were still in the neighborhood while doctors stabilized him that night. When a relative had secured an ambulance for Jebreel, they had not been allowed to go with him across the border—the Jordanian government only allowed those with life-threatening injuries to cross the border seeking medical help. Instead, they slipped out of town to call Hasna, journeying as close to the border as they could so that they could get some cell service. Jebreel was rushed to Irbed, where Samir's friend, a surgeon, was waiting for him; by the time Jebreel's ambulance arrived, Hasna, Amal, and Samir had been at the hospital for several hours.

The doctors in Irbed performed a series of surgeries on Jebreel; he was one of many patients from Syria rushed over every time the government shelled its citizens. The Jordanian government provided health care for refugees despite the exorbitant cost to their small country. Surgeons amputated what remained of his arm, stitched his face and his side, grafted skin to partially fill in the portions of his flesh the missile had destroyed.

Hasna nursed him faithfully, rarely leaving his side while he was in the hospital. When the doctors released him after his first surgery, she took him back to the apartment in Irbed. That first dinner, she helped him sit down at the seat at the head of their table; his body leaned to the left and she helped to stack pillows on that side to cushion his still-healing stitches.

She placed the dishes down for most of her family to eat together for the first time in years; the ache for Laila and Malek and Hamad was almost physical, a cavernous emptiness she felt just beneath her rib cage.

Chapter 19

US REFUGEE RESETTLEMENT, 1965–1980

O ne of the most important political victories for the American resettlement program occurred in 1965 with the passage of the Immigration and Nationality Act (INA). Built on a bill initiated by John F. Kennedy just months before his assassination, the act was a hard-won victory for Lyndon B. Johnson, who spent a great deal of political capital negotiating for its passage. He did what few presidents have been willing or able to do since then in radically overhauling the complicated American immigration system. Following on the heels of the Civil Rights Act of 1964 and the Voting Rights Act of 1965, the INA was the next step in reshaping American immigration to align more closely with the values of the civil rights movement.

President Johnson signed the bill into law on October 3, 1965, in New York beside the Statue of Liberty. In his speech, he noted that the law would "repair a very deep and painful flaw in the fabric of American justice." In abolishing what he called the "harsh injustice of the national origins quota system," in which 70 percent of the immigrants to the US arrived from England, Ireland, or Germany, the INA changed the values by which the United States accepted immigrants: "from this day forth those wishing to immigrate to America shall be admitted on the basis of their skills and their close relationship to those already here." Refugees were intrinsic to the new immigration policy. Johnson directly addressed Cuban refugees in the speech: "I declare this afternoon to the people of Cuba that those who seek refuge here in America will find it. The dedication of America to our traditions as an asylum for the oppressed is going to be upheld."

Johnson's liberalizer position was a tempered one: "The days of unlimited immigration are past." Still, by signing the bill into law on Liberty Island, Lyndon B. Johnson signaled a deliberate return to the America described in Emma Lazarus's anthem; he pointed to nearby "Ellis Island, whose corridors echo today the joyous sound of long ago voices" and said the law marked a new beginning: "today we can all believe that the lamp of this grand old lady is brighter today—and the golden door that she guards gleams more brilliantly in the light of an increased liberty for the people from all the countries of the globe." And he expressed the belief that, with the signing of this law, racist immigration policies would "never again shadow the gate to the American Nation with the twin barriers of prejudice and privilege."

THE IMMIGRATION ACT OF 1965 ESTABLISHED REFUGEE RESETTLEMENT as one of the new pillars of immigration, along with merit-based acceptance policies and family reunification. Refugee advocates hoped this would be a change from the 1950s' tempestuous, reactive presidential paroles and congressional acts providing special allotments for a limited time to refugees in specific situations. However, the limited scope of the INA still offered opportunities only for some types of refugees; "refugee" continued to imply "anticommunist," even if the INA moved away from white European as essential for American resettlement. The emphasis on anticommunism opened some opportunities for non-European immigrants, such as Cubans fleeing Fidel Castro's reign or Chinese escaping the Cultural Revolution.

But throughout the 1960s and early 1970s, refugee resettlement continued to be an uneven process based less on need than advocates would have liked. Refugee activists—including those who worked in the nonprofits, voluntary resettlement agencies, and other aid groups established in those years—labored tirelessly to get the wording of American policy adjusted so that communism was one, but not the only, type of persecution the US government recognized.

Though the policies were draped in humanitarian language, visas in the 1960s and early 1970s were predominantly given out based on US foreign interests. It's clearest in the case of Cubans and Haitians, both arriving on the shores off of Florida, where the MS *St. Louis* had docked thirty years before. Cubans—anticommunist dissenters, allies of the US cause—were welcomed. Airlifts began in 1965 to pluck Cuban bodies out of the water and went on for years; by 1973, more than three thousand flights had been logged, rescuing more than 250,000 Cubans and bringing them to their new lives in the US. Aid, federal support, legislation such as the Cuban Adjustment Act of 1966, all assisted Cubans fleeing communism.

Those same waters were also filled with Haitians. Dozens of Haitian citizens piled into the same kinds of boats as the Cubans. And yet, they did not receive anything close to the same kind of help. Haitians were fleeing persecution at the hands of a corrupt dictator who was also an American ally, President Jean-Claude Duvalier. US politicians actively denied that his people needed to flee; their language and laws classed Haitians as grasping economic migrants rather than deserving asylum seekers. While untold thousands of Haitians arrived between 1961 and 1971, they were treated with none of the special dispensations often given to Cubans. What was a life-saving policy change in 1965 for Cubans did little for Haitians fleeing a violent dictator.

In 1967, the UNHCR Refugee Protocol changed its language to acknowledge that refugees were not specific to a region or country—not just people affected by the Holocaust, for example—but could come from anywhere. It would be years before the American federal government updated its definitions to match those of UNHCR.

DESPITE THE FLAWS IN THE NEW SYSTEM, THE 1965 INA MARKED A SIGnificant and positive change for those refugees who were accepted for resettlement because of family reunification. It meant that refugees were able to have hope that their close relatives could join them in their new life. While family reunification had been a part of the Immigration Act of 1924, only about half of the visas given out before 1965 were for the purpose of reuniting families; after 1965, 74 percent of the visas brought over family members permanently. The wider scope of the INA also meant that family reunification was not exclusively available to Northern Europeans. And as resettlement demographics shifted over the next several decades, with the many partisan divides and debates, there was never serious opposition to family reunification. It was one of the few characteristics of immigration policy that restrictionists and liberalizers readily agreed on. Access to family seemed like such a basic human right that few disputed it.

The US continued the resettlement of anticommunist refugees with the Soviet Jews who began arriving in the 1960s; the resettlement of this group grew steadily in the 1970s. Resettling Jewish refugees was also something politicians from both sides of the political aisle could agree on: Not only was it a human rights issue, it also fit the foreign policy agenda of continuing to prove to the Soviet Union that the US was culturally superior. Amnesty International ran a campaign to free Soviet Jews; Jewish advocacy groups were strong supporters and, as the emergence of human rights for its own sake became a more widely accepted position, their advocacy led to many Jewish refugees choosing resettlement in the United States over Israel. Refugee advocates from HIAS and the Council of Jewish Federations also successfully lobbied the US for federal financial assistance accompanying resettlement, something Hungarians, Cubans, and Vietnamese refugees had also received but that was not yet an established part of resettlement protocol. The anti-Semitism of the 1920s and 1930s was gone, or at least more skillfully hidden; it no longer actively controlled American policy.

There were other groups that came in during those years: A few hundred Chileans fleeing the coup that brought Pinochet to power. The Cubans. Thousands of Russians. And there were groups that were overlooked, including the 2 million Nigerians displaced by the Biafran war in 1967.

But the group that defined US resettlement by the 1970s was not one group of people at all. Vietnamese, Cambodian, Laotian, and Hmong people, often referred to collectively as "Indochinese boat people," were part of one of the largest mass migrations of political refugees and economic migrants in history. The public outcry on behalf of the Indochinese boat people—with its echoes of the public goodwill the American public had not experienced since World War II—would do more to move the United States toward another peak in refugee resettlement and the creation of a permanent, stable federal program than any other humanitarian crisis.

SEVERAL EVENTS IN SOUTHEAST ASIA IN 1975 DISPLACED HUNDREDS of thousands of people. The Laotian civil war in 1974 pushed 120,000 people, particularly the Hmong, into Thailand. The fall of Saigon on April 30, 1975, and the removal of the last American troops immediately threatened the people of South Vietnam, including the translators, the children of US soldiers and their mothers, and others who had provided critical assistance to US troops. Despite the fact that the American public predominantly supported ending US involvement in the Vietnam War, the fate of those people who would be at the mercy of the North Vietnamese army weighed heavily on our national conscience. The Vietnam War had already displaced 2.7 million people; the fall of South Vietnam displaced 800,000 more.

And then in December 1975, the first internationally recognized genocide since the Holocaust occurred. The Khmer Rouge in Cambodia slaughtered more than 2 million Cambodians in an ethnic cleansing that sought to remake the country into an agricultural, Marxist state. The leader, Pol Pot, displaced thousands of urban dwellers to the north of the country. He created farm collectives and then demanded that the unskilled city dwellers miraculously figure out how to produce crops; they died in the hundreds of thousands because they starved or were beaten to death by the Khmer Rouge guards. He also executed people by the thousands in a calculated, government-led campaign.

If people could flee Vietnam or Laos or Cambodia, they did, on boats heading to Malaysia and Indonesia and Thailand. Many of them died. The US went to extraordinary lengths to save and resettle the Indochinese boat people, with the kind of airlifts they had used for the Hungarian and Cuban refugees, but advocates argued vehemently and compellingly that those efforts were not enough.

The Indochina Migration and Refugee Assistance Act of 1975 began the process of resettling more than 360,000 refugees from the region from 1975 to 1979. Rather than being fed up with helping after the initial act, public will extended the program further. One study from 1985 states that, of the "1.5 million refugees who fled Vietnam, Laos, and Kampuchea [Cambodia's name at the time under Pol Pot], approximately half have now settled in the US." By 1992, that number had risen to more than a million.

If the numbers of people resettled in the United States were unprecedented by historical standards, so, too, was the support from the American public. By the end of the 1970s, American identity—shaped by the civil rights era and forged in the Vietnam War—was turned toward humanitarianism, with an avid interest in what was happening around the globe, not just in those places where the US had a foothold.

Human rights groups exploded. John F. Kennedy's Peace Corps, established in 1961, grew exponentially: There were 370 programs in effect in 1966, and by 1971, there were 546. Membership in Amnesty International, which had been a small organization in the 1960s, grew by over 1,000 percent in the 1970s, with its Campaign Against Torture. Human Rights Watch began in 1978 with the desire to help Soviet bloc countries monitor their government's adherence to the Helsinki Accords, which had been signed on August 1, 1975.

Throughout American history, economic crises like the Great Depression have often led to a rise in isolationism and nativism, with a subsequent resurgence of anti-immigrant economic arguments. The old argument that "these people are coming to take our jobs" is often an effective restrictionist argument when the American public feels that work is scarce. Interestingly, then, though there were still active, vocal anti-immigrant groups in the United States during and after the recession from 1973 to 1975, the country as a whole did not normalize the kind of isolationism that was ubiquitous during the Great Depression. Refugees were just a portion of the immigrants coming in droves.

In addition to the end of the Vietnam War and the rise of the Indochinese boat people crisis, the Watergate scandal and the corruption revealed in the Nixon presidency contributed to the American public's humanitarian turn. In 1976, the country elected as president a peanut farmer from Georgia who campaigned with human rights as the backbone of his foreign policy. In his inaugural address in 1977, Jimmy Carter made clear his strategy for human rights around the world: "Because we are free, we can never be indifferent to the fate of freedom elsewhere. Our moral sense dictates a clear-cut preference for those societies which share with us an abiding respect for individual human rights." His warm language toward other countries echoed the Declaration of Human Rights in 1948, with its assertion that we are "all members of the same human family." As the descendants of the people who once huddled on other teeming shores, Carter's words implied, we could no longer ignore those who longed to breathe free. His administration's emphasis on human rights led to refugee resettlement on a different scale than our country had ever seen before.

In the late 1970s, the refugee crises in the world taxed the American government's short-term policies. Refugees continued to be paroled into the country by the executive branch in response to displacement with very few resources in place to extend the programs as needed. This made it difficult for federal and local authorities to be prepared for refugee admissions, and for the many NGOs and voluntary resettlement agencies around the country to budget and plan from year to year. Because it was impossible to predict how many refugees might be coming, organizations could not reliably hire the number of caseworkers they needed or ensure that they raised as much money as they should so that they could consistently cover their overhead costs. There was an outsized need for a federal program to permanently regulate the refugee visa allotments and create a more efficient system.

In 1979, the Carter administration proposed a bill to address refugee admissions permanently. The Refugee Act did two crucial things: First, it offered an allotment system that was ingeniously both predictable enough for federal budgets and voluntary resettlement agencies, and flexible enough to respond to humanitarian crises around the world. The act raised the admissions ceiling to fifty thousand, but also created a process through which the administration and Congress could work together to amend the yearly cap based on events and needs around the world. Refugee visa allocations could only be changed yearly during the formal Presidential Determination, in which presidential administrators meet with the House and Senate judiciary committees—a meeting which the act stipulated must occur before October 1. Other proposals had insisted on firm numbers for refugee admissions, but politicians' concern that the United States would need to adjust those numbers—thus leading to reactive, ad hoc policies again—kept those bills from passing congressional debate. The innovative solution proposed in the Refugee Act established a stable process with reliable numbers that could be flexible enough to adjust to the needs of the world.

The second critical aspect of the Refugee Act was that it updated the national definition of what it meant to be a refugee. The US finally amended its language to match the 1967 UNHCR Refugee Protocol. A refugee in the United States, as the US Citizenship and Immigration Services still defines it, is someone "located outside of the United States," of "special humanitarian concern to the United States," who "demonstrates that they were persecuted or fear persecution due to race, religion, nationality, political opinion, or membership in a particular social group," is not "firmly resettled in another country," and is "admissible to the United States." A refugee could not be someone who "ordered, incited, assisted or otherwise participated in the persecution of any person on account of race, religion, nationality, membership in a particular social group, or political opinion"—part of the vetting process would focus on keeping out the perpetrators of violence against others.

Leading up to this bill, refugees had generally been defined by large-scale persecution—hundreds or thousands of people fleeing at once. While that still generally remained the norm, there were now more opportunities for individuals or families or smaller groups of people who were still persecuted. Before, individual refugees were often famous, isolated incidents of Russian, Chinese, Cuban, or other anticommunist dissidents defecting; after the 1980 bill, women targeted for their gender, LGBTQ people, individuals whose opposition to people in power led to their persecution—all could now rightfully file to become a refugee. And the bill retained the US commitment to non-refoulement and the protection of asylum seekers from the 1951 UN Refugee Convention.

The bill passed the Senate unanimously—a feat in and of itself. In early 1980, in one of his last acts as president, Jimmy Carter signed the Refugee Act of 1980 into law. The act established the Federal Refugee Resettlement Program (FRRP) and the Office of Refugee Resettlement, housed within the Department of Health and Human Services, and strengthened the relationship the federal government had with the voluntary resettlement agencies that were now an integral part of the process. Because it allowed the US to formalize the foreign-policy aspects of refugee resettlement, officials at government agencies ranging from the Department of Defense to the State Department supported a stable FRRP.

For the first time in American history, the US established a bipartisan, internationally cooperative, public-private refugee resettlement program. It included a screening process for refugee admissions based on the early efforts in the 1950s to ensure that all accepted visa holders met the criteria for being a refugee; these vetting procedures would continue to be honed over the next few decades in response to restrictionists' rigorous standards. The admissions cap would never fully satisfy refugee advocates' desire for more assistance to those caught in humanitarian crises around the world. Yet, at its best, the program balanced the restrictionists' national security and economic concerns with liberalizers' and human rights activists' desires to admit people who were truly in need—people who had already endured the trauma of persecution and war.

TRAUMA MIGHT BE ONE OF THE FEW THINGS THAT REFUGEES SHARED in the years following the establishment of the Federal Refugee Resettlement Program. It was not just the trauma of witnessing one difficult incident, not the same as being in a car accident or seeing a single act of violence. The trauma that resettlement agencies came to expect from their clients is called "complex trauma."

Scientists have studied the impact of trauma on the brain since soldiers following World War I came back changed—then, they called it being "shell-shocked." Later other terms were used, such as post-traumatic stress. As scientists studied more about the impact of trauma on the brain, they gained knowledge about how multiple traumatic incidents affected brain development in children, how it changed thinking in adults on a neurological level.

Most refugees—if not all of them—who have lived through war and the stress of life in camps, or who spent years trying to find any safe place at all in an openly hostile world where they navigated danger, starvation, poverty, persecution, and other massive threats, have complex trauma. This causes structural change in the synapses that affect decision making, relational connections, and emotions.

Trauma can cause rage, sadness, and depression. Complex trauma magnifies those symptoms and includes others: distrust of other people, helplessness or hopelessness, a sense of isolation, intense guilt or shame, a change in your own view of yourself, memory loss, the sense that you're detached from your body or your mind, a desire to hurt yourself or others, alcoholism, suicidal thoughts. Many refugees arrived in the United States only to realize that the peace they sought was just as elusive as it ever was, that they'd brought the war with them in their minds.

THE PROGRAM THAT OFFERED NEW LIFE TO TRAUMATIZED PEOPLE was in no way perfect. There were the often-impossible tasks set before caseworkers, the mountains of paperwork in front of volunteers, the difficulties of creating new life for thousands upon thousands of people with different cultures and languages and expectations and personalities and priorities. There were all the normal bureaucratic hurdles, the unnecessary difficulties, the gap between what refugees needed and what they were provided, the uneven support refugees received from group to group, year to year, even month to month.

And yet, pulling back the lens to look at the process itself decades after the FRRP was established, it feels stunning that there was a time when a program like this was built, when it easily earned support from people on both sides of the political aisle, when it moved between state and mosque or synagogue or church. When the word "refugee" invoked compassion and admiration and a strong desire to help. When politicians standardized the process, and the vagaries of public opinion made the numbers ebb and flow to a certain extent, but refugee admissions continued no matter what happened in our fierce national debates about American identity.

Chapter 20

MU NAW

AUSTIN, TEXAS, USA, OCTOBER 2011

On the night Mu Naw realized that her marriage was over, Saw Doh had fallen asleep on the sofa waiting for his dad to come home. Saw Ku had missed dinner, had missed the kids' day entirely, which was nothing new by now. Even a few months ago, when the trouble seemed to be spiking between them, Mu Naw would have waited anxiously by the window, watching to see the car turn into the parking lot. That night, she waited beside Saw Doh. The lamp in the corner gave the room a soft glow. Her foot tapped vigorously against the wooden leg of the couch. She did not watch TV. She did not read a magazine.

Saw Ku was the only one who could drive; they had bought a used tan Honda Civic a few months before. At first, it had seemed like a marker of their achievement—the time saved no longer waiting on the bus was an incredible boon. But the car gave Saw Ku freedom that shifted something in their relationship. The waiting had become more common than she told anyone; she sat in the dimly lit room beside her sleeping son, thinking how much had changed in the last six months.

THE FIRST NIGHT HE HAD BEEN LATE, SIX MONTHS EARLIER, SHE HAD panicked. She had spent the day with Kachin friends in the apartment complex, walking together to pick the children up from their new school. The children's homework was finished—Mu Naw read over their shoulder while they worked to pick up English tips—and then they played outside while she made dinner. She set food on the table a few minutes before Saw Ku usually came home; she called his phone several times, but he did not answer. She stood at the window watching through the blinds; she tried to hide her fear from the children when they trooped in. Her mind was racing—if there had been an accident, would someone call her and tell her? Would he go to the hospital? How would she find him?

She could call one of the older men from the Karen Baptist church to see if he would drive her around to find Saw Ku, she decided. Maybe one of her new neighbors would help her watch her kids. She was trying to think where to go when she heard his key in the door.

The set of his jaw as he walked in let her know he was on the defensive. He held his guitar, the one he normally pulled out only on Sundays. After the church service, the Karen people who lived all over town always ate together; the women prepared the potluck, the older men sat and listened, and the young men played music. Mu Naw loved those evenings. She could see who Saw Ku might have been if they had not gotten married so young, if he'd had a chance to go to school, if he could laugh and hang out and just be the young man he was.

So, that first panicked evening, when he held the guitar up, she was only relieved, already forgiving him for the late arrival. She opened her mouth to ask him if he had gone to their friends' house, but he spoke first, eyes slightly shuttered, chin up: "Don't say anything. I was playing guitar with my friends and didn't hear you call. When I did hear, I decided to come home."

He made to brush past her to put his guitar away. She stepped in front of him. She pulled back the words.

"I cooked dinner while you were playing the guitar? I thought you were dead or in an accident or something!"

"What?" His expression of annoyance only further deepened their entrenched sides. "Why would you think I died?" He spat out the words. Mu Naw watched herself, heard her mother's voice come out of her mouth as she moved to the tips of her toes: "Because you were gone! For hours!"

"Yeah, working! One of us has to work!"

"And what do you think I do all day? You think I don't work?"

"You make, what, $20 a day? Maybe $40? That's not the same. I work for eight to ten hours every day to give you this," he gestured around at the apartment they both loved, with two bedrooms and clean vinyl blinds and a view of the tree outside, the apartment that was more expensive than the ones they'd had before and a step up from the first one where they had sat in the darkness and brooded. So many things had happened in the last four years and they had worked so hard to find each other again in this space, and yet some part of Mu Naw had always known that the end of their marriage would come and that it would look exactly like this.

"I work for $20 an hour as a translator. That's more money than you make an hour and, because I take your son with me wherever I go and because I have to be here with your children every day after school, I can't work more than a few hours at a time." Mu Naw could feel the words flowing out of her, too powerful and painful to stop, words that would obliterate his argument, that were maximized to wound him. "Honestly, I think you're jealous. I think you'd love translating. I think you'd love to speak English. That's the real problem—that I can speak English and you can't."

Mu Naw knew that was the moment when she pushed him too far. He was very sensitive about his lack of education, about his lack of English. He could not keep up with the pace of her knowledge and he had been—for a long time—proud of his brilliant wife. But there, in that pride, was also the source of insecurity for him and a power differential she had never used against him before.

That night, their fight was savage. Mu Naw found, to her surprise, that her mind no longer felt divided. She liked this strong side of herself—her anger made her feel powerful. That power was heady.

After that, Saw Ku stayed out more and more, playing video games and jamming on his guitar with the unmarried men their age.

SIX MONTHS AFTER THAT FIRST FIGHT, THE POWER SHE HAD FELT growing in that time burned away any concerns she felt about the conversation she knew would end their marriage. She felt calm as she watched her son sleep and tapped her foot against the wooden leg of the couch. Something had happened that day, something she vaguely felt was connected with her anger now; it was a connection she did not want to examine, wanting to focus instead on her rage against her husband.

While the girls were in school, Mu Naw and Saw Doh walked to the grocery store. Watching her son trudge through the weeds along the side of the busy road, Mu Naw remembered being not much older than him. She had run through long grass herself. She had been quiet so the junta would not find them. It was a visceral memory, more body sense than formed thought. The grass around her legs had been green and lush; the grass around her son's legs was reedy and dry. She had lifted her legs just as her son did.

She felt goose bumps on her arm despite the humid warmth of the day. Her heart raced. She grabbed her son's hand. She ran, the *flap-flap* of her sandals on the pavement when they left the grass for the parking lot underscoring her fear. She arrived at the grocery store. She was breathless and bewildered. The army was half a world away. The panic left her drained. It took longer than normal to walk home with her hands full of groceries. The handles of the plastic sacks left red welts on her palms.

She filled her mind with anger so she did not have to think about that memory. That night, she had decided to move Saw Ku into the children's room. She put Saw Ku's pillow on the bottom bunk bed, where Naw Wah usually slept, and moved Pah Poe's twin bed into their room, shoved beside the queen bed. The long sleeping space reminded her of the rice mat they used to sleep on as a family in Thailand, but she did not let herself remember their tiny hut infused with the idyllic memories of their first years as a family. She wanted to stay upset.

She let Saw Doh fall asleep on the couch, delighting in the pathetic image of a son waiting for his father to come home. She stewed beside Saw Doh for hours, determined to wait up. Eventually her foot tapping against the couch leg stilled.

The next morning, she woke on the couch with a crick in her neck and a sour taste in her mouth. Her son was gone. She stumbled to the bathroom, checking the time on the clock in the hall. It was early, still plenty of time for breakfast and getting the kids ready. Saw Ku was not in their room; the girls slept, arms spread and mouths wide. She looked in the children's room and thought for a few minutes that Saw Ku had not made it home at all, that Saw Doh had crawled into the top bunk on his own.

When she went to get dressed, however, sliding the closet door open silently to let the children sleep, she saw that Saw Ku's clothes were gone. Her heart lurched. She went to the children's closet. They were there, hanging in the closet. His pillow on the bed held the indentation of his head. He had slept in the bed she had made for him, moved his clothes in acknowledgment of the end of their marriage.

She realized the noise that woke her up was the sound of the door closing behind him as he left for the day, once again without seeing the children. She straightened her shoulders. Men left. Marriages ended. These were truths she never questioned, that she understood in the deepest parts of herself. She brushed her teeth, ran a brush through her hair, and woke the children up for school.

Chapter 21

HASNA

Jebreel's wounds healed; he had more surgeries to move flesh and muscle from his right calf to fill in his left side. When the procedures were over, he could move his body with slightly more ease. Hasna got used to his new walk, to speaking where he could hear her in his right ear, to helping him with any tasks that required two hands. His sons took him to physical therapy.

Khassem married the pretty girl from Daraa; they lived with her family because there was more room in their apartment. Yusef, Samir, and Khassem continued to work in whatever construction jobs they could find in Irbed and in small cities nearby, though the jobs were becoming scarcer as the numbers of refugees continued to surge. Rana thrived in school.

Hasna tried not to notice that the supply of gold that they had saved for emergencies was getting smaller and smaller—when would they have more of an emergency than now, with Jebreel still recovering and the war continuing to rage? Once Jebreel was better, when Malek and Laila were able to join them, they would more than make up the difference. If she needed to, Hasna would be willing to work as well, though she was not sure what job she could find. For now, she watched the children.

She made friends with some of her neighbors and sometimes they came over for coffee. Her granddaughters barely remembered their lives in Daraa and she told them stories about the house they would have grown up knowing had things turned out differently. Even to Hasna, some days those stories took on the sheen of fantasy; how ludicrous it felt to think that her family had once lived all together in a place of such harmony and peace.

The war in Syria only worsened. The battles raged, plain as day, on YouTube and Facebook—incontrovertible proof that Assad was attacking his own people.

The reality dawned on Hasna slowly. One day she realized she was no longer counting down the days until she could move back to Daraa. Another day, she argued with a neighbor that the US would never come, a position she had never held before. She wanted to hope that there was still a chance for international intervention, but she could not. The government was escalating its war on Syria's children. The talk continued with no action. No one was coming. No one cared.

BY THE TIME UNHCR OFFICIALS CALLED AGAIN, OVER A YEAR AFTER Hasna's initial interview, she had almost forgotten about the idea of resettlement. The officials made a file for Jebreel and suggested that he be made the head of the family. Hasna argued about it for a minute—after all, he had not wanted to be a refugee in the first place, and she was the one who was handling all of their paperwork—but it was easier, the official said. Finally, she acquiesced.

Yusef's file was joined with theirs since they were in the same household. True to the word of the first official she had met with, who had told her that families were prioritized together, officials reached out to Amal and Samir as well. The officials told them their interviews would be separate but their files would be linked. Khassem was not called. When Hasna asked him to apply for resettlement, he told her they would wait: His wife's family was all in Irbed. And besides—his eyes gleamed—they'd have to wait till after the baby was born. Hasna teared up and hugged him. And then she began to cry into the soft material of his T-shirt as she realized she might not even be here when this newest child of Syria was born in Jordan. Khassem chuckled at her, told her no country would ever want his stubborn father anyway, so not to worry, but she could see the tears in his eyes too.

There were more interviews and they happened with greater frequency. Hasna expected after each one to be told that they were no longer in consideration. In one interview, Yusef, Hasna, Jebreel, and Rana sat down in one room all together; another time they were put in different rooms. They answered the same questions over and over, separately and together, while the officials made notes. The questions became more specific: about their family connections and the timeline of when their family left Syria and what had happened when the missile struck.

As the official asked her about the loss of her house, Hasna felt, for the first time, that she was really a refugee. Somehow the balance of power shifted—as each interview passed, she realized she wanted to be resettled somewhere. She had heard the reports from friends whose family members had gone and brought them over later. Hasna tried to imagine that life and found she could not; she had no idea what American houses looked like. She always pictured some version of her own house in Daraa. But even if they had to live in trees or in holes in the ground, if her children could be with her, could have access to education, if Jebreel could have good health care, if they could work together, without the threat of hostility and with the possibility of a life ahead of them, perhaps she could envision this new future. The pressure in Jordan mounted every day and Hasna worried, in her moments of utter honesty, that life in a camp was only a year or two away.

And then, after several interviews in a row, there would be nothing again for a while. Hasna would shove her daydreams about the United States or Norway or Canada to the back of her mind and try to imagine a future here in Jordan again. It would be better to be closer to Laila and Malek, anyway. Hasna rarely stopped thinking about them; five times a day, their names were the first she uttered in her personal prayer time.

Laila and Malek continued calling, sending word through relatives, and trying to cross into Jordan at checkpoint after checkpoint. It became clear that Malek's name was on some sort of blacklist. Laila could have passed by without him at first, but she refused to leave him. And with each time they tried to leave, her chances narrowed. One time they put Hamad and Laila at the front of a group of people, with Malek standing back in the middle, and the guards stopped Laila first, comparing her ID with their computer readout. Laila was now blacklisted too. There was nothing they could do but keep trying. They gave up their scruples about crossing the border legally as the war got more desperate, but by then all the open places along the border into Jordan were closed. Hasna always kept her phone on, even at night. Eventually, the calls stopped for a long time.

Finally, after several months of silence, Laila got through late in the night. Her voice came in and out but Hasna understood two things: They had survived two more missile attacks and Laila was pregnant again. And then there was nothing. Hasna sank into the depression she had managed to hold at bay for years. Every day, she scoured her phone, afraid that in the pictures of bloody, dust-covered babies or bodies lined up in a row, she would see their faces.

Her depression spread to Jebreel. He had worked every day of his life since he was a little boy. To go to physical therapy while his sons struggled to support the family, to spend the day at home thinking of Laila and not to be able to help—Hasna could hardly live with him some days. Before, the house had been her territory while he was gone. Now, he criticized everything she did, commented on the times she took breaks from cooking. For several months, they had managed to live in a state of gratefulness that he was alive, to move past the fight that had exploded the last time she saw him before the missile hit their house. But as days and weeks without word from Laila wore away at their patience, their apartment became a crucible.

HASNA PIECED TOGETHER SHREDS OF NEWS FROM NEIGHBORS, THE truth and her imagination two sides of a terrible coin. The second attack Malek and Laila survived occurred at Malek's sister's house, in the months when the government had begun using barrel bombs on its people in Daraa. They would fill barrels with nails and explosives and launch them from helicopters—cheap explosives designed to cause maximum civilian damage. This barrel bomb hit the large, full gas tank on the roof of Malek's sister's house, exploding the top floor outright. Malek was temporarily paralyzed, unable to walk for a few weeks, from fear. As soon as he was able, they moved to other relatives' houses in villages outside Daraa, hoping that staying out of the city itself might be safer.

The third explosion was the same kind of surface-to-surface missile that had destroyed Hasna's house. They were now not sure whether the weapons were from the government or other sources. In addition to the Free Syria Army begun in Daraa, Al-Nusra, al-Qaeda, and ISIS all joined with or against other militia groups, as the country dissolved. Syrian citizens were targeted on every front. Malek, whose faith was the most important thing in his life, who had a heightened sense of right and wrong, found each of the groups suspect. He wanted to help the people, not usher in a new government loyal to Saudi Arabia, or Russia, or the United States, and certainly not ISIS or al-Qaeda. All he and Laila wanted was a place they could live in peace.

For a while, they settled in the village of Nassib, on the border between Syria and Jordan, thinking that being close to the border might give them opportunities to get through somehow. Also, because Nassib was along one of the main routes for refugees escaping the country—and thus the focus of international attention—there was less violence. At least for a while.

It was in that brief respite of peace that Laila got pregnant and told her mother in one of the few calls that made it into Jordan. Then the government began bombing Nassib. They barely made it out alive. That was the fourth bombing they survived.

The next several months were lost in chaos and smoke. They hid in relatives' houses, in shelled-out buildings. They made it back to the hospital in Nassib for Laila to give birth; the birth was complicated by her stress and she had to have a C-section. Five days later, with Laila still bleeding from her incision, the nurses came and evacuated the hospital, moments before it was destroyed by another bomb. Her wound seeped blood for days. She tried to call her mother but could not get through. It was weeks before Hasna knew the name of her newest grandson: Tawfiq.

Tawfiq was a year old when the battle for Nassib began in earnest; anti-government forces, armed with weapons from outside countries, pushed back vehemently. The Syrian government, together with Russia and Iran, fought back. Syrian citizens died at everyone's hands.

MALEK DIED IN THE FIFTH EXPLOSION. ONE DAY, IN THE APARTMENT in Irbed, Hasna opened Facebook and saw her son-in-law's face on her Facebook feed, with his birth and death dates.

A hole ripped open inside Hasna that would never be closed. Obsessively, she called Laila's phone—over and over. Nothing.

She reached out over Facebook and WhatsApp to friends of friends, asking everyone she could think of: "Have you seen my daughter? Do you know where she is? Where is Laila?"

Someone thought she had seen her and her two children with a group of refugee women trying to get to Jordan. Would she be able to make it out now that Malek was not with her? Hasna waited in eager expectation for the call from Laila that she had crossed the border, that she was in Zataari camp or at the Jaber border crossing, that she and the children were safe. She could not bear to think of the possibility that Laila and the boys had died. She dreamed of Malek at night, her tears anointing his dead brow, her hand holding his square jaw, his beard rough on her palms. She wept out apologies—she had sworn to him before he left that she would keep Laila safe. She should have tried harder, should have fought to keep Laila in Jordan. In her dreams, sometimes he was living and he had decided not to return to Syria after all, they were living next door to Amal and Samir, Laila was annoyed at her mother's repeated questions, and Hasna's heart rose in hope that dissipated the moment she awoke.

She no longer kept up the pretense of normalcy. She fed her family and swept the floors, but she did not keep coffee ready for guests, did not visit neighbors, did nothing but the most basic tasks. Every fiber of her being leaned toward her daughter, lost and alone somewhere in Syria. Messages came from friends of friends—neighbors ran into Laila somewhere outside Damascus and, through the long grapevine set up now for people to communicate with one another, passed along her greetings and her love to her mother. There was no way to know whether the news was accurate or old, whether she was really alive or if they were confused. Hasna clung to each scrap of information, repeated it to the family again and again. She woke up in the middle of the night and sat up, sure she could sense something happening to Laila.

She and Jebreel stopped bickering. Trauma and grief sometimes emptied their love for each other, sometimes filled it, like water in Lake Muzayrib dropping with drought or rising with rain.

For the most agonizing year of Hasna's life, Laila was a ghost.

THE RESETTLEMENT PROCESS CONTINUED, INTENSIVE APPOINTMENTS spread out over two years. At each appointment, they were given a different colored piece of paper to bring with them for the next appointment, so that they could easily be coded by the UNHCR workers for whichever point in the process was next. All of the appointments were in Irbed. They met with different UNHCR officials, dressed in professional Western clothes that were also appropriate for the climate—short-sleeved dress shirts and trousers, pencil skirts without hose, ballet flats instead of heels. As the meetings wore on, Hasna found herself studying the shoes of the Western women who interviewed her—if by some miracle they ended up being accepted to resettle in a Western country, she would keep her modest clothes and hijab, but she would like to have shoes that fit in with the culture. Their shoes were always practical and walkable. She bought a pair of black ballet flats one day at the market in Irbed.

The thoroughness of the interviews was almost eerie. They were clearly building a database of people who had fled Daraa. By the third visit, they asked Jebreel about things his cousins had done years ago that he had forgotten about. Jebreel's favorite question, which he repeated as a joke to anyone he talked to, was one asked by a UNHCR worker at the end: "What did your mother think when she had you, her only son, and then only had daughters after that?"

"I don't know, you'll have to go to the graveyard to ask her!" he had cackled, his infectious grin getting a smile even out of the young man with sandy blond hair whose professional demeanor never wavered. Jebreel was proud of himself for coming up with the quip in the moment. He laughed every time he told the story; Hasna stopped thinking it was funny long before he did.

It was becoming clear that the United States was the country toward which they were headed. If they passed these last UN interviews, they would be asked to go to two orientations on a US military base outside town. The woman was speaking through a translator, a young Jordanian woman who did not wear hijab and whose slicked ponytail pulled at her forehead. As they scraped back their chairs to indicate the interview was over, Hasna asked the question she had asked in every interview: "If we receive resettlement, no matter what, our children and grandchildren will be able to come?"

The US immigration official nodded and the translator watched her before responding, her tone lighter: "Yes, if they are already in the refugee process, your children and grandchildren will be in line behind you. It should take six months or so for most of them to join you. It could be as long as seven or eight months, but the US prides itself on our Family Reunification Program. You can rest assured that you are doing the best thing for your whole family. This is a once in a lifetime opportunity for all of you to have jobs and health care and a safe place to live. That's what matters most: You will all be safe. And you will all be free."

ONE AFTERNOON, HASNA ABSENTLY ANSWERED A CALL FROM A NUM-ber that she did not recognize and heard Laila's voice. The call was clearer than it had ever been from Syria.

Laila was in Turkey. Someday she would tell her mother how they had arrived, Laila said. They were out. But they were not safe. She had a place to sleep for a few days and then she would call Hasna to tell her more, to figure out a plan. After a day of not hearing from her, Hasna tried to call the number back and it did not work.

Two weeks passed with Hasna and the family seesawing between exuberance that Laila was alive and panic that something new and horrible had occurred.

THEY WERE SENT TO A US MILITARY BASE IN JORDAN A FEW HOURS away; they had taken a nice bus with others being considered for resettlement. They had interviews—together and separately—in a warehouselike building. Hasna noted with appreciation that the bus trips were provided, and the meals

were free and delicious. These seemed good omens for the resettlement process. They were searched before getting on the bus, at a checkpoint, after
leaving the bus, and before entering the building, then given lockers where
they could store their things for the day.

At one point, the men and women were separated and Hasna went with
Rana and some other women to a room where women officers asked them
probing questions in a group. Hasna felt uncomfortable; the questions seemed
designed by their very nature to get a rise out of the women. She quieted the
lioness in her. She understood she was unknown to them, that they only meant
to protect their own citizens.

"Are you intending to go to the United States to sell yourself as a sex
worker?" The translator stumbled a bit over the question that the woman officer asked unblinkingly. They were looking at Rana; Rana looked at her mother.
Hasna held her hand out, telling Rana she should respond; she smiled at her
daughter so she would know this was fine, that it was all part of the process.

"No, of course not!"

"You are an unmarried woman, but have you ever had sex?"

"No!" Rana's voice squeaked and her eyebrows shot up.

"Do you intend to go to the United States in order to participate in any
way in any activity that involves sex trafficking?" The translator's phrase felt
awkward and it took Rana a minute to understand.

"No, I just want to get married someday, but that's it! I have to go to
school first!"

Rana's response got a nervous titter out of a few of the women around
them.

The officer turned to Hasna. "And do you plan to sell your daughter to
anyone in the United States or participate yourself in any sex trafficking
activity?"

"Absolutely not." Hasna kept her face neutral and her tone level to show
Rana that she was not afraid or upset.

The officer moved on, asking similar questions of the women sitting
next to Hasna. Rana grabbed her hand and held it as the group interroga-
tion wore on.

FIFTEEN DAYS AFTER THEIR LAST PHONE CALL, WHILE SHE WAS WALK-
ing home from dropping Rana off at school, Hasna's phone started pinging.
She read the first few messages from Laila, typed out over WhatsApp from a
new Turkish number. After seven or eight messages, she stopped walking and
stood with her back against a wall, her face shaded by the awning of a store that
sold vegetables.

Ping after ping, Laila told her story in short bursts.

> Hello, my mother. How are you? I pray that you are well, that
> Allah is blessing you and my family in Jordan.

> There are many things to tell you and I can only say a few.

> Malek died.

> After, we left Daraa and we got into an area that belonged to the
> government.

> We passed many checkpoints. We paid a smuggler and he used
> bribes to get us through.

> We waited for a full day until the sun went down, and then many
> people got into big Honda trucks.

> We were on top of each other in the back.

> Hamad threw up all over me.

> Tawfiq peed, and the pee was all over me too, and it made me
> colder than I had been. The stench was unbelievable.

> The road was on rocks and it bounced dangerously.

> A pregnant woman miscarried because of how bad the ride was.

> We spent three days on that truck.

> We entered an area way up north and ISIS grabbed us.

> They hit the men.

ISIS kept me with them for seven days.

I left there in a really, really hard way. I will not talk about it.

We found a Bedouin smuggler.

I paid him almost all of my money and we walked through the desert for two days. We were trying to get from that territory to the one right next to it that was controlled by the Free Syria Army.

The bombing was going on top of us. There were airplanes going through, bombing the area where we were headed.

Before the war, it would have taken us a few minutes to drive this distance, but now, to get from Aleppo to Azaz took two days of hard walking.

On the second day, we arrived at the place held by the Free Syria Army. We were so happy; we knew we had made it.

But when we got close, we realized the Free Syria Army thought perhaps we were from ISIS or from the government forces. They could not see us well enough to tell that it was mostly women and children, we thought. That is why they shot at us.

Hamad was on my shoulders and Tawfiq was tied to my belly. I had carried them on my body all of those days in the desert. I also carried our bag with everything in it on my back.

When the soldiers started shooting at us, I threw myself on the ground. I put the children underneath me and I crawled until I found a hole in the ground.

Three people who were with me died that day.

We waited until the sun went down. And then we had to go back the way we came, back through the desert for two days to Aleppo. Each step was agony.

We stayed in a deserted house for two days until another group of people came. They were from a village outside of Daraa. We knew many of the same people.

The group from Daraa told us that the road we had taken was wrong, that what we thought was the Free Syria Army was really ISIS. Then we were glad that we had not made it through, though we were sad for the three people who died.

That group of people had better information than we had from the Bedouin smuggler, so we joined with them. I was sad I paid so much money to the Bedouin smuggler for nothing.

We kept going again, back for two days through the desert, until we got to Azaz. I carried my children and my bag. I could not feel my feet, I could not feel my back.

When we got to Azaz, my pain was so serious, I went to the hospital.

I left my children with the new friends who had known the right route.

While we were on our way to the city, Azaz had been hit by clusterbombs.

I limped into the hospital, but it was already full.

I uncovered the face of one of the bodies with a sheet over it.

It was a man whose face had been cut in half.

I put the sheet back.

The room was full of little children whose hands were cut off.

I do not know what happened—before I came into the hospital, I could barely walk. My body felt like it was coming apart with the pain.

But when I saw those children, covered in blood, with their arms ripped off, some crying for their parents, some completely silent, I forgot all about my body.

I helped. I washed their faces and helped the nurses tie tourniquets. I stayed as long as I could, and then I left.

No one was able to treat me.

I was still in pain, but my children were safe.

I walked back to the hotel. My clothes were covered in the blood of dozens of children. I took a shower, and then I went out again and bought food for my boys. Their hands were still on their bodies; they were still alive. I kissed them and then I slept.

The pain stayed with me, but I did not want my boys to end up like those children.

Two days later, we left with the family from Daraa to go to Afrin, north of Azaz.

We were driving in two different minivans, going as quickly as we could so we would not be caught.

A heat missile came from nowhere and destroyed the minivan right behind us.

In that minivan, the family from Daraa had been all together. They were the ones who had saved us and told us how to get out. With no warning, all of them were killed by that missile.

We opened the doors and jumped out of our minivan. We got out just in time.

We were a few yards away when the next missile hit our minivan. I could feel the heat when it landed.

We walked to Afrin, but Afrin was not safe.

A few days later, we left and walked to Idlib. It took many days to walk a short distance.

We found a smuggler who seemed kind and who would work with us—by then, we were almost out of money and we had no way to get more.

We stayed in a small village outside of Idlib and we slept during the day because we were going to leave at night.

We were dying from how cold it was.

The Turks were using flares to see if any Syrian refugees were trying to cross the border. When we crossed, the Turkish police grabbed us, but we hit them and ran away.

I walked in Turkey for a long time. Finally, I was able to speak with Yusef's friend who was waiting for us.

That friend came and took us to a house, where I have been for fifteen days.

If you ask me how many people are in this house, I cannot tell you. For fifteen days, I have wanted to do nothing but sleep.

Now I am lying here in bed, texting you.

I need help, Mama. I need you to come, or Yusef to come, or someone.

I cannot do this alone.

THEY ALL KNEW THE ANSWER WAS FOR YUSEF TO GO. JEBREEL COULD not help because of his injuries, and Amal had to take care of her children. Khassem jumped in to say he would go, too, but his mother told him to stop being ridiculous—their new daughter needed him. His young wife shot Hasna a grateful look.

She bought new clothes for Laila and the boys, guessing by the sizes of Amal's daughters at what might best fit her grandsons. Laila sent pictures over WhatsApp and Hasna stared at the pictures for hours, reintroducing herself to Hamad's features, scouring Tawfiq's for some familiar glimpse of his father or mother or brother. Did they look sad? Were they happy? Did they eat? There were too many questions to ask Laila all day so Hasna sent them with Yusef—make sure they have enough vegetables. Make sure they do not forget us. Tell her that, if Allah wills it, we will find a safe home for all of us soon.

It was agony to send Yusef away. As she watched his bus pull out, Hasna was split in two. She would not be whole again until her children were under her roof. She knew then, even before it became official, that they would accept resettlement if it was offered because it was the only option she could see that ended with her children together. Better to be replanted in strange soil than to die uprooted in the desert.

DAYS LATER, HASNA RECEIVED A CALL FROM A US IMMIGRATION OFFI-cial. Her hands shook while she steeped her tea, tapping the spoon against the cup in this last second before she knew the full extent of how her life would change.

They would be going to a place called Austin, Texas. She had no idea what that meant, whether it was a good city, if there would be jobs enough for all of them.

A few weeks later, US State Department officials gathered a dozen families who would be traveling to different parts of the US at the same time in a nondescript conference room on the military base and told them what to expect. Hasna understood that Jebreel would have access to the medical care he needed as well as rehabilitation. She would have to work, at least until her sons arrived. She could do anything for six months, she told herself, even working at a job for the first time in her life. Their apartment would not be as nice as they were expecting; whatever they had seen in movies or on the internet was not likely to take place. They were not going to have a lot of money, at least not at first, and there were poor places in the United States as there were in every country. There would be many kind people who would help them there, people who would give them furniture, teach them English, help them take the buses and go to the doctor. There would also be people who would not welcome them, who would be rude or even hostile to the women wearing hijabs. Here the translator's voice lowered a bit, taking on a compassionate tone—things had been changing in the US for the last several months.

Hostility was something that Hasna expected. She read the news, heard the reports from her friends and neighbors about their relatives all over the world. She understood that Muslim women in hijabs were not always welcomed in the West. She could handle it, she told herself. They would be fine.

After years of being in limbo, there was suddenly no more time: they had a week to pack everything up and leave. Hasna's first thought was of the six large gas canisters for the oven she had just refilled, now wasted money. All of their furniture—the new beds, the couches, the pillows, the table—everything she bought to return to her home in Daraa had to be sold. They gave the TV to Amal and divided up what furniture Khassem and Amal wanted. The rest they sold in a rush to their neighbors. Hasna made back a fraction of what they had spent on the household. She looked at the meager lira that they would exchange for American dollars and hoped it would be enough for them to buy some more furniture in their new apartment.

The week passed faster than she could have imagined. Noor and Maria clung to Hasna and she could not bear to put them down. She adjusted Maria's thin, blond pigtails, which had a tendency to fall down as she ran. Noor's legs had grown long and thin. She kissed the fuzzy top of Khassem's daughter's head. The thought of leaving her grandchildren until they could join her in Austin left her breathless with grief. And she thought, too, of Hamad, who was no longer the baby she had known so well, and of Tawfiq, whom she had only seen in pictures, and wept, wondering that she had any tears left. How could she leave not knowing that Laila and Yusef were already on their way? But then, how could she stay if by going she could ensure they would all be together again?

She would anchor them. She would go ahead with Jebreel and Rana so her children could find their way out of war. It was what any mother would do. Her eyes were so swollen she could barely see out of them as they headed to the airport, the good-byes gutting her. She gulped back sobs as she took the slip of paper that would bring them all a new life and boarded the airplane that took her away from everything she had ever loved.

PART 3

Chapter 22

MU NAW

AUSTIN, TEXAS, USA,
AUGUST 2014, JANUARY 2015

After the fight when he moved rooms, Saw Ku slept with his son for a few nights, and then they made up. Their marriage revived for weeks. Then they had another fight and Saw Ku moved into the children's room again. Pah Poe, whose face was most like Saw Ku's, shuttered her eyes like he did when she came home to find her bed shoved into her mother's room again. Many days, Mu Naw felt a clawing sense of grief that her children, who came from so much love, should feel the same sort of disruptive stress that she had experienced for so many years, but what could she do? Born in war, raised in strife, she had only a vague sense that there was more to life than this constant turmoil.

While her marriage ended and began again in a dizzying cycle, her mother began calling to ask Mu Naw for more money. She was sick, she said, but she was vague about the symptoms and Mu Naw couldn't tell if her mother was trying to keep her from worrying or perhaps just needed the money for other things. They wired a few hundred dollars, leaving their lights off and eating mostly packaged noodles to make up the difference. She and the other women in the apartments commiserated with one another—their family members assumed because they lived in insulated apartments and drove cars that they had endless amounts of money to spare. Back in the camps, their relatives could not fathom how difficult it was to make ends meet in this new place.

Mu Naw began to ask her American friends to help her find a new job.

Someone heard that a church preschool was hiring a teacher's assistant in the two-year-old classroom; she got the job on the day they interviewed. She could take Saw Doh with her and still be home in time to get the girls from school. That meant that she could work as a translator on Mondays for the adult ESL class and Wednesdays for the weaving cooperative and still have Friday mornings at home to clean and spend time with Saw Doh.

She had thought that the extra paycheck might stabilize her marriage. But any peace they found never lasted longer than a few months. Two years passed that way, until Saw Doh was finally old enough for kindergarten and Mu Naw decided to find a full-time job.

MU NAW PULLED INTO THE PARKING LOT FOR THE JOB INTERVIEW AT the fair-trade jewelry company. She smoothed her shirt down—the chiffon-like fabric, black with white polka dots, skimmed her torso. The hem of the black pants artfully cropped just above her ankles. Her white friends helped her pick the outfit out at the outlet mall; she kept the tags on till that morning, waiting until she had walked the children to their school bus to change into her new clothes. Everything—underwear, tank top, ballet shoes, lipstick, earrings—all of it was new. When she turned her head, she caught a whiff of citrus.

The interview felt surreal. It was as if she were watching an American version of herself she had not known existed. It was that version of Mu Naw who pushed open the heavy door and said: "I am here to meet with Madelyn," that Mu Naw who stretched into their conversation brilliantly, who was funny and charming to a stranger in English, who deftly steered the conversation around her language difficulties, who casually but kindly thanked Madelyn when the interview was over. And later that evening, when they called to offer her the job, the American version of herself was elated.

Mu Naw had never felt the difference between her past and her present as acutely as she did that night. She made an enormous pan of vegetable noodles for dinner to celebrate. When he got home and she told him the news, Saw Ku wrapped her in a hug. She reveled in the pride in his eyes. And yet, a niggling part of her worried that the girl in the hand-woven skirt that she had been, the one who had loved Saw Ku so obsessively, was now just a part of her past. Perhaps this brief warming between them actually accentuated the intractable battle lines they had drawn in the last few years. Perhaps they were too far apart to ever find lasting peace together.

THE EASY CONFIDENCE THAT PROPELLED HER THROUGH HER INTERVIEW did not return on Mu Naw's first day of work. She had tried on everything in her closet several times, hoping to achieve the effortlessly fashionable, casual but neat vibe she had glimpsed on the workers she would be sharing an office space with—leather earrings swinging, hair pulled up in topknots, tennis shoes combined with skirts, long paper beads layered with metallic chains. She knew as soon as she walked in that her outfit—a fitted green jersey top and jeans with the same black ballet flats she had worn before—was wrong. Standing beside Madelyn, whose white-blond hair was hanging almost to her waist, Mu Naw felt more like a child than she had in years. She strode through the large airy room with wooden tables in the center, metal shelves all the way to the ceilings, workstations set up and conversations taking place in a low hum around her. Everyone held coffee in their hands. Mu Naw did not like coffee.

"You'll work here. Jennifer, this is Mu Naw. This is Jennifer. She'll be showing you around." Mu Naw accepted Jennifer's handshake, trying to match her warm smile. Madelyn led Mu Naw to an empty workstation at a light wood table, explaining the inventory. "Uganda is over there, India's on that side, and this is where we're keeping Vietnam for now." Mu Naw could make no sense of these instructions. She concentrated on looking like she was listening, turning her head toward wherever Madelyn was pointing. She pulled her jersey shirt down, tugging on it a bit.

They walked through the entire second floor—the large open offices with four to five desks each. Madelyn pointed at one of the wall-size bulletin boards and said, "This is the inspiration board for the spring and summer 2016 collection. We're calling it 'Wanderlust.'" The board held curated photos: a cliff face with layers of sediment in corals and tans, tassels in various colors, the edges of a camel saddle, a collection of curlicued baskets, one gray minaret against a setting sun, and—to Mu Naw's surprise—a Karen woman walking with a gray-and-fuchsia bag slung over her shoulder up a path that looked as if it could have been on any of the hills that Mu Naw had lived on at any point in her life. She could have been that woman. But she was not.

Mu Naw wondered whether she should say something to Madelyn, point out that *her* people were on their inspiration board. She decided not to. They walked on. By the time Mu Naw returned to the workstation, she was thoroughly confused about the honeycombed office. She had seen a bathroom on their tour but had no idea where to find it now. Madelyn left after a few minutes. Mu Naw smiled and nodded, but she was retreating into herself. She did not belong in this office full of competent women.

Jennifer's eyes crinkled slightly when she asked, "How are you feeling?" She put her hand for a moment at the top of Mu Naw's arm and then withdrew it. "It can feel a little overwhelming. I felt like they'd made a mistake when they hired me because I didn't have any shipping experience."

Mu Naw's eyes widened. "*You* felt like they'd made a mistake?"

Jennifer laughed. "Yes, but that feeling goes away fast. This job isn't difficult, you just need to be ready to move quickly. In August, things are sort of slow, but by November and December, we're moving all day. It's fun, though. We have a great group in here. I'm the shift manager, so if you have any questions, you can just ask me. I thought you could shadow me this week and I'll show you everything that you need, and then next week you can start working on your own. Does that sound good to you?"

Mu Naw understood every word. Jennifer was looking at her kindly, without the condescension Mu Naw had expected, and Mu Naw smiled back without hesitation. Jennifer grabbed Mu Naw's stool and brought it over to her own table.

FIVE MONTHS LATER, MU NAW RODE WITH JENNIFER AND SOME OTHER women who worked in shipping to the annual all-hands meeting at a hotel conference room in downtown Austin. They met in the parking lot of the office early in the morning, went through a local coffee drive-thru. Mu Naw walked into the conference with her friends, chai latte in hand, and looked around with interest.

Women from all over the country filled the spacious room. They wore the fair-trade jewelry their company made, or the scarves and hats they sold, made out of knitted alpaca yarn. Mu Naw smiled in response to a joke one of the women made, pulled gently on her layered artillery bead necklace, sipped her latte, and settled in to listen to the day full of conference speakers.

The all-hands conference was an opportunity for this company's representatives who sold the fair-trade jewelry in home shows and at special events to meet one another, get training in the latest business practices, learn more about the artisan groups that made their products, and see the spring collection. Mu Naw noticed the way that some of the women watched each other, tugging at their own clothes, eyeing their neighbors' dresses and jewelry combinations rather than listening as the first speaker began, and felt a surge of gratefulness. She loved Jennifer and her colleagues and the camaraderie they had developed in her office. That feeling that someone had made a mistake in hiring her had driven her to prove they had not; by the end of the Christmas shipping season, Mu Naw not only kept up with her coworkers, she was faster than a few of them. She was good at her job. She belonged here.

During the afternoon session, the founder of the company stood up to introduce their speakers for the day, the leaders of the artisan groups whose products they would sell. The three women—one from Vietnam, one from Guatemala, and one from Uganda—sat on the stage on a soft couch with tasseled cushions. Beside them, the white company founder curled up in a small wingback chair. She said they would show the videos of the artisan groups before beginning their discussions. As the first video began to play and the Guatemalan woman spoke, the English translation in white letters at the bottom of the screen, Mu Naw moved to the edge of her chair. She breathed more quickly; her shoulders tensed.

Their videos told Mu Naw's story.

When the camera followed the Guatemalan woman up the path through the jungle to the village, Mu Naw breathed in the dank jungle air, felt the slick stalks of grass she had to push out of the way to walk, felt the slight give of the ground beneath her sandaled feet as each step rose up the mountain. Mu Naw had once been one of those sun-drenched babies, tied to her mother's back as her mother wove, loom looped to pillars on the outside of a wooden hut. Mu Naw knew instinctively that these huts were built so that the breeze through the trees would cool their homes, so that the fields nearby would get the best of the daylit hours.

When the camera stayed behind the Vietnamese woman moving through rice fields, cool water swooshed around Mu Naw's legs, thick rubber boots kept her feet oddly dry. Her hand felt the ribbed, rough edges of the bone on the lowing water buffalo the woman greeted as she might an old friend. When the camera entered the artisan studio, Mu Naw could feel how the stone walls chilled the room, how the sculpted bone fit snugly into the curve of her hand, how the knife in her other hand pushed into and carved the bone into intricate shapes that she had learned from her mother and her grandmother and all of the mothers before them.

When the camera captured the smile of the Ugandan woman—an unmitigated grin—pure joy lifted inside Mu Naw. Here in this Ugandan village, Mu Naw was the mother of these children who danced for the camera, running from every house with long arms and legs to join the song, to perform a series of moves they had been practicing for weeks. And she stood in the door of her new home, shyly pleased, as the women around her praised her and explained that women do not buy homes in this village, but this one had. This woman—the owner of this home, this model of stability and goodness and grace—stood like a queen among them. She had worked and saved her family with the strength of her hands.

When the lights came up, Mu Naw felt herself return to her body and knew—finally, utterly—who she was. She was neither the well-heeled American women around her nor the artisans on the screen, not the girl dressed in citrus-scented mall clothes or the girl in the handmade skirt—she was all of those things.

She had felt power before when she was angry at Saw Ku, but now she realized it was power of a cheap sort. The power of women who knew themselves, no matter where they were from, was rich, deep, sacred. It was available to women in villages all over the world, but she had come to the United States to find it. Mu Naw, through luck and providence, had been given the chance to receive the gifts of her sisters from all over the world, and to send those hand-made products out to people who wore their artistry with pride. She could never have asked for a more perfect job, one that gave her both a good living and a sense of purpose. She could not believe she was here, doing this, in this life.

It was only when Jennifer put her hand on her shoulder and asked her if she was all right that Mu Naw realized she had been crying.

Chapter 23

US REFUGEE RESETTLEMENT, 1980–2006

The Federal Refugee Resettlement Program in 1980 finally stabilized the high-stakes, political back-and-forth that had defined American resettlement policies up to that point. The next five presidents—Ronald Reagan, George H. W. Bush, Bill Clinton, George W. Bush, and Barack Obama—held drastically different views on almost every issue: they were certainly not aligned on immigration policies, or the scope and responsibility of the US to victims of humanitarian crises. And yet, under all of their administrations, refugee resettlement was viewed as a vital program that ensured national security, provided economic stability, and fulfilled America's humanitarian duties to the world. Those decades were not without turning points or shifts, but even the trickiest foreign policy situations—including the first attack on US soil since Pearl Harbor—did little more than cause the presidential administrations and Congress to pause the program for a handful of weeks, adjust the cap of refugees being accepted for resettlement, or turn American attention away from some regions to others.

In fact, it might be the very steadiness of the program itself in the first decades of its existence that eventually led to its greatest threat. When resettlement was culturally acceptable, broadly supported, and reasonably well funded, there was no need for educational campaigns or PR blitzes. When every new president could rely on a relatively smooth transition of this federal program and a secure partnership with nongovernment partners, it would draw less attention than other, more controversial agencies or policies. Immigration debates raged on, but people on both sides of the political aisle brought up refugees, with their now-separate admissions process, only occasionally.

If and how the nation would respond to refugee crises—once core questions of an American identity in flux—were no longer subjects of intense national debate. For thirty-five years, the questions were less about *if* or *how* than how many.

THE GENOCIDE CONVENTION, RATIFIED BY THE UNITED NATIONS IN 1948, was signed by the United States only in 1988. War-weary politicians following World War II and then the Vietnam War felt reluctant to commit US troops to any foreign conflicts even for the clearest humanitarian violations. Another reason for the delay was that many lawmakers felt that the language of the Genocide Convention indicted the United States in its historical policies against American Indians and African slaves. By signing the Genocide Convention, the United States joined other nations in pledging to do its part through intervention, aid, and resettlement when another government's actions against its people met the international legal definition of genocide. The resulting decades would be full of international debates about whether the persecution and slaughter of innocent civilians was actually genocide—and therefore required international involvement—or regrettable acts of war, tragic but not necessarily the responsibility of outside countries.

Worldwide, the number of acts of genocide increased at an alarming global rate after the 1975 Cambodian massacres, leading many historians to refer to the twentieth century as the "Age of Genocide." The Iraq genocide against Kurds in 1987, the Bosnian genocide in 1992, the Rwandan genocide in 1994, the Sudanese genocide in 2003, as well as conflicts in El Salvador, Peru, Sudan, Sierra Leone, Yemen, Liberia, Senegal, Georgia, Yugoslavia, Algeria, Tajikistan, Afghanistan, Burundi, the Congo, Cambodia, Nepal, Albania, Guinea-Bissau, and the continuing civil war in Myanmar, all created displaced populations in need of aid.

As had always been the case, US foreign policy interests significantly affected the measure of its response. The fall of the Berlin Wall in 1989, the breakup of the Soviet Union, and the first Gulf War in 1991 moved American interest away from Cold War systems of power. The expansion of the definition of "refugee" beyond "anticommunist" to displaced people fleeing targeted persecution—epitomized by the Vietnamese refugees—was an important rhetorical and cultural move. But the country intervened or not, offered resettlement or not, based more on how a conflict affected US oil supplies, or the depths of the American public's compassion fatigue, than on the actual need itself.

AND YET, ONE OF THE ASPECTS OF AMERICAN IDENTITY THAT POLITI-
cians banked on in those years was a shared sense of being the kind of nation that did its part to help refugees. Lawmakers' lofty language—often drawn from the postwar playbook—showed that, Republican or Democrat, politicians during the first decades of the program assumed a baseline of public support for refugee resettlement across the country. The United States continued to view itself as a country that defended the defenseless and welcomed the displaced.

In his last address to the nation on January 11, 1989, the image President Reagan picked to describe what it was like to lead the country through the 1980s came from efforts to resettle the Indochinese boat people. He called it "a small story about a big ship, and a refugee, and a sailor." A sailor on the carrier *Midway*, patrolling the South China Sea, "spied on the horizon a leaky little boat. And crammed inside were refugees from Indochina hoping to get to America." A crew went out from the *Midway* to rescue them. As Reagan told it, "As the refugees made their way through the choppy seas, one spied the sailor on deck, and stood up, and called out to him. He yelled, 'Hello, American sailor. Hello, freedom man.'" That image stayed with the president when he read it in a letter written by the sailor to the White House, because "that's what it was to be an American in the 1980s. We stood, again, for freedom. I know we always have, but in the past few years the world again—and in a way, we ourselves—rediscovered it."

President George H. W. Bush echoed the postwar assertions that the country could do hard things if they were right, what Truman called "our plain duty" to "join with other nations in solving this tragic problem." In a

September 11, 1990, address to a joint session of Congress, President Bush's tragic problem was a growing crisis in the Persian Gulf that he argued would require a steady hand and strong leadership in moving toward what he famously referred to as "a new world order." In the speech, he recognized that "the material cost of our leadership can be steep," but that there were some things a country couldn't run away from: "We are prepared to do our share and more to help carry that load." At the same time, the US would not enter the crisis alone, and instead "insist that others do their share as well. The response of most of our friends and allies has been good." The plain duty of the United States, joined by several allied countries, "extends to the neediest victims of this conflict—those refugees." Bush invoked the shared memories of a reluctant country later glad it assisted victims of the Holocaust as he pushed to move forward in "this purely humanitarian effort."

In 1999, President Bill Clinton relied on the international Declaration of Human Rights when he addressed US and NATO troops bound for Kosovo. It had only been a handful of years since the disastrous crises in Bosnia and Rwanda, when the United States and other NATO countries debated whether what was occurring was genocide—committing troops to fulfill the 1948 Genocide Convention—or vague "crimes against humanity," while civilians died in horrific ways. When ethnic cleansing exploded in Kosovo, Clinton and other world leaders responded with more fervor than they had in those earlier crises. In Clinton's remarks, he went back to the definition of what it meant to be a refugee: "I hope to the day you die you will be proud of being part of a nation and a democratic alliance that believes people should not be killed, uprooted or destroyed because of their race, their ethnic background or the way they worship God. . . . As long as there are innocent civilians doing nothing wrong, they're entitled to protection." Fifty years after the Declaration of Human Rights was passed—when the United Nations had hoped that the programs and agencies put in place would provide the framework to prevent genocide from ever occurring again—that same rhetoric was just as timely, the risks to people's lives just as high as when the document was written.

Even so, refugee resettlement in the 1980s and 1990s in the United States remained part of other debates that raged in those years: about the country's immigration policies on national soil; the risks and consequences of intervening in conflict zones around the world; the country's responsibility to provide aid to victims of persecution and war. But uniformly, presidents supported refugee resettlement and assumed some measure of support from the American public as well. Every year in the refugee Presidential Determination, presidents from Reagan to Obama set caps well above the 50,000-person ceiling mandated in the Refugee Act of 1980; none of those presidents came close to a ceiling that low.

Refugee resettlement was still only available to a tiny percentage of people in need around the world. In 1980, when Reagan was elected president, the number of refugees in the world expanded considerably. While it did not approach the almost 60 million estimated to have been displaced during and after World War II, the jump was alarming nonetheless. In 1951, the first year for which UNHCR has data, there were 2,116,011 refugees in the world. By 1960, that number fell to 1,656,664. But by 1980, the global number of refugees had more than quadrupled, to 8,454,937. In 1980, the US refugee/admissions ceiling was set at 231,700—a tiny percentage of worldwide refugees, but still incredibly high by American historical standards. Over the next twenty years, the American resettlement ceiling would never approach 230,000 again; as a result, the percentage of refugees resettled in relation to the global refugee crises would decrease sharply. By 1982, it was set at 142,000 and Reagan halved it four years later, with a refugee ceiling of 67,000 in 1984. The admissions ceiling rose and fell over the next two decades, with a return in 1992 to 142,000, .8 percent of the 17,838,074 refugees in the world as the Balkan and Rwandan crises in the early 1990s spiked the global number of refugees. The global refugee numbers seemed to be diminishing in the 2000s, fluctuating from 10,594,055 in 2002, to 8,661,988 in 2005, and then rising again to 11,388,967. The American ceiling decreased as well, with a low annual cap of 70,000, which would remain in effect from 2002 to 2007.

Arguably, the miracle is that, after the first attack on American soil in over fifty years, the resettlement program continued in the 2000s at all.

THE ATTACK ON THE WORLD TRADE CENTER ON SEPTEMBER 11, 2001, occurred days before President George W. Bush was to announce the year's allotment of refugee visas before the beginning of the fiscal year on October 1.

On September 14, Bush issued a "Declaration of National Emergency by Reason of Certain Terrorist Attacks," which gave the executive branch sweeping powers to respond to any potential terrorist threats in the country or outside it. In the days following 9/11, the country slotted the national identity mold developed over decades of the Cold War—the same one invoked by presidents Reagan, Bush, and Clinton—onto this new conflict. The United States defined itself almost instantaneously as antiterrorist in the same way it had been anticommunist.

While officially the language from the president and other politicians was measured, a shapeless panic directed at anyone who was Muslim, or even anyone who looked as if they could be Muslim, swept through the country. Hate crimes increased exponentially.

President Bush addressed the rising Islamophobia in a speech on September 17, 2001, given at the Islamic Center of Washington, D.C., often referred to as his "Islam Is Peace" speech: "The face of terror is not as eloquent as the true faith of Islam. That's not what Islam is all about. Islam is peace. These terrorists don't represent peace. They represent evil and war." He reminded the country that "America counts millions of Muslims amongst our citizens," and that despite the "anger and emotion, our fellow Americans must treat each other with respect." There should be no intimidation of American Muslims, and the people "who feel like they can intimidate our fellow citizens to take out their anger don't represent the best of America, they represent the worst of humankind, and they should be ashamed of that kind of behavior." But fear gripped the nation in a way it hadn't since Pearl Harbor. It was as if the anti-Japanese sentiment in the 1940s combined with the McCarthyism of the 1950s for a fierce new form of better-safe-than-sorryism. There was almost immediate public support for closing down any entry point for immigration to the United States, no matter how improbable it was that terrorists could arrive in the United States through the refugee resettlement program.

In the weeks immediately following the attack, a number of things happened swiftly to communicate to the American public that the government was taking the threat of more terrorist attacks seriously: The Bush administration suspended the refugee admissions program on October 1, including refugee processing centers under USCIS around the world; this halt affected the more than 20,000 refugees who had already passed their security clearances. For seven weeks, refugees were effectively barred from entering the United States through the resettlement program.

The military launched Operation Enduring Freedom, the war in Afghanistan aimed against Osama Bin-Laden and al-Qaeda, on October 7. The US attacks on Afghan soil contributed to a humanitarian crisis already affecting 4 million civilians in the country; Secretary of Defense Donald Rumsfeld announced 37,500 rations to aid the Afghan people, a tiny amount compared with the scale of the need of feeding millions. While advocates applauded that the US was sending aid to affected civilians, they remained concerned about the scale of the crisis, especially as the resettlement program remained closed.

The Patriot Act passed Congress on October 24. The unprecedented legislation expanded law enforcement's ability to prevent, investigate, and prosecute for terror-related crimes. It also aimed to prevent people accused of being involved in terrorist activities from entering the United States. The language was sweeping and broad, creating a complicated quagmire that would affect immigration entries, including refugee admissions, for decades.

On November 21, President Bush presented his Presidential Determination reopening the US Refugee Admissions Process with a cap of only 70,000, among the lowest numbers since the FRRP began in 1980. As part of the vast reorganization taking place at the federal level, the Office of Refugee Resettlement shared vetting with the newly created Department of Homeland Security. It took time to catch up on the backlog following the suspension of the program, especially with new vetting criteria being implemented under the DHS. Most of the allotted slots were not filled in 2002—only 27,000 refugees arrived that year. The number of refugees continued to remain well below the resettlement quota for the next few years—only 41 percent of the slots in 2003, and 75 percent in 2005.

As had happened in decades past, the mood of the American public—with the overt and underlying Islamophobia—deeply affected refugee admissions. Despite Bush and other politicians in the early 2000s promoting a differentiation between terrorist organizations and Islam as a whole, politicians on all levels learned quickly to match their rhetoric to what polls told them the public valued. The hatred and baseless fear against Muslims that took root in those years would blossom over the next decade into a national better-safe-than-sorryism on a scale not seen in the United States since the 1920s and 1930s.

AS THE WARS IN IRAQ AND AFGHANISTAN PROGRESSED, THE BUSH administration prioritized immigration for translators, informants, and others who helped US troops. In 2009, the Bush administration formalized the entry policies in the Special Immigrant Visa (SIV) program designed to give a new avenue for resettlement for those Iraqis and Afghans, many of whom were Muslim, to the US. The number of refugees from other Muslim-majority countries, or for Iraqi and Afghan refugees who did not qualify for SIV status, however, continued to remain relatively low.

In addition to the resettlement admissions process for immigrants from other countries, the US enacted several changes that affected asylum seekers on its own territory. Along with the Patriot Act of 2001 and the Homeland Security Act of 2002, the Real ID Act of 2005 and other policies and programs disproportionately targeted economic migrants and asylum seekers who arrived on American soil, mostly from Cuba through Mexico, but also those fleeing violence in Central and South America. There were even several cases of people flying from such countries as Eritrea into countries south of the United States border, such as Brazil, and then walking into the country.

As long as these asylum seekers immediately informed border guards or officials in the country, it was not illegal for them to cross the American border. It was illegal, however, to prevent people from seeking asylum or return them to danger because of the non-refoulement clauses of the 1951 Refugee Convention. But the fervor for national security overshadowed the once-effective humanitarian arguments for asylum seekers having a chance to prove their cases in a US court. The national disaster in New York had ushered in a profound new age in American politics.

With the benefit of hindsight, there are a number of things to criticize about policy decisions in the years following 9/11. The wars in Iraq and Afghanistan contributed to and caused massive humanitarian crises and essentially corroded what international goodwill the US had garnered after the World Trade Center attack. Legislation in the name of national security violated the privacy of millions of Americans. Overarching anti-immigration pushes hurt the lives of thousands of innocent people.

However, when it came to the resettlement program, the response from the federal level all the way down to local officials and community members across the country maintained the basic assumption of the previous decades: The resettlement program was an effective and worthwhile endeavor. The suspension in 2001 certainly created a backlog that it took a few years to make up; the caps were lower than they'd been since 1980. But the admission cap immediately following 9/11—67,000—still exceeded the 50,000 that the Carter administration had expected to be the norm for resettlement. There were the constant, well-founded criticisms that resettlement did not do nearly enough to mitigate the scale of humanitarian disasters around the world, but looking back, the steadiness with which the program continued despite the national emergency is awe-inspiring.

Following 9/11, even as the country slowed admissions for Muslim refugees in concerning ways, the US turned its attention to protracted refugee situations and began to finally address one of the more shameful legacies of mid-twentieth-century refugee policies.

THE REFUGEE CAMPS THAT EMERGED AS THE MODEL AFTER WORLD War II became one of the foundations of refugee aid around the world in the last half of the twentieth century. Camps played a critical role in resettlement not just to the United States, but to the other, predominantly Western countries partnering with the United Nations in offering new homes to vetted refugees. There were a number of reasons camps worked well for countries offering aid—as in postwar Europe, the countries sharing boundaries with a conflict zone took on a disproportionate number of asylum seekers and needed to set up temporary locations so as not to overwhelm their own citizens. Camps made it easier to pass out clothing, food, medicine, and other supplies to those in need. They also provided central hubs for UNHCR and other agencies to interview the refugees who might be considered for resettlement.

As the refugee crises ballooned worldwide in the 1980s, 1990s, and 2000s, so did the protracted refugee situations. For example, to help Kenya with its swelling crisis, UNHCR set up Dabaab refugee camp in 1993 for the Somalis pouring in, later joined by Ethiopian and Sudanese refugees. The camp was designed to contain 120,000 people. By 2011, 500,000 were packed in, leading to squalid, inhumane conditions. That was just one of many examples—over the next few decades, twenty-three of the camps founded in the 1980s and 1990s remained open and nine more were added in some of the most unstable regions in the world. In the first part of the twenty-first century, more than half of the world's refugee population lived in thirty-two camps.

A word in the Somali language, "bufis," means an intense desire to leave—a feeling refugees around the world understood too intimately. The average length of stay of a refugee in any camp was twenty-six years.

IN THE FIRST DECADE OF THE TWENTY-FIRST CENTURY, INTERNATIONAL refugee resettlement negotiations between the United States and other countries finally made some progress in the long-term deliberation about refugees in protracted refugee situations. A UNHCR report from April 20, 2006, advocated that countries do more than provide aid in response to "refugee emergencies" and instead, do something about refugees "trapped in situations far from the international spotlight." The month that report was issued, the United States was three years into the Iraq War; Nouri al-Maliki had just been named prime minister of Iraq. While the US attempted to frame the new government as a triumphant outcome of the war, Iraqi civilians were dying at a rate of one thousand to thirty-five hundred per month. Other countries were increasingly concerned about the scope of a war with an undetermined endgame that had such dire consequences for the civilian population.

That spring, the US agreed to accept more refugees from camps, perhaps as a way to alleviate UN pressure about the war in Iraq. Opening up resettlement to people in protracted refugee situations was also a way for the Bush administration to enact "compassionate conservativism," allowing some refugees to be resettled while still maintaining the firm restrictionist stance his base desired. Bush's compassionate conservativism relied on a private partnership with churches, many of which had been deeply involved in refugee work for years. The leaders of those churches had been advocating for years for the Bush administration to open up admissions to the people trapped in camps.

In May 2006, Secretary of State Condoleezza Rice granted an immigration waiver that allowed many of the 9,300 Burmese refugees who had been at Mae La camp in Thailand to be resettled in the United States. First Lady Laura Bush hosted a roundtable at the United Nations Security Council to raise awareness of the humanitarian crisis in September of that year. Over the next decade or so, more than 163,000 refugees originally from Myanmar would arrive in the United States. The US public, which had been supportive of refugees from Vietnam and Cambodia, naturally expanded that support to other refugees from Southeast Asia.

And it did not hurt that Christian communities in the United States often advocated for Burmese refugees because they were moved by stories of ethnic minorities in Myanmar, many of whose ancestors had converted to Christianity in the 1800s. The Rohingya Muslim refugees, equally targeted in Myanmar, got less US news coverage in those days than Karen Baptists and Karenni Catholics coming to the US to find religious freedom at last.

The resettlement of refugees from Myanmar would be one of the largest and most successful programs in US history. Refugees from Somalia and Burundi, from Bhutan and the Congo, also benefited from the Bush administration's focus on placing people from protracted situations. While there was still a stark, unmet need in the Middle East and other places, the response of the Bush administration to the better-safe-than-sorry restrictionism following 9/11 was not to end resettlement, but to open it up to groups in dire need around the world.

Chapter 24

HASNA

Hasna turned the key in the door, shoving it slightly to open it. The apartment smelled dank and mildewy. When she flipped the light on, the single yellowish bulb did nothing to dispel her sinking feeling. She took her shoes off at the door. Rana and the volunteer who picked them up at the airport in Austin were chatting and laughing as well as they could with Rana's few English words. Hasna left them to care for their five suitcases. She walked through the apartment. It did not take long.

The furniture did not match. There was a couch with holes near the cushion seams; it looked like suede, but when she rubbed her hand over it, the fabric felt too stiff, the indeterminate color neither gray nor brown. The coffee table was low and square, made out of plywood covered with a vinyl sticker that had woodgrain printed on it, the edges of the sticker peeling around the corners and the brasslike trim turning brown. When she touched it, the legs wobbled precariously. There was a table with three chairs—the table, at least, was really wood—crammed on the wall next to the couch. She took two more steps toward the bathroom and realized that from this vantage point she could see the entire home. The one bedroom had a queen-sized bed covered in a teal floral print. The dining nook, an extension of the living room, held a twin mattress on a frame; this was the second bedroom for seventeen-year-old Rana. The kitchen was a tiny corner—just room for a sink, an oven and stove, a refrigerator, and a few cabinets. She could cook and hand the dishes to Rana in bed through the peek-a-boo counter.

Opening the cabinets, Hasna realized there were no pots and pans, no way to even heat water on the stove. How could she cook with nothing to cook in? Did they also not cook in this country? There was a stove and a refrigerator that were not unlike the ones she had had back in Jordan and Syria, though this one seemed to be electric and not gas. She would not have to buy gas canisters, at least. She had wondered how she would know the vendors were coming anyway, or how she would negotiate with them if she could not speak the language. And the dishes—she couldn't stop picturing the beautiful china and cutlery she had lovingly placed in boxes before leaving Daraa, the full sets she had invested in over time. Even the simple plates and cutlery in Jordan had at least matched.

This kitchen held only three of everything, none of it coordinating: two blue plates stacked on top of a thick pottery plate with a cream center and a dark green circle. One of the bowls was blue with red apples, one was pink, one was baby blue. The three bowls weren't even the same sizes; neither were the three mugs. She couldn't stack them, which didn't matter because what was the point of stacking three of anything?

The volunteer made sympathetic noises as Hasna stumbled to sit down on the sludge-colored couch. She could tell from the way the woman was gesturing that the volunteer assumed they were physically tired. It was regret, not fatigue, that made Hasna's knees feel as if they were about to buckle. She thought with almost physical pain of the gleaming wooden furniture she had sold off or given away in Jordan in the week that passed between getting the news they were coming to the US and leaving on the plane. All of the gold that she had used to garner things for a life back in Syria—their entire savings spent on appliances and furniture that, in the end, she had begged her neighbors to take. It had been less than forty-eight hours since she had held her grandbabies' cheeks to her face. And she had left them for this—a bleak existence in a country whose language she could not speak.

The volunteer closed the door and locked it, showing Rana how to turn the deadbolt. Hasna watched dully. Before the war, she had never locked her door in Daraa. She thanked the woman who had picked them up at the airport. As the woman left, Hasna felt herself cratering.

She focused on Rana, on giving her a shower and making sure her sheets were clean and that the bed was comfortable. She put Rana to sleep as she hadn't since Rana was a little girl, stroking her hair until her breathing became deep and regular. Only then did Hasna take her own shower, dig through one of the suitcases until she found her pajamas, slide in beside Jebreel in bed with damp hair chilled by the air-conditioned air.

After several minutes of trying unsuccessfully to fall asleep, she sat up on the edge of the bed, eased off the mattress so she wouldn't wake Jebreel. She went to check on Rana again. They were not used to such chilly air-conditioned air. It would make Rana sick. She pulled the covers up around her. Rana stirred for a minute, her full lips parting.

Hasna looked out the sliding glass door that led to the small back porch in the living room, pulling apart the blinds that hung from the top of the door. The blinds rattled gently, but Rana did not stir. Suddenly Hasna wished desperately to walk outside, to feel real air on her face instead of the tin can air whirring inside. But she did not want to wake up Rana or Jebreel.

Streetlights outside illuminated a tennis court and a lawn between apartments, with sidewalks leading from one building to another. As they drove in from the airport, Hasna had noticed that the apartment buildings were centered on courtyards; she liked the inclusion of green space and trees within the buildings. She also liked that she could see out of the window and that there was no wall; the thought registered as a slight betrayal, having loved her walled home, but now that she had lived in homes with windows where she could see out, she recognized its charm. From the apartment window in Ramtha, she had watched the dogs in the field outside for hours. She wondered what she would see out of this window.

She pictured what it would be like when her children arrived. She had counted the doors as she came down the long breezeway—four downstairs, including theirs, and four upstairs. That meant there were eight apartments per breezeway and she had noticed two breezeways per building. They had driven past multiple buildings on their way into the complex; there must have been a dozen at least. Surely people moved often—worst-case scenario, her children would be in a building on the opposite side of the complex for a while. But so much better if they could live across this courtyard—Laila's boys would love to ride bikes on those sidewalks.

They would buy small outdoor chairs, she thought, which they could leave set up in the breezeway as they had in the villa in Ramtha. They could line them along the wall. Perhaps there were bigger apartments in the complex, better than this small one, one with a separate bedroom for Rana. They would need at least three bedrooms when Yusef came. They could try to get all of the apartments on the bottom floor. Amal and Samir and their girls in one, Khassem's family in another, Laila and her boys in the third. Yusef would need a wife, which would mean a fifth apartment, and a sixth when Rana was older. Hasna chuckled softly to herself. Of course she should begin looking for Yusef's wife before she started worrying about a husband for Rana—her son was old enough to settle down and marry, something to look forward to once the whole family was here. What she needed was a piece of paper so she could write these ideas down.

She was immediately buoyed by the idea of a to-do list, the ability to codify and prioritize all that needed to happen. First, the stools to sit outside in the breezeway—though that should probably wait until they had at least one more apartment to store things in. She would not write down a wife for Yusef, not yet, but she would start putting feelers out among the women around her. Surely there were other Syrians nearby; she looked forward already to connecting with them, to hearing Arabic in this unfamiliar place. On the list would go some matching dishes, more than three coffee cups, and pots and pans. She would need food as well, and spices to cook with. She hoped there would be women to help her find these things.

She looked once more at the courtyard and felt a surge of affection for its possibilities. Laila and the boys were so exhausted; this place would give the children room to play, something they had not had in years. If her older children worked during the day, Rana could finish school and she and Jebreel could watch the grandchildren after school every day. Her grandchildren would run into her apartment just as her children ran into her gate in Daraa, laughing and bickering. They could clean and paint the apartment, save up for good wood furniture.

She would have food simmering on the stove every afternoon. They would take turns eating dinner in one another's houses; maybe there would even be room on the lawn to set up a table outside. She would hang fairy lights like the ones they had had in Daraa on the trees outside the window. She might invite her neighbors over; these Americans who had just the right number of dishes for the people who lived in their home would be hungry, would love the food she would make them. She pictured her family walking out of their apartments in time for dinner, everyone carrying a dish as they caught up with one another's days, while she carried out a large pan of maftul, plates of hummus, platters of salad. They would gather in the courtyard and eat lingeringly. At night, the cousins would run barefoot on the grass.

Perhaps the neighborhood was not unsafe, just unfamiliar. With her children around her, she would not worry about locking her doors. She walked back to her bed, lay down, and went to sleep.

THE FIRST KNOCK ON HER DOOR THE NEXT MORNING WAS A SYRIAN woman who lived a few buildings over. Hasna was so grateful to see her and hear her Arabic with its thick Aleppo accent, she nearly cried. The woman was short with gray eyes and a sharp set to her mouth that reminded Hasna a bit of one of the small dogs she had watched in Ramtha—a small, determined terrier. They greeted each other, kissing cheeks briefly, and the woman introduced herself as Um Khalid. She told Hasna she had come to make sure that she had everything she needed. Hasna told her all about the three-cup debacle of a kitchen and Um Khalid laughed grimly: "It is like they follow the exact instructions but do not think. Did they not assume that you would ever have other people to eat? Or that you might sometimes want more than one plate per person?" She rolled her eyes and Hasna felt cheered immediately.

Some of the other women dropped by later in the day, kissing cheeks and clucking sympathetically when Um Khalid told them that Hasna had only received three of everything in the kitchen and no pots or pans. Within hours, the women had organized a meal for them. In the afternoon, one of the women who could drive took Hasna to the local halal market to buy what she needed; she had been given cash by the IOM representative who helped them and she used almost two hundred dollars buying a cheap tin pot-and-pan set and a full set of glasses and plates for their home and food for the next few days. She worried about spending so much money so quickly, before she found out where the rest of the money was going to come from, but truly, there was no choice. The other women agreed with her—she could not live in a home in which she could not cook.

Her Syrian neighbors eased Hasna's first day considerably. That night, they were invited over for dinner at one of the Syrian families' apartments. The women who had taken her to the store brought their children and they talked late into the night, answering all of Hasna and Jebreel's questions. There, Hasna finally learned the full scope of what they had taken on.

They would have to pay back the US government the full amount of their plane tickets, a debt that already felt daunting to Hasna. Whatever they had been told in the orientation or in the months leading up to their resettlement, it didn't matter. In fact, when Hasna named some of the things, they only laughed: A year's worth of financial support? They would not be able to afford rent past the first month and they were in a six-month lease contract. Free medical care? They would be eligible for Medicaid but they would need to stay on top of their paperwork or they would lose their coverage. Disability payments? They would come in a few months, but they should expect some snafu that would delay payments.

An older man, balding but with a ring of thick black hair, ranted for long minutes about the United States. He told Jebreel and Hasna that the United States did not care for them, but his tirade only made Hasna feel that he was asking too much of this new country. Why should anyone give them free health care and money without their working for it? Those were not things that she wanted. His beginning premise—"sure, they let our children go to school and they help us bring our families over"—were the beginning and end of what she hoped for. If she had her children and Rana could be educated, that would be enough.

Many in the group readily acknowledged that the US system did help their families stay together. Some of them had already welcomed relatives. Hasna could see that many of the most bitter people were also the most vocal. She suspected that several of the others did not feel as strongly as the loudest voices in the room.

She sensed, even through her despair and worry, that there was a great kindness in this new country. The system was not perfect, but Americans did not cause the war in Syria and were not responsible for fixing it. And yet, they had paid for these people to come from Jordan all the way over to Austin, Texas; there were thousands more refugees from Syria all over the country. What kind of people built into their laws and culture an infrastructure to care for refugees from all over the world? Good people. Every country had people they were not proud of, who caused problems—Syrians, of all people, could understand that. But this was a country that took responsibility to provide a new home for people who had lost theirs to war. By the time the man's wife succeeded in her not-so-subtle campaign to get her ranting husband to stop and go home, Hasna was convinced of the goodness of the people of the United States.

THE NEXT MORNING, THEY SAT IN A ROOM FULL OF PEOPLE FROM ALL over the world at Refugee Services of Texas as one of the caseworkers—a tall former Iraqi refugee with a square jaw and milk-chocolate brown eyes—explained to them some of the things they had already been told by their neighbors. She was grateful she had had a chance to process the information first. He leveled with them that yes, their expectations and reality in the United States would not always match up, but the people at RST truly did want to help them. He told them as much as he could about what they could now expect in the weeks to come.

A Syrian-American man who introduced himself as Natheir Ali came over that evening, entering their home deferentially, and spent more than an hour asking Hasna and Jebreel about their home, their life in Daraa, their children and grandchildren, their jobs and educations, what they were hoping to find here. They clicked with him immediately; he held himself with the quiet containment Hasna associated with the people who had served in the military in Syria, a kind of power that could spring forth at any time but that usually did not. But there was no violence in his power; it was a coiled energy and sense of purpose. He was tall and almost too thin, charismatic, but in a self-deprecating way—he used his sense of humor to put them at ease. When he laughed, his deep voice lightened into a high-pitched giggle which Hasna found endearing. He knew all of their neighbors and told them everything he could about the Syrian refugee population in Austin. There were more than a hundred people from various parts of Syria in Austin; most of them were children. They were concentrated in a few of the apartment complexes, including this one, and their children attended a handful of schools. He teased Rana mercilessly and she scolded him back and they all laughed. Hasna fed him dinner and he accepted, praising her cooking till she blushed. He told them about his own family and his friends who were there to help with whatever they needed.

Things were going to be hard, he told them, but there were good people, many originally from Syria and others who were not, who would be there to help them for the next several months. A family like theirs, with no adult children to work for them, was in one of the more difficult positions. Most of the other Syrian families in Austin had either two adults who could work or at least some adult children who could help. He couched it gently, so they would not take offense, but to Hasna, his assessment was a relief—she was not wrong that their life would be incredibly difficult, that what they were undertaking was harder than what most people would have to endure.

When he left, Hasna looked at him with tears in her eyes: "I have been denied my sons for a time but look: Allah has brought us a son, and he has brought us a brother. Thank you." Natheir's eyes filled with tears too.

The air shifted. She could feel that this room in the middle of America had also become Syria: a place where people clasped hands and refused to forget, to lose heart, to let go of their love for their country and for each other. It gave Hasna hope and it filled her with despair.

Chapter 25

MU NAW

AUSTIN, TEXAS, USA, MAY 2015

Saw Ku's sister, Soe Paw, tried to call Mu Naw several times. Assuming she wanted to give Mu Naw advice about her marriage with Saw Ku—it would not be the first time—Mu Naw ignored the calls. Her life was so busy with work and home that several days passed without her finding a minute to call Soe Paw back. Finally, on a Friday afternoon as she was picking up the house and thinking about dinner, her sister-in-law in Austin, Deh Deh, called.

"Why have you not answered your phone? Soe Paw has been calling you for days!" Mu Naw was surprised at Deh Deh's sharp tone. Her voice sounded raspy.

"Because Soe Paw just wants to tell me what to do and you know how she is. I didn't want to hear it." Saw Ku had been gone again the night before—Mu Naw hoped at Jaw Jaw's house—and she was glad to talk to Deh Deh, who was always on Mu Naw's side. "Did she call you first? Was she full of advice again?"

The pause at the other end of the line was too long. Finally, Mu Naw stopped picking up the children's toys and turned the television down.

"What? What is it?"

Her sister-in-law's voice caught while she spoke. "It's your mother. She's gone."

Mu Naw sat down on the couch.

THE CHILDREN FOUND HER LATER IN HER CLOSET, HER BODY SHAK-
ing with sobs. She would not answer them when they asked what was wrong;
she could not form the words. She waved them away, too overcome to worry
about the scared looks on their faces.

In the dark, small space of the closet, Mu Naw could see her mother's face,
could almost feel her presence. A few weeks ago, her mother had asked for
money again and Mu Naw had wired as much money as they could afford to
her in Mae La camp. Though her mother did not accuse her of being stingy,
of not caring, of forgetting who they were and where they had come from, Mu
Naw knew that other relatives did—Soe Paw had told her that more than once.
It was not true that she was stingy—they did everything they could—but the
accusations stewed in her, layered onto the guilt she already carried for leaving her mother behind.

Before, when she felt guilty, it was easy to put off all thoughts of her mother.
She had taken comfort in her long-term plan: When she saved up enough for
herself and was on her feet, when the children were older, when they could
buy a home, she would call her mother and beg her to come. She would finally
convince her, do everything in her power to help them set up a new life.

That plan lay in pieces on the closet floor. It was hepatitis C, Deh Deh had
told her. Mu Naw had not even known that her mother had hepatitis C. Her
requests for money had always been for school or minor medical issues for Mu
Naw's younger half siblings. She broke down again at the realization that her
mother had kept the news from her. Mu Naw would have bankrupted her
family to save her mother.

Her mother knew that. Of course she did.

Mu Naw's unholy wailing could be heard from the parking lot. Saw Ku
rushed home when Deh Deh called Jaw Jaw; his brother had promised to
explain it to their manager at the hotel where they worked as housekeeping
staff. Saw Ku flung the closet door open and pulled Mu Naw to him. She clung
to him for a moment, her wails subsiding into hiccups, and then she crawled
into the closet again.

He left her there, went to hug the children hovering tearily in the hallway.

He gave them baths and fixed them dinner, cleaned up the living room, and put them in front of the television before going back in to Mu Naw with a plate of food in his hand.

MU NAW WAS LOST IN A SWIRL OF MEMORY. HER MIND DRIFTED THROUGH images of her mother: Her face in the dim light spilling from the doorway of her hut on the night when Mu Naw showed up after years apart. Her mother's hair coming out of her braid as she leaned over Mu Naw's baby sister with a look of sheer joy. Laughing at a joke Mu Naw told her one day while they hung laundry out to dry on the line strung behind their hut at Mae La. She remembered her mother leaning out the window in their first hut in Nu Po camp— young, sharp-featured—calling Mu Naw in from playing. She watched her mother walk, shoulders hunched, away from her on that day she left Mu Naw with the grandmothers, right before the junta attacked Nu Po. She felt her mother's hand caressing her cheek, tracing her jaw, when she was sick as a teenager.

She caught at one of the memories and held it: the story of how her parents married. Her father loved to tell it, usually when he'd been drinking. Mu Naw had heard it dozens of times as a little girl. She could still hear her father's resonant voice, slightly slurred. She had never heard her mother tell it.

In this dark closet in a country thousands of miles away, that story took on a new cast.

YEARS AGO, IN HER HOME VILLAGE, MU NAW'S MOTHER DANCED IN FRONT of everyone for the Karen New Year celebration.

She had grown up poor and she had landed a job as an indentured servant in the home of some of the richest people in their village. The rich people paid her family for her services and she worked night and day for them. She had very little time off, but she managed to sneak away to spend time with her new boyfriend. Their love was bone-deep and easy. It made the years of hard labor seem survivable; when her family had saved up enough of a bride price, she would marry this good man.

That night, she danced with abandon, aware that his eyes were on her.

Mu Naw's father thought she was more beautiful than any woman he had ever seen. His need to possess her became a consuming passion. He knew that he was a good-looking man and he had never really been denied anything that he wanted. He had no doubt that she would be lucky to marry a man like him. And watching her slim body move beneath her finest skirt, he knew it would be tonight.

Mu Naw's mother returned in the dark of night to the home of the rich family, smiling as she remembered the things her boyfriend told her.

She never saw the men waiting for her around the bend in the path. They put a sack over her head and covered her mouth so she would not call out. They carried her to a hut across the village.

There, they ripped the sack off her head. Laughing men surrounded her. None of the men were her gentle boyfriend. They all left except for one, closing the door behind them. The men stayed outside all night to prevent her from leaving.

Mu Naw's father had always said that was their wedding night. Now, with a deep intake of breath, Mu Naw realized her father had raped her mother into marriage.

That night changed everything, because it ruined her mother's reputation. Mu Naw's mother could no longer work in the job that supported her family. She could never marry the man whom she loved, the one she'd kissed just hours before.

The news spread instantaneously around their small village, spurred on by Mu Naw's father's friends, who were proud of their capture. For Mu Naw's grandparents, the news was a mixed blessing: Mu Naw's daughter could no longer work, but they no longer had to pay the expensive bride price because she was damaged goods. Mu Naw's father's method was not even that unheard of; other women had been forced into marriage in the same way.

"He's so handsome! Look at his light skin!" Mu Naw's mother's friends told her. "You should be pleased. He will make a very handsome husband. Your children will be so beautiful."

Either that first night or in the nightmarish ones that followed, Mu Naw was conceived.

Her mother served her husband faithfully. She worked hard to create a home for him. She cooked him dinner, cleaned him up when he staggered home drunk, endured his swinging bouts of anger, made no comments when he gambled away their money. She brought his two daughters and one son into the world. But she never, not once, loved him.

When her father told the story of how he made her mother marry him, guffawing over his own cleverness, Mu Naw noticed that her mother never laughed. As she grew older, she noticed her mother's jaw clenched with each telling.

And now she knew: her mother had left her father at Nu Po camp all those years ago because she wanted to be free. It was not inevitable for marriages to end in conflict. Her parents' marriage had never been anything like the one she shared with Saw Ku.

MU NAW STOPPED SOBBING. SHE COULD STILL HEAR MUFFLED NOISES from inside and outside her apartment—the TV in their living room, neighbors yelling at each other in Spanish, cars coming in and going out of the apartment complex, feet on the stairs and in the neighbors' apartment above.

She realized that her face was pressed against her Karen dresses hanging in the back of the closet, dresses that she had once worn every day and now wore only for special events, that had become more costume than clothes. She could feel the knotted designs with her fingers even if she couldn't see them in the dark. She jerked a skirt off of the hanger, bunched it in her fist, buried her face in its supple folds.

All these years, Mu Naw had blamed her mother for the things she had not had—a loving home, a stable life, a connection to her past, access to school, some idea about how to navigate the world. She had, without realizing it, carried this rage and resentment for years, heavy and dense, since the fire in the camp when she could not find her mother and she had no choice but to flee with her grandmothers.

And then, in a way she could not explain, her mother was here with her, closer than she had been in years, closer than she had perhaps ever been. The closet was infused with her scent, the fruity shampoo she used, the clean smell of her skin. Mu Naw felt her mother's warm breathing, felt the pressure of her arms around her, felt the release as her mother unclasped the burden of grief and guilt and anger and fear Mu Naw had carried for so long.

In that moment, Mu Naw understood several things at once. Mu Naw might have been born of rape and violence, but her mother had adored her, had stayed in the home of her rapist for the sake of her tiny, tenacious daughter and the children who came after. Her mother had so few choices in her life: children she had not wanted with a man she never loved, the desecration of their home, the loss of everything they had ever known, a half-life in a camp, the constant search for money to care for them all, the years when she had not known whether her children were dead or alive, the resentment of a teenage daughter who came back after years only to hate her within weeks, the disappointment of a second marriage that had brought equal parts happiness and pain, the daily disgrace of living in a tiny space with small-minded people who taught her daughter she was a source of shame instead of a source of boundless, indomitable strength.

As Mu Naw felt regret well up in her, her mother offered forgiveness, bright and warm, flowing through her body. Her mother knew everything, knew the remorse Mu Naw felt for those lost years.

Her mother's forgiveness washed her shame away like a burst of afternoon rain in Myanmar—sharp and quick and cool.

When Saw Ku finally opened the closet door, Mu Naw had fallen asleep with her face cradled in the folds of her Karen skirt. The light hit her eyes and she opened them; they were swollen from crying and her legs and the arm she had slept on tingled painfully. She struggled to sit up and Saw Ku reached out his hand to pull her up.

He did not embrace her. He kept his hand on her arm and they looked at each other for a long time. Mu Naw knew then, with some regret, what she had to do.

Chapter 26

US REFUGEE RESETTLEMENT, 2008–2015

By the time President Obama entered office in 2008, the Refugee Admissions Process (RAP) had become a well-honed system. Agencies built on the security practices started in the 1950s and 1960s added such new technology as biometrics and international security databases as they became widely available in the 2000s, making it the most secure entry process for anyone coming to the United States. The RAP numbers remained consistent with President Bush's. For his first several years as president, Obama did not significantly raise the admissions ceiling during his Presidential Determination—his administration capped refugee admissions at 80,000 from 2009 to 2011, lowered them in 2012 to 76,000, then again in 2013 to 2015 to 70,000. He only raised it his last year in office, 2016, to 85,000; it was still significantly lower than the highest ceilings set by Ronald Reagan and George H. W. Bush (142,000 in 1982 and 1993) or Bill Clinton (121,000 in 1994).

Under the Obama administration, the admission process was at its pinnacle. Refugees around the world identified themselves to UNHCR officials to receive aid and benefits; no matter the country they were in or whether resettlement was an option for them, declaring that they were a refugee with UNHCR was always the first step. UNHCR officials conducted initial interviews, gathered documents, began a file with data including names, former addresses, birth dates, family relationships, date of border crossings, and other details. In the initial vetting interviews, officials asked the same questions over and over, pushing against stories and comparing data collected from one interview with those provided by neighbors or family members to form a holistic picture of backgrounds of the refugees they were interviewing. At the end of that time, a handful of refugees who UNHCR determined had a verified need for resettlement were recommended to overseas Refugee Support Centers, US government offices that prescreen refugees, administer their case files, and prepare them for interviews.

American RSCs were federally funded, and officials from various agencies combed through the initial interviews from UNHCR and repeated the process again until refugees had been interrogated thoroughly by multiple officials over several months. Before 2003, those RSC interviews were handled by the State Department or agencies with a State Department contract; after that year, with the institution of the Department of Homeland Security, they fell under the jurisdiction of the new US Citizenship and Immigration Services (USCIS). Depending on the region and the conflict, the FBI or the National Counterterrorism Center, as well as other agencies within the intelligence community, might be involved. The level of information these agencies discovered about refugees—their relationships, their known associations, their habits, their livelihoods, their interests—was often staggering to the interviewees themselves. It was only when they had passed the biographical security checks—which once more weeded out a number of applicants—that RAP candidates' files were passed on to highly trained USCIS officers.

These officers collected biometric data such as fingerprints in addition to reconducting the already reconducted interviews, digging further for any red flags or changed answers or signs that refugees had attempted to deceive officials with their stories. The biometric information was screened against a number of databases—FBI, Department of Defense, Department of Homeland Security. This was the point at which Syrian refugees received an enhanced Fraud Detection and National Security (FDNS) review, which looked at social media and other sources; individual cases might be recommended for the enhanced review as well.

If they passed these tests, refugees underwent medical examinations; anyone with tuberculosis or other communicable diseases was denied resettlement. After the medical examinations, refugees attended a cultural orientation that attempted to prepare them for life in the United States. Based on a wide range of factors—including refugees' relationships within the US and regional availabilities at the time—various agencies chose their resettlement location. Finally, when every part of the process was finished, the International Organization for Migration booked their travel; refugees were screened again by Customs and Border Patrol, and then by Transportation Security Administration officials. After enduring scrutiny at every step in a process that took at the very least eighteen months, though often much longer, refugees arrived in the United States.

Because it was a long-term, complicated process, if the executive branch of the United States raised the refugee cap with the yearly Presidential Determination, there were not always enough refugees ready for resettlement, which was why some years actual resettlement numbers were below the visa allotment ceiling. On the other side, if the cap was lowered, the process bottlenecked. People in camps, or making do in hostile urban areas, waited longer and longer, with the threat of violence or chaos, growing resentment, or suffocating hopelessness.

After refugees finally arrived in the United States, their first few months fell under the jurisdiction of the nine different voluntary resettlement agencies—the volags—with State Department contracts: Church World Service; Ethiopian Community Development Council; Episcopal Migration Ministries; Hebrew Immigrant Aid Society; International Rescue Committee; Lutheran Immigration and Refugee Service; US Committee for Refugees and Immigrants; United States Conference of Catholic Bishops Migration and Refugee Services/Catholic Charities USA; and World Relief. Those agencies either resettled refugees within cities themselves or partnered with smaller agencies—such as Refugee Services of Texas in Austin—that were established in almost every city in the country. Some smaller affiliates contracted with more than one national agency to receive resettlement allotments. At the end of the Obama administration, the nine volags managed or partnered with 350 affiliate sites throughout the country; the agencies had varying amounts of money to help refugees in those first few months, depending on the federal budget of the Office of Refugee Resettlement and the amount of donations each agency received or the funding of their agencies. Their caseworkers, employment specialists, therapists, and translators were the frontline support—along with faith communities and volunteers and schoolteachers and hospitals and employers and other aid workers—in helping refugees start their new lives. The refugees who arrived were truly in need of resettlement and the joy of watching entire families or small diasporas of people find new life made even the hardest, most difficult times worth it to those involved at every stage. It was the unlikeliest thing—a bureaucratic program laced with goodwill and hope.

DURING PRESIDENT OBAMA'S YEARS IN OFFICE, WHILE AMERICAN admissions numbers remained relatively static, the global refugee crises spiked again. In 2007, UNHCR began including people in what the agency termed "people in a refugee-like situation" in their calculations of global risk, causing an even greater jump in refugee numbers around the world. The previous calculations (including the numbers cited in earlier chapters) covered only refugees recognized under the 1951 Convention relating to the Status of Refugees. For UNHCR, actual registered refugees became a subcategory of the larger "persons of concern" designation. In adding other groups to this larger umbrella—including asylum seekers, internally displaced persons (IDPs), returned refugees and returned IDPs, stateless persons, and others in vulnerable or precarious situations—the agency acknowledged that the often-narrow definition of refugee from 1951 did not necessarily match the needs of the world in the twenty-first century. Even without their expanded definitions— just using the traditional definition for refugee—the numbers rose alarmingly while Obama was president. At the end of 2008, there were 10,489,812 global refugees and 34.46 million persons of concern. By the end of 2016, there were 17,187,488 global refugees and 67.75 million persons of concern.

In those eight years, no conflict escalated at the rate and scale of the Syrian crisis. The Obama administration, along with most of the international community, did not respond to the Assad regime's attacks on its own civilians in a way that might have prevented—or at least mitigated—the worst humanitarian crisis since World War II. The reasons for America's inaction were much the same as the reasons for doing nothing in the 1930s: The economic recession of the 2000s fueled the same kind of strong public lack of interest in spending money on any foreign policy situation as had the Great Depression. After long-lasting, complicated conflicts in Iraq and Afghanistan, the US public exhibited the type of war fatigue that had swept through the nation in the decades following World War I. And the widespread, racialized antiterrorist rhetoric and sentiments after 9/11 made it much easier to dehumanize the victims of the Assad regime. Despite the brilliant diversity of the Syrian people, the fact that Christians and Muslims and Druze and others had lived together in harmony for centuries and were now facing equal threats under Assad, because the country was in the Middle East, from the very beginning, there was low American public support for assisting the Syrian people.

Karen Christian refugees from Myanmar remained an easy sell in those years; the program begun under Bush flourished under Obama. Muslim refugees from Syria—victims of the same kinds of targeted attacks by their own government—would never enjoy that widespread support.

OBAMA CAMPAIGNED ON A PLATFORM OF WITHDRAWING FROM IRAQ. In 2011, the year the war in Syria began, Obama began the process of pulling the US military out of Iraq. Whether that withdrawal was too early—and fomented the creation of the Islamic State—remains a matter of debate among historians and political scientists, journalists and pundits. But having staked political capital on that decision, the Obama administration was not in a position to push for strong intervention on behalf of civilians when the war in Syria began—in the first heady days when the US or European allies flexing their muscles at the Assad regime might have actually stopped what was to come.

The war in Syria got very bad very fast. Obama issued a White House statement on August 20, 2012, saying, "We cannot have a situation where chemical or biological weapons are falling into the hands of the wrong people." In what many at the time took to be an escalation of US policy toward Syria, Obama warned Assad and "other players on the ground" that "a red line for us is we start seeing a bunch of chemical weapons moving around or being utilized." If that happened, it "would change my calculus; that would change my equation."

But when the red line was crossed on August 21, 2013—when the Assad regime attacked rebel-held enclaves in Damascus with chemical weapons and when amateur footage from cell phone cameras showed mouths foaming from sarin gas, parents clutching dead babies, bodies lining hospital floors—the US did not intervene. In what would become a hallmark of the Syrian war, viral photos and videos clearly provided footage of what was happening almost in real time. With no free press to monitor the government, and revolutionaries who had learned from the Arab Spring the value of social media and cell phone coverage, what happened in Syria was instantly available around the world. There was now no need for the violin-laden newsreels of the 1940s, the solemn newscasts of the 1960s to the 2000s, or even the breathless coverage of the cable news era. Syrians on the ground sent videos via text or WhatsApp to people who uploaded them to YouTube or Twitter, Facebook or Reddit, within minutes of any attack.

Military officials in the United States were ready for what seemed to be inevitable strikes, quietly scheduled over Labor Day weekend. On Saturday, August 31, President Obama issued a statement:

> Our intelligence shows the Assad regime and its forces preparing to use chemical weapons, launching rockets in the highly populated suburbs of Damascus, and acknowledging that a chemical weapons attack took place.... All told, well over 1,000 people were murdered. Several hundred of them were children—young girls and boys gassed to death by their own government. This attack is an assault on human dignity.

In addition to the danger to Syrian citizens, he called the attack "a serious danger to our national security," "a mockery of the global prohibition on the use of chemical weapons," and said it endangered US allies that bordered Syria, which "could lead to escalating use of chemical weapons, or their proliferation to terrorist groups who would do our people harm." National security and humanitarian duty were the cornerstones of his address. Therefore, he concluded: "this menace must be confronted."

And then, the speech made a surprising turn. Rather than announcing the strikes or military action against Syria his "red line" comment had implied,

Obama announced that, as "president of the world's oldest constitutional democracy," he decided to "seek authorization for the use of force from the American people's representatives in Congress."

The day before, the British Parliament had rejected the resolution, backed by Prime Minister David Cameron, for military action against Syria. Without allies willing to cooperate, the case became more complicated before Congress. Still, there was reason to think that military force was still an option. On September 3, House Speaker John Boehner and House Majority Leader Eric Cantor both endorsed military action. But it became clear over the next few days that the vote would not pass the full Congress—many representatives did not want to go back to war-weary constituents having voted for yet another Middle Eastern conflict.

At the G20 Summit in Russia Obama attended on September 5–6, world leaders were reluctant to back up the American military. Without congressional support at home or allied support abroad, the Obama administration faced two almost equally intolerable foreign policy possibilities. The first was not intervening when a country employed chemical weapons against its own civilians, thus signaling to Syria and any other foreign actors that there would be no punitive action in future uses of those same kinds of weapons. This would cause political and rhetorical predicaments with possibly disastrous consequences in the future, either on US soil or for American troops abroad, not to mention civilians in Syria and elsewhere. The second was to commit American troops and American funds to another long slog of a war with the nebulous goal of regime change.

The Obama administration agreed readily when Russia presented a proposed solution on September 9 to broker a deal for Syria to hand over its chemical weapons supply. Obama called on Congress to postpone the scheduled vote on Syrian military action. He hailed the "diplomatic solution," but warned that the talks with Russia couldn't be a "stalling tactic." He used language of international cooperation to ensure that "Assad gives up his chemical weapons so that they can be destroyed."

But as it would turn out, those talks were only mildly successful—a stalling tactic at best. Certainly, the Syrian government gave up some chemical weapons when it joined the Chemical Weapons Convention in September

2013 and allowed UN inspectors to destroy its chemical weapons or remove them in late 2013 and early 2014. But gas attacks against civilians continued. Some attacks were clearly the work of Syrian government forces, others were possibly by ISIS or other actors in the increasingly complicated political terrain.

Civilians endured documented gas attacks in April 2014, September 2014, March 2015, April 2015, August 2016, December 2016, March 2017, April 2017, April 2018, and November 2018; with chlorine and sarin and sulfur mustard gas; in Talmenes and Sarmin and Marea and Aleppo and Hama and Damascus and Douma and Khan Sheikhoun.

The weapons employed against civilians in Syria were not just chemical. There were FROG missiles. Scud missiles. Antitank guidance missiles. T-55, T-62, and T-72 tanks. Su-22 and MiG-23 warplanes. Sniper rifles, assault rifles, anti-material rifles, antitank rifles, carbine assault rifles, heavy machine guns, light machine guns, submachine guns, semiautomatic pistols. Rocket-propelled grenade launchers. Automatic grenade launchers. Shoulder-fired rocket launchers. Mortar weapon systems. Improvised explosive devices. Barrel bombs. The brutal torture chambers in Sednaya Prison and every prison throughout the country. The horrible, mind-gripping fear of a people so thoroughly traumatized, with such justified fear of their own government, that their collective PTSD seeped into the DNA of their children.

Syrians fled. And fled. And fled. They ran on a massive scale—refugees, asylum seekers, internally displaced, all looking for any place safe. Many escaped their government to die at the hands of ISIS, or in a boat trying to get to Europe, or of starvation along the road to any other place at all. By 2014, 4 million refugees had fled Syria to the neighboring countries—2 million to Turkey, 1 million to Lebanon, 1 million to Jordan. Those countries closed borders rapidly; routes that had been available even days or weeks before were suddenly gone.

Hasna, like many Syrians, points to moments in those years when she thought the world would finally wake up and help. In 2011, when the government attacked the parents of the tortured children in Daraa. In 2013, when the US almost followed up when Assad barreled through Obama's red-line policy. In spring 2015, when it became clear that chemical weapons were still being used against Syrian civilians even after the UN inspectors had come and gone. In fall 2015, when the world saw the body of drowned three-year-old Alan Kurdi wash onto the sand of a Turkish beach. In April 2017, when photos of Abdel Hameed al-Youssef clutching the blue-lipped bodies of his gassed, nine-month-old twins after the chemical weapons attacks in Khan Sheikhoun horrified social media and journalists alike.

These are the moments summed up by that thin diplomatic phrase, "assault on human dignity."

THE FIRST SYRIAN REFUGEES TRICKLED INTO THE UNITED STATES through the resettlement program in October 2011, just a few in the beginning: 31 the first year, 36 the second, 105 the third. In 2015, 1,682 Syrians were admitted for resettlement; by the end of the year, the UN identified 6.75 million people of concern from Syria alone. And Syria was not the only country with epic, continuing crises: Conflicts in Afghanistan and Somalia, as well as many other places, led to the ever-increasing rise in refugee numbers. The fact that American resettlement represented the tiniest of drops in an ocean of need had never been clearer.

But by the end of 2015, the American public was in no mood to calculate the humanitarian need—not after the Paris attacks on November 13–14, 2015. Over the course of two days, suicide bombers and mass shooters terrorized Paris. 130 people were killed, over 400 injured, in the deadliest attacks in the country since its occupation during World War II. Reports trickling out in the days and weeks after the attacks indicated that ISIS in Syria had at least some connection to the bombers, some of whom trained in the ISIS-held city of Raqqa. At least two Iraqi bombers arrived in the Schengen area claiming to be Syrian refugees (their passports were later found to be fabricated). The European Union's unique border policy meant that once migrants passed through an external boundary checkpoint, they could move unimpeded through the region. Thousands of unvetted economic migrants and asylum seekers flooded the countries, many of them from Syria.

Europe experienced a massive wave of anti-immigrant sentiment following the Paris attacks, and the bombings in Brussels a few months later. Like the

Islamophobia in the United States after 9/11, it was a misplaced, harmful swing of public opinion that equated terrorists with victims in other countries who were fleeing terrorists. The broad-brush fearmongering spread quickly to the United States. Despite the fact that the undocumented migrants and asylum seekers in Europe had a completely different path from the well-vetted Syrian refugees who were accepted for resettlement—after years' worth of interviews, background checks, and identity verification by highly trained US and UNHCR officials, including an enhanced review for Syrian cases—the backlash in the United States was fierce.

In November 2015, thirty-one US governors issued statements declaring that Syrian refugees would not be welcome in their states. Presidential candidates like Ted Cruz and Donald Trump, congressional representatives like Michael McCaul, and governors like Mike Pence of Indiana and Greg Abbott of Texas all began to speak out against refugees. For the first time since the establishment of the Federal Refugee Resettlement Program, the term "refugee" no longer immediately implied "victim of persecution" in the imagination of the American public. Decades' worth of unobtrusive, widespread government and private-sector support left the American people with little working knowledge of what refugee resettlement actually entailed.

In the last two years of his presidency, as President Obama framed the response of the United States to the Syrian crisis as one of the great moral predicaments of our time, for the first time in decades, the national debate about refugees turned back to whether we should resettle them at all.

ON SEPTEMBER 20, 2016, IN REMARKS BY PRESIDENT OBAMA AT THE Leaders' Summit on Refugees, he outlined the enormous necessity for countries to do more. He returned to shared international security as a major determiner in refugee assistance: "Not because refugees are a threat. . . . They are victims." But because "when desperate refugees pay cold-hearted traffickers for passage, it funds the same criminals who are smuggling arms and drugs and children. When nations with their own internal difficulties find themselves hosting massive refugee populations for years on end, it can risk more instability." National security underlined the argument echoed from President Bush before him: that there was great risk in "reinforcing terrorist propaganda" by reifying the stereotype that "nations like my own are somehow opposed to Islam" when Muslim refugees are disproportionately turned away for resettlement.

But the greatest danger Obama identified was a "test of our common humanity—whether we give in to suspicion and fear and build walls, or whether we see ourselves in another." In failing to act, the US could "betray our deepest values," "deny our own heritage" as a country "built by immigrants and refugees," ignore a "teaching at the heart of so many faiths that we do unto others as we would have them do unto us," and cause a "stain on our collective conscience" like the one the country earned when it turned away Jewish refugees. How the United States and other countries responded to refugees and immigrants would be a bellwether of our own ability to live by our deepest values, and "history will judge us harshly if we do not rise to this moment."

In August 2016, the 10,000th refugee from Syria arrived in the United States. An editorial by the *Washington Post* editorial board noted the relatively small measure of this accomplishment: "the United States could do much more. Hundreds of thousands of Vietnamese were resettled in this country after the war there. More than 120,000 Cubans came to the United States in the course of a few months during the Mariel boatlift in 1980." It was a reminder of how embattled the topic of refugees had already become; the editorial called it a "craven resistance to any resettlement." On September 28, in Obama's last Presidential Determination on refugees, the Obama administration announced the resettlement ceiling would jump to 110,000.

Less than two months later, Donald Trump was elected president of the United States.

Chapter 27

HASNA

Six weeks after they arrived in the United States, Hasna started the first job of her life. She had never worked outside the home. Natheir asked her one day if there was a job she had always wanted. For a second, she thought of saying architect, but that long-ago dream felt childish and absurd. But she surprised Jebreel when she said, "Hairdresser."

"Really?" Jebreel's face was mildly perplexed.

"Yes, really! I always colored my own hair and our neighbors' back in Daraa."

"Well, yes, but . . ."

"Well, I want to be a hairdresser." Her voice sounded firm and she felt pleased. This would be a good fit for her, something she could be proud of.

A few weeks later, Natheir called and told her he had found a place for her, a high-end salon downtown managed by a woman named Nawal, who was Muslim but did not wear a hijab over her highlighted hair. The women in the apartment complex helped Hasna figure out the bus routes and Hasna left two hours earlier than she needed to, arriving with thirty minutes to spare. Nawal's dark-paneled salon had low couches, gilded mirrors, dark-paneled walls. The aroma of sandalwood and lemongrass lingered in the air. Hasna felt out of place, and apologized for arriving early, but Nawal waved it away and told Hasna she'd be able to talk when she finished cutting her client's hair. Hasna watched her fingers closely, the way she pulled the comb out at an angle to snip expertly, the way she stepped back and pursed her lips slightly while evaluating the length.

When she was finished, Nawal pulled Hasna back into the office and talked to her about the job. Hasna was disappointed to learn that she would not be able to cut hair and was only going to be allowed to wash and mix colors. She told Nawal that she was very good at the right hair color—she even pulled off her hijab to show Nawal her honey-colored hair, explaining the formula she used, the proportions of bleach to olive oil, and how she was quick at pulling the hair with the thin hook through the rubber cap for highlights so that it hurt less. Nawal nodded but stated firmly: Hasna could neither cut nor color the clients' hair. In the United States, you had to have a certificate before you were allowed to work as a cosmetologist; technically, Hasna was not supposed to be on the floor at all, but Natheir was an old friend of Nawal's and she was doing him a favor in employing Hasna.

Hasna was disappointed—"hairdresser's assistant" did not have the ring to it that "hairdresser" did—but she was determined to prove herself. She had heard stories from the women about the jobs available here, how the Iraqi chemists and doctors, engineers and college professors, were all working now in hospital kitchens or as custodians. She wanted to stay in this salon, with its gilded sheen and perfumed air.

The first few days, she was humble when Nawal explained to her the proper way to shampoo hair, the right temperature, the words to ask—"Mint? Or lavender?"—when letting clients choose that month's shampoo scents. The women whose hair she watched Nawal wash were sleek, their eyebrows curved in perfect lines, their cheeks contoured by their makeup, their lips slightly pursed and always glistening with lipstick. They did not speak to Hasna, but some of them smiled. She watched Nawal fold foils of gel around her clients' hair and thought this American method of highlighting was superior to what she had done; her head always burned for a few days after pulling at her hair and then dousing it with bleach.

Hasna swept eagerly and tried to avoid tripping up Nawal or the other hairdressers while getting the hair out from under their feet. Nawal asked her once to wait until they were done, so Hasna stood eagerly to the side. When she scrubbed the desk thoroughly, she only lightly splashed the appointment book sometimes.

RANA STARTED SCHOOL AND STRUGGLED TO CATCH UP TO HER PEERS; she spent hours every night studying on the rickety table in their apartment. Hasna was confident it would not take Rana long to learn English, but Rana did not share her mother's assurance. Their RST caseworker helped them apply for Medicaid and they went to doctors' appointments with translators. The doctors admired the skill with which Jebreel's torso and shoulder had been reconstructed.

Jebreel seemed to be pulling into himself more and more. While she was gone at work, he straightened up around the house, but that did not take long. He spent many hours with other Arabic-speaking men in the apartment complex, sitting on the couches smoking and talking about politics. Many days, Hasna came back from a backbreaking day to find the men in her living room and her home filled with smoke. She never liked smoke but in Daraa she understood that she had joined her husband in his home when they married and smoking had always been a part of that. Except now, she was the one working for their rent and the acrid stink of stale smoke clung to her clothes in the pristine salon. Their irritation with each other seeped into the fabric of their home. In Daraa, there had been space when they had fought, neighbors and daughters to vent to and laugh with, work that kept Jebreel occupied all day. Now, those buffers were gone.

Jebreel's disability checks did not come and did not come. She looked at him one day when she walked in the door, sitting alone on the couch checking the news on his phone, and realized that he was old. At some point in the last three years, he had aged significantly and, for the first time since she had been a teenage bride, she felt the gap between their ages was wide. Every day she felt an inexorable pull out of the apartment, a desire to learn English and to find out what was happening around them in Austin. She loved to watch the women in the salon, her mouth twisting itself into English whenever she could. She had already learned to shop, to ride the bus, to find her neighbors' homes in the labyrinthine complex. His world by contrast was becoming the small, isolated world of an old man.

The children and grandchildren coming would help immensely. Perhaps he could stay with them while she worked and the children worked too—more income would be better for all of them. Jebreel at home with the babies, Hasna out all day . . . she wondered if she could convince him to cook, and smiled—that was a funny thought.

Her wages from the salon and their refugee stipend coming from RST only barely covered rent. They had four months left before they had to pay back the government for the plane tickets and the money from RST was over. Hasna fervently hoped that the disability checks would help.

Natheir came as often as he could and brought them a few pieces of better furniture, usable dishes, groceries for several weeks—all gifts from Syrian Americans, he told them. Hasna kept a new list in her head of everything they received, so she could pay them back, or at least help them pay for someone else in the future. When Amal and Samir got here, and then Yusef and Laila after that, they would work together to dig their way out of the debt they were accumulating.

Even if they could break their six-month apartment contract, Natheir told them there was no place in Austin they could afford. The city was built like a target and the closer you were to the center, the more expensive the apartments were. The buses in Austin were not designed for real people with real jobs—it took eight minutes for Hasna to drive to the salon when she could get a ride with a neighbor in a car, but it was an almost two-hour bus ride, depending on whether the buses were on time or not.

The sheer difficulty of navigating their lives left no room for the English she desperately wanted to learn. Hasna could not make the words stay in her brain. Her mouth formed and then lost them again. She tried writing them down, even phonetically in Arabic, but it didn't help.

She kept depression at bay only by focusing on her children. She and Amal talked almost daily over WhatsApp about what they were packing—she requested several items, including clothes, because she had not brought enough—and what they would do when they arrived. Khassem and his wife were expecting another baby; he regularly sent pictures of his daughter.

Yusef and Laila spent weeks trying to apply for refugee status in Turkey. The country was openly hostile to Syrian refugees and it felt as if every interaction took ten times as long as it should have. Their bureaucratic nightmares put into perspective for Hasna and Jebreel how long it took to get anything done in the United States. Their apartment was not what they might have wished, but at least they had a place—Laila and Yusef were in a constant state of flux waiting for their documents, staying with relatives' friends.

At every call to prayer that sounded—now from their phone app rather than ringing throughout the city—she prayed faithfully for each of her children and grandchildren by name. They were the most pressing thing in her heart.

WITH THE HELP OF A TRANSLATOR FROM RST, HASNA AND JEBREEL met with an immigration lawyer, a young woman in a suit and heels, who confirmed what Hasna had heard in all of the other meetings: Family reunification was an integral part of the US resettlement program. Her children would be given priority. They gave the lawyer Amal and Samir's names and information, as well as those of Khassem's family, even though they were not as far along with their paperwork. They also told her Yusef's and Laila's information in Turkey. The lawyer told them she would make the calls she needed to so that their names would be attached to Jebreel's case files; the situation for Yusef and Laila in Turkey might take longer than Jordan because they had not been there as long, but there was no reason to think they wouldn't be able to make it as well. The US was one of the top destinations for refugees from Turkey, the lawyer told them. It could be as early as seven months after Hasna and Jebreel arrived, maybe as long as twelve, for Amal and Samir and their girls, since they were in the system already. The lawyer gave them the paperwork they needed to fill out in order to get their green cards and told them how to file the papers.

The next day, she started writing in the green card application. Several days later, she mailed it off with as much hope as she had had for weeks. She was Syrian and her heart would beat for Syria until she died. But this was one small step she could take toward permanently reuniting her family.

HASNA HAD BEEN AT THE HAIR SALON FOR TWO MONTHS WHEN NAWAL pulled her aside and told her that there was a problem. The woman who owned the salon had discovered that Hasna did not have the correct certification to work there even as a hairdresser's assistant. Nawal was sorry, but she was going to have to let Hasna go. Hasna asked if she could stay through the end of the day, to finish sweeping and to clean everything up. She tried not to let Nawal see her cry while she straightened the bottles of shampoo one last time. Nawal avoided her eyes.

Hasna was not sure where to go that afternoon after she was done at the salon. She ended up taking the bus to the grocery store and buying a cake. As long as she had money, she would buy this cake. It was creamy, soaked in milk with icing between the layers. That night after dinner, she sprinkled pistachio nuts on top of it and served it with Turkish coffee and cardamom. After they had finished eating, Hasna told Jebreel about getting fired.

She spent two months without a job and Natheir Ali raised money to help her pay for the rent. Jebreel smoked cigarettes. Hasna cleaned. Rana studied. The apartment felt small and cramped and yet Hasna was desperately afraid that they would lose it. Where would they go? What happened to people when they could not pay their rent in the United States? It was not something she had ever considered, even though they had had some lean months in Syria; in Jordan it had loomed over her as she watched the dwindling supply of gold and saw how many more refugees arrived every day to compete for the scant jobs that kept their family afloat. Natheir told them that he would not allow them to be on the street. The thought that they were living on other people's charity was a heavy blanket on her shoulders, one she could never take off.

One of her friends told her that there was an opening in the hotel where a few of the women in the apartment complex worked, the Hyatt Downtown. They were looking for an entry-level person to join the housekeeping crew. She asked whether Hasna would be interested in the job. A few months ago, the idea of working for the cleaning crew in a hotel had seemed like the worst possible fate. Now, Hasna was grateful for the chance. In Daraa she would have felt it was beneath her station. Here she saw many other people doing whatever they needed to do in order to survive; she respected them and resolved that she would have to view this job as admirable rather than shameful.

The next morning, she was able to speak to Amal's daughters over video chat. Just to see their little faces brought her joy. She wished that she could pull their hair back again; it kept getting in their eyes. They kept grabbing the phone and reaching toward her, asking her to come play with them.

TWO WEEKS LATER, HASNA PULLED THE CART OUT INTO THE HALL-way to begin her day. She yawned. She had to leave the house by 5:30 in order to be on time for her 7:45 shift. She ended the day at 4:00 and was able to make it home in time for dinner most days. Rana had taken over most of the cooking, which was a relief to Hasna. The twelve-hour days wore on her. She noticed that her muscles were getting stronger, but every day her feet were swollen by the time she got home.

In the morning, she filled up the cart with everything she needed to clean the rooms for the day: sheets, towels, shampoos and soaps, hairdryers, toilet paper, ice buckets, glasses, cleaning supplies. She had to appear professional but also to blend in with her surroundings. She was allowed to smile pleasantly, but not engage with people unless they asked her questions. No one ever asked her questions.

Every morning, she received a list of rooms to be cleaned. At first, she cleaned like a Syrian. She used buckets of water with soap, scrubbing down everything, including the walls. Her Arabic-speaking shift manager, a woman with beautiful eyes from Iraq, had not been angry but had laughed and told Hasna that here in America, they used disinfecting spray and did not scrub very much. She showed Hasna how to spray and wipe down the bathroom in a few minutes' time.

Now she could clean each room quickly. She refilled the coffee station, laying the tea bags out nicely and placing the wrapped paper cups facedown beside the coffee pot. She made sure to tuck the clean sheets tightly around the mattress as she had been taught. After she put the blankets and the pillows back on the bed, she vacuumed the room well. Then she dusted, placing the pad of paper with the hotel logo at right angles with the edge of the desk. The pen went diagonally across the pad of paper.

Then she tackled the bathroom. Shower, toilet, sink, mirror, new soap, folded-edge toilet paper, fresh towels, new glasses. She took out the trash last, checking to make sure that there was an extra trash bag underneath the empty one. Finally, she would spray the room with perfume. In Syria, they did not use perfume. They just used plenty of soap.

That night on the ride home from work, as the bus started and stopped in its long winding route to her apartment, Hasna overheard two people talking about the election. She recognized the words "president" and "Donald Trump." She had known that the US was electing a president but had barely paid attention to the process since she could not listen to news in English. They received their news from Arabic sources over their phones and through their friends' posts on Facebook or WhatsApp—she knew much more about what was happening in Syria and Jordan than here in the United States. Like all the Syrians she knew, Hasna wanted Hillary Clinton to win. Secretly, Hasna liked the idea of living in a country with a woman president. Mostly the headlines in the Arabic-speaking news agencies were full of the things that Donald Trump had said about Muslims. Hasna liked the people that she had encountered in the United States. She assumed that they would not support someone who said the kinds of things that Donald Trump said as their leader. Or—as seemed likelier to someone who had lived most of her life reading between the lines of the Syrian media—the reports were greatly exaggerated. Surely no world leader talked that way.

But she heard the two people in front of her say the name Donald Trump several times in disbelief, looking at their phones. She pulled hers out and checked the news in Arabic. The headlines talked about the presidential election, but no one knew the winner. She went home that night and ate the simple dinner that Rana had prepared. She slept. When she woke up, she checked the news again. It was true—Donald Trump was the new president. Hasna felt sad for the people she knew who really wanted Clinton to have won, but really, what did it have to do with her? The president of the United States felt far away from her daily life. She hurried to shower before praying and running out the door to catch her bus.

Chapter 28

MU NAW

AUSTIN, TEXAS, USA, MARCH 2016

Mu Naw walked up to the door of her new house. The papers were signed, the fees all paid. For the first time in her life, she was a homeowner. She would have to water the front lawn; she would have to buy a lawn mower. She had seen people with small buzzing machines trimming the grass around the edges—she supposed she would have to buy one of those too. The list of things she would need—washing machine and dryer, curtains and blinds, lawn care equipment—just to make it through the next few weeks felt daunting. There were entire rooms to furnish, blank cream walls to hang pictures on, drawers and cabinets to fill.

Smoothly, without fiddling at all, she unlocked the door of her new home. She could have opened the garage door with the new remote—she pressed a button and an entire door rose at her command—but she had not. She had wanted to walk into her new home by the front door. She stood back to let the children spill in first, racing each other, all arms and legs and shouting voices that echoed through the empty rooms. She took a deep breath and looked behind her.

The moving truck was parked haphazardly in the driveway, loaded with almost a decade of life in a new country. She was in awe of everything she had, grateful for her new home, although leaving had been incredibly difficult— dinner the night before had been full of tears and prolonged good-byes.

Saw Ku came around the corner. He put down the box he was holding and looked at Mu Naw for a long moment. Then, without warning, he walked up to her. He grinned, the lopsided smile of complete happiness that he reserved only for her, and kissed her. She knew that he was thinking back to that lock on the door in their first apartment.

Just before she walked in the door, Saw Ku tugged at her hand. His voice was quiet, meant only for her. "This is because of you, my love." He leaned in to kiss her forehead. "This house and everything we have is because of you."

EVERYTHING HAD CHANGED FOR MU NAW ON THE NIGHT SHE FOUND out her mother had died. The overwhelming grief that still came in waves did not dilute the clarity she had felt. She had seen herself as her mother saw her, as she could imagine seeing her own daughters years from now, and realized that she and her mother had both done their best to love and support each other, that she and Saw Ku loved each other but were not sure how to find each other again through the pain of their past, that all of them had made the best decisions they could with the information they had available at the time.

The epiphany was simple, but the ramifications were profound. Mu Naw knew she *did* want to be like her mother—like the best sides of her mother. She had within her the strength to make it on her own. But she wanted to fix things with Saw Ku.

She stepped out of that closet with a new resolve to save her marriage. It was not easy. The damage they had done to each other was deep. It would take years to undo their way of communicating, the arguments and the stinging comments that always seemed to be their go-to. But in the first few days after her mother's death, it was clear that he had been struck by the same resolve. He came home from work earlier, took on more of the chores around the house, played with the children as he had not in months. He was tender and kind; he gave her time for herself and let her go to bed early on days when she could hardly function without crying. He hugged her more; he held her hand in public. He went to church with her several Sundays in a row. And, one day, he asked if he could move back into her bedroom.

At church, Mu Naw began asking the older Karen women for marriage advice. One of them handed her a magazine published by a Karen Baptist press with an article in it outlining how to have a family devotional. The woman told Mu Naw to keep the magazine and she took it home and read the article until she almost had it memorized. The author suggested that reading the Bible and praying together as a family was the single most important thing she had done—it was clear the article had been translated from English and that the woman's ideas were perfect for an American context. Mu Naw wasn't sure how the article would go over in Karen communities in Thailand, or in Myanmar—did it seem ludicrous to plan for family mealtime after work when everyone lived together, all day with no jobs, in one tiny hut? How would the chipper tone be received in Karen families where Dad wasn't just distracted, he was off fighting in the jungle with the Karen National Army? What did a family devotional look like for the life she had once led?

But it fit her life now. It gave her a plan and a way forward.

She left the article with a bookmark on Saw Ku's side of the bed; she noticed when she came in from washing her face one night that he was reading the magazine. She did not say anything; she did not even act as if she noticed. A few days later, she told Saw Ku that she and the children were going to begin to have a family devotional on Wednesday nights. She did not ask him to join. She mentioned it only in passing.

The first night they had the family devotional, she prayed first that her heart would be right. She found the passages that she wanted to read aloud in the Bible, in both Karen and English so that her children—who now read English better than Karen—would truly understand. After dinner, when the dishes were put away and the children bathed, she called them into the living room. Saw Ku turned off the TV and went into the bedroom; he was not tense, he was just uninterested. She tried not to be disappointed. She decided to say nothing. She had the girls, first Pah Poe in Karen and then Naw Wah in English, read aloud: "Do not be anxious about anything, but in everything, by prayer and petition, present your requests to God. And the peace that passes all understanding will guide your hearts and minds in Christ Jesus." She felt that peace infuse her. She wanted that peace in her home. She wanted to feel that peace every day.

She began praying every day for peace between her and Saw Ku. The older woman who gave her the article gave her more magazines and Mu Naw read them voraciously, finding nuggets of wisdom in each article that talked about families, serving one another, and speaking to each other with love. Mu Naw was not sure if God—or how God—worked on Saw Ku, but she knew that praying for Saw Ku increased her own awareness of his life.

Saw Ku worked hard every day at a job where no one talked to him but his brother; if his coworkers did speak to him, he barely understood them. He was drained from the hard physical labor of cleaning hotel rooms—moving the sheets in and out of the laundry piles, pushing large furniture around to clean, hauling carts up and down the hallway. It was often disgusting work—it was shocking to both of them the things that people would do and the messes they would leave in an anonymous hotel. And it was mindless work—it was not the kind of work he loved. What he loved was providing for his family; and he loved to play the guitar, one of the few times a week when he could let his mind and body go, when he was confident in the way his fingers flew on the strings, when he knew who he was and what he was doing.

Mu Naw began asking Saw Ku if he would like to go with the guys on Saturday nights to play video games and jam together. The first time she offered, he squinted at her suspiciously—he wanted to see what she hoped for in return. But he went and she asked for nothing and a week later, she suggested he go again. That night became habit and she made sure to ask him before scheduling translating gigs after work at night. In turn, he asked her before he left the house, or called when he thought he would be late.

One day, several weeks into her new routine of having a family devotional, Saw Ku came out of the bedroom and joined them. The kids, following their mother's lead, acted as if it were normal for him to be there. When she asked Pah Poe to read aloud from the Karen Bible, Saw Ku took it and read the verse himself. When he was finished, Naw Wah read it confidently in English. He told his little daughter she had done well. Saw Ku caught her eye and they smiled at each other. A year later, they moved into the new home they could afford because of Mu Naw's good job.

Chapter 29

US REFUGEE RESETTLEMENT,
2015–2018

In 2015, while President Obama was making the case for resettling more Syrian refugees, the massive unraveling of public support for refugee resettlement in the United States began relatively quickly. The spark might have been the Paris attacks at the end of 2015, as well as the attacks in Brussels in early 2016, but this particular restrictionism had been simmering in the country since 9/11.

Social media spread fear of refugees in a new way, but the underlying messages and racialized tropes were virtually unchanged since the United States immigration debates in the 1880s. One meme that went viral in the United States and Europe showed four images of heavily built men crossing gangplanks. The caption, "Refugees?" in white letters in the middle of the picture was followed by red-rimmed, disintegrating letters at the bottom: "Is it sinking in yet?"

Another meme lifted an image from *The Atlantic* of a Free Syria Army officer posing with his assault weapon outside Aleppo in January 2015 and then seeking asylum in Greece in fall of 2015. The image—shared by an anti-immigrant advocate in the UK, Peter Lee Goodchild, with the caption, "Remember this guy? Posing in ISIS photos last year—now he's a 'refugee.' Are we suckers or what?"—was shared more than seventy thousand times before Goodchild removed the post.

"Sucker" was the same word used by the announcer in the postwar Army-Navy newsreel when he posed the question about why the United States and other Allies were helping refugees. The argument put forth at that time—that aid was effective not just for humanitarian reasons but because, if the US didn't "help these people now, then the chaos will continue indefinitely, and the seeds of a third World War will take root"—was not as effective in 2015 as it had been in the late 1940s. Instead, to paraphrase the Chinese Exclusion Act cartoon, the memes represented "The Great Fear of the period—that the United States would be consumed by terrorists." As had happened in the 1930s, this rhetoric conflated the victims of terrorism with its perpetrators, but, unlike the 1930s, the intensive—one might even say extreme—vetting processes put people accepted in the United States for refugee resettlement in a completely different category. The Refugee Admissions Process was an all but impossible avenue for terrorists to enter the country. The American public did not turn against people holding tourist or student visas, which were the way most of the actual non-American terrorists in the twenty-first century had gained admittance to the country. Stoked by fear-based social media, however, that logical argument did little to stem the tide of public sentiment.

This view—that any humanitarian impulse toward Muslim refugees was a product of suckers who were welcoming poorly disguised terrorists—was not limited to biased posts on social media. Antirefugee rhetoric became more and more mainstream. Politicians once again presented better-safe-than-sorryism as commonsense policy. They used phrases almost identical to those in the starkly racist debates that culminated in the Immigration Act of 1924 and the closed-door refugee policies of the 1930s and early 1940s.

TRUMP GAVE A SPEECH ON REFUGEES ON JANUARY 12, 2016, WHILE campaigning in Cedar Falls, Iowa, almost eighty years after Lindbergh's 1941 Iowa "war agitator" speech, that played up that great fear. He had just begun using the slogan "America First," which journalists and historians at the time connected with Lindbergh and the original America First Committee. Trump framed Syrian refugees, and Muslims in general, as an enemy to the American people:

> They don't have paper work, they have no documentation whatsoever—they have no documentation! And then we're bringing them into this country? We don't know who they are? And you look at what happens in California? And you look at some of the things that happen, including, by the way, flying airplanes into the World Trade Center? Why are we doing this?

He conflated all Syrian refugees (and, in other speeches, all Muslims) with San Bernardino shooters Syed Rizwan Farook (who was from Riverside, California) and Tashfeen Malik (who was originally from Saudi Arabia and Pakistan), as well as the al-Qaeda-associated September 11 hijackers who came to the US on tourist and student visas from Saudi Arabia, United Arab Emirates, Egypt, and Lebanon. Syrian refugees, who had years' worth of paper trails backing up their stories from the intensive vetting process across multiple agencies and international databases, were the people he said had "no paperwork."

But the speech was just weeks after the Paris attacks, and news outlets in the United States were still tracing some of the terrorists back to ISIS in Syria—whether or not any of Trump's referents were factual at all, his audience's shared context made those appeals effective in a way they might not have been in another time.

At the same rally, to describe his immigration policy, Trump put on his reading glasses and read Oscar Brown Jr.'s lyrics to "The Snake." The story line is simple: a woman finds a cold snake, takes it into her home to warm it up, and then it bites and kills her. For emphasis, Trump added the word "vicious" before the word "snake" every time he read it. When he arrived at the end of the lyrics, he emphasized each word: "You knew damn well I was a snake before you took me in." At this point Trump paused, took off his glasses while the audience applauded, and asked, "Does that make sense to anybody? Does that make any sense? Does that make sense? And hopefully that's not going to be the case. I read it and I just put it together." The simplistic, sing-song rhythm felt like a children's nursery rhyme, a concept so easy to grasp even a child could understand: a country naïve enough to bring in "snakes" deserves what it gets.

Lindbergh's anti-Semitic "America First" speech in 1941 destroyed his reputation. Trump's Islamophobic "America First" speeches in 2015–2016 led to his becoming president.

ON FRIDAY, JANUARY 27, 2017—HOLOCAUST REMEMBRANCE DAY— President Trump instituted one of the first acts of his administration. Effective immediately, the sweeping "Executive Order Protecting the Nation from Foreign Terrorist Entry into the United States" restricted entry by citizens of seven different countries—Iraq, Iran, Libya, Somalia, Sudan, Yemen, and Syria—for ninety days. The travel ban issued a call for new immigration screening processes in addition to the ones implemented under Bush and Obama, what Trump called in other speeches "extreme vetting."

The order suspended the refugee program for four months, longer than the Bush administration's suspension after 9/11. In a striking deviation from every other president before him, Trump's order overturned Obama's Presidential Determination to resettle 110,000 refugees and capped the admissions ceiling at 50,000.

In the order, Trump also banned all Syrian refugees. As he said in his announcement speech, "I hereby proclaim that the entry of nationals of Syria as refugees is detrimental to the interests of the United States and thus suspend any such entry." Once the resettlement program reopened, priority would be given to refugees for whom "the religion of the individual is a minority religion," meaning that Christian refugees from Muslim-majority nations would be much likelier to receive resettlement than their fellow citizens.

There were no exceptions made—not even for family members of those who had already been resettled, the first time since 1965 that the United States would challenge family reunification as a pillar of immigration. Soon the Trump administration would rebrand family reunification as "chain migration"; Vice President Mike Pence would promise to abolish it. Presidential senior policy adviser Stephen Miller—whose uncle wrote a scathing op-ed in *Politico* revealing that his family was the product of "chain migration"—and other officials in the Trump administration would work tirelessly against allowing families to reunite in a series of policies affecting all immigrants, but particularly targeting refugees.

ON THE DAY THE ADMINISTRATION ISSUED ITS TRAVEL BAN, THERE was an immediate explosion of demonstrations in airports across the country. News outlets shared stories of those affected—people with legal visas sent back without being able to disembark, refugees who had sold everything unable to board their planes after years of vetting. Lawyers and reporters jostled with sign-holding protesters for days at almost every international airport in the United States. There was an overwhelming public outcry against the president's language asserting that all immigrants from the seven Muslim-majority countries were "foreign terrorist entries."

Lawsuits filed by the ACLU and other groups on Saturday, January 28, led to a temporary injunction from a federal judge in New York by the next morning. Four other federal courts agreed with the judge in New York. While the courts sorted out what was legal and what was not with the order—unprecedented both in scope and in the rapidity of its implementation—officials allowed refugees and other immigrants with legal visas and imminent arrival times who had been banned to enter the United States.

The real impact came for those who were not on airplanes, for refugees at various points in the resettlement process, for voluntary resettlement agencies that had prepared for arrivals that were stopped, for immigrants whose paperwork was still under consideration.

On March 6, 2017, Trump signed a narrowed version of the ban, which took off Sudan and Iraq but added Chad to the countries whose citizens would not be admitted (the Trump administration would later remove Chad from the list in April 2018). A federal judge in Hawaii halted implementation of the ban on March 15. In May 2017, a judge in Maryland upheld a lower court ruling in an International Refugee Assistance Project lawsuit against the government.

In July 2017, the Supreme Court agreed with a ruling by a lower court that exempted not just immediate family members from the travel restriction but also grandparents, grandchildren, brothers- and sisters-in-law, uncles and aunts, cousins, nieces, and nephews—anyone with what it termed a "bona fide relationship."

In September 2017, the Trump administration countered with a third version of the executive order, which this time added North Korean citizens to the list of those restricted from coming into the country, as well as some Venezuelan officials. The justices allowed the travel ban to remain in effect while the courts considered challenges.

On June 26, 2018, in a 5–4 decision in *Trump* v. *Hawaii*, the US Supreme Court upheld the third version of the Trump administration's executive order. Chief Justice John Roberts noted at the time of the ruling that many of the statements made by the president of the United States, including his promise to instill a "total and complete shutdown of Muslims entering the United States" could not be considered by the court; their job was not to decide "whether to denounce the statements" made by the president—in fact, he stated he would "express no view on the soundness of the policy." Instead, the order on which they deliberated fell within the "scope of Presidential authority" and therefore outside the jurisdiction of the Supreme Court: "The admission and exclusion of foreign nationals is a fundamental sovereign attribute exercised by the government's political departments largely immune from judicial control." The third version of the executive order stood.

THE TRAVEL BAN IN THE UNITED STATES MIGHT HAVE BEEN AN EXTREME policy, but resettlement numbers were down across the globe as restrictionism rose worldwide. There was every reason to think that there should be more resettlement opportunities—the number of countries partnering with UNHCR had risen from fourteen in 2005 to thirty-seven in 2016. And yet the number of people accepted anywhere for resettlement declined sharply as well, from 189,000 people worldwide in 2016 to 103,000 in 2017.

At the same time, the number of refugees reached a record high in 2017: 25.4 million by the end of the year. The number rose more than 2 million from 22.5 million at the end of 2016, and there were now 71.44 million persons of concern in the world.

If it were possible to gather the persons of concern into one country, by population it would fit between Thailand (69.3 million) and Germany (82.4 million). By population, if the 103,000 people resettled collectively anywhere in the world were a city in the United States, it would be about the size of Wichita Falls, Texas; Rialto, California; Davenport, Iowa; South Bend, Indiana; or Las Cruces, New Mexico.

IN 2017, IN HIS FIRST PRESIDENTIAL DETERMINATION, TRUMP ANnounced a refugee admissions cap of 45,000, the lowest ceiling since 1980. Only 22,491 refugees actually arrived in the United States in fiscal year 2018. For the first time since the establishment of the Federal Refugee Resettlement Program, the US no longer led the world in resettlement. Canada surpassed the United States, with admissions just under 30,000.

The vast majority of refugees, 7,883, came from the Democratic Republic of Congo; 3,555 arrived from Myanmar. True to his administration's promises, the arrivals were 68 percent Christian, though the stark decrease in the overall number of refugees meant that the number of Christian refugees was down significantly from 22,637 Christians the year before. There were still a handful of people—369 total—resettled under the "bona fide relationship" exemptions to countries listed in the travel ban.

In 2018, the Assad regime systematically regained control of the country, unimpeded by the international community and backed by Russia and Iran, and UNHCR estimated 13.1 million people were in need in Syria. There were now 3.3 million Syrian refugees in Turkey, 1.5 million in Lebanon, over a million in Jordan.

In 2018, the US resettled 62 Syrian refugees.

BECAUSE THE REFUGEE ACT OF 1980 PUT REFUGEE ADMISSIONS UNDER the jurisdiction of the president, it is one of the few aspects of immigration over which any president has almost unimpeded control. The Trump administration set out to curb immigration in the United States through a number of restrictionist actions in 2017 and 2018: ending the Deferred Action for Childhood Arrivals (DACA) program; ending the Temporary Protected Status (TPS) for people from Haiti, Nicaragua, Sudan, Honduras, and Nepal; targeting undocumented immigrant populations, even those who had been ignored by previous administrations, for arrest and deportation; separating families at the border as a matter of policy; turning asylum seekers away in a violation of American non-refoulement agreements. Some of those attempts were more successful than others; federal courts stopped the administration's attempts to cancel DACA; public outcry against the family separation policy mitigated it to some degree.

When it came to this item on their agenda, however, the Trump administration was enormously effective. Miller's remarks at a White House meeting with officials from the State Department, the Department of Homeland Security, and the National Security Council on June 5, 2017, in a story recounted to Jonathan Blitzer at *The New Yorker*, showed the administration's focus. Miller notes that, unlike past administrations, "the President views this as a homeland-security issue." As an unnamed official understood it, resettlement would no longer "be looked at from the typical lens of foreign policy," but instead it became "a domestic-policy issue, an immigration issue." Previous administrations took pains to separate refugees, with their unique admissions process, vetting procedures, humanitarian needs, and foreign-policy considerations, from larger national immigration discussions. The Trump administration erased those divisions and special considerations, lumping refugees with almost all immigrants—this administration's new "undesirables."

THE CHANGES EFFECTIVELY CONSTRAINED THE RESETTLEMENT NETwork that had grown up since the passage of the FRRP in 1980. By adding extra procedures to the vetting process, the Trump administration impeded the ability of the FBI and other government agencies to conduct routine security reviews—one of the main reasons why less than half of the allowed 45,000 people actually arrived in 2018. The same way that McCarthyism stringently over-vetted refugee admissions in the early 1950s, so restrictionist officials were able to slow the process under the Trump administration. But in the 1950s, the Eisenhower administration worked to ensure that those officials did not wield a disproportionate amount of power. In 2018, the restrictionist officials were within the administration itself.

The drastic cut in admissions came with steep financial implications for organizations that often already worked on a shoestring budget. The federal government provided each refugee a grant that partially funded agencies' work and with lower arrivals, their budgets fell immediately. In early 2018, based on the lower number of arrivals, the State Department adjusted the number of contracts it offered to the nine national private voluntary resettlement agencies—effectively, it no longer approved some places to work with refugees and, without that approval, the organizations could no longer do the work they had done for years. By early 2018, there were 324 resettlement offices operating in the country under the nine volags with a State Department contract or their affiliates. The State Department announced in February 2018 that 40 sites would be forced to reduce their operations and 20 others would close completely. By April 2018, in Florida alone, 12 of the 25 resettlement agencies closed or moved away from resettlement. Those site closures represented the loss of experienced caseworkers and translators, community partners and volunteer coordinators—the kinds of workers that would be incredibly difficult to replace should resettlement numbers go up again in the future.

The cuts didn't affect just new arrivals. Refugees qualified for services for the first five years after they arrived in the country; most agencies, if they had the funding and capacity, would offer that help longer if they could, especially for more vulnerable populations. Those services included English classes and mental health counseling and employment help. When sites closed and agencies were forced to make choices about what they could offer, the repercussions for traumatized people whom the United States committed to support were instantaneous.

The radio program *This American Life* documented the last week for an International Rescue Committee office in Garden City, Kansas. The producer, Zoe Chace, recorded site manager Amy Longa as she tried to wrap up the work of an office that was an integral part of the community. Amy could not finish packing up the office because people kept coming in and asking questions:

How do I get a birth certificate for my new baby daughter? How much does it cost? How is my green card application doing? . . . How much is it to go to the dentist? Should I pull this tooth out of my mouth? If I pull the tooth, should I replace it with a new tooth or leave the gap? And what will people around here think if I have a gap? Is that bad? Where is the dentist's office?

As Chace noticed, "Amy has this ability where it's like she imagines all the thoughts in their head. She can picture the entire thought process of the person who's sitting in front of her." A former refugee herself, Amy knew how to be empathetic, capable, kind, efficient, firm, and loving all at once. The tacit knowledge in her mind—the ability to intuit what her clients were going to ask or need—could not be replicated. For most people who stayed in it for any amount of time, resettlement work became more of a calling than a job. The loss of Amy Longa and hundreds, if not thousands, of experienced caseworkers and administrators like her was a devastating blow to the entire process.

WHAT MADE IT ESPECIALLY DIFFICULT WAS THAT THE TRUMP ADMIN-istration continued to invoke the same lofty, inspiring language of every president since Truman. In September 2018, Secretary of State Mike Pompeo announced the Presidential Determination for a devastatingly limited refugee admissions ceiling of 30,000 refugees.

In his speech, he conflated two separate admissions processes, referring to 310,000 refugees and asylum seekers who would come to the United States as if they arrived through the same program. The 30,000 refugees accepted for resettlement came through the Refugee Admissions Process. The 280,000 asylum seekers were part of a different, discrete route; mostly from Central America, their cases would go through the US immigration courts and the vast majority would never be considered for asylum. But putting the two together masked the stark deviation from previous administrations' tactics—those who were unaware of the resettlement figures under the Reagan, George H. W. Bush, Clinton, George W. Bush, and Obama administrations might think

310,000 was on par with or even ahead of those decades. It certainly sounded impressive.

Pompeo also borrowed statistics from the Bush and Obama administrations to note "the over 800,000 asylum seekers who are already inside the United States and who are awaiting adjudication of their claims," as well as "over one and a half million people ... admitted as refugees or granted asylum" since 2000, and the "hundreds of thousands of people who have received temporary and permanent humanitarian protection under other immigration categories such as victims of trafficking, humanitarian parole, temporary protected status, and special immigrant" visas. He touted "these expansive figures" that demonstrated "the United States' long-standing record as the most generous nation in the world when it comes to protection-based immigration and assistance"—while he announced cuts that took the once-generous resettlement program to a new historic low.

FOLLOWING THAT ANNOUNCEMENT, EVEN MORE AGENCIES SHUTTERED. Not all organizations had a closure as dramatic as that of the IRC in Garden City, Kansas. Some of the sites shifted their focus to other vulnerable populations. Caritas of Austin, an affiliate of Catholic Charities and one of two agencies working in Austin, Texas, announced in September 2018 it would no longer accept refugees for resettlement. Only a few years before, the nonprofit employed twenty-seven staffers serving as case managers, or employment and education specialists; by 2018, there were five staffers left who had worked with refugees and they focused on Austin's homeless populations by the end of the year. In October 2018, Refugee Services of Texas—now the only affiliate agency serving refugees in Austin—did an internal analysis that showed they could make it for two more years at their current budget without losing any of their staff. As RST CEO Russell Smith put it, the goal for the nonprofit was to "survive until we can thrive. . . . By 2021, we need to be able to ramp up."

That sentiment echoed across refugee resettlement agencies—the desire to hunker down and wait out the changes in a way that would allow agencies to be prepared for an eventual uptick in resettlement. The bureaucratic connections and processes that had taken years to develop would take time to reinstitute if and when the US could begin accepting refugees at the rate it once did. Private donations made up for some of the losses from the cut federal funds, but the years were lean ones for the volags and affiliates that did manage to keep their doors open. One anonymous source estimated that there were eighty-six sites total that had either closed or shifted away from refugee assistance by early 2019: 25 percent of the once-thriving, well-protected humanitarian agencies in cities across the United States.

The Trump administration took aim at various aspects of the refugee process. Officials publicly toyed with the idea of moving the Bureau of Populations, Refugees, and Migration (PRM) from the State Department to another agency, an idea that refugee advocates managed to successfully petition first Secretary of State Rex Tillerson and then Secretary of State Mike Pompeo not to do. A planned closure of twenty-three USCIS field offices in twenty different countries in early 2019 would hold up a significant number of refugee applications at the earliest stages. The administration's proposed 2020 budget called for a 90 percent reduction to PRM's budget. As of the writing of this book, the administration was reportedly considering zero refugee admissions for its 2020 Presidential Determination. No matter the number that would be proposed, the Trump administration effectively demonstrated its intention to stop or slow resettlement with every tool in its arsenal: bureaucratic, rhetorical, political, and financial.

Those refugees who could no longer reunite with their families or who were no longer eligible for resettlement in the United States were not the only ones these lowered numbers and focused closures affected. Since 1948, restrictionist and liberalizer presidential administrations had raised and lowered the cap. They paroled in displaced persons or ended programs in response to specific crises. They advocated fiercely for some refugees while ignoring the plight of others based on US foreign policy interests. There were many shifts and changes in the more than seven decades of focusing on refugees as a group of immigrants with a unique set of considerations.

Still, the actions of the Trump administration were truly unprecedented: for the first time in history, the government branch tasked with overseeing the refugee admissions process instead brought the entire resettlement system to the edge of collapse.

Chapter 30

HASNA

Amal told Hasna over video chat they had already begun the first security screening, which meant they were reaching the end of the process. Her earliest estimate for the date when Amal and her family might arrive was March. Every day, Hasna eyed her neighbors, wondering if any of them were going to move. Even with her job and Jebreel's disability checks, they still barely had enough money every month to pay for rent and groceries and bills and their debt to the US government. Still, she managed to set a little bit aside every month to save for some good dishes for Amal and clothes for the children. Natheir told her that he had friends who would help them get better furniture than the particle-board table—Hasna wanted Amal's family to begin their new lives with some things that could last.

Yusef and Laila continued to move to various places in Turkey, staying first with one friend and then another. There was a time when the fact that Laila was a widow might have been cause for other people to help her, but now most Syrian women were widows, most children half orphans. Hamad and Tawfiq were whiny. Over video chat, Hasna could tell Laila was stressed that they had to continue to impose on other people's hospitality. Hasna tried to amuse the boys, showing them her apartment and the neighborhood kids playing on their bikes outside the picture window. Perhaps they would get Laila's boys bikes when they arrived, she told them. Laila laughed—her face was so young when she smiled—and said she hoped that would be true. She could not wait for that day.

Rana was still struggling in school. She could not understand the English words and there was much she had to catch up on. More difficult for her were the lack of other young women in hijabs at school. They had always lived in Muslim countries; the stares of people around them took some getting used to, and at seventeen, Rana was at an age when she was profoundly uncomfortable with being different. It was not that she thought about taking off her hijab, which she'd been wearing since she was in Ramtha, but that she resented other people for not realizing it was normal. A girl in her ESL class asked her one day why she wore it and she tried to explain that it was a sign of her devotion to God, but the girl argued with her and told her that she was oppressed. Rana had to look the word up later and it upset her.

She and Hasna talked about it that night, now more like friends than mother and daughter. The Americans they met seemed to think that Syria was full of terrorists and that women were being abused. Hasna found it confusing—Syria had always been a warm and open society, where Christians and Muslims and Druze, Circassians and Kurds, blended their lives beautifully. Muslim women were not judged for leaving their heads uncovered—hijabs were almost taboo in the years Hasna was having babies, when she had left her hair uncovered and worn miniskirts. Later, as the association with the Muslim Brotherhood faded and it became more acceptable to show outward forms of religion, more and more women wore the hijab while others chose not to, and both decisions were fine.

Hasna hated that this war had erased the good things in Syria, that people only knew about her country because of the refugee crisis. She wished she had the words to tell people in English that the word "Syria" was not one to invoke pity or fear. It tasted like honey on her tongue.

Things were easier for Rana in the apartment complex. Hasna was glad she was making friends. Several of the families had young girls around Rana's age and they met with other young women at a club for refugee teenagers. Hasna liked that strong, devout young Syrian women surrounded her daughter at home.

ON A COLD FRIDAY NIGHT AT THE END OF JANUARY, HASNA WALKED into the apartment, shaking off the cold. The space was too full of men. She wished again for the large, comfortable living space in Daraa, where the men would have reclined on her velvety Persian rugs against low pillows. She would have served them tea on her filigreed brass tray. She tucked the wish away. This was where she was and what she had. She greeted them and began walking to the back to hang up her coat in her room.

"Hasna!" Jebreel's voice was sharp but his eyes were not on her, they were on his phone. She realized that she had been thinking about smoke and couches and not noticing the mood in the room—the men were on the edges of their seats.

"What? What's going on?" Hasna had her arm out of her coat sleeve when there was a knock on the door and Um Khalid walked in without waiting to be bid. Her husband, Abu Khalid, was sitting on the couch by some of the other men. A cigarette dangled from his fingertips; his black hair was carefully slicked back to minimize the balding spots on either side.

"Peace be with you, Um Khalid." Hasna slid the other sleeve of her coat off.

"Peace be with you, Um Yusef. I'm so sorry." Um Khalid's sympathetic expression softened her normally sharp features.

"What?"

"Hasna." Jebreel looked up now. Rana walked in with a tray of tea and Um Khalid moved to take it before Hasna could. In an instant, Hasna registered her pride at Rana's initiative—the tray was the long clear dish from the inside of their microwave and the teacups were mismatched, but the tea, at least, was stout black tea from Turkey and Rana had sliced bananas, fruit, and grapes artfully onto small plates with forks and napkins—and her slight irritation that Um Khalid felt it was her place to serve in Hasna's home.

But the other part of her brain was already detaching itself, becoming aware that something had happened. Her family—someone had been killed. She fumbled for a chair, clutching her coat like a baby to her chest.

"Hasna, there's been an announcement. An official proclamation from the president."

"It's an 'executive order,'" Um Khalid interrupted. Her husband shot her a side glance and she shrugged her shoulders. Hasna's mouth was open slightly. Were they being sent back to Syria?

"They are not allowing any more Syrians to come to the United States. As of today. Even the ones on the planes are being turned back."

She tried to focus on Jebreel's face. She realized there were tears in his eyes.

"But Amal is coming."

"I know."

"And Samir. And the girls."

"Yes." Now the tears were spilling out of his eyes. Saying their names, she could almost conjure them in her living room.

And if Amal couldn't come, then Laila . . . "And the boys. And Yusef. And Khassem . . ."

"I know."

"Here, habibti. Drink your tea." Um Khalid shoved a hot cup of tea, brimful with sugar, into her hand. Hasna gulped it. The liquid scalded her tongue but she felt that if she did not drink it, she might sink into the floor.

Rana came to sit by her and Hasna snuggled her into the crook of her arm. Rana was pale and her body shook occasionally with sobs. And then Hasna sat up.

"No. This can't be right. They told us. Everyone told us about family reunification . . ."

Abu Khalid hung up the phone and listened to her, but she tapered off. When she did not speak anymore, he nodded as if she had made an excellent point. "Natheir Ali has been on the phone with dozens of people. Abu Adnan's brother was at the airport in Turkey. They had sold everything and were standing at the airport with their tickets in their hands." Um Khalid gasped quietly.

"The US has turned them away."

"They cannot do that." Hasna was surprised to find that she was the one speaking. She stood up. "They promised us. Those people will have sold all of their possessions and let go of their apartment. They don't have any place left to go."

Abu Khalid kept nodding. "And yet, they've done this thing. Made this 'executive order.' And that means they can do whatever they want."

Hasna was shaking her head. "I do not believe that this will last. Surely Americans will let them come. They have all of their paperwork. They have one security clearance left." And she realized she was talking about Amal and not Abu Adnan's brother and suddenly she was crying into her sleeve and she went to the bathroom, closing the hollow plywood door behind her.

LATER, THEY HEARD A FLURRY OF STORIES OF HORROR AND HOPE: Abu Adnan's brother and family were rerouted and then, after a number of weeks, allowed to finally arrive in Houston—Abu Adnan told them himself. A woman on the plane to Washington, D.C. to join her husband was almost sent back, except a governor and three US senators went down to the airport and demanded she be allowed to stay. Hundreds, maybe thousands, of people went to the airport with signs, yelling against this travesty—those protests they read about on the news on their phones. Hasna watched video after video of angry Americans—not bombed or gassed by their government, allowed to yell out their rage at this executive order. Hasna took heart in these stories. The American people's anger at injustice, the people who got through—they made the following weeks bearable.

For the next several weeks, the tension she felt was exactly like what she had endured when her boys were in prison back in Syria. It was as if her body, having the memory of that stress, returned to that state again. Her shoulders were rigid. Her heart raced when she was sitting still. Her back ached, both from her job and from holding her body with such constant stiffness.

One day, she sat down next to a man on the bus and he immediately got up. He was an older white man with a grizzled chin and glasses. He moved to the front of the bus and stood there, glaring at her malevolently.

A few days later, one of her coworkers snapped when Hasna asked whether the new bottles were cleaning fluid—the hotel had switched brands and the colors were different. The woman stood close enough to Hasna that a speck of spit landed on her forehead. "Why don't you bother to learn our language? You should go back where you came from if you don't even want to try to speak English."

Hasna had been speaking English. She nodded and walked away, pushing the cart aimlessly along the hall before realizing she had left behind the list of rooms she was supposed to clean. She stayed around the corner on the other end of the hall until she heard the elevator ding that indicated her coworker had gone.

About a month after she learned about the executive order, Amal called from Jordan. They had finished their last interview and had been offered resettlement—to Canada.

She kept repeating the city after Amal, "Quebec? Que-*bec*?" as if, by saying the name, she might undo the cavern opening in front of her.

She could not breathe when she thought of it. Amal and Samir, starting a new life in a cold city, Quebec. Her granddaughters in coats and scarves, learning English and French. They would live in a small apartment with wood floors, she thought; there would be snow caked in the windows, maybe a fireplace. She looked at the most recent picture of the girls on her phone and imagined their chubby legs lengthening, the lines of their faces becoming more angular. She would miss it, miss all of it. One government decided her city was worth destroying, another government decided their lives weren't worth saving, and now her family was shattered.

The next day was her day off. She left her bed only to pray and to use the restroom and drink water occasionally. Rana and Jebreel must have made lunch or dinner, she did not know. She stared at the play of light on the ceiling in her darkened bedroom for an entire day.

AMAL CALLED HER WHEN THEY ARRIVED IN CANADA AND HASNA pressed her face close to the phone as if she might reach through it to her granddaughters. They were tired. It was cold—February in Quebec felt dark and daunting. Amal had asked the Canadian officials when her parents could come, or she could go visit them in the States. They were kind, she said, they apologized profusely, but for now, it seemed, it was better to wait.

Amal pressed: how long? Her voice paused.

"What did he say?"

When she looked into the video, they could not make eye contact—Amal looked down slightly, at Hasna's face, and Hasna caught the way she twisted the side of her mouth to keep from crying. "They said definitely we should wait until you get your green cards and possibly until we're citizens, or you are."

"That's five years or more." Hasna's voice was a whisper.

Amal could only nod.

TIME MOVED DIFFERENTLY AFTER THAT FOR HASNA. AT SOME POINT in late winter or early spring, Laila called to say they were going to Greece. They would not go on a boat, she said. But they could not stay in Turkey anymore. It was almost as dangerous in Turkey as it had been in Syria. Hasna did not ask what that meant. She did not think Laila would tell her.

A few weeks later, Yusef called—they were in Greece, in a tent near the beach. They were going to try to find someplace safer. They would call when they could. As she had every day that Laila had been in Syria while she was in Jordan, Hasna kept her phone on and charged all day and night.

Hasna now recognized that the worst agony she could imagine was not death—it was her children being in danger or stressed when she was powerless to help.

ONE MORNING WHEN HASNA HAD BEEN WORKING AT THE HYATT Hotel for eight months, she was cleaning a room obviously occupied by young men. That day, she had more rooms on her list than she usually did. She was working quickly, her mind on the latest phone call with Yusef—he was looking for work in a small Greek town whose name she could not pronounce—when she tugged too hard on the bed sheets. They came off suddenly and she stumbled back. Her foot caught on a ten-pound free weight she had not seen by the bed; her arms tangled in the sheets, she tried but failed to catch herself on the desk behind her. She sat, stunned, for a few minutes, then pulled herself up as best she could. She tested her ankle—it was sore, but she could stand on it. She stumbled through her day, her wrist swelling alarmingly as the day went on. At the end of her shift, she took her loaded cart to the laundry area where she was supposed to leave the sheets and towels. She filled her arms with sheets, turned to drop the load, and collapsed. Something in her ankle cracked.

The next day, Um Khalid drove her to the doctor. She had sprained her ankle and broken her wrist. The doctor told her she could not work for several weeks. He gave her crutches and a wrist brace. When Hasna called her Arabic-speaking shift manager, she was sympathetic, but the hotel could not hold her job open for her. She told Hasna to call as soon as her arm and foot were healed enough to stand comfortably for several days and to load the heavy sheets. She admired Hasna and wanted to hire her again, but there was no medical leave policy for housekeeping.

Hasna had no choice but to call the Syrian Americans who had supported them before when she lost her last job and ask for their help again. One of the mosques kept a fund for Muslim refugees in need, and they promised to help pay for their rent for a few months. Their caseworker had put them on a list for a housing assistance apartment when they were still under the care of RST; if they got accepted for that program, their rent would be a fixed percentage of their income, but the waiting list was at least two years deep. Until then, there was nothing cheaper around her. It galled Hasna to take charity yet again, but she could see no other option.

Within the last six months, many of their friends had already moved on to other apartments—with one or two adults in the family who could find jobs, especially if a grandmother or teenager could care for the younger children, they could afford nicer places. Hasna had gone to visit them on her days off, feeling an absurd spurt of jealousy of these women with their slightly larger kitchens.

But that night, when Um Khalid dropped her off—driving smoothly in a black sedan her son had helped her finance and heading to her new apartment several minutes away—Hasna realized she was not jealous because of their kitchens. She was jealous because, without her children, her body would be the only thing that propelled them forward. She had never imagined a life where she was the only person working, where there would not be sons and daughters to bring energy and drive, where she was not the hub of an ever-spinning wheel but a solitary pole supporting Jebreel and Rana.

In the middle of the night, Hasna woke up unable to catch her breath. She felt she would stifle in the close apartment. Careful not to wake Jebreel or Rana, she limped to the front door, where she had leaned the crutches above her black ballet slippers. She opened the front door and slid outside. The night was not cool, but there was a breeze and she gulped in air gratefully.

She went to sit on the benches beside the tennis courts the local boys used as a soccer field. After a few minutes, she struggled to her feet. She could feel her ankle swelling, so she lifted it behind her, but she could not bear to be still. Slowly, agonizingly, she followed the sidewalks between the buildings, making her way from one end of the complex to another, the rhythm of her movement— *crutches*, foot, *crutches*, foot—comforting her. By the time she went to bed, dawn was lightening the sky.

At least once a week, and often for several nights in a row, Hasna haunted the apartments. When her ankle healed, she no longer used the crutches, shuffling on her still-unsteady ankle, clutching her wrist to her side, walking.

UM KHALID'S DAUGHTER, WHO WAS A LITTLE OLDER THAN RANA, GOT married. A friend of a friend knew of an eligible young man in a nearby town looking for a bride. They negotiated the marriage contract and Abu Khalid asked Jebreel and some of their former neighbors to come and serve as relatives at the jaha. Later, Hasna and Rana rode with some friends who had a car to the rented conference room at a strip mall a few miles away where the women would have the henna night.

Hasna tried to imagine what it would be like in a few years when Rana married; she wondered how they would find anyone suitable in this new country. The difference between this small, dank hall where they gathered with the dozen Syrian girls near Rana's age and the large clan gathering for Laila's wedding with Malek was stark. White circle tables with bouquets of flowers dotted the floor where the girls took selfies and checked lipstick and compared manicures, their rented formal dresses rustling as they moved self-consciously.

The mothers, wearing their nicest black dresses, told stories of the nights they remembered in Syria, comparing regional traditions and foods in the never-ending small talk at their get-togethers that kept their country alive.

One of the other women came from Aleppo but had grown up in a village not far from Daraa in the Horan region. When Hasna mentioned an old song about a bride's grief at leaving her mother's home, sung at henna nights in Horan for generations, that woman remembered it. Hasna and her relatives had sung it for Amal and Laila on their henna nights. She began it now and the other woman joined in.

> *Please prepare my pillows.*
> *Tonight I am sleeping with you.*
> *Tomorrow I am leaving my sisters.*
> *Oh mother, oh mother.*
> *I left the house*
> *and did not say good-bye to my sisters.*
> *Oh my daughter, don't cry,*
> *You will make me cry.*
> *Your brother is very loving,*
> *he will come see you on Eid night.*
> *Oh how beautiful were*
> *the nights and the parties and the singing.*
> *How beautiful, the sleeping*
> *among my sisters and cousins,*
> *staying up late on the roof*
> *with my sisters.*
> *Oh mother, oh mother.*
> *I left the house*
> *and did not say good-bye to my sisters.*

Hasna could barely finish the song. How beautiful they had been, the nights of feasting and throwing candy and staying up late playing backgammon and discussing children and watching them fall in love and holding her grandbabies under the grape-laden arbor and soft fairy lights of her jasmine-scented courtyard. Her voice wove a lament to everyone she had lost, everything she would never have again.

AS THE BRIDE LEFT THE HENNA NIGHT TO JOIN HER GROOM, HASNA watched her daughter. Soon Rana would leave too. So often her life in this new country felt unreal to Hasna, as if everything here were made from cardboard when at home it had been stone. But watching the bride cast eyes at the groom when he arrived to pick her up, and the giggles of Rana and her friends, Hasna realized it was not the same for Rana—in a few years, this new life might even feel more real than their life in Daraa ever had.

Assad had done everything in his power to do away with the Syrian people who rebelled against him. International forces had made it clear that Syrian lives did not matter to them. Though many people had been kind to her in this country, Hasna knew many of her friends also sensed the hostility that rankled just beneath the surface. It felt as if the world would have been happy if Syrians were wiped off the face of the earth.

And yet, this boy and this girl had found each other. She might not be able to find a bride for Yusef—she might never see Yusef again—but she would someday find a groom for Rana. They would create new lives together here. There would be children born in this country, Allah willing, new little ones who carried the basalt stubbornness of the people of Daraa in their veins. And Rana's children would always be bound to Hasna's other grandchildren, even if her darlings were scattered around the world, even if they were never in the same room again in this life.

After they got home, Hasna prayed, long past the allotted time, late into the night. Rana slept in the dining room nook, her gentle breathing punctuating Hasna's prayers. Jebreel went to bed and Hasna knelt until her feet were as numb as Laila's had been on the truck ride to Aleppo, until she felt her body wither and atrophy into itself. She prayed and prayed. She had been praying that Allah would bring her children here, but that night, her prayer shifted.

She begged Allah to keep his hands on her loved ones all around the world. Hasna's hope diminished to one thin thread: If they could not be together, inshallah, that they would at least be safe.

Epilogue

MU NAW

AUSTIN, TEXAS, USA,
JANUARY 2016

Naw Wah is eleven and she is running. It is unseasonably warm for January, even in Austin; her shoes are off, and she is racing with bare feet through clipped grass. Saw Ku mowed the lawn early yesterday morning with their new lawn mower so that the children could enjoy the backyard. Mu Naw steps out of the kitchen to call them in to eat, but she pauses first. Her three children running in their backyard with their cousins and closest friends is a sight that takes Mu Naw's breath away. They have no idea, these children ranging from toddlers to Mu Naw's oldest—a newly minted teenager—what they mean to their parents gathered in the house. It is dusk and they are screaming to one another, encouraging Mu Naw's niece, who is chasing the others. It is a game they learned in school and Mu Naw does not understand it, but she doesn't have to. All children all over the world play some variation of this game; she did too. Except her children play it in a place with no war, no starvation, no brilliant minds wasting away in a village school taught by teachers who are barely literate themselves.

Almost a decade has passed since they arrived in Austin, and her children don't even think in terms of safety and freedom anymore. Those things are such a part of their lives, they rarely feel grateful for them. But their parents never forget, never take their joy for granted. She and Saw Ku passed their citizenship test a few years back; they raised their hands to pledge allegiance to this new country that wanted them and Mu Naw cried when she heard Lee

Greenwood sing ". . . at least I know I'm free." In ten more years, perhaps this same group will return to this house as doctors, engineers, nurses, teachers. She is struck by the profound simplicity of that thought—they can be anything they want to be. And they will. Their parents' every choice has led to this: children in the backyard she and Saw Ku own, raising their voices and laughing without realizing that their laughter is a miracle, is a gift, is the most impossibly precious noise in the world.

MU NAW AND SAW KU INVITED THE ENTIRE KAREN BAPTIST CHURCH over for tonight's house blessing, all fifty people. Saw Ku, his brother, and two of their friends from church had gone to purchase and slaughter the live goat they needed for many of tonight's dishes. They brought the goat meat back to Mu Naw and spent hours cutting it into the sizes she needed. Mu Naw sniffed, tasted, stirred, mixed, and simmered various dishes. The meat marinated all night and they finished as many salads as they could prepare in advance, but she still got up at 5:00 a.m. to cook everything else.

The children helped during the day, peeling garlic cloves, cutting carrots and shallots, preparing the beans, singing while they worked, chopping and snapping in time to Karen praise songs, Burmese pop songs, American folk music.

Mu Naw felt again in her kitchen the familiar sense of capability she often did when cooking—she was good at this and she loved it. She could time her dishes down to the second so they all came out hot. She knew how many spices to add—when to boil, when to lower the heat. As she cooked, she allowed herself to dream about the garden they would plant in the spring. They had already picked out the plot for their raised bed, based on the area of the yard that got the best morning sunlight; they were debating now where to plant the trees.

The feast that took shape under her hands held flavors from every region she had lived in—Burmese meat dishes, Thai soups, American salads. She pushed their table to the side—it was their original table, the one with the white tile center and the blond-wood trim; she added folding tables she had borrowed from a friend. A few minutes before the guests arrived, she filled the tables with large foil-covered aluminum pans.

Saw Ku answered the doorbell. For thirty minutes or so, as each family arrived, she showed them around the house, smiling and laughing and receiving their compliments. They peeked behind doors, opened cabinets, explored every inch of the rooms. The women could see their home as it took shape in Mu Naw's mind—the walls they would fill with colors, the pictures they would hang, the furniture they would buy.

MU NAW STANDS AT THE BACK DOOR TO CALL THE CHILDREN AND they run into the house; several mothers yell out for them to wash their hands and a sweaty, jostling line forms outside the downstairs bathroom. They gather in a circle in the living room, parents' hands on children's shoulders.

As their voices quiet, they look at Mu Naw expectantly. After the prayer for the meal, they will grab heaping paper plates full of food and squat on the dark wood floor. The children will snatch plates from their parents and run to eat outside. They will let the children play until it is too dark to see, and the parents will gather in each of the rooms to pray blessings on every part of this new home, because they are Christians and they cannot accept the full bounty of God's goodness without thanking him first and asking him to keep his hands on those he has protected for so long, those he has brought so improbably far.

But Mu Naw realizes that here, in this expectant moment with a houseful of beloved friends and family members, the blessings have already come. She breathes in, the fusion scent of pepperoni and som tom, of sticky rice and goat meat, the faint vanilla aroma of the house spray she likes, the earthy smell of children running in grass. She breathes out, takes in each of the faces that have walked with her through every difficult and wonderful part of the last several years, who are family, who make this home.

She looks at Saw Ku. He smiles at her, his eyes full of love, and reaches out to take her hand before turning: "Thank you all for coming tonight." Mu Naw can hear the slight catch in his voice. "It means so much to us that you are here." He pauses. She squeezes his hand. He nods once. "Let us pray."

AFTERWORD

I met Mu Naw when she was pregnant with Saw Doh, six months after she first arrived in the United States, at a fall festival in Austin outside on the grounds of a church that doubled as the neighborhood community center. We struck up a quick, languageless friendship watching our children play—her girls were five and two; my daughter was ten months old, dressed in an overly hot plush octopus costume and wriggling in her stroller. Mu Naw indicated her belly to show me she was pregnant. I demonstrated for her daughters how to bob for apples and toss the rings and stood in line while they waited to jump in the bouncy castle.

I made so many mistakes in the beginning of our friendship, it's impossible to recount them all: I knew nothing about refugees. I did not understand that Mu Naw came from a no-person's-land within Thai borders where her body, her clothes, her language, her mannerisms, everything about her marked her as a member of an ethnically distinct group—the Karen people—and therefore persecuted in her home country and reviled in Thailand. I blithely spoke my taxi-Thai, picked up from spending two summers in northern Thailand just hours from Mae La camp. Mu Naw responded with what Thai she knew—her capacity for language is really extraordinary—and we bumped along. Over months spent sitting together watching our daughters play, I got to know the extraordinary organizations scaffolding refugees' lives in Austin. I became friends with several of the caseworkers at Refugee Services of Texas; it was small then, only around fifteen people in Austin, and I've stayed in touch with some of my first contacts as the nonprofit has grown into an agency that resettles close to 3 percent of all refugees accepted into the United States.

We started a Tuesday night ESL class that turned into a women's cooperative for Mu Naw and her friends, most of whom were weavers. Mu Naw asked my friend Caren George and me one day if we could sell their bags. First, we sold what they had, then we helped them order new yarn and, as we built trust with one another and as Mu Naw's language skills exploded, it grew into a nonprofit. For seven years, as long as there were women who wanted to earn supplemental income with their weaving and sewing and jewelry making, Caren, my husband, Jonathan, Mu Naw, and I, along with more volunteers than I can name, partnered with Burmese refugee artisans, producing thousands of bags and earrings and scarves and dolls and bibs made of rice bags and other items. We sold their handmade goods at fair trade festivals before Christmas and produced wholesale orders for companies in Austin (including the one that eventually hired Mu Naw). There were more than thirty artisans who came and went; a handful stayed in Austin and we're friends still. Mu Naw was the hub of it all.

After the nonprofit successfully ended when the last artisan got a job, Mu Naw and I occasionally met in the summer for playdates with our kids. We were both now working full-time. We talked on the phone sometimes and caught up every few months. When I told her over lunch one day in 2016 at Cherrywood Café in East Austin that I was thinking about writing a book, she was excited. I knew she and others wanted their story to be told; we had talked about it some over the years. We had created artisan profiles on our website and I'd interviewed the women we were working with, often with Mu Naw as our translator, to tell the story of our nonprofit for some blogs and publications. We kept coming back to a recurring theme—the women were afraid the world had forgotten what happened to them in Myanmar and in the camps in Thailand.

While the book was still a proposal, I began to interview Mu Naw more regularly. I thought, because I had been there almost from the beginning, that I understood quite a bit about her life after coming to the United States; I even thought I had a decent grasp on what had happened before. I learned almost immediately that I was drastically wrong. There were many things I had never known. I thought becoming a refugee was her greatest trauma; as it turned out, that was not the case. War and a refugee camp and resettlement in the US profoundly affected her, but it was only the situation in which she lived out her story. The story itself was one that only she could define.

I tell you about our friendship first because that is the frame through which I've made every decision in writing this book. My relationships with Mu Naw and later with Hasna are the core of this narrative. If they are displeased with how this book is written, if I have done a disservice to their lived experiences, then I have failed.

IN 2015, WITH THE RAPID RISE IN ANTIREFUGEE RHETORIC IN OUR political conversations, Mu Naw and I both felt—as many did living in our community, where an average of one thousand refugees a year had peacefully settled and become part of the fabric of Austin—an urgent and outsized need to correct the public understanding of what it meant to be a refugee. Before, in every interaction I had ever had with anyone in Texas, people were either like me when I first met Mu Naw—ignorant about what it meant to be a refugee—or happily supportive of them. Almost without warning, a term that had once inspired compassion and a program that quietly enjoyed bipartisan support for decades became hot-button political issues. "Refugee" became weirdly, wildly synonymous with "terrorist."

I realized as that shift happened almost overnight that we couldn't wait for the years to pass before their children were old enough to pick up the narratives. To be clear: The writers who must lead these conversations and must be centered in any discussion are those who once identified as refugees. They must always speak first. But not every refugee today has the language capacity, time, or inclination to write down their stories. Our country also desperately needs to hear from refugees who came a few years or a few months or even a few weeks ago, whose lives have been permanently upended by current policies.

I began offering the people I knew the opportunity to tell their stories in a way that hid their identities. I sent out a few texts and suddenly couldn't pitch or write fast enough to keep up with requests I was receiving from friends of friends who wanted to make sure the world knew what they had gone through. That was when I met Hasna, in December 2016. I began working on an as-told-to piece with her; it was published by *Vox* days after the Trump administration's executive order on January 27, 2017, restricting arrivals from seven different countries.

That article settled my method for me. I realized what a writer who has had long-term relationships in the refugee community can do: My role is to hide what needs to be hidden and tell what needs to be told. By using a pseudonym and changing some of the identifying details of her life, Hasna could speak out without fear of repercussions. This is the delicate balance I've tried to achieve: to write in a way that tells their stories now, in all of their raw urgency, while still keeping everyone as safe as possible.

As I did in that first piece with Hasna, throughout this book I have tried to use many of the tactics of a cowriter—allowing Hasna and Mu Naw to have as much narrative control as possible, privileging their viewpoints of events. Some of the characters, such as Mu Naw's children, are not as fleshed out, because they are still young and a book like this, even with pseudonyms, can have a strong impact on a kid; that's a decision we've made together. Instead of the first-person as-told-to format, I decided early on to use the third person because, no matter how many questions I've asked, no matter how deep we dive into any specific moment, I cannot write an entire book in their voice. I have never been a refugee and third person felt like the only appropriate way to acknowledge that distance for a longer narrative.

Mu Naw and Hasna chose their pseudonyms and their family's names in the book; Mu Naw picked hers because she liked the name and Hasna picked "al-Salam" because it means "peace." We have given pseudonyms to the people I refer to who have not given us permission to use their stories (Jane I tried to find but could not, Bob I know how to get a hold of but never want to contact, for obvious reasons). Not one single person I interviewed for the narrative portions of the book wanted to use their real name—not the former refugees or the resettlement caseworkers or the translators or the Syrian American community members who serve as cultural liaisons. With my editor's over-sight, Mu Naw and Hasna worked closely with me to change some physical attributes or other characteristics of the people who are involved in this story so that this book does not put anyone at risk. Safety has been our highest narrative consideration.

The Burmese junta is openly targeting Rohingya people and renewing attacks in the Kachin states and certainly keeps tabs on anyone who has had any ties to a dissenter; anyone who thinks there is peace in Myanmar has not heard the stories of those persecuted citizens. The Syrian government took back the city of Daraa during the summer of 2018, while I was working on this manuscript. The reach of the Assad regime is long and I have picked up a portion of the Syrian community's fear that even small details could result in their loved ones disappearing or dying, on Syrian soil or in other countries in the world.

As Viet Thanh Nguyen writes in the introduction to *The Displaced*, "True justice is creating a world of social, economic, cultural, and political opportunities" where refugees and displaced persons can "tell their stories and be heard, rather than be dependent on a writer or a representative of some kind." I fervently hope someday for that kind of justice, for a time when Hasna and Mu Naw and their families will be able to speak out proudly without fear and tell the world exactly what happened to them. Until then, I have partnered with them to ensure that I accurately and ethically represent them well.

This is very far from being the only, the best, or the most complete version of this story. Refugees' stories are as diverse and individual as the tellers themselves. At the end of the book, you'll find a short list of books that either were written by refugees or represent the story of refugees through methodical research and interviews; I hope you'll read them as well.

I CANNOT POSSIBLY DESCRIBE THE DELIGHT AND JOY OF SPENDING almost two years interviewing Mu Naw and essentially reliving our decade of friendship again, this time filling in the pertinent details, the life-altering shifts, the undercurrents I never understood. I think we made it through at least one or two interviews without crying, but those were rare. Neither of us can quite believe this is how the story ended.

For Hasna's side of the narrative, we used a translator, Amena, a friend of a friend who is from Syria but who has lived in the United States for several years. Amena's story is also worthy of a book but, as with most of my Syrian American friends, can never be told because it would put people she loves in danger. Her natural empathy makes her one of the most gifted translators I have ever met. Translation is an almost impossible art—an app can bring words from one language to another, but a translator provides context, cultural equivalents, detailed descriptions. Amena brought Hasna's story to life.

My interviews with Hasna did not follow the well-organized trajectory of my sessions with Mu Naw. Instead, they were disjointed moments that sometimes connected and sometimes did not; often, she repeated the same events over and over, which gave me the chance to pick up new details every time. There were many reasons for the repetition—I did not know Hasna as well when we began and I found that, in letting her tell me things in her own time, I learned what was important to her. But also, Mu Naw's trauma is a scar that she points to on occasion; Hasna's trauma is real and continuing. These events just happened. That trauma is still wreaking havoc on her life and her mind.

There are some caveats I have in writing Hasna's narrative. The first is that I have never been to Syria or Jordan; I was with Mu Naw in most of the places she went in Austin and have been to both Thailand and—very briefly— Myanmar. I was not with Hasna for the bulk of her story. I have asked a thousand questions, watched dozens of videos that Hasna sent me, researched to the best of my ability, but my descriptions are limited to what I thought to ask. I am certain there are mistakes, and they are all mine; I'm incredibly grateful to Amena and the other Syrian American readers who have asked to remain anonymous in helping me make my settings and historical timelines as accurate as possible.

Second, Hasna and Jebreel are both insistent about some details that I still cannot confirm are accurate—for example, she is adamant that the boys who wrote in chalk on the wall at the al-Banin school were young, fourth or fifth graders, and every source I've read has shown that they were older. In that and a few more situations in the text, I made note of the discrepancies. The source of her knowledge was often rumor on the ground, which gives a flavor for what the stories were as they spread but does not always equal definite truth.

That leads to my third caveat: Researching the Syrian revolution is a difficult task because of the lack of a free press in the country. Many of the battles in the war are on YouTube and Reddit, so finding firsthand sources is easy in many ways, but verifying facts is almost impossible. I do not speak Arabic and I stopped asking my Arab-speaking friends to help me translate some of the video captions when I realized the depths of trauma I was triggering with my questions. During the months when I was fact-checking Hasna's story within Syria, I watched video after video in which government forces shot children point-blank, tortured civilians, bombed houses. I don't have the Teflon skin I associate with many of my journalist friends and their ability to move past trauma to the heart of the story. I will never get some of those images out of my head; I still dream often about the missiles I watched destroying houses in Aleppo. I will never be able to understand what it is like to have lived through that reality; the images alone were enough.

Because of the trauma that Hasna endured, there are important gaps in her story. She is unsure of some of the timelines; the war and then bureaucratic tension made time move differently for her. She and Laila argued frequently over WhatsApp about when Hasna actually left Jordan and when her children and grandchildren came and went; in the details we could back up with visas and paperwork, Laila was almost always right. Ultimately, the gaps in Hasna's story are consistent with what occurs under complex trauma. I have not always tried to fill them in with the narrative; the result reads, I think, disjointedly in some places. But those holes and fragments are as much a part of her journey as the hoopoe birds on the rooftop in Ramtha, or the scent of jasmine and coffee and the music of Fairuz in her beloved home in Daraa.

WHEN THE NARRATIVE ENDS, LAILA AND YUSEF HAD JUST MADE IT TO Greece. They had some hope that things would be better once they were in Europe. That has not turned out to be the case. Since we began our interviews, Laila has been in a WhatsApp group with Hasna, Amena, and me, and we have followed along with her journey. Greece is swamped by refugees; more than a thousand refugees on average arrived every day in 2017. Yusef and Laila and the boys spent some time in a small city in Greece and then moved to Athens. Despite the fact that Greece was struggling under more than 50 percent unemployment, Laila was able to get a job for a while as a waitress at a restaurant owned by a Syrian man; Yusef watched the boys while she worked. She could barely make enough money to cover rent in a hostel for refugees, called a "squat" in Greece, and food for the boys. She was mugged and lost her cell phone, which had all of her pictures of Malek on it. Their lives in Greece were incredibly stressful; there were almost constant fights outside the door of their squat. She video chatted with us sometimes—she looks and sounds very much like Rana. Laila would hold her camera up to show us the rooms they were living in, the concrete walls and sparse beds with not enough blankets. They left Greece when Laila lost her job.

As of the writing of this Afterword, Laila has joined Yusef in another country in Europe and they are hoping to receive permission to work there. The boys are in school, but their situation is tenuous. Because Laila and Yusef filed for resettlement in Europe, even without the travel ban, they would not be able to join their family in the United States. Had they stayed in Turkey and had the travel ban not been put in place, there is every reason to think they would be here by now.

When I've told people what Laila has gone through, I often get a few surprised reactions, especially that Hasna and her family keep in such constant contact around the world. They talk multiple times a day. The world after social media is an incredibly small place—a battle takes place in Syria and I can watch the bombs fall moments later on YouTube and read in-depth analysis on Reddit by people all over the world. Hasna can talk to her grandchildren as soon as they're home from school every day.

But the immediacy of those interactions also outlines the difficulty Hasna and Jebreel have in being in the United States while most of their children are not. Hasna's emotional health rises and falls with the dramatic events that Yusef and Laila endure, and with the deteriorating political situation in Syria. She and Jebreel do not sleep much still. They often stay up all night watching videos about what is happening in Syria. Their hearts and their bodies are not in the same place.

ONE DAY, AFTER SHE HAD BEEN IN TEXAS FOR ALMOST TWO YEARS, Hasna stepped in an ant pile. The dirt was soft and her foot, in the black ballet flats she always wore, sank into the mound. Small red ants swarmed, stinging her repeatedly. Later that week at an interview at my house, she propped her foot on my coffee table to show us the big red welts. Amena tsked sympathetically and we talked about how horrible fire ants are in Texas, especially during the hot months. Scorpions and snakes Hasna knew to look out for, but who would have guessed the ants in Texas would be this vicious?

It had been an incredibly hard week for Hasna. Her loved ones who still lived in Syria were sending word—sometimes over WhatsApp and, more often, through oral messages passed to people outside the country who then conveyed them to Hasna via Facebook messenger—about the threats they faced. She was edgy, shifting her body often. They were frantic and she was too. She told us that she refreshed her Facebook feed over and over—that's where she found out about Malek's death, and she was afraid she would see other faces she loved. We could say nothing to make her feel better.

She was crying when she told us, "What if it's all memories? What if I never get to see them again in this life?"

She felt like one of those ants—fierce and tenacious, she had fought for her home, but she was still tiny. There was nothing she could do against the forces that destroyed her country. Like floodwaters washing away an ant pile, the war had erased her home and scattered everything she had known or loved. The world cared about her less than about an ant swept away by water.

Then I told her about the fire ants we had seen in our backyard a few years back, when a Memorial Day flood overflowed the creek bed around our house. Most of our yard was under at least a foot of water by the time the rain stopped. When we walked out onto the back porch, we noticed an odd red clump in the backyard.

It was a flotilla of fire ants. Until I saw it in our backyard, I had never known that fire ants possessed this particular skill. They have developed an incredible biological ability to create long-lasting rafts that save their entire colony when it is threatened by water. They work together, placing the weakest members on the top. Ants can hold on to one another the same way they climb up walls and trees. They connect to one another, leaving pockets of air between them. Soon the whole group drifts on the surface of the water. These rafts can hold for months. By reaching toward one another, these fierce ants avoid being washed away when disaster comes.

Instead, they float.

Acknowledgments

"Mu Naw" and "Hasna" and their families have opened their lives throughout this process with one goal—for others to know what refugees really go through. I'm grateful for the deeper friendship we've built through writing this book. I can never thank them enough for trusting me with their stories.

This book would not exist without the artisans of Hill Country Hill Tribers and the team of people that gathered to address large and small needs in those early years of the Burmese resettlement movement. Out of a desire to hide the identities of the more than thirty artisans who partnered with us, I will have to issue a general "thank you" that feels profoundly insufficient. In addition, Nang and Nan, Dr. Salai Tun Than, Meagan Brown, Jenny Blackmon, Erika Hassay, Terra Brimberry, Holly Fullerton, Chez Dishman, Ashley Luksys, Kelsi Klembara, Scott Warner, Adam Black, and Denise Black were integral to Hill Tribers, the Village Center, and Artreach—the projects that grew out of those years. I'm convinced after those years that Constance Dykhuizen secretly runs the world, or at least that we'd all be better off if she did. I'm eternally grateful to Caren George, who taught me the art of structured flexibility and pairs deep compassion with dark humor better than anyone I know.

Partnering with "Amena" as a translator was one of the most immense gifts of my life; she quickly became one of my dearest friends. Her steadiness, empathy, and perceptiveness shaped this book in incalculable ways. "Natheir Ali" provided me with more connections than I can name, as well as invaluable comprehension of Syrian historical and cultural contexts. I wish I could name each of them publicly, but the tireless Syrian American advocates in Austin who helped newly arrived refugees are heroes. I'm especially in debt to the Syrian American beta readers who helped me hone and shape Hasna's narrative so that it was accurate, and who allowed me to grieve with them for the destruction of their beloved, singular country.

The caseworkers, English teachers, therapists, advocates, volunteers, and friends surrounding the Austin and national refugee community are fierce. I am grateful to the insights of Russell Smith, Melissa Helber, Erika Schmidt, Lubna Zeidan, Erika Hughes, Aaron Rippenkroeger, Jacqueline Mize-Baker, Meg Erskine, Chris Kelley, Matthew Soerens, and Joanna Mendez through interviews and critiques of early drafts of this book.

Joy McGlaun generously connected me on many occasions to people for book research, but more importantly, as we tried to make sure that Laila and her little family and other Syrians were safe at various critical moments in their journeys. I believe firmly there's no one on earth Joy couldn't help within twenty-four hours. Cynthia Bajjalieh in Senator Richard Durbin's office answered a number of questions when we thought there was a chance Laila and Yusef could be reunited with their family; her thoughtfulness meant a great deal to us.

I loved my time with an Austin-based book club reading an early draft of this book: thank you especially to Kathryn Cantrell, Anna Prendergast, and Staci Woodburn for the attentive notes.

This book simply would not exist without my writing group; Christiana Peterson, Stina Kielsmeier-Cook, D. L. Mayfield, Kelley Nikondeha, and Amy Peterson have wrestled with me through years of figuring out how to tell these stories well. I cannot imagine my writing life without them. I went to the Collegeville Institute twice, once at the beginning and once at the end of the manuscript-writing process, and I'm profoundly grateful for that space and the people I was with there. This book is better for the incisive criticism and profound encouragement of Lauren Winner, and the brilliant mind, wry wit, and endless passion of Kate Bowler.

Kurt Heinzelman has provided advice and encouragement in my eclectic career over the years, for which I'm extremely grateful.

Ann Reese, Holly Mock, and Amy Carder forever keep me grounded and give me room to cry or laugh when I've needed it most. I'm indebted to smart friends who work through ideas with me, such as Nyssa Wilton, Erin Raffety, Amy Bench, and Corie Humble.

I will forever grieve that Stephanie Odom was not here to see this book finished but I'm a better writer for having known and loved her. This work began, in many ways, with Rachel Held Evans's support of Hill Tribers and the way she constantly centered marginalized stories. Her loss is incalculable.

My mom loves people so well, and the lessons she taught me through a life of serving others are ones I tried to emulate throughout this book-writing process, as I do every day. Some of my earliest memories are connecting historical and political moments in fascinating ways with my dad; this book draws from the kinds of compassionate insights he taught me to make. I'm deeply grateful to Karen, Randy, Jocelyn, Mark, Jay, Mary Kate, Jared, April, Joel, Cari, Marta, Kyle, Adam, and Rachel, as well as the world's funniest, most wonderful nieces and nephews: I love you all dearly.

No one has ever enjoyed working with their agent and editor more than I have. This book exists because of the tireless advocacy and insight of the best of all agents, Mackenzie Brady Watson, and the keen mind and unrelenting patience of the best of all editors, Emily Wunderlich. I'm grateful to the entire Stuart Kritchevsky Agency, especially Ross Harris and Aemilia Phillips, and the incomparable team at Viking Books, particularly Emily Neuberger, Sean Devlin, Colin Webber, Ben Petrone, Bel Banta, Alicia Cooper, Nidhi Pugalia, Bridget Gilleran, and Kate Hudkins.

To my girls: you have never known a time when refugees weren't some of your closest friends and I have learned so much from watching the way you love people effortlessly and unconditionally. Raising three strong, spirited daughters is one of the greatest joys of my life. I love you.

And to Jonathan: You are the love of my life and the most fascinating person I know. I have no idea at this point where my ideas end and yours begin; your influence is everywhere in this book. Our adventurous life is the only one I can imagine leading.

Notes

PART 1

CHAPTER 1

7 **Mu Naw stood on the landing:** The International Organization for Migration is an agency that was established in 1951 and currently has 173 member states (according to its website, iom.int). While they address a number of areas that affect vulnerable migrants around the world, one of the things they are known for is helping resettled refugees arrive in their new country. Traveling with the blue and white plastic bags featuring the IOM logo is one of the things that many refugees in the United States have in common.

9 **The camp where she had lived in Thailand:** Mae La camp is the largest of the refugee camps in Thailand, with a population of around 40,000 refugees, that started in 1984 and was originally intended for 1,000 people. For further reading, see the website of The Border Consortium, an NGO focused on human rights issues in Myanmar, especially their information about the camps along the Thai border (https://www.theborderconsortium.org/where-we-work/camps-in-thailand/).

CHAPTER 2

14 **US lawmakers, with the unprecedented support of constituents across the country:** There were exceptions to these views, of course. Throughout these history chapters, as I trace the hegemonic narrative that controlled refugee policy, I'm not mentioning the many opposed views or groups that worked against, within, or around those policies and milieus. American identity is as varied as the millions of individuals who have lived in the country over the centuries; my academic work focuses on the way writers push back against these dominant cultural narratives at every turn. It is outside the scope of my project to identify and trace all—or even most—of those counternarratives, but I want to provide a caveat here and throughout the rest of the book: The history stories I'm telling immediately demand to be contextualized within their sociohistorical moments and there will be multiple exceptions to the broad strokes of my argument. As often as I can, I provide sources for further

reading that have informed my thinking and that I hope can provide more depth and complexity, as well as important exceptions and nuances, to the history I tell.

14 **World War II left more than 10 million displaced people:** Carl Bon Tempo, *Americans at the Gate* (Princeton: Princeton University Press, 2008), 7.

14 **On June 25, 1948, President Harry S. Truman:** The legislation was originally for a two-year period and was extended for another two years in 1950, thus doubling the original 200,000 to 400,000. For further reading on the Displaced Persons Act, see Displaced Persons Act of 1948, S. 2242, 81st Cong. (1948); Atina Grossmann and Tamar Lewinsky, "Displaced Persons," in *A History of Jews in Germany Since 1945: Politics, Culture, and Society,* ed. Michael Brenner, trans. Kenneth Kronenberg (Bloomington: Indiana University Press, 2018), 57–84; and Kathryn M. Bockley, "A Historical Overview of Refugee Legislation: The Deception of Foreign Policy in the Land of Promise," *North Carolina Journal of International Law and Commercial Regulation* 253 (1995), http://scholarship.law.unc.edu/ncilj/vol21/iss1/6.

14 **At the time, the US immigration system:** There were critical exceptions, including the Chinese refugees who fled Shanghai; two excellent books about that time period are Helen Zia, *Last Boat Out of Shanghai: The Epic Story of the Chinese Who Fled Mao's Revolution* (New York: Ballantine, 2019), and Diana Chang, *The Frontiers of Love* (Seattle: University of Washington Press, 1956).

15 **But still he pressed Congress:** Harry S. Truman, "Annual Message to the Congress on the State of the Union," 80th Cong. (January 6, 1947).

15 **Every other option was equally impossible:** Harry S. Truman, "Special Message to the Congress on Admission of Displaced Persons," 80th Cong. (July 7, 1947).

15 **The American public listening to Truman:** Barack Obama, "Remarks by President Obama at Leaders' Summit on Refugees," United Nations, New York, September 20, 2016: https://obamawhitehouse.archives.gov/the-press-office/2016/09/20/remarks-president -obama-leaders-summit-refugees.

16 **Less than ten years before, in 1939:** For further reading on the MS *St. Louis,* see Sarah A. Ogilvie, *Refuge Denied: The St. Louis Passengers and the Holocaust* (Madison: University of Wisconsin Press, 2006), and Gordon Thomas and Max Morgan Witts, *Voyage of the Damned* (New York: Stein and Day, 1974).

16 **While the refugees sailed, blissfully unaware:** Among many sources, I'm especially indebted to Catherine Cassara, "To the Edge of America," *Journalism History* 42, no. 4 (2017): 225–38.

16 **Their telegram to President Roosevelt begged:** R. Hart Phillips, "Cuba Recloses Door to Refugees; 48-Hour Limit on Offer Expires," *The New York Times,* June 7, 1939, 1.

16 **The subheading on the story:** R. Hart Phillips, "907 Refugees Quit Cuba on Liner; Ship Reported Hovering Off Coast: Rumor That United States Will Permit Entry Is Spread to Avert Suicides—Company Orders St. Louis Back to Hamburg," *The New York Times,* June 3, 1939, 1.

16 **Refugee advocacy groups worked tirelessly:** For further reading on Roosevelt's refugee policies, see Richard Breitman, *FDR and the Jews* (Cambridge: Harvard University Press, 2013); Verne W. Newton, ed., *FDR and the Holocaust* (New York: St. Martin's Press, 1996); and Henry L. Feingold, *Bearing Witness: How America and Its Jews Responded to the Holocaust* (Syracuse: Syracuse University Press, 1995).

16 **As the ship moved toward Europe:** "Ship Steams Away to Return Refugees to Reich," *Washington C.H. Record-Herald,* June 9, 1939, 8.

16 **More than a month:** Ogilvie, *Refuge Denied,* 175.

16 **But within the year, Nazi troops:** Ogilvie, *Refuge Denied,* 174.

17 **The United States ended World War II:** This isn't to say that the US was the only world leader—not at all—but to acknowledge the framework that was almost ubiquitous in popular and political rhetoric in the country at the time.

17 **It was a message hammered in the 1940s:** Television sets were not yet affordable for most people; in 1946, a third of Americans went to the movies at least once a week. See Richard Maltby, *Hollywood Cinema* (Malden, MA: Blackwell, 1995), 20.

17 **It was in every scene:** *Stagecoach*, directed by John Ford, featuring John Wayne as "Ringo Kid" (Walter Wanger Productions, 1939).

17 **The underlying message of these movies:** Following World War II, several groups deeply questioned the fact that, in almost all of the movie portrayals as well as the political examples, the leaders were always white men; the early subversive work that led to the civil rights movement and second-wave feminism was already well under way.

17 **In one film, a cheery newscaster:** "United News, Release 166" (Los Angeles: United Newsreel Corporation, 1945), 10 min.

17 **The films asked Americans:** "United News, Release 194" (Los Angeles: United Newsreel Corporation, 1946), 9 min.

18 **The camp model provided:** Ibid.

18 **"If we don't help these people now":** "Spotlight Displaced Persons," *The Army-Navy Screen Magazine*, no. 2 (Washington, DC: Army Pictorial Service, 1945). Also, I want to acknowledge the incredibly problematic formulation of "one half" of the world being the United States of America and "the other half" being once-Nazi-occupied European nations.

18 **Harrison's letter belied the chipper tone:** Report from Earl G. Harrison to President Harry S. Truman, August 3, 1945, United States Holocaust Memorial Museum, https://www.ushmm.org/exhibition/displaced-persons/resourc1.htm.

19 **The Nuremberg trials were a start:** "History of the United Nations," the website for the United Nations, http://www.un.org/en/sections/history/history-united-nations/.

19 **In 1948, the UN voted:** "Convention on the Prevention and Punishment of the Crime of Genocide," December 9, 1948, 78 U.N.T.S. 277: https://treaties.un.org/doc/publication/unts/volume%2078/volume-78-i-1021-english.pdf. Article 1 states: "The Contracting Parties confirm that genocide, whether committed in time of peace or in time of war, is a crime under international law which they undertake to prevent and to punish." Article 2 states: "In the present Convention, genocide means any of the following acts committed with intent to destroy, in whole or in part, a national, ethnical, racial, or religious group, as such:
"(a) Killing members of the group;
"(b) Causing serious bodily or mental harm to members of the group;
"(c) Deliberately inflicting on the group conditions of life calculated to bring about its physical destruction in whole or in part;
"(d) Imposing measures intended to prevent births within the group;
"(e) Forcibly transferring children of the group to another group."

20 **The 1951 Refugee Convention:** "Convention and Protocol Related to the Status of Refugees," United Nations Commissioner for Refugees, July 28, 1951: https://www.unhcr.org/3b66c2aa10.

20 **A filmmaker captured:** "DP Neg 237 Reel one-two," (Bremerhaven, Germany: US Holocaust Memorial Museum, gift of Julien Bryan Archive, 1947), 7 min., https://collections.ushmm.org/search/catalog/irn1003638.

20 **The October 20, 1948, headline:** Harold Faber, "813 Refugees Sail for the U.S. Today," *The New York Times*, October 21, 1948, 13.

CHAPTER 4

41 **No one came:** Mu Naw no longer had an RST caseworker by the time I met her six months after her arrival and no longer remembers her name, so I was unable to verify this part of the narrative. I feel the need to defend other caseworkers there, some of whom I'm still friends with, in saying that leaving clients for several days was not even close to a normal practice for RST, at that time or any other. In fact, caseworkers are supposed to return within twenty-four hours of dropping a client off. None of my resettlement agency beta readers could believe this part of the story—they'd never heard of anything like it. My educated guess is that Mu Naw was under the care of an overworked caseworker and that her family slipped through the cracks in those first few days. This incident points to the dangers of a fluctuating system—too many high-needs arrivals at once, like what began to happen when the US resettled people from protracted refugee situations in Myanmar, Burundi, and Somalia in 2006 and 2007—could leave dangerously overworked caseworkers without enough resources to sufficiently help their clients. A steady program with experienced caseworkers benefits everyone involved.

CHAPTER 5

48 **She put her hands to her ears:** For the spelling of these phrases and all transliterated Arabic throughout the book, I've deferred to the preferences of Amena, the translator for my interviews with Hasna.

51 **After ten days of violent clashes:** Julian Borger, "Tunisian President Vows to Punish Rioters After Worst Unrest in a Decade," *The Guardian*, December 29, 2010: https://www.theguardian .com/world/2010/dec/29/tunisian-president-vows-punish-rioters.

53 **He hired a Western PR firm:** Bill Carter and Amy Chozick, "Syria's Assad Turned to West for Glossy P.R.," *The New York Times*, June 10, 2012: https://www.nytimes.com/2012/06/11 /world/middleeast/syrian-conflict-cracks-carefully-polished-image-of-assad.html?_r=2& ref=todayspaper.

53 **She could sense a Syria:** The fascinating story of Buck's trip to Syria to interview Asma al-Assad, the subsequent publication of the piece, unfortunately titled "Asma al-Assad: A Rose in the Desert," in *Vogue* in February 2011, and Buck's back-and-forth with the editors at *Vogue* is worth reading in its entirety: "Joan Juliet Buck: Mrs. Assad Duped Me," *The Daily Beast*, July 30, 2012: https://web.archive.org/web/20120730110710/http://www.thedailybeast .com/newsweek/2012/07/29/joan-juliet-buck-my-vogue-interview-with-syria-s-first-lady .html.

53 **Hasna's neighbors told her:** Hasna is adamant that the boys were elementary aged, but her personal account differs pretty widely from one of the more comprehensive stories about them: Mark MacKinnon, "The Graffiti Kids Who Sparked the Syrian War," *The Globe and Mail*, December 2, 2016: https://beta.theglobeandmail.com/news/world/the-graffiti-kids -who-sparked-the-syrian-war/article33123646/?ref=http://www.theglobeandmail.com&.

CHAPTER 6

61 **In zones A and B:** Orapin Banjong, Andrea Menefee, Kitti Sranacharoenpong, Uraiporn Chittchang, Pasamai Eg-kantrong, Atitada Boonpraderm, and Sopa Tamachotipong, "Dietary Assessment of Refugees Living in Camps: A Case Study of Mae La Camp" (paper presentation, United Nations University Fifth International Conference on Dietary Assessment Methods, Chiang Rai, Thailand, January 26–29, 2003): http://archive.unu.edu /unupress/food/fnb24-4-3.pdf.

CHAPTER 9

88 **By Hasna's count:** While I have been able to independently verify many of the details in Hasna's narrative, including the major dates of the battles she describes, several details like this one are impossible for me to back up with outside research. The lack of a free press in Syria makes almost every source amateur; accounts of some of the smaller skirmishes or neighborhood battles depend entirely on her account or on unverifiable YouTube and Reddit videos. Since I don't know the source of many of those videos (and because some of the ones I watched for this portion of the narrative have subsequently been deleted or changed), I will issue the caveat that these details remain unconfirmed.

CHAPTER 10

94 **From the 1880s into the 1910s:** For further reading about the racialized aspects of immigration policies from 1880 to 1945, see Michael Grossberg and Christopher Tomlins, eds., *The Cambridge History of Law in America, Vol. II: The Long Nineteenth Century* (Cambridge, U.K.: Cambridge University Press), particularly Chapter 6, "Citizenship and Immigration Law, 1800–1924: Resolutions of Membership and Territory," by Kunal Parker, 168–203; Mae M. Ngai, *Illegal Aliens and the Making of Modern America* (Princeton: Princeton University Press, 2014); Natalia Molina, *How Race Is Made in America: Immigration, Citizenship, and the Historical Power of Racial Scripts* (Berkeley: University of California Press, 2014); and Desmond S. King, *Making Americans: Immigration, Race, and the Origins of the Diverse Democracy* (Cambridge, MA: Harvard University Press, 2000).

95 **Chinese people made up a tiny percentage:** For further information about the Chinese Exclusion Act, see Bill Ong Hing, *Making and Remaking Asian America Through Immigration Policy, 1850–1990* (Stanford: Stanford University Press, 1993); Kristofer Allerfeldt, "Race and Restriction: Anti-Asian Immigration Pressures in the Pacific Northwest of America during the Progressive Era, 1885–1924," *History*, 88.1 (Hoboken, NJ: Wiley, 2003), 53–73; and *The Chinese Exclusion Act: A Special Presentation of American Experience*, directed by Ric Burns and Li-Shun Yu, Coproduction of Steeplechase Films and the Center for Asian American Media (New York: PBS, 2018), among many other sources.

95 **One political cartoon from the years:** "The great fear of the period That Uncle Sam might be swallowed by foreigners: The problem solved" (San Francisco: White & Bauer, between 1860 and 1869); found online at the Library of Congress website: https://www.loc.gov /resource/cph.3a23482/.

96 **This cartoon was one of dozens:** The term "naturalized" formed the basis of the Naturalization Act of 1790, the first law about American citizenship, which decreed that any free white person who could prove they had resided in the United States for two years or longer was eligible to become a US citizen. "Naturalized" was therefore synonymous with "white citizen."

96 **Declaring the statue the "Mother of Exiles":** Emma Lazarus, "The New Colossus," *Emma Lazarus: Selected Poems and Other Writings*, edited by Gregory Eiselein (Peterborough, Ontario, Canada: Broadview Press, 2002), 233.

97 **Liberalizers had effectively blocked bills:** For further reading on immigration in the Progressive Era, see Cybelle Fox, *Three Worlds of Relief: Race, Immigration, and the American Welfare State from the Progressive Era to the New Deal* (Princeton: Princeton University Press, 2012); *A Companion to the Gilded Age and Progressive Era*, edited by Christopher McKnight Nichols and Nancy C. Unger (Oxford, U.K.: Wiley Blackwell, 2017); and Steven J. Diner, *A Very Different Age: Americans of the Progressive Era* (New York: Hill and Wang, 1998).

97 **On the list of "undesirables":** See especially James A. Tyner, *Oriental Bodies: Discourse and Discipline in U.S. Immigration Policy, 1875–1942* (Lanham, MD: Lexington Books, 2006); Anders Stephanson, *Manifest Destiny: American Expansionism and the Empire of Right* (New York: Hill and Wang, 1995); and Mark Elwood Lincicome, *Imperial Subjects as Global Citizens: Nationalism, Internationalism, and Education in Japan* (Lanham, MD: Lexington Books, 2009).

97 **Politicians argued for:** For more information on the Johnson-Reed Act and the role of eugenics at the time, read "Outstanding Features of the Immigration Act of 1924," *Columbia Law Review* 25, no. 1 (1925): 90–95; David M. Reimers, "Post–World War II Immigration to the United States: America's Latest Newcomers," *The Annals of the American Academy of Political and Social Science*, 454 (1981): 1–12; Thomas C. Leonard, "Retrospectives: Eugenics and Economics in the Progressive Era," *Journal of Economic Perspectives*, 19, no. 4 (2005), 207–24; Meredith Roman, "Making Race in the Twentieth- and Twenty-First-Century United States," *Journal of American Ethnic History*, 35, no. 3 (2016), 99–103; among other sources.

97 **In an April 9, 1924, speech:** Senator Ellison DuRant Smith, speaking on H.R. 7995, on April 9, 1924, 68th Cong., 1st sess. *Congressional Record*, 65. See also Adam Serwer, "White Nationalism's Deep American Roots," *The Atlantic*, April 2019: https://www.theatlantic.com/magazine/archive/2019/04/adam-serwer-madison-grant-white-nationalism/583258/.

98 **The act also actively barred:** See Leo M. Alpert, "The Alien and the Public Charge Clauses," *Yale Law Journal*, 49 (1939): 18–38.

98 **The racist views of the 1920s:** Hitler wrote Grant in the 1920s and called *The Passing of the Great Race* his "bible" (Serwer, par. 6).

98 **The brand of "better-safe-than-sorryism":** "Better-safe-than-sorryism" is my own term for this kind of restrictionism; it came from a Facebook exchange with a friend. In a private message debating the move in Texas politics to limit Syrian refugee arrivals to the state in 2016 and 2017, this friend commented that it was better to be safe than sorry. After that conversation, I began to notice how often that phrase was the underlying warrant of so much of the anti-refugee rhetoric and policies in this decade and throughout American history.

99 **Better to be safe by forcibly detaining:** To learn more about President Roosevelt's Executive Order 9066 and the Japanese internment camp program, see Richard Reeves, *Infamy: The Shocking Story of the Japanese Internment in World War II* (New York: Henry Holt, 2015); Matthew M. Briones, *Jim and Jap Crow: A Cultural History of 1940s Interracial America* (Princeton: Princeton University Press, 2012); and Lawson Fusao Inada, ed., *Only What We Could Carry: The Japanese American Internment Experience* (Berkeley: Heyday Books, 2000).

99 **Their spokesman, Charles Lindbergh:** Charles Lindbergh, "Who Are the War Agitators?" speech at an "America First" rally, Des Moines, Iowa, September 11, 1941. Full transcript: http://www.charleslindbergh.com/americanfirst/speech.asp.

99 **The cost of "sorry" was a genocide:** A Polish lawyer and linguist, Raphael Lemkin, coined the word "genocide" from *geno* ("race" in Greek) and *cide* ("killing" in Latin) to describe the slaughter enacted by the Nazis, who exterminated 49 members of his own family. See Philippe Sands, *East West Street* (New York: Knopf, 2017), for the fascinating and necessary story of the two men who made "crimes against humanity" and "genocide" internationally accepted legal definitions after World War II.

CHAPTER 11

102 **It was ludicrous:** Again, this is another detail that I cannot confirm with outside research and for which I'm relying on interviews with Hasna, Jebreel, Rana, and Laila.

CHAPTER 13

128 **The government shut off:** There are several videos whose origin I am unable to trace: "Syrian Army attacking Daraa on 24th April 2011," uploaded by freeknight2011 on YouTube, https://www.youtube.com/watch?v=hIdiRpUWZ0U; "Tanks were entering Daraa early today April 24," uploaded by Mohammad Al Abdallah on YouTube, https://www.youtube.com/watch?v=dUVdeawzkvg (the date is given in various sources ranging from April 24 to 26; Hasna is uninterested in the actual dates and remembers the story based on how it affects her family, so I've followed her lead in the narrative); "syria syrian government forces tanks in daraa 1," uploaded by sssammmiiii; all accessed May 12, 2019. See also "Syria: Lift the Siege of Daraa," the Human Rights Watch website, May 5, 2011, https://www.hrw.org/news/2011/05/05/syria-lift-siege-daraa). For more in-depth coverage of the Syrian war in 2011, see Samar Yazbik, *A Woman in the Crossfire: Diaries of the Syrian Revolution,* translated from the Arabic by Max Weiss (London: Haus Pub, 2012); Nikolaos van Dam, *Destroying a Nation: The Civil War in Syria* (London: I. B. Tauris, 2017); Rania Abouzeid, *No Turning Back: Life, Loss, and Hope in Wartime Syria* (New York: W. W. Norton, 2018); Fouad Ajami, *The Syrian Rebellion* (Stanford, CA: Hoover Institution Press, 2012); Stephen Starr, *Revolt in Syria: Eye-Witness to the Uprising* (London: Hurst, 2012); and Janine Di Giovanni, *The Morning They Came for Us: Dispatches from Syria* (New York: Liveright, 2016).

129 **That day, many people had their phones:** See "Killing of freedom protesters in Daraa on 29th April 2011," published by freeknight2011 on YouTube, https://www.youtube.com/watch?v=jrutMwHMZPE, accessed May 12, 2019, among many other videos.

135 **Weeks before, seven defecting officers:** See one of the original videos made by seven Syrian officers who formed the Free Syrian Army on "Syria Comment," a website for "Syrian politics, history and religion," authored by Joshua Landis, "Free Syrian Army Founded by Seven Officers to Fight the Syrian Army," July 29, 2011: http://www.joshualandis.com/blog/free-syrian-army-established-to-fight-the-syrian-army/; accessed May 12, 2019.

PART 2

CHAPTER 15

149 **And their part of the Jordanian border:** According to Human Rights Watch, "Jordan's border with Syria was mined prior to the current conflict within Syria, but it is not known if Syrian forces have laid new mines on its border with Jordan" (par. 17); from Hasna's description, the border into Jordan became more difficult to traverse because of land mines, though I have been unable to independently verify that the Syrian army laid more mines than before. However, according to this article and other sources, they were laying more land mines on the borders into Turkey and Jordan, so it seems possible: "Syria: Army Planting Banned Landmines," Human Rights Watch website, March 13, 2012, https://www.hrw.org/news/2012/03/13/syria-army-planting-banned-landmines.

CHAPTER 16

163 **For the twenty years following World War II:** From María Christina García, *The Refugee Challenge in Post–Cold War America* (Oxford: Oxford University Press, 2017): "US policymakers... were greatly influenced by Cold War geopolitics. Escape from a communist country was often sufficient to gain admission to the United States, and the terms 'defector,' 'escapee,' 'refugee,' and 'parolee' were used interchangeably by policymakers as well as journalists" (4).

163 **There were no airlifts:** This figure came from the website for the United Nations Relief and Works Agency for Palestine Refugees in the Near East (UNRWA), https://www.unrwa .org/palestine-refugees.

163 **There were no US-government-promoted:** See John P. Burns, "Immigration from China and the Future of Hong Kong," *Asian Survey* 27, no. 6 (1987): 661–82.

163 **There were no visas allotted:** See Christopher Paul, Colin P. Clarke, Beth Grill, and Molly Dunigan, "South Vietnam, 1960–1975: Case Outcome: COIN Loss," in *Paths to Victory: Detailed Insurgency Case Studies* (Santa Monica, CA: Rand, 2012), 177–97, and Amelia H. Lyons, "French or Foreign? The Algerian Migrants' Status at the End of Empire (1962–1968)," *Journal of Modern European History*, 12, no. 1 (2014): 126–45.

164 **In October 1956, student protesters:** See Rupert Colville, "Fiftieth Anniversary of the Hungarian Uprising and Refugee Crisis," UNHCR website, October 23, 2006: http://www .unhcr.org/en-us/news/latest/2006/10/453c7adb2/fiftieth-anniversary-hungarian-uprising -refugee-crisis.html; and Peter Pastor, "The American Reception and Settlement of Hungarian Refugees in 1956–1957," *Hungarian Cultural Studies*, vol. 9 (2016), 10.5195/ahea.2016.255.

164 **To present it more effectively:** In this overview, I'm particularly indebted to Bon Tempo's research since I had not heard of the PR blitz before reading his book; though I've verified his analysis with my own primary source research, his chapter "Refugees from Hungary" (60–85) is excellent and worth reading in its entirety.

164 **The announcer relied on lyrical language:** "The Flight from Hungary," *The News Magazine of the Screen*, vol. 7, no. 5 (Warner-Pathe News, 1957): https://archive.org/details /0081NewsMagazineOfTheScreenTheVol7Issue5.

165 **It followed one family's arrival:** "They Pour In . . . And Family Shows Refugees Can Fit In," *Life*, January 7, 1957, 20–27.

166 **The nationalist quota system:** In 1952, Senator Patrick McCarran, a Democrat from Nevada with an impeccable restrictionist background, proposed a bill to limit admissions along the lines of the nationalist quota system. The bill adjusted the numbers in favor of Northern and Western Europeans; there were some concessions to liberalizer views, such as a few slots for Asian countries, but it was largely a restrictionist bill. Together with Representative Francis Walter, a Democrat from Pennsylvania, and other advocates, McCarran successfully led the passage of the Immigration and Nationality Act of 1952, popularly called the McCarran-Walter Act. Truman vetoed the bill, but a congressional majority overrode his veto, and the bill stood. See E. P. Hutchison, *Legislative History of American Immigration Policy, 1798–1965* (Philadelphia: University of Pennsylvania, 2016).

166 **Eisenhower and other liberalizers:** Refugee Relief Act of 1953, Pub.L. 83-751, 68 Stat. 1044 (1953). The act defined refugees as lacking "the essentials of life" and focused both on World War II and on Soviet victims; in addition to 45,000 people who lived in countries with communist regimes, the act opened the door to 60,000 Italians and 17,000 Greeks barred under the McCarran-Walter Act, as well as 17,000 Dutch citizens.

166 **During his tenure, Eisenhower "paroled":** See Bockley, "A Historical Overview of Refugee Legislation." Bockley's coverage of this moment in American history is especially helpful: "Despite the growing conflict over its expanding use, Congress did not challenge the executive branch's expansive use of parole authority. Actions that had formerly been taken only after Congressional approval became a regular aspect of the Executive's refugee policy. Because no standardized procedures were adopted to regulate its use, refugee admission under the parole power of the Attorney General was manipulated readily by foreign policy. Furthermore, due to the discretionary nature of parole power, it was outside of the scope of judicial review. After its discovery in 1956, parole authority became a primary means of concealing

the ad hoc nature of refugee admissions" (268). The rest of the section on parole authority provides excellent insight into the debates happening in the country at the time.

CHAPTER 17

172 **Seeing a man in the shadows:** Bob was eventually arrested on another case by detectives in Austin and received a three-year sentence for "indecency with a child, sexual conduct," but was later released on parole. The detective who tried to get evidence from the Burmese community told us that Bob was one of the top five most egregious pedophiles he had encountered in his many years on the force; the officers worked doggedly for weeks to convince the community to speak with them but, as far as I know, they were not successful. His eventual arrest was for sexual conduct with a child who was not a member of the refugee community. As of the writing of this book, he's free again and living within a couple of miles of where he was; at one-point he was living across the street from a middle school. As the detective informed us, "Unfortunately, there are no restrictions on [Bob] about where he can live" (email to the author, September 18, 2012). I've verified his arrest records on family watchdog.us; he had a previous arrest for "indecency with a child by exposure."

CHAPTER 19

184 **President Johnson signed the bill:** "President Lyndon B. Johnson's Remarks at the Signing of the Immigration Bill," Liberty Island, New York, October 3, 1965, LBJ Presidential Library website, http://www.lbjlibrary.org/lyndon-baines-johnson/timeline/lbj-on-immigration.

186 **Airlifts began in 1965:** See "Refugee Timeline," U.S. Citizenship and Immigration Services website: https://www.uscis.gov/history-and-genealogy/our-history/refugee-timeline.

186 **While untold thousands of Haitians arrived:** Because of the lack of documentation, the actual number is hard to ascertain. In 1971, Jean-Claude "Baby Doc" Duvalier ascended to the presidency. Because he was a US ally, American border policies were more lenient with earlier waves of Haitian arrivals—many of whom were part of the educated or wealthy classes in the beginning—than they were with later groups who were actively fleeing Baby Doc. For further reading, see Gil Loescher and John A. Scanlan, "Human Rights, U.S. Foreign Policy, and Haitian Refugees," *Journal of Interamerican Studies and World Affairs*, vol. 26.3 (August 1984): 313–56; María Cristina García, *Havana USA: Cuban Exiles and Cuban Americans in South Florida, 1954–1994* (Berkeley: University of California Press, 1996); and Jake Miller, *The Plight of Haitian Refugees* (New York: Praeger Publishers, 1984).

186 **While family reunification had been:** See Philip E. Wolgin, "Family Reunification Is the Bedrock of U.S. Immigration Policy," Center for American Progress website, February 12, 2018: https://www.americanprogress.org/issues/immigration/news/2018/02/12/446402/family -reunification-bedrock-u-s-immigration-policy/.

186 **And as resettlement demographics shifted:** Carly Goodman, "For 50 years, Keeping Families Together Has Been Central to U.S. Immigration Policy. Now Trump Wants to Tear Them Apart," *The Washington Post*, December 17, 2017: https://www.washingtonpost.com/news /made-by-history/wp/2017/12/17/for-50-years-keeping-families-together-has-been -central-to-u-s-immigration-policy-now-trump-wants-to-tear-them-apart/?utm_term= .d5822da26a38: "Family unity was a strong shared value that transcended partisan and ideological divides, despite its different interpretations and meanings to different people. And with a few tweaks over the years, the family immigration framework created in 1965 remains at the core of U.S. immigration admissions today."

187 **The US continued the resettlement:** See Steven J. Gold, "Soviet Jews in the United States," *The American Jewish Year Book*, 94 (1994): 3–57.

187 **But the group that defined US resettlement:** See particularly the overview of Hmong culture and refugee situation in Anne Fadiman, *The Spirit Catches You and You Fall Down: A Hmong Child, Her American Doctor, and the Collision of Two Cultures* (New York: Farrar, Straus and Giroux, 1998).

188 **The Laotian civil war in 1974:** See Lydia DePillis, Kulwant Saluja, and Denise Lu, "A visual guide to 75 years of major refugee crises around the world," *The Washington Post*, December 21, 2015: https://www.washingtonpost.com/graphics/world/historical-migrant-crisis/.

188 **Despite the fact that the American public:** Sixty percent of people in a Gallup poll taken in January 1973 "thought sending US troops to Vietnam was a mistake," and in March 1973, only 32 percent expressed "a great deal of confidence" in the American military leadership. See Tom Rosentiel, Jodie T. Allen, Nilanthi Samaranayake, and James Albrittain, Jr., "Iraq and Vietnam: A Crucial Difference in Opinion," Pew Research Center website, March 22, 2007: http://www.pewresearch.org/2007/03/22/iraq-and-vietnam-a-crucial-difference-in -opinion/.

188 **The Vietnam War:** Chapter 4, "Flight from Indochina," *The State of the World's Refugees 2000: Fifty Years of Humanitarian Action*, UNHCR website, January 1, 2000: https://www.unhcr .org/3ebf9bad0.pdf.

188 **The Indochina Migration and Refugee Assistance Act:** Drew Desilver, "Executive Actions on Immigration Have Long History," FactTank: News in the Numbers for the Pew Research Center, November 21, 2014: https://www.pewresearch.org/fact-tank/2014/11/21 /executive-actions-on-immigration-have-long-history/.

188 **Rather than being fed up:** Jacqueline Desbarats, "Indochinese Resettlement in the United States," *Annals of the Association of American Geographers*, 75, no. 4 (1985), 522.

189 **By 1992, that number:** "The Largest Refugee Resettlement Effort in American History," International Rescue Committee website, July 28, 2016: https://www.rescue.org/article/largest -refugee-resettlement-effort-american-history.

189 **If the numbers of people resettled:** According to a Gallup poll taken in 1979, when asked if Indochinese refugees would be generally welcomed in their neighborhood, 57 percent of people answered that they would. And when asked if they would personally like to see Indo- chinese refugees in their community, 47 percent of people said they would, compared to 40 percent who would not. See Frank Newport, "Historical Review: Americans' Views on Ref- ugees Coming to the U.S.," Pew Research Center website, November 19, 2015: https://news .gallup.com/opinion/polling-matters/186716/historical-review-americans-views -refugees-coming.aspx.

189 **Human rights groups:** See especially the excellent book *The Breakthrough: Human Rights in the 1970s*, edited by Jan Eckel and Samuel Moyn (Philadelphia: University of Pennsylvania Press, 2013).

189 **John F. Kennedy's Peace Corps:** *Peace Corps: Tenth Annual Report* (Washington, DC: Peace Corps, 1971): https://files.eric.ed.gov/fulltext/ED209551.pdf.

189 **Membership in Amnesty International:** *Amnesty International Annual Report 1969–1970* (Amnesty International, 1970): https://www.amnesty.org/en/documents/pol10/001/1970/en/.

189 **Human Rights Watch began in 1978:** See "History," Human Rights Watch website: https:// www.hrw.org/history.

189 **"Our moral sense dictates":** "Carter and Human Rights, 1977–1981," *Milestones in the His- tory of U.S. Foreign Relations* blog, Office of the Historian website: https://history.state.gov /milestones/1977-1980/human-rights.

190 **In 1979, the Carter administration:** See especially David A. Martin, "The Refugee Act of 1980: Its Past and Future," *The Michigan Journal of International Law* 93 (1982): 91–123, and

George Packer, *Our Man: Richard Holbrooke and the End of the American Century* (New York: Knopf, 2019).

191 **A refugee in the United States:** Refugee Act of 1980, Pub. L. No. 96-212, 94 Stat. 102 (1980).

192 **The trauma that resettlement agencies:** See "Complex Trauma Disorder," The Center for Treatment of Anxiety and Mood Disorders website, September 15, 2018: http://center foranxietydisorders.com/complex-trauma-disorder/; Susannah Radstone, "Trauma Theory: Contexts, Politics, Ethics," *Paragraph* 30, no. 1, 2007: 9–29; and Devon E. Hinton and Byron J. Good, *Culture and PTSD: Trauma in Global and Historical Perspective* (Philadelphia: University of Pennsylvania Press, 2016). I'm especially indebted to Joanna Mendez, Community Wellness Counselor at Refugee Services of Texas (interview with the author, April 18, 2018).

193 **There were all the normal bureaucratic hurdles:** See Andrea Freiberger, "The United States' Response to Humanitarian Refugee Obligations: Inconsistent Application of Legal Standards and Its Consequences," *Washington University Journal of Law and Policy* 33 (2010), 297–327.

CHAPTER 21

208 **We waited for a full day:** The small trucks used for transporting goods across the country, smaller versions of the eighteen-wheelers we have in the US.

212 **I cannot do this alone:** Drawn verbatim from Laila's WhatsApp messages and translated by Amena. Her words have been lightly condensed and edited for clarity, but otherwise this section is entirely in her own words.

PART 3

CHAPTER 23

225 **Worldwide, the number of acts of genocide increased:** See Samantha Powers, *"A Problem from Hell": America and the Age of Genocide* (New York: Basic Books, 2002).

226 **Lawmakers' lofty language:** In following the rhetoric of American identity in relation to refugee resettlement, I'm glossing over many of the larger immigration policies and controversies that raged in those years, such as Ronald Reagan's amnesty bill in 1986; George H. W. Bush's 1990 Family Unity Program; and Bill Clinton's hard-line immigration policies beginning in 1996, among many others.

226 **He called it:** "Farewell Address to the Nation," President Ronald Reagan, January 11, 1989, Ronald Reagan Presidential Library and Museum: https://www.reaganlibrary.gov/011189i.

226 **In a September 11, 1990, address:** "Address before a Joint Session of Congress," President George H. W. Bush, September 11, 1990: https://millercenter.org/the-presidency/presidential -speeches/september-11-1990-address-joint-session-congress.

227 **In Clinton's remarks:** Linda D. Kozaryn, "Clinton Salutes U.S., Allied Troops," for the U.S. Department of Defense website, June 23, 1999: http://archive.defense.gov/news/newsarticle .aspx?id=42798.

228 **While it did not approach:** See Chauncy D. Harris and Gabriele Wülker, "The Refugee Problem of Germany," *Economic Geography* 29, no. 1 (1954): 10–25. As this contemporary article makes clear, the number "60 million" is an estimate of the number of displaced persons; as the guidelines and registration process for refugees solidifies in the twentieth century, there will be a distinct difference between the exact number of registered refugees in any country and the estimation of "persons of concern."

228 **In 1951, the first year:** This interactive chart of the UNHCR Population Statistics Database is incredibly helpful: "UNHCR Statistics—The World in Numbers," UNHCR website:

http://popstats.unhcr.org/en/overview. This number does not differentiate between "refugees" and "persons of concern" (see note above).

228 **By 1960, that number fell:** All numbers in this section are from "UNHCR Historical Refugee Data," UNHCR website: http://data.unhcr.org/dataviz/.

228 **But by 1980, the global number:** Those numbers included people who were internally displaced—and therefore not eligible for aid or resettlement because they were still within their countries—in addition to those who crossed borders to flee persecution or war. Under Brazil's military government, 24,000 were internally displaced. In Ethiopia, the country with the most refugees in the world in 1980, the country had 2,567,990 refugees throughout the world, including 10,930 internally displaced people. See Catherine Dauvergne, *The New Politics of Immigration and the End of Settler Societies* (Cambridge: Cambridge University Press, 2016), 42.

228 **By 1982, it was set at 142,000:** Figures for US resettlement ceilings in this paragraph are from "U.S. Annual Refugee Resettlement Ceilings and the Number of Refugees Admitted, 1980–Present," Migration Policy Institute website: https://www.migrationpolicy.org/programs/data-hub/charts/us-annual-refugee-resettlement-ceilings-and-number-refugees-admitted-united.

228 **The global refugee numbers:** See "How Draconian Are the Changes to the US Asylum Law? A Monthly Time Series Analysis (1990–2010)," *Human Rights Quarterly*, 37, no. 1 (2015): 153–87.

229 **On September 14, Bush issued:** "Proclamation 7463—Declaration of National Emergency by Reason of Certain Terrorist Attacks," issued on September 18, 2001, has been renewed every year since the George W. Bush administration by both Presidents Obama and Trump: https://www.govinfo.gov/content/pkg/FR-2001-09-18/pdf/01-23358.pdf.

229 **Hate crimes increased:** The FBI recorded 93 assaults against Muslims in 2001, and then the numbers stayed in the 30s to the 50s until 2015, when they reported 91 assaults, and 2016, when there were 127 according to Katayoun Kishi, "Assaults Against Muslims in U.S. Surpass 2001 Level," *FactTank: News in the Numbers*, Pew Research Center website, November 15, 2017: https://www.pewresearch.org/fact-tank/2017/11/15/assaults-against-muslims-in-u-s-surpass-2001-level/.

229 **There should be no intimidation:** "Remarks by the President of the United States at the Islamic Center of Washington D.C.," September 17, 2001. A pdf of the remarks is available at https://georgewbush-whitehouse.archives.gov/news/releases/2001/09/20010917-11.html.

230 **The US attacks on Afghan soil:** George Monbiot, "Folly of Aid and Bombs," *The Guardian*, October 9, 2001: https://www.theguardian.com/society/2001/oct/09/1.

230 **On November 21, President Bush:** Bon Tempo, *Americans at the Gate*, 204.

230 **Most of the allotted slots:** "U.S. Annual Refugee Resettlement Ceilings and the Number of Refugees Admitted, 1980–Present," Migration Policy Institute website: https://www.migrationpolicy.org/programs/data-hub/charts/us-annual-refugee-resettlement-ceilings-and-number-refugees-admitted-united.

230 **The number of refugees:** Bon Tempo, *Americans at the Gate*, 205.

231 **It was illegal, however:** The growing fear that rose after 9/11 led to a sharp decrease in the number of people receiving asylum. In American border states, the fear that terrorists would infiltrate the border routes morphed with anti–undocumented immigrant language. The 2003 Homeland Security Act restructured immigration in a number of crucial ways under the Department of Homeland Security, including creating a new agency, US Immigration and Custom Enforcement (ICE). The restructuring led to immigration enforcement falling more clearly into the jurisdiction of the same agencies concerned with national security. See

Andrew I. Schoenholtz, "Refugee Protection in the United States Post–September 11," *Columbia Human Rights Law Review* 36 (2005), 323–64: https://scholarship.law.georgetown .edu/facpub/564/.

233 **In the first part:** Figures in this paragraph come from Alexander Betts and Paul Collier, *Refuge: Rethinking Refugee Policy in a Changing World* (Oxford: Oxford University Press, 2017), 53.

233 **A word in the Somali language:** Maggie Fick, "In Kenyan Refugee Camp, Hope of New Life in U.S. Fades and Suicide Rate Rises," *Reuters*, April 9, 2018: https://www.reuters.com /article/us-refugees-usa-somalia/in-kenyan-refugee-camp-hope-of-new-life-in-u-s-fades -and-suicide-rate-rises-idUSKBN1HG0YW.

233 **The average length of stay:** Betts and Collier, *Refuge*, 53.

233 **A UNHCR report:** Those refugees were trapped in camps "in the world's poorest and most unstable regions," their conditions "frequently the result of neglect by regional and interna- tional actors." The cost was high: "The consequences of having so many human beings in a static state . . . include wasted lives, squandered resources and increased threats to security," according to "The State of the World's Refugees 2006: Human Displacement in the New Millennium," UNHCR website, April 20, 2006: https://www.unhcr.org/publications/sowr /4a4dc1a89/state-worlds-refugees-2006-human-displacement-new-millennium.html.

233 **While the US attempted to frame:** The Pentagon doesn't keep statistics on civilian deaths and there is a great deal of divergence about the number of civilians dying. See especially "The Iraq War: 2003–2011," The Council on Foreign Relations website: https://www.cfr .org/timeline/iraq-war.

234 **In May 2006, Secretary of State:** Because of the provision in the Refugee Act of 1980 that stated that a refugee could not be someone who "ordered, incited, assisted or otherwise participated in the persecution of any person on account of race, religion, nationality, mem- bership in a particular social group, or political opinion," many of the refugees fleeing the conflict in Myanmar had been barred from resettlement to the United States. The US waived this provision for this specific conflict under international and domestic pressure from ref- ugee advocates, who argued that people who had defended themselves against ethnically targeted violence were not "inciting or assisting" persecution, they were resisting it. The Bush administration's change in tack opened the door to people in one of the most dire and protracted refugee situations in the world. For more information, see "Rice Allows Myanmar Minority to Seek Asylum," NBC News, May 5, 2006: http://www.nbcnews.com/id/12649433 /ns/us_news-security/t/rice-allows-myanmar-minority-seek-asylum/#.XG6PNS3MzUI, and the speech by then–assistant secretary of state Ellen Sauerbrey, at the High-Level Dialogue on International Migration and Development of the United Nations General Assembly, New York, September 16, 2006: https://2001-2009.state.gov/g/prm/rls/2006 /72316.html. Sauerbrey states, "The Karens had been declared ineligible for asylum because the Homeland Security Department determined they had 'provided material support' to the Karen National Union, a 58-year-old resistance group opposed to central government control."

234 **First Lady Laura Bush:** "Burma: A Human Rights Disaster and Threat to Regional Secu- rity," Bureau of Public Affairs Fact Sheet, Washington, D.C., September 19, 2006: https:// 2001-2009.state.gov/r/pa/scp/2006/72840.htm.

234 **The Rohingya Muslim refugees:** See Patrick Winn, "The Biggest Group of Current Ref- ugees in the US? Christians from Myanmar," *PRI's The World*, May 7, 2017: https://www.pri .org/stories/2017-05-04/biggest-group-refugees-us-christians-myanmar,

234 **The resettlement of refugees from Myanmar:** Bradley Graham, "Immigration Waiver Granted to Refugees," *The Washington Post*, May 5, 2006: http://www.washingtonpost.com /wp-dyn/content/article/2006/05/04/AR2006050402062.html.

CHAPTER 26

249 **He only raised it:** "U.S. Annual Refugee Resettlement Ceilings and the Number of Refugees
Admitted, 1980–Present," Migration Policy Institute website: https://www.migrationpolicy
.org/programs/data-hub/charts/us-annual-refugee-resettlement-ceilings-and-number
-refugees-admitted-united.

249 **Under the Obama administration:** From "Infographic: The Screening Process for Refugee
Entry into the United States," from the White House of President Barack Obama website,
November 20, 2015: https://obamawhitehouse.archives.gov/blog/2015/11/20/infographic
-screening-process-refugee-entry-united-states, among many other sources, including first
person interviews.

250 **At the end of that time:** "The Resettlement Process," Refugee Council USA website: http://
www.rcusa.org/resettlement-process.

250 **This was the point at which:** "Written testimony of USCIS Director Francis Cissna for a
House Committee on the Judiciary, Subcommittee on Immigration and Border Security
hearing titled 'Oversight of the United States Refugee Admissions Program,'" Homeland
Security website, October 26, 2017: https://www.dhs.gov/news/2017/10/26/written-testimony
-uscis-director-house-judiciary-subcommittee-immigration-and-border.

251 **At the end of the Obama administration:** Through February 2019, the UNHCR website
continued to list 350 affiliate sites, despite the fact that other sources quoted that figure as
much less with the closures of many of the local sites (see Chapter 29). "Refugee Resettlement Facts," UNHCR website, February 2019: https://www.unhcr.org/resettlement-in-the
-united-states.html.

252 **By the end of 2016:** "UNHCR Statistics—The World in Numbers," UNHCR website:
http://popstats.unhcr.org/en/overview.

253 **In 2011, the year the war:** See Jasmine El-Gamal, "Trump Is Making the Same Mistakes
in Syria That Obama Did in the Middle East," *The Washington Post*, December 22, 2018: https://
www.washingtonpost.com/outlook/2018/12/22/trump-is-repeating-obamas-mistakes
-syria/?utm_term=.ef16a0954abe; Tim Arango and Michael S. Schmidt, "Last Convoy of
American Troops Leaves Iraq," *The New York Times*, December 18, 2011: https://www
.nytimes.com/2011/12/19/world/middleeast/last-convoy-of-american-troops-leaves-iraq
.html?mtrref=www.google.com.lb&gwh=C7EF213277238BA5BFD621A017D4F332&gwt=
pay; and Alice Fordham, "Fact Check: Did Obama Withdraw from Iraq Too Soon, Allowing
ISIS to Grow?" NPR, December 19, 2015: https://www.npr.org/2015/12/19/459850716/fact
-check-did-obama-withdraw-from-iraq-too-soon-allowing-isis-to-grow.

253 **Whether that withdrawal:** See James Franklin Jeffrey, "Behind the U.S. Withdrawal from
Iraq," *The Wall Street Journal*, November 2, 2014: https://www.wsj.com/articles/james
-franklin-jeffrey-behind-the-u-s-withdrawal-from-iraq-1414972705.

253 **Obama issued a White House statement:** "Remarks by the President to the White House
Press Corps," The President Barack Obama White House website, August 20, 2012: https://
obamawhitehouse.archives.gov/the-press-office/2012/08/20/remarks-president-white
-house-press-corps.

254 **But when the red line:** See the final report of the United Nations Mission to Investigate
Allegations of the Use of Chemical Weapons in the Syrian Arab Republic, from the
Secretary-General of the United Nations to the President of the General Assembly and
the President of the Security Council, December 13, 2013: https://undocs.org/A/68/663.

254 **On Saturday, August 31, President Obama:** "Statement by the President on Syria," The
President Barack Obama White House website, August 31, 2012: https://obamawhitehouse
.archives.gov/the-press-office/2013/08/31/statement-president-syria.

255 **On September 3, House Speaker:** See David Jackson, "Boehner, Cantor Back Obama on Force Against Syria," *USA Today*, September 3, 2013: https://www.usatoday.com/story/news /politics/2013/09/03/obama-syria-strike-chemical-weapons-congress-g-20-russia /2756991/; and Mark Landler, Michael Gordon, and Thom Shanker, "House Leaders Express Their Support for Syria Strike," *The New York Times*, September 3, 2013: https:// www.nytimes.com/2013/09/04/us/politics/obama-administration-presses-case-on-syria .html.

255 **He used language of international cooperation:** "Weekly Address: Pursuing a Diplomatic Solution in Syria," The President Barack Obama White House website, September 14, 2013: https://obamawhitehouse.archives.gov/photos-and-video/video/2013/09/14/weekly -address-pursuing-diplomatic-solution-syria#transcript.

256 **Some attacks were clearly:** See Reese Erlich, *Inside Syria: The Backstory of Their Civil War and What the World Can Expect* (New York: Prometheus Books, 2014).

256 **Civilians endured documented gas attacks:** See "Timeline of Syrian Chemical Weapons Activity, 2012–2019," Arms Control Association website: https://www.armscontrol.org /factsheets/Timeline-of-Syrian-Chemical-Weapons-Activity; and "Chlorine Likely Used in Attack on Syria Town Douma, Says OPCW," *Al-Jazeera*, March 2, 2019: https://www.aljazeera .com/news/2019/03/chlorine-attack-syria-town-douma-opcw-190302063053270.html.

256 **Improvised explosive devices. Barrel bombs:** See "Weaponry Used by Different Factions," on the Syrian Civil War Map Project's website: https://syriancivilwarmap.com/weaponry -used-different-factions/; "Syria War: Weapons Key Players Have at Their Disposal," *BBC News*, April 12, 2018: https://www.bbc.com/news/world-middle-east-43730068.

257 **In fall 2015:** See Annalisa Merelli and Caitlin Hu, "These Photos Will Change How the World Sees the Syrian Refugee Crisis," *Quartz*, September 2, 2015: https://qz.com/494068/these -photos-will-change-how-the-west-sees-the-syrian-refugee-crisis/; and Tima Kurdi, *The Boy on the Beach: My Family's Escape from Syria and Our Hope for a New Home* (New York: Simon & Schuster, 2018).

257 **In April 2017:** See Michael Edison Hayden, "Father Loses 9-Month-Old Twins in Syrian Chemical Attack," *ABC News*, April 5, 2017: https://abcnews.go.com/International/father -loses-month-twins-syrian-chemical-weapons-attack/story?id=46596223.

257 **In 2015, 1,682 Syrians:** "UNHCR Statistics—The World in Numbers," UNHCR website: http://popstats.unhcr.org/en/overview.

257 **Reports trickling out:** See Paul Cruickshank, "The Inside Story of the Paris and Brussels Attacks," *CNN*, October 30, 2017: https://www.cnn.com/2016/03/30/europe/inside-paris -brussels-terror-attacks/index.html.

258 **Despite the fact:** "Refugee Resettlement—Security Screening Information," Human Rights First website, Feb. 1, 2017: https://www.humanrightsfirst.org/resource/refugee-resettlement -security-screening-information.

259 **How the United States and other countries:** Obama, "Remarks by President Obama at Leaders' Summit on Refugees," United Nations, New York (September 20, 2016): https:// obamawhitehouse.archives.gov/the-press-office/2016/09/20/remarks-president-obama -leaders-summit-refugees.

259 **In August 2016, the 10,000th refugee:** Haeyoun Park and Rudy Omri, "U.S. Reaches Goal of Admitting 10,000 Refugees. Here's Where They Went," *The New York Times*, August 31, 2016: https://www.nytimes.com/interactive/2016/08/30/us/syrian-refugees-in-the-united -states.html.

259 **More than 120,000 Cubans:** Obama, "Presidential Determination—Refugee Admissions for Fiscal Year 2017," Memorandum for the Secretary of State, September 28, 2017: https://

obamawhitehouse.archives.gov/the-press-office/2016/09/28/presidential-determination
-refugee-admissions-fiscal-year-2017.

259 **On September 28:** Editorial Board, "America Has Accepted 10,000 Syrian Refugees. That's Still Too Few," *The Washington Post*, September 2, 2016: https://www.washingtonpost.com /opinions/global-opinions/america-has-accepted-10000-syrian-refugees-thats-still-too -few/2016/09/02/470446e2-6fc0-11e6-8533-6b0b0ded0253_story.html?utm_term= .ce0f2188358c.

CHAPTER 27

264 **The US was one of the top destinations:** "IOM Turkey Helps Resettle Over 21,000 Refugees in 2016," International Organization for Migration website, January 17, 2017: https:// www.iom.int/news/iom-turkey-helps-resettle-over-21000-refugees-2016.

CHAPTER 29

272 **The caption, "Refugees?" in white letters:** See Lizzie Dearden, "The fake refugee images that are being used to distort public opinion on asylum seekers," *The Independent*, September 16, 2015: https://www.independent.co.uk/news/world/europe/the-fake-refugee-images-that -are-being-used-to-distort-public-opinion-on-asylum-seekers-10503703.html; and Mike Wendling, "Laith Al Saleh: This viral photo falsely claims to show an IS fighter posing as a refugee," *BBC News*, September 7, 2015: https://www.bbc.co.uk/news/blogs-trending-34176631.

273 **He had just begun using:** See Frank Rich, "Trump's Appeasers," *New York* magazine, November 1, 2016: http://nymag.com/daily/intelligencer/2016/11/charles-lindbergh-is-a-cautionary-tale -for-republicans.html. As Rich comments, Lindbergh's speeches "sounded like the Ur-text for much of Trump's America First campaign."

273 **Trump framed Syrian refugees:** Ali Vitali, "'The Snake': Trump Poetry Slams Syrian Refugees with Allegorical Song," *NBC News*, January 12, 2016: http://www.nbcnews.com /politics/2016-election/snake-trump-poetry-slams-syrian-refugees-allegorical-song -n495311; and "FNN: Donald Trump Reads 'Snake' Poem to Syrian Refugees," Fox 10 Phoenix, January 12, 2016: https://www.youtube.com/watch?v=V-NaN1ujo_0.

274 **He conflated all Syrian refugees:** "Everything We Know About the San Bernardino Shooting Terror Investigation," *The Los Angeles Times*, December 14, 2015: http://www.latimes.com /local/california/la-me-san-bernardino-shooting-terror-investigation-htmlstory.html.

274 **At the same rally:** As several journalists noted at the time, Brown based his lyrics for the song sung by Al Wilson in 1968 on one of Aesop's fables. Brown's grandson, Sidakarav Dasa, wrote a Facebook post on January 13, 2016, the day after Trump's rally, to protest that it is "a relationship allegory, a dialog between two persons, and it is not supposed to be taken as an indictment of an entire nationality, or race, or religion." Sidakarav Dasa tagged Trump in the post and suggested another of Oscar Brown Jr.'s poems, "Debris," as being more appropriate to Trump's campaign; he also suggested Trump, and not the Syrian people, was the snake. The Facebook post has since been removed.

274 **The simplistic, sing-song rhythm:** Princeton professor Josh Zeitz noted the direct correlation between the rhetoric being used in the 1930s by the America First movement and the rhetoric Trump and other politicians used in 2016 about refugees: "Then as now, skepticism of religious and ethnic minorities and concerns that refugees might pose a threat to national security deeply influenced the debate over American immigration policy." Josh Zeitz, "Yes, It's Fair to Compare the Plight of the Syrians to the Plight of the Jews. Here's Why," *Politico*, November 22, 2015: http://www.politico.com/magazine/story/2015/11/syrian-refugees-jews -holocaust-world-war-ii-213384.

275 **Effective immediately, the sweeping "Executive Order":** Donald Trump, "Executive Order Protecting the Nation from Foreign Terrorist Entry into the United States," Executive Order issued by the President of the United States, January 27, 2017: https://www.whitehouse .gov/presidential-actions/executive-order-protecting-nation-foreign-terrorist-entry -united-states/.

275 **In a striking deviation from every other president:** While the ensuing court battles about the ban would keep the Trump administration from being able to completely overturn the Obama administration's Presidential Determination, they successfully kept admissions for fiscal year 2017 close to their 45,000 target, with slightly more than 53,000 refugees actually admitted. See Dara Lind, "Under Trump, Refugee Admissions Are Falling Way Short— Except for Europeans," *Vox*, September 17, 2018: https://www.vox.com/2018/9/17/17832912 /trump-refugee-news-statistics.

275 **Soon the Trump administration:** Mike Pence, Vice President of the United States, "We're going to BUILD THE WALL. We're going to END CHAIN MIGRATION. We're going to END THE VISA LOTTERY PROGRAM, and we're going to address DACA. But this administration is going to do it in a way that will meet the expectations of the American people. #MAGA," Twitter, January 10, 2018: https://twitter.com/vp/status/951251616514084864 ?lang=en.

275 **Presidential senior policy adviser Stephen Miller:** David S. Glosser, "Stephen Miller Is an Immigration Hypocrite. I Know Because I'm His Uncle," *Politico*, August 31, 2018: https:// www.politico.com/magazine/story/2018/08/13/stephen-miller-is-an-immigration-hypocrite -i-know-because-im-his-uncle-219351.

276 **Lawsuits filed by the ACLU:** "Timeline of the Muslim Ban," ACLU Washington website: https://www.aclu-wa.org/pages/timeline-muslim-ban.

276 **On March 6, 2017:** See Kaitlyn Schalhorn, "Trump Travel Ban: Timeline of a Legal Journey," Fox News, June 26, 2018: https://www.foxnews.com/politics/trump-travel-ban-timeline-of -a-legal-journey, among many other sources.

277 **"The admission and exclusion of foreign nationals":** *Trump, President of the United States, et al., v. Hawaii, et al.*, 585 U.S. ___ (2018).

277 **There was every reason to think:** The countries listed by UNHCR are: "Argentina, Australia, Austria, Belarus, Belgium, Brazil, Bulgaria, Canada, Chile, Croatia, Czech Republic, Denmark, Estonia, Finland, France, Germany, Hungary, Iceland, Ireland, Italy, Japan, Republic of Korea, Latvia, Liechtenstein, Lithuania, Luxembourg, Netherlands, New Zealand, Norway, Portugal, Romania, Spain, Sweden, Switzerland, United Kingdom, United States of America, Uruguay." "Information on UNHCR Resettlement," UNHCR website: https://www.unhcr.org/information-on-unhcr-resettlement.html.

277 **And yet the number of people accepted anywhere:** Phillip Connor and Jens Manuel Krogstad, "For the first time, U.S. resettles fewer refugees than the rest of the world," *FactTank: News in the Numbers*, Pew Research Center website, July 5, 2018: http://www .pewresearch.org/fact-tank/2018/07/05/for-the-first-time-u-s-resettles-fewer-refugees-than -the-rest-of-the-world.

277 **The number rose more than 2 million:** "Population Statistics," UNHCR website: http:// popstats.unhcr.org/en/overview.

278 **If it were possible:** "Countries in the World by Population (2019)," Worldometers website: http://www.worldometers.info/world-population/population-by-country.

278 **By population, if the 103,000:** American FactFinder, the Census Bureau website: https:// factfinder.census.gov/.

278 **For the first time:** Connor and Krogstad, *FactTank: News in the Numbers*, Pew Research Center website.

278 **Canada surpassed the United States:** Nadine Yousif, "Canada's Resettlement of Refugees Highest in the World for First Time in 72 Years, New Data Shows," *The Star* (Edmonton, Alberta, Canada), January 23, 2019: https://www.thestar.com/edmonton/2019/01/23/canadas -resettlement-of-refugees-highest-in-the-world-for-first-time-in-72-years-new-data -shows.html.

278 **True to his administration's promises:** Paige Winfield Cunningham, "The Health 202: The Trump Administration's Refugee Policy Is Dismantling the Infrastructure That Cares for Them," *The Washington Post*, December 19, 2018: https://www.washingtonpost.com /news/powerpost/paloma/the-health-202/2018/12/19/the-health-202-the-trump -administration-s-refugee-policy-is-dismantling-the-infrastructures-that-cares-for -them/5c193e8a1b326b2d6629d4e3/?utm_term=.11b02d064754.

278 **There were still a handful:** Nayla Rush, "Refugeee Resettlement Admissions in FY 2018," for the Center for Immigration Studies website, October 1, 2018: https://cis.org/Rush /Refugee-Resettlement-Admissions-FY-2018; and Cunningham, "The Health 202," *The Washington Post.*

278 **In 2018, the Assad regime:** "Syria Emergency," UNHCR website: https://www.unhcr.org /syria-emergency.html.

278 **There were now 3.3 million:** "Operational Portal, Refugee Situations: Syria Regional Refugee Response," UNHCR website, "Lebanon": https://data2.unhcr.org/en/situations/syria /location/71 and "Jordan": http://reporting.unhcr.org/sites/default/files/UNHCR%20Jordan %20Fact%20Sheet%20-%20June%202018.pdf.

279 **As an unnamed official understood:** Jonathan Blitzer, "How Stephen Miller Single-Handedly Got the U.S. to Accept Fewer Refugees," *The New Yorker,* October 13, 2017: https:// www.newyorker.com/news/news-desk/how-stephen-miller-single-handedly-got -the-us-to-accept-fewer-refugees.

279 **By adding extra procedures:** Dan De Luce and Julia Ainsley, "Trump admin intentionally slowing FBI vetting of refugees, ex-officials say," NBC News, August 24, 2018: https://www .nbcnews.com/politics/immigration/trump-admin-intentionally-slowing-fbi-vetting -refugees-ex-officials-say-n903346.

280 **The federal government provided each refugee:** Scott Bixby, "The New Collateral Damage in Trump's War on Refugees," *The Daily Beast*, September 24, 2018: https://www .thedailybeast.com/the-new-collateral-damage-in-trumps-war-on-refugees.

280 **The State Department announced in February:** Mica Rosenberg, "Exclusive: Dozens of Refugee Resettlement Offices to Close as Trump Downsizes Program," *Reuters*, February 14, 2018: https://www.reuters.com/article/us-usa-immigration-refugees-exclusive/exclusive -dozens-of-refugee-resettlement-offices-to-close-as-trump-downsizes-program-idUSKCN 1FY1EJ.

280 **By April 2018, in Florida alone:** David C. Adams, "U.S. Refugee Resettlement Offices Close as Flow of Arrivals Dries Up Under Trump," *Univision News*, April 24, 2018: https://www.univision .com/univision-news/united-states/us-refugee-resettlement-offices-close-as-refugee-flow -dries-up-under-trump.

280 **The radio program *This American Life*:** "Let Me Count the Ways," *This American Life*, episode 656, September 14, 2018: https://www.thisamericanlife.org/656/transcript.

281 **In September 2018:** "Presidential Determination on Refugee Admissions for Fiscal Year 2018," Presidential Determination No. 2019-01, October 4, 2018: https://www.federalregister .gov/documents/2018/11/01/2018-24135/presidential-determination-on-refugee-admissions -for-fiscal-year-2019.

282 **It certainly sounded impressive:** Asylum seekers are processed under DHS. In Fiscal Year 2016, 73,081 people applied for asylum and 20,455 received it, which is about 28 percent

(Zuzana Cepla, "Fact Sheet: U.S. Asylum Process," the National Immigration Forum website, January 10, 2019). While the number of asylum seekers has risen, the percentage of those who would actually receive asylum would remain statistically low throughout 2019.

282 **He touted "these expansive figures":** "Remarks to the Media," Michael R. Pompeo, Secretary of State on the U.S. Department of State website, September 17, 2018: https://www .state.gov/remarks-to-the-media/, accessed May 20, 2019.

282 **Caritas of Austin:** Nancy Flores, "As Refugee Flow Dwindles, Caritas to End Resettlement Program," *Austin American-Statesman*, September 26, 2018: https://www.statesman.com/news /20180926/as-refugee-flow-dwindles-caritas-to-end-resettlement-program.

282 **As RST CEO Russell Smith:** In a Wednesday, October 3, 2018, interview with the author.

283 **One anonymous source estimated:** Private email to the author in March 2019.

283 **Officials publicly toyed with the idea:** See Didi Martinez and Nahal Toosi, "Pompeo Urged to Not Cut State Department Refugee Office," *Politico*, July 23, 2018: https://www .politico.com/story/2018/07/23/mike-pompeo-state-department-refugee-office-735801; and Dan De Luce and Robbie Gramer, "White House Weighs Taking Refugee Programs Away from the State Department," *Foreign Policy*, May 2, 2018: https://foreignpolicy.com/2018/05 /02/white-house-weighs-stripping-state-department-of-control-over-refugee-policy-u-s -agency-for-international-development-trump-pompeo-immigration.

283 **A planned closure:** Vanessa Romo, "Trump Administration Seeks to Close International Immigration Offices," NPR, March 12, 2019: https://www.npr.org/2019/03/12/702807908 /trump-administration-seeks-to-close-international-immigration-offices.

283 **The administration's proposed 2020 budget:** Carol Morello, "Budget Calls for Deep Cuts to Foreign Aid, Especially for Refugees and in Humanitarian Crises," *The Washington Post*, March 11, 2019: https://www.washingtonpost.com/world/national-security/budget-calls-for -deep-cuts-to-foreign-aid-especially-for-refugees-and-in-humanitarian-crises/2019/03 /11/4acc1d2f-bcd1-4022-8514-6f49b7321881_story.html?utm_term=.6c4573edee22.

283 **As of the writing of this book:** See "Former Refugee, Advocates, and Experts Respond to Reports that Trump Administration Plans to Cut Refugee Admissions to Zero," Refugee Council USA blog, July, 22, 2019: http://www.rcusa.org/blog/former-refugee-advocates-and -experts-respond-to-reports-that-trump-administration-plans-to-cut-refugee-admissions -to-zero-a-r.

283 **No matter the number:** "A Budget for a Better America," Fiscal Year 2020, Budget of the U.S. Government, website for the White House of President Trump: https://www.white house.gov/wp-content/uploads/2019/03/budget-fy2020.pdf.

283 **The government branch tasked:** Priscilla Alvarez, "America's System for Resettling Refugees Is Collapsing," *The Atlantic*, September 9, 2018: https://www.theatlantic.com/politics /archive/2018/09/refugee-admissions-trump/569641/.

CHAPTER 30

288 **A woman on the plane:** Jessica Goudeau, "In Trump's America, Regular People Are the New Freedom Fighters," *Muftah*, January 31, 2017: https://muftah.org/american-people -new-freedom-fighters/#.XOLqXi_MzUJ.

EPILOGUE

295 **She and Saw Ku passed:** She still cries when she hears that song—I played it for her to make sure I had the right one because she just knew it was something about the United States and freedom (which describes a number of songs) and when we finally got to that one, she teared up immediately.

AFTERWORD

299 **I became friends:** That figure came from Russell Smith, director of Refugee Services of Texas, in an interview with the author, October 3, 2018.

301 **In 2015, with the rapid rise:** Nancy Flores, "Austin Nonprofits Brace for Further Drop in Refugee Admissions," *Austin American-Statesman*, September 18, 2018: https://www.statesman.com/NEWS/20180918/Austin-nonprofits-brace-for-further-drop-in-refugee-admissions.

305 **Greece is swamped by refugees:** "Greece," UNHCR website: https://www.unhcr.org/en-us/greece.html.

306 **Despite the fact that Greece:** Steven Zeitchik, "With Jobless Rate Above 50%, Disillusioned Greek Youths Becoming a 'Lost Generation,'" *The Los Angeles Times*, June 2, 2015: https://www.latimes.com/world/europe/la-fg-greece-youth-economic-woes-20150602-story.html.

307 **They have developed:** Nathan J. Mlot, Craig A. Tovey, and David L. Hu, "Fire Ants Self-assemble into Waterproof Rafts to Survive Floods," *Proceedings of the National Academy of Sciences of the United States of America* 108, no. 19 (May 2011): 7669–73.

Further Reading

Abdelrazaq, Leila. *Baddawi*. Charlottesville: Just World Books, 2015.

Ahmedi, Farah, and Tamim Ansary. *The Other Side of the Sky*. New York: Gallery Books, 2005.

Barghouti, Mourid. *I Saw Ramallah*. Translated by Ahdaf Soueif. New York: Anchor Books, 2003.

Beah, Ismael. *A Long Way Gone: Memoirs of a Child Soldier*. New York: Farrar, Straus and Giroux, 2008.

Bhutto, Fatima. *The Shadow of the Crescent Moon*. London: Penguin Books, 2014.

Brauen, Yangzom. *Across Many Mountains: A Tibetan Family's Epic Journey from Oppression to Freedom*. Translated by Katy Derbyshire. New York: St. Martin's Press, 2011.

Bui, Thi. *The Best We Could Do*. New York: Abrams Press, 2018.

di Giovanni, Janine. *The Morning They Came for Us: Dispatches from Syria*. New York: Liveright, 2017.

Dorfman, Ariel. *Homeland Security Ate My Speech: Messages from the End of the World*. New York: OR Books, 2017.

Fadiman, Anne. *The Spirit Catches You and You Fall Down: A Hmong Child, Her American Doctors, and the Collision of Two Cultures*. New York: Farrar, Straus and Giroux, 1997. Reprinted with a new afterword by Fadiman, 2012.

Fleming, Melissa. *A Hope More Powerful Than the Sea: One Refugee's Incredible Story of Love, Loss, and Survival*. New York: Flatiron Books, 2017.

Gourevitch, Philip. *We Wish to Inform You That Tomorrow We Will Be Killed with Our Families: Stories from Rwanda*. New York: Farrar, Straus and Giroux, 1998.

Hemon, Aleksandar. *The Book of My Lives*. New York: Farrar, Straus and Giroux, 2013.

Jones, Ann. *War Is Not Over When It's Over: Women and the Unforeseen Consequences of Conflict*. New York: Metropolitan Books, 2010.

Kingsley, Patrick. *The New Odyssey: The Story of the Twenty-First-Century Refugee Crisis*. New York: Liveright, 2017.

Kurdi, Tima. *The Boy on the Beach: My Family's Escape from Syria and Our Hope for a New Home*. New York: Simon & Schuster, 2019.

Malek, Alia. *The Home That Was Our Country: A Memoir of Syria*. New York: Nation Books, 2017.

Mengestu, Dinaw. *The Beautiful Things That Heaven Bears*. New York: Riverhead, 2008.

Moorehead, Caroline. *Human Cargo: A Journey Among Refugees*. New York: Henry Holt, 2005.

Murad, Nadia, and Jenna Krajeski, with a foreword by Amal Clooney. *The Last Girl: My Story of Captivity, and My Fight Against the Islamic State*. New York: Tim Duggan Books, 2017.

Nayeri, Dina. *The Ungrateful Refugee: What Immigrants Never Tell You.* New York: Catapult, 2019.

Nguyen, Viet Thanh. *The Refugees.* New York: Grove Press, 2017.

———, ed. *The Displaced: Refugee Writers on Refugee Lives.* New York: Abrams Press, 2018.

Pearlman, Wendy. *We Crossed a Bridge and It Trembled: Voices from Syria.* New York: Custom House, 2017.

Sirees, Nihad. *The Silence and the Roar.* New York: Other Press, 2013.

Yang, Kao Kalia. *The Latehomecomer: A Hmong Family Memoir.* Minneapolis: Coffee House Press, 2008.

———. *The Song Poet: A Memoir of My Father.* New York: Metropolitan Books, 2016.

Index

Al-Abbas mosque, 50, 88
Abbott, Greg, 258
Abu Adnan, 287–88
Abu Ahmad, 89–90
Abu Khalid, 286–88, 292
ACLU, 276
Afghanistan, 225, 257
Afghanistan War, 230–32, 253
African Americans, 98, 225
Alawites, 25, 35, 52
Aleppo, 24, 154, 159, 209, 239, 256, 272,
    293, 305
Algeria/Algerians, 51–52, 163, 225
Amal (Hasna's daughter), 156, 181–82,
    238, 266
  brother-in-law detained, 158–59
  childhood of, 27–29
  in Daraa, 32, 36, 49, 87, 111, 152–53
  denied resettlement in US, 287–89
  education of, 27–29, 177
  interviews for resettlement, 200, 289
  in Jordan, 129–30, 136–37, 150, 154, 160,
    212–13
  marriage of, 29–31, 293–94
  moves to Irbed, 177–78
  religious life of, 27–28
  resettles in Canada, 289–90
  seeks resettlement in US, 263–64, 284
America First campaign, 273–75

America First Committee, The, 99,
    273, 275
American Indians, 225
American Life, This (radio program), 280–81
Amjad (Hasna's son), 26–28
Amnesty International, 187, 189
anti-immigrant sentiments, 95–96, 98, 189,
    213, 232, 257–58, 272–75, 301
anti-Semitism, 99, 187
anticommunism, 185–87, 191, 226, 229
antiterrorism, 229, 253
Arab nations, 24–26
Arab Spring, 51–56, 254
Arabic-speakers, 53, 102, 169, 179–80, 238–39,
    262–63, 266–67, 291
Armenia, 96
Asia, 97–98
al-Assad, Asma, 52–53
al-Assad, Bashar, 154, 156, 177
  attacks own citizens, 159, 200,
    252–56, 294
  curates his image, 52–53
  inner circle/loyalists of, 35, 54
  opposition to, 53, 71, 76, 253–54, 256
  regains control, 278, 303
  tortured schoolboys and, 54–56
  uses chemical weapons, 178, 253–57
al-Assad, Bassel, 52
al-Assad, Hafez, 25–28, 35, 52–54, 71, 154

asylum seekers, 252
Haitians as, 186
Jewish refugees as, 16
"non-refoulement" and, 20, 191, 231, 279
refugee camps for, 232
Syrians as, 256–58, 272
US and, 97, 185, 231, 281–82
Atlantic, The, 272
Austin-Bergstrom Airport, 7–9, 44
Austin, Texas, 304
English classes in, 79, 82–83, 168, 173–74, 213, 300
fair-trade jewelry co. in, 218–23, 300
jobs for refugees, 171–72, 265
Karens resettle in, 62, 64, 80, 82, 113–14, 142, 296–97, 299
Myanmar community in, 167–69, 173
refugee agencies of, 282, 299–300
refugees no longer accepted in, 282
refugees welcomed in, 167–69, 301
Syrian refugees resettle in, 213–14, 235–42, 260–67
Syrians not welcome in, 289, 294
women's cooperative in, 167–68, 173, 218, 300
See also Karen Baptist church (Austin, TX); Mu Naw; Refugee Services of Texas (RST); al-Salam, Hasna
Australia, 10, 180
Austria, 98, 164–65

Bangkok, 7–8, 67–68
al-Banin schoolboys, 53–56, 129, 256, 304
Baptists, 61–62, 169, 195, 234, 269–70, 296–97
Belgium, 16. *See also* Brussels
Bin-Laden, Osama, 230
biometric data, 249–50
bipartisan politics, 192–93, 225, 301
Blitzer, Jonathan, 279
Bob (Austin church volunteer), 82–84, 119, 122, 142, 168–72, 302
Boehner, John, 255
Bosnia/Bosnians, 225, 227–28
Bouazizi, Mohamed, 51
Brackenridge Hospital (Austin, TX), 143–46

British Parliament, 255
Brown Lloyd James, 53
Brown, Oscar Jr., 274
Brown, Peter, 53
Brussels, 257, 272
Buck, Joan Juliet, 53
Budapest, 164
Buddhists, 2, 10, 61–62, 66
Bureau of Populations, Refugees, and Migration (PRM), 283
Burmese, 62, 116, 296
junta, 2, 303
language, 57, 60, 83, 173
refugee artisans, 300
resettle in US, 114, 168–71, 234
target ethnic minorities, 2, 66, 142
Burundi, 79, 114, 169, 225, 234
Bush, George H. W., 224, 226–27, 229, 249, 281
Bush, George W., 259
compassionate conservatism of, 233–34
immigration policies of, 224, 231, 249, 281–82
Karen Christian refugees and, 253
and Sept. 11, 2001, 228–30, 234, 275
suspends refugee admissions, 229–30, 275
Bush, Laura, 234

Cambodians, 10, 187–89, 225, 234
Cameron, David, 255
Campaign Against Torture, 189
Canada, 10, 201, 278, 289–90
Cantor, Eric, 255
Carter, Jimmy, 189–91, 232
cartoons, political, 95–96, 273
caseworkers, 38, 57–60, 80–84, 168–72, 190, 193, 241, 251–52, 262, 280–82, 291, 302
Castro, Fidel, 185
Catholic Church, 234, 251, 282
Central America, 231, 281
Central Presbyterian Church (Austin, TX), 79, 85, 174
Chace, Zoe, 280–81
Chad, 276
chain migration, 275–76
chemical weapons, 178, 253–57

Chemical Weapons Convention, 255–56
child abuse, 170–71
Chile/Chileans, 187
Chin people/state, 2, 61–62
China/Chinese, 62, 95–97, 163, 185, 191
Chinese Cultural Revolution, 163, 185
Chinese Exclusion Act of 1882, 95–96, 273
Christians, 2, 10, 51
    Karen people as, 43, 61–62, 85, 234, 253, 297
    of Myanmar, 61–62, 66, 234, 253
    in Syria, 35, 253, 285
    welcomed in US, 234, 253, 275, 278
    church groups
    aid Karens in US, 12–13, 81–82, 114, 139
    aid refugees, 167, 234, 251
    and Bush's conservatism, 233–34
    offer English classes, 79, 140
    See also specific churches
citizenship, 20, 52, 96, 290, 295–96
Civil Rights Act, 184
Civil Rights movement, 166, 184, 189
Clinton, Bill, 224, 227, 229, 249, 281
Clinton, Hillary, 267
Cold War, 25, 163–64, 226, 229
communism, 163–65, 185–87, 191
compassionate conservatism, 233–34
concentration camps, 16, 18–19, 99
Congo, 225, 234, 278
Convention on the Prevention and
        Punishment of the Crime of
        Genocide, 19
crimes against humanity, 19–20, 227
Cruz, Ted, 258
Cuba/Cubans, 16, 184–88, 191, 231, 259
Cuban Adjustment Act, 186

Dabaab refugee camp, 233
Damascus, 24, 47, 52, 56, 72–73, 76
    attacks on, 159, 178, 254, 256
    college in, 35–36
    men carried off to, 88, 101, 105, 110
    men imprisoned in, 126, 128
Daraa, Syria, 178, 294
    ancestral relations/feuds in, 54
    barrel bombs used in, 202–3, 256
    Free Syria Army founded in, 203
    full-scale attack on, 128–33, 135, 137

"Great Friday Protests" in, 128–29
    looters in, 155, 175–76, 178
    men rounded up in, 77–78, 87–89,
        108, 129
    mukhabarat officers of, 50, 54
    protests in, 49–56, 71–72, 102, 154
    recaptured by government, 303
    residents flee from, 124–25, 205
    schoolboys tortured in, 53–56, 129,
        256, 304
    sheikhs of, 27–28, 48, 50, 54
    siege of, 89–93, 101–12, 124–25, 175–76
    war escalates in, 112, 149–50, 152,
        154, 159
    wedding customs in, 31–33
    women in, 106–9, 130
    See also Omari mosque (Daraa, Syria);
        al-Salam, Hasna
Declaration of Human Rights, 190, 227
Deferred Action for Childhood Arrivals
        (DACA) program, 278–79
Deh Deh, 80, 83, 85–86, 173, 243–44
Democratic Party, 94–95, 165–66, 226
    displaced persons, 303
    lack of assistance for, 163–64, 187
    of Southeast Asia, 187–88
    US and, 21, 91, 165, 187, 190, 226, 283
    WWII and, 14–20, 100, 163, 228
    See also internally displaced persons
        (IDPs); refugees
Displaced Persons (DP) Act, 14–15,
        19–20, 94
Displaced, The (Nguyen), 303
Druze, 253, 285
Duvalier, Jean-Claude, 186

economic
    migrants, 186, 187–89, 231, 257
    recession, 29, 189, 252–53
Egypt, 36, 51–52, 149, 156, 274
Eisenhower, Dwight D., 164–66, 279–80
England, 16, 52, 98, 178, 184, 255
Eritrea, 231
ESL classes, 83, 218, 285, 300. *See also* Austin,
        Texas: English classes in
ethnic cleansing, 188, 227
eugenics, 97–98, 163

Europe, 163
  anti-immigrant sentiments in, 257–58
  conflict in, 97–98
  displaced people in, 14–21, 100, 163
  Hungarian refugees in, 165
  immigrants from, 97–98, 184–85, 189
  postwar, 19, 232
  refugee meme and, 272
  refugees resettle in, 180, 256–58, 305–6
European Union, 257
"Executive Order Protecting the Nation from
    Foreign Terrorist Entry into the
    United States," 275–78

Facebook, 136, 178, 200, 204, 254, 267, 307
fair-trade jewelry, 218–23, 300
family reunification, 200
  and Immigration Act of 1924, 186
  and Immigration Act of 1965, 185–87
  Trump opposed to, 275–76, 283
  valued by US, 180, 206, 240, 264
family separation policies, 279
Farook, Syed Rizwan, 274
FBI, 250, 279
Federal Refugee Resettlement Program
    (FRRP), 191–93, 224–26, 230, 258,
    278–79
Florida, 16, 98, 186, 280
foreign aid, 15–17, 19, 163–65, 186, 225,
    232, 249
foreign policy, 17, 253
  on displaced persons, 163–64, 225–26
  Jewish refugees and, 187
  of President Carter, 189–92
  on refugee resettlement, 192, 224, 279, 283
  and Syrian crisis, 255, 253
  visas and, 185–86
France, 16, 154, 178, 257, 272, 274
Fraud Detection and National Security
    (FDNS) reviews, 250
Free Syria Army, 135–37, 154, 177, 203,
    209–10, 272
Friday prayers, 36, 47–50, 55–56, 103

G20 Summit, 255
Gaddafi, Muammar, 51
Garden City, Kansas, 280–82

gender, 20, 191
genocide, 19–20, 96, 100, 188, 225, 227
Genocide Convention, 225, 227
George, Caren, 300
Germany, 14–20, 98–100, 184, 225
Ghouta, Syria, 178
Golan Heights, 26
Goodchild, Peter Lee, 272
Grant, Madison, 97
Great Depression, 98, 189, 253
Greece, 98, 272, 290, 305–6
green cards, 264, 290
Guatemala, 221–22
Gulf War, 226

Haiti/Haitians, 95, 186, 279
Hama, Syria, 26–27, 52, 71, 154, 256
Hamad (Laila's daughter), 214
  and Daraa, 175, 181–83
  escapes to Turkey, 208–12, 284
  and father's detention, 158–60
  in Jordan, 149–50, 201
Hamad (Laila's son), 34, 49, 87, 89, 91–93,
    108–11, 124
Harrison, Earl G., 18–19
hate crimes, 229
Hawaii, 276–77
Hebrew Immigrant Aid Society (HIAS),
    187, 251
Helsinki Accords, 189
Hezbollah, 102–3, 125
hijab, 22, 28, 33, 74–75, 106–7, 205, 213,
    260–61, 285
Hitler, Adolf, 98. *See also* Nazis
Hmong people, 10, 61, 187–88
Holocaust, 14, 19, 21, 98–100, 186, 188,
    227, 275
Homeland Security Act, 231
al-Homsi, Fahad, 103–5, 108–10, 112, 125–26,
    130, 135–36
Honduras, 95, 279
Horan region, Syria, 23–24, 54, 129, 293
human rights, 19–20, 187, 189–90, 192, 227
Human Rights Watch, 189
humanitarian crises
  in Afghanistan, 230–32, 257
  Indochinese boat people and, 187

in Myanmar/Thailand, 234
in Persian Gulf region, 227, 231–33
Refugee Act of 1980 and, 190
and refugee resettlement, 232, 234, 283
in Syria, 252–54, 257–58
US's duty towards, 224–25, 227–28
humanitarian efforts
under Bush, 224, 227
under Obama, 224, 254, 257, 272–73
for Syrians, 129, 254, 257, 272–73
US and, 185–86, 189–93, 224, 231, 279, 282
and WWII refugees, 15, 18, 99–100, 227
Hungary/Hungarians, 164–65, 187–88
Hyatt Hotel (Austin, TX), 265–67, 290–91

Immigration Act of 1917, 97
Immigration Act of 1924, 97–98, 163, 166,
    186, 273
Immigration and Nationality Act (INA),
    184–87
immigration debate
American identity and, 94, 96, 100, 166,
    189, 193, 225–26
economics and, 95–96, 98–99, 192
liberalizers and, 94–97, 165–66, 185, 187,
    192, 283
and liberalizers vs. restrictionists, 94–98,
    165–66
racism and, 94–98
and resettling refugees, 192, 258, 272
See also restrictionists/restrictionism
immigration lawyers, 264
immigration system
executive order and, 277, 287–89, 302
extreme policies for, 275–78
and merit-based acceptance, 185
overhaul of, 184–85
policies for, 14–16, 94–95, 184–87, 224,
    227–28
quotas for, 14, 94, 165–66, 184, 230
and racism, 94–98, 185
Trump's policies for, 278–80
See also family reunification
India, 2, 62, 163, 219
Indochina Migration and Refugee Assistance
    Act, 188–89
Indochinese boat people, 187–89, 226

internally displaced persons (IDPs), 62,
    252, 256
International Organization for Migration
    (IOM), 7–8, 11, 44, 239–40, 251
International Refugee Assistance
    Project, 276
International Rescue Committee (IRC)
    (Kansas), 280–82
internment camps, 99
Iowa, 273–74
Iran, 27, 102–3, 178, 203, 275–76, 278
Iraqis, 52, 225, 257
banned from US, 275–76
as refugees in US, 85, 169, 231, 233, 241,
    261, 266
and US interference, 125
US war against, 178, 231–33, 253
Irbed, Jordan, 155, 157, 177–79, 199–200,
    204–5
Irish, 95–96, 184
ISIS, 203, 208–10, 256–57, 272, 274
Islam, 28
Islamic State, 253
Islamophobia, 229–30, 258–59, 275
isolationism, 94, 189
Israel, 25–27, 125, 154, 163, 187
Italians, 95, 98–99

Jane (Austin church volunteer), 139–40,
    142–46, 302
Japanese immigrants, 97, 99, 229
Jaw Jaw, 80, 83, 173, 243–44
Jebreel (Hasna's husband), 294, 304
black market IDs and, 134
business of, 23, 34–35, 103, 125
confronted by soldiers, 125–28
and Daraa protests, 49–51
disability checks for, 262–63, 284
executive order and, 286–87
family denied resettlement in US,
    286–89
family/home life of, 23–26, 29–32, 36–37,
    47–48
and imprisoned sons, 105–6, 110, 124
interviews for resettlement, 200–201, 205–7
and Omari mosque attack, 73, 75
opposes registering as refugee, 155–57

Jebreel (Hasna's husband) (*cont.*)
 protects family home, 130, 137–38, 152,
  175, 180
 resettles in Austin, 213–14, 237–42, 260,
  262–67
 school explosion and, 132–33
 and siege of Daraa, 91–93
 supported by Hasna, 292
 taken by soldiers, 77–78, 87–88, 101
 trauma/grief of, 205, 306
 visits family in Jordan, 149, 155–57
 wounded by missile, 181–83, 199, 201–2,
  212, 262
Jewish refugees, 14–19, 98–100, 163,
  187, 259
Johnson, Lyndon B., 184–85
Jordan, 24, 51, 241
 cracks down on refugees, 149,
  158, 202
 funds refugees' education, 153
 king of, 159–60
 offers refugees medical help, 182–83
 refugees flee to, 178–79, 199, 203–4, 256,
  264–65, 278
 refugees register in, 153–57
 Syrians not welcome in, 151, 201
 US military base in, 205–7, 213
 See also Ramtha, Jordan; refugee camps: in
  Jordan
journalists, 53, 101–2, 129, 257, 273, 305

Karen Baptist church (Austin, TX), 195, 234,
  269–70, 296–97
Karen people, 2, 173, 253, 303
 as ethnic minority, 2, 61, 142, 299
 and family devotionals, 270–71
 language of, 8, 57, 114, 169, 270
 marriage customs of, 245–47
 in refugee camp, 61–62, 65–66
 resettle in US, 10–11, 62, 64, 79, 82, 113–14,
  169, 172–74
 return to Myanmar, 69–70, 116–17
 See also Mu Naw; Saw Ku
Karenni people, 2, 61, 114, 169, 173, 234
Kennedy, John F., 184, 189
Kenya, 233
Khan Sheikhoun, Syria, 256–57

Khassem (Hasna's son), 30, 47, 89, 158, 238
 childhood of, 25–28
 construction jobs of, 154, 156, 199
 in Daraa, 49–51, 56, 181–82
 education of, 35–36
 imprisonment of, 76–77, 124–25, 127–29,
  131, 133–34
 in Jordan, 134–36, 212–13
 marriage/family of, 199–200, 263
 moves to Irbed, 177–78
 seeks resettlement in US, 263–64, 287
 in Syrian army, 23, 36, 71–73, 103, 112,
  128, 134
 visits Lake Muzayrib, 71–73
al-Khatib, Hamza, 129
Khmer Rouge, 188
Kosovo, 227
Kurds, 225, 285

Laila (Hasna's daughter), 36, 156,
  238, 294
 on blacklist, 201–2
 childhood of, 28–29
 and Daraa home, 49, 152–53, 181–83, 199
 flees to Jordan, 124, 128–29, 136–37,
  149–50, 157
 flees to Turkey, 206, 208–12, 214, 264,
  284–85, 306
 forced back to Daraa, 158–61, 175–77
 husband's imprisonment and, 87–89
 leads protest, 106–9, 111–12, 132
 marriage of, 29–34, 292–93
 resettles in Greece, 290, 305–6
 seeks resettlement in US, 263–64, 287
 and siege of Daraa, 91–93, 104–12
 survives missile strikes, 202–3, 211
Lake Muzayrib, Syria, 71–73
Laos/Laotians, 10, 187–89
Lazarus, Emma, 96, 185
Leaders' Summit on Refugees, 258
Lebanon, 27, 51–52, 256, 274, 278
LGBTQ people, 191
Libya, 51, 275–76
Life magazine, 165
Lindbergh, Charles, 99, 273, 275
literacy test, 97
Longa, Amy, 280–81

Mae La refugee camp, 59, 168
  Burmese refugees in, 234
  clinic in, 143
  daily life in, 13, 38, 40–41, 121, 245, 248
  description of, 10, 60–62
  Karen people in, 61–62, 142, 299
  Myanmar refugees in, 7–11, 40–45, 80, 114,
    117–19, 140–41, 172, 217, 244
  See also Mu Naw; Saw Ku
Mafraq, Jordan, 154, 156, 158, 177
Malaysia, 2, 62, 188
Malik, Tashfeen, 274
al-Maliki, Nouri, 233
Maria (Amal's daughter), 136, 160,
    177, 214
marriage customs
  of Myanmar/Thailand, 140–41, 245–47
  of Syria, 24, 29, 31–34, 238, 292–94
Marshall Plan, 19, 94, 163
Massacre on Saida Bridge, 129
McCarran-Walter Act (1952), 166
McCarthyism, 166, 229, 279
McCaul, Michael, 258
McGuire Air Force Base (New Jersey), 165
media, 102, 129, 163, 254, 305
Medicaid, 84, 139–40, 145, 240, 262
Meh Bu, 114, 120–22
Mexico/Mexicans, 95, 231
Middle East, 98, 176, 234, 253, 255
Miller, Stephen, 275–76, 279
missionaries, 61–62, 65–66, 140
movies, 17, 20, 99
Mu Naw
  anger of, 41, 118, 173–74, 196–97,
    247–48
  arrives in Austin, 7–9, 11–13, 44, 172
  becomes homeowner, 268–69, 271
  caseworker of, 57–58, 60, 80, 82–84
  childhood of, 1–3, 62, 65–70, 114, 116–17,
    197, 245
  deep grief of, 64–65, 70, 82, 86, 113, 121,
    172, 269
  education of, 44, 66
  English classes and, 79–80, 82–83, 113–14,
    120, 122, 140, 142
  fair-trade jewelry job of, 218–23, 300
  finds power in US, 222–23

  first days in Austin, 38–41, 43–46, 57–60,
    62–65, 70
  flees from Myanmar, 1–3, 65
  grateful for new US home, 295–97
  as Karen, 174, 299
  language skills of, 299–300
  leads women's cooperative, 167–68, 173,
    218, 300
  in Mae La refugee camp, 7–11, 38, 40–45,
    60–62, 114, 121, 168
  marriage ceremony in Mae La, 140–41
  marriage of, 173, 243, 247–48
  marriage troubles and, 194–98,
    217–19, 222
  mother's death and, 243–45, 247–48, 269
  in Nu Po refugee camp, 65–69, 142,
    245, 247
  parent's marriage and, 245–47
  pregnancy of, 84–86, 113–16, 121–22,
    139–40, 299
  relationship with husband, 42–43, 119–22,
    268–71
  religious life of, 43, 61–62, 85, 270–71, 297
  returns to Myanmar, 69–70, 116–17
  reunited with mother in Mae La, 117–19,
    245, 248
  and son's birth, 142–46, 167, 173
  struggles to pay bills, 80–85
  struggles with apt. manager, 115–16,
    119–23
  tells her story, 221–23, 299–304
  thrives in Austin, 167–68, 171, 173–74
  trauma of, 217, 247–48, 301, 304
  works as translator, 169–70, 172–74, 196,
    218, 271, 300
Mubarak, Hosni, 52
mukhabarat, 50, 54–55, 129
Muslim Brotherhood, 26–28, 52,
    154, 285
Muslim-majority countries, 275–78, 302
Muslims, 291
  face opposition, 229–32, 253, 259, 273
  in Myanmar, 234
  in Syria, 35, 253, 274, 285
  Trump's views on, 267, 274–277
  women, 213, 260, 285
  See also travel ban

Myanmar, 270, 300, 304
  armed forces of, 1–2, 68–70, 86, 142
  civil war in, 10, 61–62, 70, 116–18,
      141, 225
  ethnic minorities of, 2, 57, 61–62, 142,
      234, 299
  weaving traditions of, 167–68, 173
  women raped in, 116, 246, 248
Myanmar refugees
  flee country, 1–3, 61–62, 65–66
  persecution of, 299, 303
  resettle in US, 10–11, 80, 114, 167–69, 173,
      234, 278
  return to homeland, 69–70, 116–17
  US's support of, 253
  See also Mu Naw; Saw Ku

Nassib, Syria, 203
Natheir Ali, 241–42, 260–61, 263, 265,
      284, 287
National Counterterrorism Center, 250
National Security Council, 279
national security, 15, 254
  and conflict in Europe, 97–99
  Obama on, 254, 258–59
  refugee resettlement and, 224
  restrictionists and, 97–98, 166, 192,
      after Sept. 11, 2001, 231–32
Native Americans, 61
nativism, 189
NATO troops, 227
Naw Wah (Mu Naw's daughter), 64
  arrives in Austin, 7, 13, 39–41
  childhood of, 119–23, 145, 197, 295
  education of, 113, 168
  and family devotionals, 270–71
  in refugee camp, 141
Nazis, 14, 16–18, 98–100, 163
Nepal, 62, 225, 279
New York, 184, 231, 276
New York Times, 16, 20
New Yorker, The, 279
news outlets, 99, 254, 267, 274, 276
newsreels, 17–18, 100, 164–65, 254, 273
NGOs, 43, 190
Nguyen, Viet Thanh, 303
Nigeria/Nigerians, 187

Nixon, Richard, 165, 189
Noor (Amal's daughter), 34, 49, 129–30, 160,
      177, 214
North Korea, 277
North Vietnam, 163, 188
Norway, 201
Nu Po refugee camp, 65–69, 142,
      245, 247
Nuremberg trials, 19, 94

Obama, Barack, 224, 251, 281–82
  global refugee crisis and, 252
  and Karen Christian refugees, 253
  refugee admissions cap of, 228, 249,
      259, 275
  on Syrian crisis, 253–56, 258, 272
Office of Refugee Resettlement, 191,
      230, 251
oil supplies, 226
Omari mosque (Daraa, Syria),
  attack on, 74–77, 102–3, 128
  Friday prayers at, 36, 48, 50, 55
  and the protesters, 50–51, 55–56, 73, 128
Operation Enduring Freedom, 230–31
Operation Safe Haven, 165

Pah Poe (Mu Naw's daughter)
  arrives in Austin, 7, 13, 39–41, 44–46
  childhood of, 113, 119–22, 145,
      197, 217
  education of, 168
  and family devotionals, 270–71
  in refugee camp, 140–41, 143
Pakistan, 163, 274
Palestine/Palestinians, 51, 149, 163
Paris, France, 257, 272, 274
Passing of the Great Race, The, 97
Patriot Act, 230–31
Peace Corps, 189
Pence, Mike, 258, 275
Persian Gulf, 227
Philippines, 97
Pol Pot, 188–89
Politico, 275
Pompeo, Mike, 281–83
post-traumatic stress disorder (PTSD),
      192, 256

poverty, 51, 192
PR campaigns, 53, 163–65, 224
Presidential Determination, 251
    under Bush, George W., 228–30
    under Carter, 190–91
    under Obama, 228, 249, 259, 275
    under Reagan, 228
    under Trump, 275, 278, 281, 283
presidential election (2016), 267,
    273–74

al-Qaeda, 203, 230, 274
Quran, 28–29, 48, 102

race
    and antiterrorism, 253
    Nazis and, 99
    refugee quotas and, 163
    and refugees, 20, 191, 227, 272
racism
    immigration policies and, 94–98,
        185, 273
    restrictionists and, 95–97
    See also genocide
Ramtha, Jordan
    and Daraa residents, 133, 135, 149, 175
    Hasna al-Salam's home in, 136, 177,
        237, 305
    Syrian refugees in, 124–25, 130, 133, 149,
        156–57, 161–62
    women in, 151, 285
Rana (Hasna's daughter), 72, 178,
        292, 306
    childhood of, 28, 32–33, 37, 47, 49, 53
    cooks for family, 266–67
    education in Austin, 262, 265, 285
    education of, 103, 112, 136, 153, 155–57, 177,
        199, 240
    family denied resettlement in US,
        287, 289
    flees to Jordan, 133, 136
    and friend's wedding, 292–94
    interviews for resettlement, 201, 207
    resettles in Austin, 214, 235–40, 242,
        285–87
    school explosion and, 131–33
    settles in Jordan, 150, 152, 285

    and unrest in Daraa, 73–75, 77–78, 87–88,
        91–93, 125, 130
Reagan, Ronald, 224, 226, 228–29,
        249, 281
Real ID Act, 231
Reddit, 254, 305–6
Refugee Act of 1980, 190–92, 228, 278–79
Refugee Administration Process (RAP),
        249–52
Refugee Admissions Process, 230,
        273, 281
refugee camps
    average length of stay in, 233
    crucial role of, 232–34
    in Europe, 15, 18–19, 163
    in Jordan, 152, 158–59, 177, 179,
        201, 204
    poor conditions in, 18–19, 233
    refugees trapped in, 62, 232–34, 251
    in Thailand, 2, 62, 300
    trauma and, 192
    See also Mae La refugee camp; Nu Po
        refugee camp
Refugee Convention (1951), 20, 231, 252
Refugee Relief Act (1953), 166
Refugee Relief Program, 166
refugee resettlement
    admissions cap for, 185, 190–93, 224, 228,
        249, 251–52, 259
    admissions cap lowered for, 230–32, 275,
        278–83
    after WWII, 14–21, 96, 100, 163–64
    agencies for, 80, 185, 190–93, 232–33,
        250–52, 276, 280–83, 299–300
    applying for, 141–42, 172, 176
    current policies for, 301
    decline in, 277–78, 283
    economic stability and, 224
    lack of support for, 252–53, 258, 272–75,
        278–80
    policies for, 14–16, 19–21, 100, 163–66,
        185–86, 232, 273
    process of, 179–80, 193, 205–7, 225, 231,
        249–52, 273, 283
    suspended after 9/11, 229–32, 234, 275
    suspended by Trump, 275, 302
    in US, 185–93, 231, 249–52, 259, 273–76, 278

refugee resettlement (*cont.*)
  US public's support for, 187, 189, 193,
    226, 234
  See also specific cities, countries
Refugee Services of Texas (RST), 251
  caseworkers of, 168–73, 241, 262, 291, 300
  assists Hasna al-Salam, 241, 262–64, 291
  assists Mu Naw, 58–59, 62–64, 168–69
  under Trump administration, 282
Refugee Support Centers (RSC), 250
refugees
  airlifted by US, 186, 188
  ballooning crises of, 232–33, 252–53
  definition expands for, 184–86, 191–92,
    226–27, 252
  definition of, 20, 96, 100, 163,
    258, 301
  denied resettlement, 250, 259, 283
  extreme vetting of, 273–76, 279
  financial assistance for, 187, 240, 251,
    263, 280
  fleeing persecution, 185–86, 191–93,
    225–26, 228, 258
  growing number of, 228, 258, 277–78
  hire smugglers, 62, 208–11, 258
  laws protecting rights of, 19–20
  mental health counseling for, 280
  and "non-refoulement," 20, 191,
    231, 279
  persecution of, 61, 142, 191, 299, 303
  protracted situations of, 232–34
  racialized trope and, 272–73
  restricted entry of, 275–78, 302
  return to homelands, 163
  services offered to, 206, 280
  tell their stories, 299–308
  unique position of, 14–15, 185, 279, 283
  US duty to, 224–28, 241, 254
  vetted by US, 166, 180, 191–92, 230, 232,
    249–52, 258
  as victims of war, 14–16, 19, 192,
    225, 228
  white Europeans as, 163–65
  See also anti-immigrant sentiments
religion, 43, 227, 275, 285, 297
  family devotionals, 270–71
  Friday prayers, 47–50, 55

Karen people and, 61–62, 270–71
  and persecution of refugees, 191
  Syrians and, 27–29
  See also Karen Baptist church; Omari
    mosque; *churches, specific denominations*
religious freedom, 20, 191, 234
Republicans, 165–66, 226
restrictionists/restrictionism
  Bush administration and, 233–34
  on family reunification, 187
  rise in, 97–98, 100, 166, 272, 277
  slows refugee admissions, 279–83
  and "take our jobs" rhetoric, 98, 189
  Trump administration and, 278–80
  vetting refugees and, 166, 192
  want quotas/limited admissions, 94–95
Rice, Condoleezza, 234
Roberts, John, 277
Rohingya refugees, 2, 234, 303
Roosevelt, Franklin, 16
Rumsfeld, Donald, 230
Russia/Russians, 178, 187, 191, 203,
    255, 278
Rwanda/Rwandans, 225, 227–28

al-Salam, Hasna
  cares for injured husband, 181–83, 199, 202
  and children in Jordan, 133–34, 136–37
  clan life of, 23–25, 29, 31–33, 78, 292
  confronted by soldiers, 125–28
  Daraa home destroyed, 181–82, 201
  Daraa home of, 22–24, 31, 36–37, 47–48,
    73–74, 125, 138, 236–37, 305
  and Daraa protests, 49–51
  and daughter's escape, 208–12
  and daughter's protest, 106–9, 111–12, 132
  deep grief of, 72–73, 151, 162, 176, 202,
    205, 214
  faces hostility, 289, 294
  family denied resettlement in US, 287–89
  first revolutionary thoughts of, 27–28,
    35–36
  flees to Jordan, 137–38, 153
  and friend's wedding, 292–94
  friendship with soldier, 103–5, 108–10,
    135–36
  on girls' education, 27–29, 31, 112, 155–57

gold savings of, 91–92, 126, 128, 138, 154, 178, 182, 199, 236, 265
hopes for intervention, 178, 256
husband/sons taken away, 77–78, 87–89, 101
and imprisoned sons, 124–25, 133–34, 288
interviews for resettlement, 200–201, 205–7
jobs in Austin, 260–67, 288–92
Jordan home of, 236–38, 265, 305
"Lebweh" nickname of, 111–12, 132, 207
on looting of home, 175–76, 178
and Malek/Laila's return to Daraa, 158–61
marriage/family of, 23–37, 47–49, 78, 150
moves to Irbed, 177–81
offered resettlement, 176, 179–80
and Omari mosque attack, 73–78, 132
politically unengaged, 25–26, 35, 130–31, 155
registers as refugee, 153–57, 200
religious life of, 27–28, 43, 47–49
resettles in Austin, 213–14, 235–42, 260–67, 305
returns to Daraa, 149
school explosion and, 131–33
settles in Jordan, 149–53, 175–76
and siege of Daraa, 89–93, 101–12, 125, 129–30, 133, 135, 176
sons released from prison, 105–6, 110–12
stays connected to children, 306–7
struggles to pay bills, 263, 265, 284, 291
Syrian neighbors of, 239–42
tells her story, 301–8
trauma of, 76, 125, 304–7
visits Lake Muzayrib, 71–73
al-Salam, Malek, 156, 177, 306
on blacklist, 201–2
brings family to Jordan, 149–50, 152, 157–59
in Daraa, 48–49, 181–83, 199
death of, 204, 208, 307
forced back to Daraa, 158–61, 175
imprisonment of, 105–6, 124
in Jordan, 124, 128, 136
marriage of, 29–34, 292

release of, 109–11, 125, 131
survives missile strikes, 202–3
taken by soldiers, 87–88, 101
Samir (Amal's husband), 156, 182, 238
construction jobs of, 154, 199
family/home life of, 29–31, 111
flees to Jordan, 129–30, 136
interviews for resettlement, 200
moves to Irbed, 177–78
resettles in Canada, 289–90
seeks resettlement in US, 263–64, 287
and unrest in Daraa, 49, 87–88
San Bernardino shooters, 274
Saudi Arabia, 51, 203, 274
Saw Doh (Mu Naw's son), 144–46, 167, 194–98, 218, 299
Saw Ku (Mu Naw's husband)
arrives in Austin, 7–9, 11–13
caseworker of, 57–58, 60, 80, 82–84
and death of Mu Naw's mother, 244–45, 248
first days in Austin, 38–41, 43–46, 57–60, 62–64
grateful for new US home, 295–97
jobs of, 82–83, 115, 195–96, 271
in Mae La refugee camp, 10–11, 40–43, 59, 121, 141–42
marriage of, 140–41, 243, 247
marriage troubles and, 194–98, 217–19, 222
relationship with Mu Naw, 42–43, 61–62, 119–22, 268–71
and son's birth, 142–46, 173
struggles to pay bills, 80–85
takes English classes, 79–80, 82
thrives in Austin, 167–68, 171, 174
and wife's pregnancy, 84–85, 113, 140
security databases, 249–50, 274
security, international, 249, 258–59
Sednaya Prison, 76–77, 256
September 11, 2001, 224, 228–32, 234, 253, 258, 272, 274
Shan people/state, 61–62
al-Shari, Thamer Muhammad, 129
Smith, Ellison DuRant, 97
Smith, Russell, 282
"Snake, The" (Brown), 274–75

social media
    Free Syria Army video on, 135–36
    provides news source, 158, 178, 254, 267
    spreads fear, 272–73
    Syrian war on, 129, 200, 202, 204, 254, 257,
        305–7
    used for vetting refugees, 250
    See also Facebook; Reddit; WhatsApp;
        YouTube
Soe Paw, 243–44
Somalia, 79, 85, 114, 169, 233–34, 257,
        275–76
South America, 98, 231
South Vietnam, 188
Southeast Asia, 61, 188, 234
Soviet Union, 25, 164–66, 187, 189, 226
Special Immigrant Visa (SIV) program, 231
St. Louis, 16–17, 20, 98–99, 186
starvation, 192, 256
Statue of Liberty, 96
Sudanese, 225, 233, 275–76, 279
Sunni Muslims, 35, 52
Switzerland, 165
Syria
    Alawites in, 25, 35, 52
    banks not trusted in, 91–92
    current conditions in, 306–7
    disappeared people in, 25–26, 76, 303
    diverse people of, 253, 285
    education in, 24, 27–29, 31, 34–36
    ethnic minorities of, 25, 52
    gains independence, 25
    "Great Friday Protests" in, 128–29
    lack of free press in, 102, 129, 254, 305
    Muslims slaughtered in, 26–27, 52, 71, 154
    police in, 48, 54–55
    political engagement in, 25–28, 35
    residents flee from, 124–25, 178–79, 241, 256
    sanctions against, 27
    secret police in, 50, 54–55, 129
    US inaction concerning, 252–59
    war in, 133, 135–37, 149–50, 159, 178, 241,
        285, 305
    war worsens in, 200, 202–3, 253–57
    women in, 24, 27–34, 112
    See also al-Assad, Bashar; Daraa, Syria;
        Hama, Syria; al-Salam, Hasna

Syrian army, 154
    attacks innocent people, 135–36
    mandatory service in, 36
    school explosion and, 131–33
    and siege of Daraa, 76–78, 102–9, 112,
        124–29
    soldiers defect from, 135–37
    See also Free Syria Army; Khassem (Hasna's
        son): in
Syrian army
Syrian government, 102, 303
    attacks own citizens, 182, 200, 202–3,
        252–56, 305
    attacks rebels, 254
    bloody assaults in Hama, 26–27, 52, 71, 154
    Syrians fearful of, 256
    uses chemical weapons, 253–57
Syrian refugees
    enhanced vetting of, 250, 258, 274
    flee to Europe, 256–58
    flee to Jordan, 203–4, 256, 264–65, 278
    growing number of, 252–53, 256, 278
    lack of support for, 213, 253, 272–75
    registering as, 154–55
    resettle in US, 180, 205–6, 213–14, 235–42,
        257–59, 264, 272, 278
    in Turkey, 264, 278, 306
    turned away by Trump/US, 275–76,
        287–89, 306
    unwelcome, 256, 258, 264, 274, 285, 294

Tatmadaw, 1–2, 68–70, 86, 142
Tawfiq (Laila's son), 202–3, 208–12, 214, 284
Temporary Protected Status (TPS), 279, 282
terrorism, victims of, 258, 273. See also
        antiterrorism
terrorists
    and Sept. 11, 2001, 228–30, 253, 258–59
    synonymous with refugee, 273–74, 301
    in Syria, 102, 254, 274, 285
    and Trump travel ban, 275–76
Thailand, 81, 197, 234, 296, 304
    ethnic minorities in, 61–62, 299
    Hmong refugees in, 188
    Karen communities in, 270
    See also Mae La refugee camp; Nu Po
        refugee camp; Tatmadaw

Tillerson, Rex, 283
trafficking, 207, 258, 282
Transportation Security Administration, 251
trauma, of refugees, 192–93, 205, 256, 280, 301, 304–7
travel ban, 275–78, 302, 306
Truman, Harry S., 14–16, 18–19, 226, 281
Trump, Donald
    and the election, 258–59, 267, 273–74
    immigration policies of, 273–83
    refugee admissions caps of, 278, 281–83
    travel ban of, 275–78, 302
    views on Muslims, 267, 274–77
Trump v. Hawaii, 276–77
Tunisia, 36, 51–52
Turkey, 27,
    Syrian refugees in, 206, 208, 212, 256, 278, 284, 287, 306
    Syrians not welcome in, 264, 290
Twitter, 254

Uganda, 219, 221–22
Um Ahmad, 23–24, 35, 89–93, 111, 130, 176
Um Ibtihal, 75–78, 106, 108, 130, 176
Um Khalid, 239, 286–87, 291–92
UN Refugee Convention, 191
undocumented immigrants, 258, 279
unemployment, 51, 95, 306
United Arab Emirates, 24, 274
United Kingdom, 52, 272. See also England
United Nations, 7–8, 177, 227
    destroys chemical weapons, 256–57
    founding of, 19, 94
    landmark declarations of, 19–20
    Myanmar refugees and, 10–11, 62, 69, 141–42
    peacekeeping forces of, 69, 125
    and refugee camps, 232–33
    Syrian refugees and, 257
United Nations High Commissioner for Refugees (UNHCR), 228
    countries partnering with, 277
    expands definition of "refugee," 186, 191, 252
    interviews refugees, 141, 179–80, 201, 205–6, 232, 249–50, 258
    Myanmar refugees and, 141–42

and refugee camps, 232–33
and refugee vetting process, 249–51
Syrian refugees and, 176, 179–80, 200–201, 205–6, 278
United Nations Relief and Rehabilitation Administration, 18
United Nations Security Council, 234
United States
    aids Hungarian refugees, 164–65
    "better-safe-than-sorryism" of, 98–100, 229, 231, 234, 273
    census of 1890, 98
    "closed-door" refugee policy of, 273
    cultural dominance of, 164, 187
    European immigrants in, 184–86, 189
    European refugees resettle in, 14, 20–21, 163–66
    immigration courts of, 281
    large numbers migrate to, 94–97, 187–90
    and nonwhite immigrants, 97–98, 163–64, 185–87
    protection-based immigration and, 282
    protests in, 276, 288
    and protracted refugee situations, 232–34
    refuses Jewish refugees, 15–16, 20, 98–99, 259
    sends rations to Afghanistan, 230
    and Syrian crisis, 125, 154, 178, 252–59
    as world leader, 17, 21, 100
Universal Declaration of Human Rights, 19–20
US Citizenship and Immigration Services (USCIS), 191, 229–30, 250, 283
US Congress, 14, 166, 190, 230, 255
US Department of Defense, 192, 250
US Department of Health and Human Services, 191
US Department of Homeland Security (DHS), 230, 250, 279
US State Department, 192, 213, 250–51, 279–80, 283
US Supreme Court, 276–77

Vietnam, 95, 222
    displaced persons of, 163–64,
    refugees from, 187–89, 221–22, 226, 234, 259

Vietnam War, 10, 188–89, 225, 259
visas, 163, 276, 305
    and 9/11 terrorists, 273–74
    "special immigrant," 231, 282
    US foreign interests and, 185–86
    US regulations for, 190, 192
    US's allotment of, 190, 228–29, 251
        during WWII, 14, 16
Vogue, 53
Voting Rights Act, 184
Vox, 302

Washington Post, 259
Wayne, John, 17
WhatsApp, 158, 204, 208, 212, 254, 263, 267, 305, 307
World Refugee Day, 174
World War I, 192, 253
World War II, 252, 257
    and Jewish refugees, 98–100
    leaves displaced people, 14–21, 100, 163, 228
    and postwar American identity, 17–18, 21, 94
    refugee camps and, 232

and refugee resettlement, 14–21, 96, 99, 100, 165
    US involvement in, 99

Yemen, 51–52, 225, 275–76
al-Youssef, Abdel Hameed, 257
YouTube, 129, 200, 254, 305–6
Yugoslavia, 164, 225
Yusef (Hasna's son), 23, 47–48, 238, 294
    and brother-in-law detained, 158–60
    childhood of, 25–28
    confronted by soldiers, 125–28
    construction jobs of, 154, 156, 199
    and Daraa protests, 49–51
    flees to Jordan, 128–30, 135–36
    imprisonment of, 105–6, 124, 126–27
    interviews for resettlement, 200–201
    moves to Irbed, 177–78
    and Omari mosque attack, 73
    release of, 109–12, 125, 131
    resettles in Greece, 290, 305–6
    seeks resettlement in US, 263–64, 287
    taken by soldiers, 77–78, 88, 101
    in Turkey, 212, 214, 264, 284, 306
    works with father, 34–36